EVOLUTION OF INDIAN EDUCATION

EVOLUTION OF INDIAN EDUCATION

From Colonial Stranglehold to Resurgent India

(A critical study, in an historical perspective, of the development of Indian education during the period 1813 to 2013)

Professor (Dr.) Jagdish Lal Azad
Ex-chief of Education Division
Planning Commission
Government of India
New Delhi

GYAN

ISBN: 978-81-212-1211-3

Price: ₹ 1150

First Published 2014

Published by

Gyan Publishing House
23, Main Ansari Road
Daryaganj, New Delhi-110002
Phones: 23282060, 23261060
Fax: 91-11-23285914
E-mail: books@gyanbooks.com

Laser Typesetting: Deepak Shukla, Delhi

Printed at: Chawla Offset Printers, Delhi

Cataloging in Publication Data--DK

Courtesy: D.K. Agencies (P) Ltd. <docinfo@dkagencies.com>

Azad, J. L. (Jagdish Lal), 1920-

Evolution of Indian education : from colonial stranglehold to resurgent India : a critical study, in an historical perspective, of the development of Indian education during the period 1813 to 2013 / Jagdish Lal Azad.

p. cm.
Includes bibliographical references (p.) and index.
ISBN 9788121212113

1. Education--India--History. 2. Education and state--India--History. I. Title.

DC 370.954 23

Dedicated with Profound Love and Reverence to

Late Smt. Daya Wati Azad

(1-7-1925 to 30.1.2009)

Smt. Daya Wati Azad was a divine benediction, who sanctified our lives with her unparalleled devotion, piety and self-sacrifice. She was an epitome of love, affection and self-abnegation. She was my constant companion and inspiration during our joys and sorrows; the rough and tumble of life. She rendered invaluable help to me all through the onerous task of collection of data/facts from various sources; mainly from the records at the National Archives of India, Central Secretariat Library and other institutional libraries. But for her untiring zeal, continuous encouragement and unflinching support, the Study would not have seen the light of the day.

Deeply and reverentially remembered by Saroj, Harish, Karuna, Pritam, Madhu, surender; grand and great grand children.

May God, the Almighty, grant eternal peace to her soul!

Jagdish Lal Azad

Smt. Daya Wati Azad - A Brief Life Sketch

Daya Wati was born in a small village - Sarai Sidhu - in Multan district in West Punjab (Now in Pakistan). Her father, Dr. Ganga Ram, was a practising Unani physician in the village. Unfortunately, at a comparatively young age, he developed - possibly oral cancer - and before any diagnosis could be made, he passed away. This was a stunning blow to the family because he was the sole earning member of the family. On the advice of the elders, Daya Wati was married at a very young age - both of us were in teens.

Daya Wati made significant contribution to the upkeep of our family. During post-partition days, when our lives were in shambles and we had no means of making both ends meet in an alien land to which we were forcibly deported, she got employment as a teacher in a remote village in Haryana. Her meagre salary sustained us till I had completed my education and got employment.

True to her name, she was compassion incarnate, ever-ready to help the persons in need. Most of the NGOs, concerned with helping the poor and needy, were recipients of financial help from her. She was deeply religious and would recite Vedic hymns regularly twice a day. She was a voracious reader. Munshi Prem Chand, Bankim Chandra Chatterji, Sarat Chandra and Shivani were her favourite writers.

On 13th April 2007, Daya Wati developed cerebral disorientation, which was diagnosed as the dreaded Dementia. This severely affected her comprehension and memory. It also affected her immune system. In October, 2008, she was hospitalised because of failure of vital organs. During the middle of January, 2009, she suffered from cardiac arrest and was put on ventilator - never to get out of it. On the morning of January 30, 2009, when India was observing the Martyrs' Day, her Soul left her tormented mortal frame to merge with Eternity!

Daya Wati is no more with us in physical form but the enchanting fragrance of her adorable personality; the resonance of her sweet voice; her unbounded love, devotion and humaneness, will always illuminate our lives and will be a guiding force for our family for all times to come.

A Prayer

au revoir, Daya Wati, my gracious soul mate; my invaluable life partner.

Our profound gratitude to the Almighty for giving us blissful companionship –so long; so joyful; so contented!

In your Heavenly abode, be at the Lotus feet of the Lord, sing His glory and pray with me that God, the Merciful, in His unbounded beneficence, may bless us to meet again; somewhere, sometime! … amen

Ever Yours,
Jagdish

Contents

Foreword

Writing history of Indian education is indeed a very daunting task. Undoubtedly, India has had a very long and ancient legacy of pursuit of knowledge through well organised institutions. It is the opinion of many scholars that the British rule created discontinuity in the spread of education in the subcontinent by disrupting the natural evolution of the education system to cover common people in the form of mass education. In fact, Mahatma Gandhi is on record complaining in 1930s that Indian population was more literate before the advent of British rule. However, there are others who consider British sowed the seeds of modern education which facilitated Indians to acquire modern scientific knowledge and move towards industrialisation. While the nature and extent of impact of British rule on Indian education development is debatable, it is clear that what exists today is built on the edifice of an education system left behind by the British. For a meaningful understanding of the progress of education during the contemporary period, it is imperative that one looks to the historical evolution of the system during the British rule through the more than six decades of independent India. This is what Dr. J.L. Azad has attempted in this volume *Evolution of Indian Education - From Colonial Stranglehold to Resurgent India: A critical study in an historical perspective of the development of Indian Education during the period 1813 to 2013*, covering two hundred years of history of Indian education.

Covering the progress of education in as complex a setting as India over a period of two hundred years is a very challenging task. In this book, Dr. Azad, in his own unique style, takes us through the historical events and policy shifts in education in the subcontinent over this long period. The narratives punctuated by introduction of extracts from original documents makes for a gripping story. The style is simple and straight forward, rich in information supported by personal insights, from someone who has lived through the two sides of the history - before and after independence. Events and processes are seen and interpreted through the eyes of a professional planner as Dr. Azad had direct engagement in shaping the development of education in the country as educational advisor to the Planning Commission at a period in the history when the Mahalnobis model of economic development planning was the main instrument for designing development policy and programmes in India. As Dr. Azad mentions in the Introduction, it 'is not in the nature of the usual survey of education in an historical perspective'. It is anchored around selective episodes in education that have significantly influenced the course of education development in India. Reflections on the role of important individuals like Raja Ram Mohan Roy, Lord Macaulay, Swami Dayanand, Rabindra Nath Tagore, Sir Syed Ahmad Khan and Mahatma Gandhi brings in new insights in understanding how these personalities influenced the contours and contents of education during the British Period. The narratives on education development in post-independence period has a personal touch as Dr. Azad was part of the planning establishment. Through the hardcore planned development era, moving into the era of liberalisation and getting more and more entrenched in a market centric development framework - the volume is vivid as Dr. Azad has seen it all analysing the developments from a professional lens.

Dr. Azad is one of very few in contemporary India who could travel back and forth in memory and articulate a professional narrative on the changes that span over 200 years. It was a pleasure reading the book and I am quite sure that it will be a very valuable addition to the collections on Indian education.

R. Govinda
(Vice Chancellor)
National University of Educational
Planning and Administration
New Delhi

Acknowledgements

The author expresses his profound gratitude to Professor R. Govinda, Vice-Chancellor of the National University of Educational Planning and Administration who, in spite of his very busy schedule, was gracious enough to write a very thought provoking Foreword to the Study.

The author is beholden to Dr. T.N. Dhar for giving unstinted help at all stages of the Study. He went through the drafts of the Report and gave very useful comments/suggestions about the contents of the Report. The author also benefitted immensely from his papers/notes, some of which have been, partly, incorporated in the Report. The author also gratefully acknowledges the very encouraging comments made by Dr. K.L. Gandhi. The author also thanks Justice (Retired) R.N. Mittal for reviewing the legal aspects of the Right to Education Act and offering useful suggestions.

The author is beholden to Dr. Perti, the then Director of the National Archives of India, for providing access to the papers/reports/books/files maintained at the Archives. He is also thankful to the staff of the Archives particularly, Shri Malik and his colleagues, for promptly supplying the requisite materials, books, files and other papers as also providing facilities for photocopying.

The author also appreciates the assistance rendered by Librarians and staff of the Central Secretariat Library and the NUEPA Library for making available books and other publications as also for providing photocopying services.

The author does not find adequate words to express his sincere thanks to Shri Sudhir Dagar for providing ungrudging help and assistance all through the prosecution of the study. He made significant contribution in drafting/redrafting of the Report. It was through him that the author could lay his hands on books/monographs/reports relevant to the study. Without his very competent, timely and untiring assistance, it would have been very difficult to complete the study.

Last, but not the least, the author expresses this gratitude to the Gyan Publishing House for their keen interest in publishing the study. He is also thankful of the editorial staff of the Publishing House for their efficient and prompt services as the various stages of the Publication.

Introduction

The foundation of the British rule in India was laid in 1618, when Sir Thomas Roe, the ambassador appointed by the British King in 1614, succeeded in prevailing upon the then Mughal emperor Jahangir to sign a contractual agreement granting a licence to the East India Company to trade in India. Ironically, Jahangir could not have imagined, in the wildest of his dreams, that this innocuous document will lead to the emergence of the British Raj, which would extinguish the Mughal Empire and one of his great, great grandsons, Bahadurshah Zafar, would be deposed and incarcerated in a far off land to die a most humiliating death!

The East India Company which was formed in London on the last day of 1600 was initially intended to finance trading voyages to India and other South Asian countries including China. After the death of Aurangzeb in 1707, the vast Mughal kingdom was in a decadent state with many provinces breaking away to form independent fiefdoms. Further, Marathas established their dominions over Mughal provinces in Malwa, Berar and Bundelkhand and the Rajputs consolidated their authority over territories in Western and Southern India. The Jats also showed their mettle by occupying large tracts of land in Northern India. The Mughal Empire was, thus, in a state of utter disarray.

In these circumstances the East India Company found an opportunity to spread its tentacles wide and become a ruling power. Besides occupying the remnants of the Mughal Empire, it had also to contend with its European rivals, particularly the French and the Portuguese. With the combined strength of military power, subterfuge and diplomacy, the Company was able to hold its sway over large tracts of Indian land. It was, however, the Battle of Plassey fought in the sweltering heat of June, 1757, which enabled the British to establish their military superiority and win the day. The battle was, however, won because of the betrayal of friends and relatives of the unfortunate Nawab Siraj-ud-Daula and the treachery of Mir Jafir, about whom Iqbal said in a Persian couplet:

Jafir Az Bengal, Saadiq Az Deccan,
Nang-e-Millat, Nang-e-Deen, Nang-e-Watan.

Rendered in English, it would read like this:

"Jafir (Mir) from Bengal;
Saadiq from Deccan; (are)
"Shame for the Community; Shame for
the Religion; Shame for the Country.

Be that as it may, from that day on, there was no looking back for the Company. By the Treaty of Allahabad, the Company got the Diwani of Bengal, Bihar and Orissa; the right of administering these territories and collecting revenues. Within 100 years from 1757, after the victory in Plassey, the British Colonialists had captured the entire Indian sub-continent. Its European rivals, the French and the Portuguese were squeezed out to small tracts of land in South and West. Although the Company had shed off its pretence of a trading concern in 1833, and become a ruling power, it was the Revolt of 1857, which led to its demise. The British Crown took over the administration of the vast expanse of the Indian Empire.

Progress of Education

We have discussed in detail the progress of Indian education during the Colonial rule, the policy paradigms, the system of finance - its magnitude, inter-sectoral priorities etc. in separate chapters.

It has been observed that during the first sixty years of the Colonial rule ending 1813, the Company was engaged in expansion of territories through war, deception and other acts of high handedness. It was only in 1813, that an infinitesimally small amount of Rs. one lakh per annum was provided for the education of the natives. In actual fact, the Colonialists' interest in education started from 1835, when the government decided to spend this amount on the promotion of European education through English. It may, however, be conceded that the modern Indian education rests on the edifice built up during the Colonial rule.

Political and Other Developments

We have discussed some of the natural and man-made events that effected the course of Indian education during the Colonial period. These events included the famous Indian Revolt (1857) against the British rule-euphemistically called the 'Sepoy Mutiny'; the natural catastrophes like the bubonic plague, cyclone and earthquakes that devastated the socio-economic fabric of certain regions of the country in the last decade of the Nineteenth century. Further, the First World War (1914-18) between the British Imperialism and the German expansionism, in addition to causing unprecedented loss of human life, brought about a period of prolonged economic recession that forced the British administration to curtail or keep on hold some of the important schemes of educational development. The period also witnessed political turmoil culminating in the Non-Cooperation

Movement that altered drastically the complexion of Indian education and gave rise to the creation of a number of national institutions that have survived to this day despite the apathy and cynicism of the British bureaucracy towards them.

The Constitutional Reforms introduced by a hesitating British oligarchy also impacted the administrative system of Indian education. Under the Reforms, education, with some very crucial exceptions, became a transferred subject under the charge of Indian ministers. Notwithstanding the half-hearted approach of the British, the Reforms had their impact on the policy paradigms relating to education and its progress in various fields.

The post First World War period saw the British repression at its worst. The much maligned Rowlatt Act was imposed in 1919, which authorised the detention of any Indian without trial. This was followed by the Jallianwala Bagh massacre in which thousands of unarmed Indians were brutally murdered. This period also witnessed the execution of Bhagat Singh, Raj Guru and Sukhdev as also the martyrdom of Lala Lajpat Rai. The Quit India Movement in 1942 led to revolt against the British rule. The World War-II reduced the British Empire's capacity to hold the countries under its rule. The events, thereafter, followed with much rapidity till the British announced their decision to quit India.

India Attains Freedom

It is not intended to analyse the circumstances leading to the decision of the British Government to quit India even after attaining a victory over the so called Fascist powers and Japan in a prolonged war of attrition extending to over six years (1939-45). It could be that as a consequence of the War, the emergence of the two superpowers - the USA and the USSR - eclipsed the once mighty British Empire, which, even otherwise, had suffered a great economic loss. Further, the strident Indian nationalism culminating into Mahatma Gandhi's launching of the Quit India Movement and his call to the people of India to 'Do or Die' forced the saner elements among the British die-hards to realise that the 'White Man's Burden' was becoming too burdensome and that they must quit gracefully before it became too difficult for them to hold on.

The British Government relinquished its Indian Empire on the 15th of August 1947, almost ten months before the previously announced date of 3rd June, 1948. On this day, the country threw away its yoke of slavery, which had held India's conscience in its vicious stranglehold for centuries. Before quitting, however, the wily Britishers saw to it that this ancient land was partitioned into two sovereign states on the basis of religion. This was based on the infamous policy of the British Government of '*divide et empera*', which they had followed all along during their suzerainty over India.

The Aftermath of Partition

The partition of the country unleashed, on an unprecedented scale, the process of death and destruction, social turmoil and pathological antagonism between the two newly created States. It also led to massive population transfers between the two countries. Based on 1951 census of the displaced persons, 7.266 million Muslims went to Pakistan immediately after partition, while 7.249 million Hindus and Sikhs moved to India. 11.2 million or 78 per cent of the population transfer was on the western periphery of India, with Punjab on both sides accounting for most of it. It also led to unabated slaughter of innocent people, which occurred on both sides of the border as the newly formed governments were completely unequipped to deal with migration of such staggering magnitude. Estimates of death vary from two hundred thousand to one million!

Blow to Indian Economy/Education

Under the circumstances prevailing in the country during the period immediately following the unplanned partition of a vast sub-continent like India, one can imagine the heavy blow that it would have caused to the Indian economy, its socio-cultural moorings and the systems of education.

We have dealt with these issues in relevant chapters. Suffice it to say that the situation was precarious, perhaps too serious to require a drastic plan of concrete action.

Objectives of the Study

In the backdrop of these developments extending to about 134 years of the British Colonialism and about 66 years of independent India, it would be useful to critically examine the various contours of the development of Indian education- its progress, problems and perspectives. The study will, however, have to be done separately for the two periods:

1. India under the Colonial rule and
2. India as an independent country.

The major objectives of the study are:

1. To discuss the policy paradigms relating to education that were evolved by the respective governments;
2. To analyse the various stages of educational development - over all as well as sectoral;
3. To make an analytical study of the financial investment in education; its quantum, inter-sectoral/inter-regional priorities;
4. To highlight the nature and extent of significant events that impacted Indian education during the two periods; and
5. To study the profiles of important personalities, who attempted to alter the course of educational development according to their perception and the extent to which they were successful.

A Clarification

It needs to be mentioned that the study is not in the nature of the usual survey of education in an historical perspective. It analyses selected episodes in education under the Colonial rule as also in independent India. In analysing the various episodes, however, the historical sequence has been kept in view.

Another important aspect of the study is the discussion about the effect of significant events that occurred during the two periods and impacted the educational system. The study also discusses profiles of personalities who attempted to change the course of education according to their perceptions. The extent to which they were successful in their mission has also been examined.

As already stated, the study has been presented in two parts which, though interlinked, stand apart. The first part is an analysis of the development of education under the Colonial rule; its policy paradigms, financial systems etc. The second part relates to the analysis of almost the same aspects of education in the post-independence period. It may, however, be clarified that the study does not aim at giving a comparative picture of the state of Indian education during the periods under review. In fact, in view of the vastly different administrative systems, policy paradigms, quantum of financial investments, the geographical dimensions of the provinces/native states during the two periods, no valid comparison can be arrived at. One can, however, view the state of education by juxtaposing the situation emerging under the two periods.

Collection of Data

The data/facts in respect of the various aspects of the study were collected mainly from the National Archives of India, the Central Secretariat Library, Planning Commission, the Central Statistical Organisation and institutions like the National University of Educational Planning and Administration, National Council of Educational Research and Training, University Grants Commission, and All India Council of Technical Education. Besides, some important reports/publications were also studied.

Limitations of the Study

The study is based on the data/facts obtained from the files of the National Archives of India; Reports of some Commissions/Committees on various aspects of education appointed by the Government of India/provincial governments from time to time. In view of the absence of any standing mechanism of data collection for a long time in the initial stages of the Company's rule, there is no possibility of ensuring continuity and authenticity of the data relating to the different periods. Further, in view of the fast changing systems of school and college education, it has not been possible to attempt at comparing the findings of the different periods of study. Also it is difficult to compare the magnitude of financial investment in education and the priorities given to various sectors because of the vast changing purchasing power parity (PPP). In spite of these limitations, an attempt has been made to analyse the data and facts and to draw some meaningful conclusions.

It has also been observed that in spite of the genuine efforts made by Government agencies like the National and State Archives and the libraries to preserve old documents, the ravages of time have taken their toll, particularly on those documents that belong to the eighteenth and nineteenth centuries. In some cases the wear and tear of some pages made it difficult to decipher the contents fully. Further, some pages of the Reports have become so brittle that unless extra care is taken, the pages could be torn. It has also been seen that at some places the write up had become very indistinct; almost illegible. In such cases one had to take resort to making a guess of the contents - not a very scientific, but the only way of basing one's analysis on such contents. Mercifully, the number of such documents is not very large and, therefore, this deficiency has in no way affected the authenticity of the facts stated and the conclusions drawn, in the study.

It is hoped that the study will give a new dimension to the history of educational development under the Colonial rule and in post-independence India. It will also enable those concerned with Indian education to develop an insight into the entire spectrum of Indian education, past and present; its bright spots, failings and oddities in order to give an objective raison d'être for educational development in India in times to come.

PART-I— EDUCATION DURING THE COLONIAL RULE

This part discusses the development of Education mainly during the period 1813 to 1947. It also analyses the policy paradigms evolved by the colonial masters; the development of education – sector-wise; significant events that impacted Indian education and the profiles and contribution of important personalities – Indian and British – who attempted to alter the course of Indian education.

This part has been divided into 8 chapters, a list of which has been given in the 'Contents'.

1

Educational Policy

"Education in India under the British Government was first ignored, then violently and successfully opposed, then conducted on a system universally admitted to be erroneous and finally placed on the present footing." (Arthur Howell, Education in British India: Prior to 1854 and in 1870-71, Calcutta, Government Printing, 1872)

The East India Company, established in 1600 AD, did not pay any attention to education of Indians, over whose destinies its progeny had the privilege to preside for about two hundred years. In the initial stages, the Company concentrated mainly on trade and commerce, besides expanding its territories by aggression, subterfuge and deceit. It was only in 1698 that the Charter Act enjoined on the Company to maintain priests in schools in its garrisons. Proselytisation was an important objective of the Company's rule. By winning the Battle of Plassey in 1757 and with the grant of Diwani in 1765, the Company became a ruling power. Education, however, did not attract their attention. There were some sporadic efforts by individuals like Warren Hastings, William Adam, etc. to start educational institutions providing instructions in Sanskrit and Arabic.

Rudiments of Some Policy Framework

The sporadic efforts made by individual members of the ruling class and the sentiments of some Indians about the shape that education should take could not be regarded as the emergence of a policy framework for guiding the development of Indian education. It would, however, not be out of place to mention some of the pioneering efforts - regardless of their sinister motivation-to draw up some policy guidelines that would determine the shape of Indian education.

The much talked about, among the policy makers, relating to the shape that education of the natives of India should take, was Sir Charles Grant (1746-1823), who proposed an 'education plan' based on a 'healing principle' fired by an uncanny evangelistic zeal. Grant heaped scorn over religions, social customs and the way of living of the two communities - the Hindus and the Muslims. He asserted that both these communities were morally and socially bankrupt and the only way to save them from the abyss of depravity was to remove their ignorance, which was possible only by exposing them to 'our arts, our philosophy and our religion'. He vehemently advocated the conversion of the natives of this ancient land to protestant Christianity.

We will give some details about Grant, his motivation to work out a policy paradigm as also the problems that could have emerged from the implementation of that policy. It may, however, be noted at this stage that fortunately better counsels prevailed on the Government of that time and no tangible action was taken to implement Grant's long winding treatise, which contained abuses and derogatory references to the Indian communities in plenty. In fact, Grant's 'healing principle' was submerged in the labyrinth of the fast developing events that followed.

Before discussing Grant's plan of action relating to Indian education, it would be appropriate to draw up a brief biographical sketch and a summary of the views of this self-proclaimed crusader for spreading Christianity in India so as to 'civilize' the natives who inhabited this country.

Charles Grant (1746-1823)

Charles Grant came to India in 1776 as an army officer. Later, through the recommendations of his friends and acquaintances, he was raised to the position of Superintendent Overall of the East India Company's trade in Bengal. Lord Cornwallis, the then Governor General, appointed Grant as a member of the East India Company's Board of Trade in 1787 and later as Chairman of the Company's Court of Directors. In 1792, he wrote his much publicised essay entitled 'Observations on the State of Society Among the Asiatic Subjects of Great Britain, particularly with Respect to Morals; and on the Means of Improving It'. This essay was presented to the East India Company and the House of Commons in 1813 and printed in that year. The main points made by Grant in his treatise are discussed briefly: Grant's main thesis was built on his perception that the Indian society was rotten to the core; it was debased and corrupt and required a full scale surgical operation to remove the cancerous applications. He believed that Company's rule in India was a necessity of the time. But it was always at stake due to the immoral character of the Indian people. In order to perpetuate the Company's rule, a radical transformation of the moral, religious and social character of Indian society was imperative and this could be possible only through the introduction of Christianity.

Grant charged the Hindus - the majority in India - with dishonesty, corruption, fraud, mutual hatred and distrust. According to him, the Indian social system was in a universal state of degradation, depravity and degeneration. "It was the despotic nature of Hinduism, its failure to teach virtue and its positive encouragement of immorality, which was the cause of the degeneration of Indian society"[1].

About Muslims, Grant was equally condemnatory. He considered the Muslims not very different from the Hindus but worse than the Hindus in morals, supported by political power. He depicted Muslims as proud, fierce, lawless and superstitious and made by success, more proud, sanguinary, sensual and bigoted. According to him, the Muslim government was a violent despotism, devoid of all restraint of morals; practising oppression, atrocities and cruelties. He said the Muslim rule in India was a divine punishment for the immoral Hindus in the form of 'successive treacheries, assassinations and usurpation".[2] Grant asserted that to make matters worse, the intercourse of two communities had led to further debasement of both because each had imbibed the vices of the other. He therefore stressed that the Company was under no obligation to protect the creed of the Hindus, which was monstrous and subversive of the first principles of reason, morality and religion.

Grant took the high moral ground of reforming the natives who, according to him had descended into the abyss of depravity and moral degradation. He argued that the main method of *civilizing* (emphasis added) the Indian society and its morality and religion would, for the Company, be to allow Christian missionaries into India along with Christianity's legal establishment.

After his malicious, highly provocative and vituperative condemnation of the religion, culture and social moorings of the two Indian communities, Grant was 'gracious' enough to unfold his education plan. He pleaded that the Company should apply a 'healing principle'. He stopped short of suggesting the use of the mighty force that 'we possess to destroy the distinctions of castes and to demolish their idols'. Instead, he suggested that the Hindus' ignorance which was the primary cause of their moral and social degradation could be countered by dispensing knowledge to them. According to him, the Hindus err because "they are ignorant and their errors have never fairly been laid before them. The communication of our light and knowledge to them would prove the best remedy for their disorders..."[3]

In short, the remedy suggested by the great 'Messiah' of the eighteenth century was the imposition of protestant Christianity of the colonial masters on the hapless subjects and of the arts and sciences of Europe, which he called the 'superior lights' of the west.

The 'superior lights' were to be communicated not through the Indian languages, but through the language of rulers, viz. English. Backed by the brutal force that the colonial masters commanded, he brazenly declared: "...it is perfectly in the power of this country (England) by decrees to impart to the Hindoos our language; afterwards, through that medium, to make them acquainted with our easy literary compositions upon a variety of subjects; and let not the idea hastily excite derision, *progressively with the simple elements of our arts, our philosophy and our religion*. (emphasis added). These acquisitions would silently undermine and at length subvert the fabric of error and all the objections that may be apprehended against such a change, are, it is confidently believed, capable of a solid answer. The first communication, and the instrument of introducing the rest, must be the English Language; this is a key, which will open to them a world of new ideas, and policy alone might have impelled us, long since; to put it into their hands".[4]

It is not difficult to question the bonafides of Grant in denouncing the tenets of Hindu religion in the most crude and prejudicial manner. It is also doubtful whether the 'healing principle' advocated by him was really workable on the scale on which it could be effective when an organised educational system was still to make any headway. Further, Grant failed to recognise the resilience of the Hindu religion, which had withstood the onslaught of foreign rule for about ten centuries.

It seems that Grant was so much fired by the evangelistic zeal that he did not think of verifying his facts about the state of Indian society at that time. He thought that the best way to propagate Christianity was to denounce vehemently and demolish the existing social customs and religious beliefs of the Indian communities. He, however, nowhere mentioned the basis of such a fierce and rabid condemnation of the Indian society. Instead, he did not hesitate to build the edifice of education on an infirm foundation of ignorance and hatred.

In his zeal for converting the Indian population to Christianity, the method suggested by him - the introduction of English as the medium of instruction - was also violative of the accepted principles of transmitting knowledge at the school stage through mother tongue. It is universally accepted that the best way of educating children - at least in the lower stages - is to teach them through their mother-tongue. Grant's emphasis on classroom teaching through a foreign language had the potential of stultifying the minds of the children and retarding their creativity. In his zeal for conversion of the populace to Christianity, Grant had no qualms in suggesting an absurd, unrealistic and unworkable plan of education.

The First Policy Directive

Fortunately the fulminations of this utterly biased 'reformer' were drowned in the policy guidelines contained in the Charter Act of 1813, which enjoined on the Governor General in Council to apply a sum of not less than Rs. one lakh each year to the 'revival and improvement of literature and the encouragement of the learned natives of India and for the introduction and promotion of a knowledge of sciences among the inhabitants of the British territories of India".[5] The Despatch of 1814, which announced the grant (the first educational Despatch of the Court of Directors) clarified that the 'sciences' referred to were oriental sciences - the many excellent systems of ethics contained in the Sanskrit language "with codes of laws and compendiums of the duties relating to every class of people; tracts of merit and the virtues of plants and drugs and many other things, the study of which might do much to those natives, who may be destined for the judicial department of the government".[6]

The Controversy Erupts

The clear direction given in the Despatches of 1813 and 1814 - that the amount be spent on promotion of education in 'oriental sciences; and the many systems of ethics contained in the Sanskrit Language - led to a very fierce controversy as to the manner in which the amount earmarked for education should be spent. The main contenders were Lord T.B. Macaulay and H.T. Prinsep, Chairman and member of the Committees of Public Instruction respectively. The different facets of the controversy have been discussed in a separate chapter. The controversy ended with the hastily taken decision of Lord William Bentinck, that the promotion of western sciences and the introduction of English language should be the objective instead of the Indian vernaculars. The places for oriental learning were, however, to be retained as long as there was demand for them.

The possible dangers of this development were early observed. Raja Radhakant Deb wrote: "Nothing should be guarded against more carefully than the insensible introduction of a system whereby, with a smattering knowledge of English, youths are weaned from the plough, the axe and the loom to render their ambitions only for the clerkship for which hosts would besiege the government and mercantile offices, and the majority being disappointed (as they must be) would (and with their little knowledge inspiring pride) be unable to return to their trade; and would necessarily turn vagabonds. The evil is not wholly imaginary. But it is often exaggerated. Justice has not been done to vernaculars. But no system that could have been invented would have been flawless."[7]

The Despatch of 1854

The Despatch of 1854, which, according to the Calcutta University Commission (1917-19) was, in its main conception, a bold, farseeing and statesman-like document, declared that 'among many subjects of importance none can have a strongest claim to our attention than that of education', "it is one of our most sacred duties to be the means, as far as it in us lies, of conferring upon the natives of India, those vast moral and natural blessings, which flow from the general diffusion of useful knowledge, and which India may under providence, derive from her connection with England. For although, British influence has already, in many remarkable instances, been applied with great energy and success to uproot demoralising practices and even crimes of deeper dye, which for ages had prevailed among the natives of India, the good results of those efforts must, in order to be permanent, possess the further sanction of a general sympathy in the native mind, which the advance of education alone can secure."[8]

Notwithstanding the unnecessary and uncalled for sanctimonious and holier than thou tenor of the opening statement of the Despatch, it may be conceded that its most notable feature was the emphasis, which it laid upon elementary education, hitherto disregarded by government and therefore its implicit repudiation of the more extreme forms of the 'Filtration' theory. To implement its intent, the Despatch recommended the creation of a Department of Public Instruction in every province with a staff of inspectors, anticipating that this Department would implement and supervise the recommended educational policy, an expectation which was not fulfilled, especially in Bengal.

The Despatch also laid emphasis on the proper inspection of schools, the setting up of universities in the then Presidency towns; the establishment of teacher education institutions; maintenance of the existing government colleges and high schools and increase in their number, whenever necessary, increased attention to vernacular schools, both for primary and secondary education and the introduction of the system of grants-in-aid.

The System of Grant-in-Aid

In the belief that government activity alone could never be sufficient to create such a system as was contemplated, the Government broke away definitely from the practice followed since 1835, when most of the available public funds had been expended upon a few government schools and colleges. It instituted a systematic policy of 'grants in aid' to be distributed by the Departments of Public Instruction to all institutions, which should reach an approved standard. The Government "looked forward to a time, when any general system of education entirely provided by the government might be discontinued, with the advance of the system of grant-in-aid and when many of the existing government institutions, especially those of a higher order may be safely closed or transferred to the management of local bodies, under the control of and aided by the state. Further, after taking the view that 'public funds' would be most profitably used if they were employed to benevolence, it even contemplated the ultimate abandonment by the government of direct control over many of its existing institutions, while recognising the necessity of their maintenance for the present."[9] This policy was modelled upon the educational policy followed in Britain by the British government of that date. "The plan was that every honest educational agency, whether religious or not, should be encouraged to the utmost, under the inspection and direction of a government department, and with the encouragement and assistance of the local officers of Government upon the value of which emphasis was laid".[10]

We have given detailed description of the Grants-in-Aid system in a separate chapter.

The Modus Operandi

In order to carry out its policy, the Despatch of 1854 laid down the following conditions:

1. The constitution in each Presidency and Lt. Governorship of a department of education for administration of education with an adequate system of inspection;
2. The establishment of universities in the Presidency towns; it may be stated that the universities were established on the basis of the Resolution of the Government on India on 12th December, 1856. The Resolution was based on recommendations of a Committee appointed by the Government of India on 26th of January, 1855. The Committee submitted its report on the 7th August, 1856;
3. The establishment of institutions for the training of teachers for all classes of schools;
4. The maintenance of the existing government colleges and increase in their numbers, wherever necessary;
5. Increased attention to vernacular schools both for secondary and primary education;
6. Emphasis on female education;
7. No use of government influence for proselytisation.

The Despatch ended by endorsing the hope expressed by Sir Thomas Munro that any expense, which may be incurred for this object (education) "will be amply repaid by the improvement of the country; for the general diffusion of knowledge is inseparably followed by more orderly habits; by increasing industry; by a taste for the comforts of life; by exertion to acquire them and by the growing prosperity of the people."[11]

The Despatch of 1859

The Despatch of 1859 reviewed the progress in education achieved till then and advocated the adoption of further steps for the promotion of primary education, including the levy of a special cess on land for financing vernacular education.

It would be seen that the British government in India took some halting steps to evolve a policy framework for education of the natives. As already stated, the first Policy Directive (1813) gave rise to a controversy between what were called the 'Anglicists' and the 'Orientalists'. It was only in the mid nineteenth century that the Government of India was able to arrive at a decision. The "first war of independence" (1857) was probably a reason which diverted the attention of the government away from education although it resulted in the government taking control of the administration of the colony. The Education Commission of 1882 attempted to refocus the government's attention on education. It is, however, difficult to say the extent to which the Commission was able to draw government's attention towards education. It may, however, be conceded that one major achievement of this period was the introduction of the grants-in-aid system, which encouraged the setting up of educational institutions - religious or secular - by the private bodies. Although the system did not help in developing an education system that would meet the needs of the country, it facilitated the expansion of education in India to a significant extent. The system is still in vogue with some modifications. Another major achievement was the setting up of universities in three presidencies of Calcutta, Madras and Bombay in 1857. Later, the Punjab University was established in 1882.

Other Developments

Indian Education Commission (1882-83)

In 1882, the government appointed Indian Education Commission, popularly known as the Hunter Commission to review the progress of Indian education and to suggest measures that would 'further extend' the system for India's teeming millions. The review was to be carried out in the context of the implementation of the recommendations made by the Despatch of 1854. The main recommendations of the Commission were:

(a) Indigenous Education

(i) All indigenous schools set up by natives should be recognised and encouraged. Their teachers should be given professional training. The curriculum should contain all that is valued by the people.

(ii) The schools should be given grant-in-aid and should be subject to inspection by government inspectors. The aid should be given by local and municipal boards. Schools should be given freedom to develop in their own way.

(iii) The local inspecting officials should be ex-officio members of the Municipal or District School Boards.

Primary Education

The recommendations of the Indian Education Commission about primary education have been given in detail in the relevant chapter. Briefly it may be stated that the Commission referred to primary education as the education of the masses, which should be imparted through vernaculars. Further, funding of primary education should be the first charge on government and local revenues. The Commission also recommended that the curriculum should be based on the local needs and practical aspect should be emphasised.

(b) Secondary Education

(i) In the upper classes of high schools, there should be two divisions - one leading to the entrance examination of the universities and the other of a more practical character to fit youth for commercial or other non-literary pursuits.

(ii) High and middle schools be merged to be called secondary schools.

(iii) An examination on the principles and practices of teaching be instituted, success in which should, hereafter, be a condition for permanent employment as a teacher in any secondary school.

(iv) A scheme of scholarships by open competition should be launched. Scholarships should be paid out of public funds, including educational endowments.

(c) Collegiate Education

(i) Aid to colleges should be determined by the strength of staff, expenditure on maintenance, efficiency of the institution and the needs of the locality.

(ii) Attempt should be made to prepare a moral text book, based upon the fundamentals of various religions.

(iii) Fees at the highest rate, consistent with the undiminished spread of education, should be levied. No aided college should levy fees at the same rate as charged in a neighbouring government college.

(iv) There should be a provision for scholarships particularly tenable for post graduate students.

(d) Female Education

(i) Female education should be considered as a legitimate charge on local, municipal and provincial funds and receive special encouragement; eligibility conditions for aid to girls' schools should be relaxed.

(ii) Rules be framed for the gradual replacement of male by female teachers in girls' schools.

It would be seen that the Commission made comprehensive recommendations for accelerating the process of educational development. Keeping in view the suggestions made in the Despatches of 1854 and 1859, the focus of recommendations was on school education, particularly primary education, which was brought under the local boards. The government, however, provided assistance to the boards, which eased their financial position. Indigenous schools were also brought under the control of local boards. At the secondary stage, the Commission's recommendations on diversification of courses did not attain much success. At the collegiate stage, there was a spurt in the setting up of institutions by private bodies. In this context, mention may be made of reformers like R.P. Paranjpe, Bal Gangadhar Tilak, Triplankar Iyanger, Surendar Nath Banerji and Mahirishi Dayanand Saraswati, who did pioneering work in setting up of educational institutions in the country.

Policy during the Twentieth Century

The educational policy of the Government of India in the twentieth century could be discussed in two phases:

Phase-I - 1900-1920 (inclusive of the First World War 1914-18)

Phase-II - 1920-47 (Post War period culminating in India's independence)

Phase 1 - 1900-1920

The education policy during this period was determined by two important events that took place within a span of the first 12 years of that century. They were:

1. The policy paradigms emanating from Lord Curzon's address to the Educational Conferences organised by the Government of India in September, 1901[12] and again in September, 1905.[13]
2. The recommendations of the Indian Universities Commission, 1902.

The main recommendations made in the above addresses/conferences are briefly summed up below:

1. *Lord Curzon's Views* - The two addresses delivered by Lord Curzon made a comprehensive review of the Indian education scenario at that time. They also contained suggestions for taking steps to modify the system. He stated:

(a) Primary Education

"...in primary education, we have realised that improvement means money; we have laid down that primary education must be a leading charge on provincial revenues; and in order to supply the requisite impetus, we gave in our last budget a very large permanent annual grant of Rs. 35 lakhs to be devoted to that purpose alone. This will be the real starting point of an advance that ought never to be allowed henceforward to slacken. Most of the money will go in buildings, to begin with, and a good deal in maintenance afterwards...I look as the result of the policy to see a great development in elementary education in the near future. It is apt to be neglected in India in favour of the louder calls and the more showy results of higher education. Both are equally necessary, but in the structure of Indian society, one is the foundation and the other the coping stone; and we, who are responsible, must be careful not to forget the need of the voiceless masses while we provide for the interests of the more highly favoured minority, who are better able to protect themselves".[14]

(b) Secondary Education

"The fruit of these is the degree to which it is being carried out by the Government policy as laid down by the Education Commission of 1882-83 and by subsequent Resolutions - viz. that private effort should be encouraged by every possible means, and that government should gradually withdraw from the direct management of secondary schools. This seems to me to be a very difficult question, for while it cannot be doubted that the principles underlying this policy are sound, and progress in that direction should be our aim; secondary education is not yet, in most parts, in a position to stand alone. The existence of a limited number of well managed government schools undoubtedly serves to keep up a high standard in aided school, and their disappearance would probably be followed by a serious diminution in the quality of the secondary education. My view is that a *pari passu* development will probably for sometime longer be found desirable, but that government should be careful to regard its own institutions, not as competitors but as models..."[15]

"In secondary education, the faults were largely the same and the remedies must be the same also. More teachers are the first desideratum, more competent teachers the second, more inspectors the third, next comes the reform in courses of study and buildings..."[16]

(c) Higher Education

"....the first reflection that strikes every observer of the Indian system, who is familiar with the older English universities, is the fundamental contrast, both of character and conception. Oxford and Cambridge are incorporated institutions, composed of colleges, which constitute and are embodied in the corporate whole. The two together make the university..."[17]

"How different in India! Here the university has no corporate existence in the same sense of the term: it is not a collection of buildings, it is scarcely even a site. It is a body that conducts courses of study and sets examination papers to the pupils of affiliated colleges. They are not part of it. They are frequently not in the same city, sometimes not in the same province. The affiliated colleges of the Calcutta University are scattered in regions as remote as Burma and Ceylon. Then look at the colleges. They are not residential institutions, with a history, a tradition, a *genius loci*, a tutorial staff of their own... They are bound to each other by no tie of common feelings, and to the university, by no tie of filial reverence. On the contrary, each for the most part regards the others as rivals, and pursues its own path in self-centered and sometimes jealous isolation...."[18]

"Is it not equally our duty to maintain a high standard in the affiliation of colleges? I have examined the system in vogue in different university areas, and find that no two are alike and that in some cases, carelessness has crept in. I think that we want to exercise great caution and vigilance in the recognition of these affiliated institutions and that incentives should be given to their maintenance of initial standard....

"Higher Education ought not to be run either by politicians or by amateurs. It is a science; service of human life and conduct in which we must give a fair hearing and a reasonable chance to professor."[19]

The **Indian Universities Commission**[20] was appointed in 1902 under Mr. T. Raleigh. Its main objective was to inquire into the conditions and prospects of the universities established in British India; to consider and report upon any proposals, which have been, or may be, made for improving their constitution and working, and to recommend to the Governor General in Council such measures as may lead to elevate the standard of university teaching and to promote the advancement of learning.

The Commission made important recommendations about the development of higher education as also the augmentation of resources. It recommended that till changes proposed by the Commission for the constitution and working of existing universities have been tested by experience; no new university should be set up.

University Bodies

1. The legal powers of the older universities should be enlarged so that all of them may be recognised as teaching universities. Under-graduate education should be left to the colleges. The universities may make better provision for post-graduate and advanced courses.
2. The Commission made detailed recommendations about appointment of Fellows to the senates of various universities.
3. It is not necessary to insist on uniformity in the arrangement of faculties
4. The Senate may appoint such Boards of study as it thinks necessary from among its own members.
5. The syndicate should not be a large body. The minimum number may be nine and the maximum 15. The syndicate should be elected by the senate.
6. New affiliation rules should be framed giving justification for the application of an institution and its financial viability.
7. A college should have a regularly constituted governing body, adequate teaching staff, adequate provision for teaching various courses, etc.

Other Recommendations

(i) The examination system should be modified and simplified;
(ii) Minimum age of matriculation should be sixteen;
(iii) Second grade colleges should be gradually closed;
(iv) Teaching of law in arts colleges should be revived;
(v) Teaching of agriculture sciences should be encouraged;
(vi) Quality and status of courses in Indian classical languages should be improved.

University Finances

About university finances, the Commission's suggestions were:

(i) All institutions maintained by the State must refrain from competing with aided or private institutions by charging lower fees and the Departments of Public Instruction and the managers of private institutions should cooperate to raise fees gradually and cautiously in all colleges. This policy aims at rendering the institutions, aided or maintained by the state, less dependent on assistance from public revenues, and is also designed to secure greater efficiency and success in private institutions.

(ii) The primary considerations that should be observed in the settlement of fees would be: "that they must not be pitched so high as to check the spread of education, and secondly, that they must not be fixed so low as to tempt a poor student of ordinary ability to follow a university course, which is not to his real interest to undertake... No poor but really able student should be excluded, by reason of his poverty, from the advantages of higher education, but these should be secured for him not by charging nominal fees, or by the indiscriminate bestowal of free-studentships, or the establishment of free colleges, but by a comprehensive and liberal system of scholarships..."[21] A further consideration is that no college under private management should be required to levy fees at the same rate as in force in a neighbouring government college.... It is, however, impossible to suggest a minimum scale of fees, which should be made applicable to all privately managed colleges.[22]

"....We consider that the first thing towards improvement must be a raising of the present very low level of fees now charged at some colleges. We, therefore, recommend that the syndicate of each university should, in consultation with the managers, prescribe a minimum rate of fees for the colleges affiliated to it, after taking into consideration local circumstances, the demand for higher education, and the ability of the class of students, who are likely to attend the institution, to pay adequate fees for each instruction. This rate will be primarily applicable to the circumstances of colleges, which obtain no pecuniary aid from government. The State has in its power to regulate the rates of fees at both the government and aided colleges, and should, in our opinion, fix the fees at both these classes of colleges, at a rate higher than the rate, at the former being necessarily fixed higher than at the latter class of colleges.[23]

Besides fees, the Commission made the following suggestions for the creation and augmentation of university resources:

(i) The principle should be recognised that if the universities are to incur additional expenditure in order to improve the education of their students, it is not unreasonable that they should charge higher fees, and each university should consider how far it can, by means of resources already at its disposal and by raising its fees, find funds for new expenditure.

(ii) The scale on which government supports and aids the colleges may be recommended in view of the increased expenditure to which the acceptance of the foregoing recommendations must lead. Unless, by Government aid or otherwise, the financial position of the universities can be materially strengthened, the prospect of any thorough change for the better must be indefinitely postponed".[24]

Government of India's Resolution (1904)

In the backdrop of these recommendations, the policy of the Government of India was enunciated in a Resolution of the Government in 1904[25], which accepted the Education Commission (1882)'s suggestions about the continuous withdrawal of the Government from primary, secondary and collegiate education and its devolution to the private sector. It also reaffirmed the intention of the Government not to enter into any competition with private enterprise. The Resolution, inter-alia, stated:

1. The Government of India recognised the extreme importance of the principle that in each branch of education, government should maintain a limited number of institutions as models for private enterprise to follow. In order to uphold direct management, it was considered essential that government should retain a general control, by means of efficient inspection, over all public educational institutions.
2. The Resolution reiterated the views of the Commission of 1882 in regard to the importance of primary education. It stated that promoting education had received inadequate attention and insufficient funds and that its provision should be made a leading charge on provincial revenues. It also stressed that teaching in rural schools should be adapted to the needs of the rural community.
3. Female education should be promoted.
4 The university bodies should be streamlined. Universities should be given teaching powers in addition to their examining powers. Financial aid to universities should be enhanced. They could also receive funds from private sources.

Important Developments

During the period 1904 and 1913, the following important developments took place:

(1) The introduction of a bill in the Imperial Legislative Council for the extension of elementary education, which would have made the provision of compulsory primary education permissible, that is subject to the consent of the local authorities and local governments.[26]
The Bill was officially opposed on the grounds that there had been no popular demand for the measure, that local governments were opposed to it and the few, though not of the majority of non-officials, were also hostile; while the idea of additional local taxation was thoroughly opposed...[27]
(The subject has been dealt with thoroughly in a separate chapter; 7).

(2) In April 1905, the Government of India established the Agricultural Research Institute at Pusa in Bengal. From this establishment emerged the Central

College of Agriculture, which was given 1.30 lakh pounds for research, education and demonstration. The Institute has since been shifted to Delhi.

(3) The Tata Institute of Science at Bangalore was given a legal status on 27th May, 1909. The Institute was given an initial grant of Rs. 30 lakh by Sir Jamsetji Tata, who originally conceived of this post-graduate centre for research in Chemistry and Medicine.

(4) On 18th July 1911, the Government of India approved the proposal of establishing the Muslim University at Aligarh. Four years later, the Beneras Hindu University was set up. Both these institutions are now central universities.

(5) A conference of vice-chancellors of universities was held on December 5, 1911. The Conference made the following recommendations, particularly about research in universities.

At present, there is very little desire for research. The main reasons for this are:

1. Our system of education, as at present organised, does not lead students naturally to continue beyond a certain point to regions of research;
2. A subsidiary reason is that there are at present not many opportunities for research in the country.

The Conference recognised that it was an essential part of university to stimulate and conduct research. Further, it was necessary to give encouragement to research students by means of fellowships which will support them comfortably during their study and lead to some academic appointment afterwards. It is out of question financially for the universities to provide really adequate means of research. But a beginning should be made, if the universities of India or groups of universities combined to induce some really eminent professor in his own subject to give a course of lectures. This, however, would require to be financed by the government. The universities could not do more than cooperate and possibly send a few students to a centre.

Further Developments: 1913 Onwards

The policy of the Government of India regarding Indian education was further elaborated in the Resolution of 1913,[28] which declared the major intent of their policy as formation of character of scholars and undergraduates under tuition. The main features of the Resolution were:

1. It reiterated its policy of not acceding to the introduction of compulsion in primary education due to financial and administrative reasons. It, however, reaffirmed its resolve to make available resources for improving and expanding primary education on a voluntary basis.
2. It advocated the teaching of hygiene and medical inspection of schools.
3. It stressed the need for improving and multiplying middle schools, provision of competent teachers and improving their training.
4. It underlined the need for expanding facilities for girls' education and increase in the number of women teachers.

5. It reaffirmed the policy of relying mainly on private effort in secondary education with the assistance of a more elastic system of grant-in-aid.
6. It endorsed the view that the secondary school final examination should be conducted by organisations other than the universities - a precursor to the creation of Boards of Secondary Education.
7. It recognised the necessity for improving the pay and prospects of teachers in the educational services.
8. It reported improvement in the condition of the five existing universities (Calcutta, Bombay, Madras, Allahabad and Punjab) but advocated reduction in the jurisdiction of these universities and the establishment of teaching facilities at their centres, with adequate libraries. It also announced the setting up of teaching and residential universities particularly at Dacca, Benaras and Aligarh. It also urged the necessity for providing facilities for research in every branch of learning.

The First World War and Political Unrest

Educational development in India came to a grinding halt due to the First World War (1914-18). India, under the British hegemony, had to divert all its resources to fight a war in which it had no stake. Under the post - war political reforms of 1920, education became a transferred subject, with provincial governments principally responsible for it.

Economic Depression

The devastating war heralded a period of economic distress and political unrest. The long continuance of the war led to economic depression. "The cost of education rose with the price of food and clothing and school material. Employment proved hard or impossible to get...."[29] Further, the Non-Cooperation Movement launched in 1920, "succeeded in crippling some schools beyond recovery; in disorganising the work of others for six months or a year and in ruining the careers of many promising scholars...."[30] The nationalist parties like Indian National Congress, issued an appeal to the student community to break away from the control of government... The power of appeal was strengthened by a very genuine discontent with a course of education, which appeared to lead to nothing, but the acquisition of a degree, an honour no longer worth the money spent on acquiring it. The political appeal was thus supported by economic considerations. Finally, it must be admitted that the appeal was made to the most inflammable material (the students).[31]

Phase II - 1920-1947

Political Reforms

It is not intended, at this stage, to dwell upon the educational implications of the political upsurge caused by the non-cooperation movement launched by the Indian National Congress in its Nagpur session of 1920. It may, however, be pointed out that the 'attack' (non-cooperation movement) came in waves, which were not simultaneous in all provinces... It may safely be inferred that "non-cooperation movement was responsible during that year (1920-21) for a substantial, though not alarming, reduction in enrolment of higher and middle Anglo vernacular schools...".[32] The movement was followed by constitutional reforms under which education became a provincial transferred subject. By declaring education as a provincial subject, the Government of India Act did little more than state and define the existing position. The provincialisation of education, however, did not deprive the Government of India of all its educational functions. To enable it to exercise its functions and give advice on questions of educational policy, a Central Advisory Board of Education (CABE) was established in 1921, with the Bureau of Education to act as its secretariat.

Curtailment of Education Budgets

Despite signs of improvement in the economy during 1922-27, education budgets continued to be curtailed affecting the growth of educational development. Retrenchment committees were set up by the Government of India as well as by some provincial governments. Some of these committees suggested definite reduction in educational budgets.

The Central Retrenchment Committee[33]

The Retrenchment Committee appointed by the Government of India, known as the Inchcape Committee, made far reaching recommendations, most of which were unfortunately accepted. In particular, it suggested heavy reduction in the expenditure on education in areas directly controlled by the Government of India. It was a very short sighted recommendation, since all these areas were educationally backward. Further, it recommended the closing down of the Delhi University, which had just come into existence by an Act of Legislature in 1921. This caused a furore in the academic circles. Fortunately, wisdom dawned on authorities and the proposal was not accepted. The other recommendation, which was accepted, resulted in amalgamation of the Department of Education and Health with that of Revenue and Agriculture - a rather bizarre combination!

The Committee also proposed the abolition of the newly created Central Advisory Board of Education and the abolition of the post of Education Commissioner to the Government of India. Though the CABE and the Bureau of Education were abolished, the Education Commissioner was not sacked but saddled with some non-educational responsibilities. The strength of the Department of Education was considerably reduced although the number of subjects entrusted to it was formidable.

It was felt that although the extent and quality of education are fundamental to national life, there was no coordinating agency, which could look at the problems of education from an all India perspective. Further, under the Government of India Act, the Central Government was prohibited from making contribution towards subjects, which had been provincialised. This was an unfortunate development.

It had also been realised that the system of education, at that time, had been top heavy and needed to be placed on a really firm and stable basis. This meant a determined attack on the problem of providing universal primary education. The first step was to plan this attack in the light of local conditions and the resources available and the second was to translate it into action.[34]

It had been also felt that the education provided was not practical enough and sufficiently in touch with the child's environment and experience and not related to his other needs in later life. Secondary education was, in particular, too academic and suffered from a lack of variety. It accentuated the drift of unsuitable pupils towards higher literary education. There was considerable wastage in primary schools, which retarded progress towards attainment of literacy; there was lack of control by provincial governments over local bodies and the absence of coordination in the educational activities. All this led to serious consideration of the question of educational reconstruction.[35]

On the Threshold of Political Emancipation — Changing Policy Paradigms

As India moved towards independence from foreign rule, cataclysmic changes occurred in the government policy towards Indian education. The Central Advisory Board of Education, which was revived after being in a limbo for a few years, drew up what could be termed as the National Policy of Education (the Sargent Plan) and the first attempt at working out a broad framework of educational policy for India.[36]

It was realised that India was spending a very meagre amount per head on education; it was almost half a rupee in 1938-39 against about Rs. 33 in Great Britain.[37] It was also felt that while the aim of Indian education should be to attain a standard already attained in Great Britain and other western countries before the world war (1939-45), it should adopt methods best suited to Indian conditions. Further, because conditions prevailing in different parts of the country varied considerably, there could not be any attempt to impose some kind of uniformity on Indian education system.

It was also realised that the education of the future citizens should be based on certain fundamental principles, which should hold good regardless of time and space. The Board said: "...They (the Board) cannot conceive that any form of social or political community will prosper unless the importance of fostering, in the rising generation, such attributes as physical fitness, intelligence and integrity of character, receive the fullest recognition....at all stages of education, training of the intellect and the training of character must proceed side by side".[38]

The Board's specific recommendations concerning different stages of education are summarised below:

Basic (Primary and Middle) Education

(i) The age range for compulsory school education should be from six to fourteen years. Children may, however, be encouraged to attend school at the age of five. Universal compulsory education must be free.

(ii) Basic (Primary and middle) education embodies many of the educational ideas contained in the original Wardha Scheme, whose main principle of learning through activity has been endorsed by educationists all over the world. At the lower levels, activity would take many forms, leading gradually to basic craft suited to local conditions. The entire curriculum should be harmonised with this general conception. The three R's by themselves cannot be regarded as an adequate equipment for efficient citizenship. Education at the lower stages cannot be expected to be self-supporting.

(iii) Basic education, while preserving its essential unity, will consist of two stages, 'the Junior (or primary) stage covering three years and the senior (or middle) of three years.

(iv) The various types of post primary schools (other than Senior Basic Schools) should provide for a variety of courses extending over a period of at least five years after the age of eleven. These courses should prepare pupils for entry to industrial and commercial (and agricultural) occupations as well as to universities.

(v) English should not be introduced as a subject in the curriculum of Junior Basic Schools nor in the Senior Basic schools. Final decision may, however, be left to the provincial education departments.

(vi) The pay and status of teachers should be considerably improved. Emphasis on craft work, and correlation of other subjects thereunto, needs a high level of teaching skill, if it is to be successful. The minimum qualification for a basic school teacher should be matriculation followed by a two or three year course of professional training. At least three-fifth of the teachers in junior basic and one half of them in senior basic schools should be women.

(vii) An adequate provision of pre-primary education in the form of nursery schools should be an essential component of any national system of education.

High School Education

(i) High school course should cover six years with normal age of admission being eleven years.

(ii) Entry to high schools should be on a selective basis.

(iii) High schools should be of two main types - (a) academic and (b) technical. The objective of both should be to provide a good all round education, combined with some preparation in later stages for the careers which pupils will enter on leaving school.

(iv) The curriculum in all cases should be varied as circumstances permit and should not be unduly restricted by the entry requirements of universities.

University Education

(i) Indian universities, as they exist today, despite many admirable features, do not fully satisfy the requirements of a national system of education.

(ii) In order to raise standards all around, the conditions for admission must be revised with the objective of ensuring that students are capable of taking full advantage of university courses.

(iii) The present intermediate courses should be abolished. Ultimately, the entire course should be covered in high school but, as an immediate step, the first year of the intermediate stage should be transferred to high school and the second to university.

(iv) The minimum length of a university degree should be three years.

(v) The importance of establishing a high standard in post graduate studies and particularly in research in pure and applied sciences should be emphasised.

(vi) An Indian University Grants Commission should be established on the lines of the University Grants Committee of Great Britain. Its main function will be to exercise a general supervision over the allocation of grants to universities. The Commission, which should be a statutory authority, should coordinate university activities with a view to avoiding overlapping and for adjusting, as far as possible, the output of universities to the economic needs of the country.

Technical, Commercial and Art Education

1. In view of the prospective needs of post-war industry and commerce for skilled technicians and in order to cater to the aptitudes of those who will derive greater benefit from a practical course, the establishment of an efficient system of technical education at all stages is a matter of great urgency. This would necessitate:
   (a) making technical education system fulfil the needs of industry and commerce for properly trained workers of all grades and;
   (b) providing a suitable form of education for those boys and girls, whose natural abilities can best be developed by instruction on practical lines.
2. Instruction and training for women should be provided through the following main types of technical institutions:
   (i) Junior technical or industrial schools;
   (ii) Technical high schools; and
   (iii) Senior technical institutions.

Adult Education

1. Literacy is a means, not an end in itself. Although the main emphasis in the beginning should be on the liquidation of illiteracy, adult education in full sense of the term must be provided for all those already literate. With elimination of illiteracy, the stress should be on adult education and not only on literacy.
2. The quality of teachers is of primary importance. The difficulty of obtaining sufficient number of teachers, particularly women, should not be under-estimated.

Training of Teachers

1. The capacity of existing training institutions is barely sufficient to train the requisite number of teachers. New training institutions would be required to supply additional teachers.
2. Prospective teachers should be selected from educational institutions.
3. Training courses provided should be practical in nature. No fees should be charged in training colleges. Poor students should be liberally supported.

Cost of the National System of Education

The estimated gross annual cost of the programme of educational development, envisaged by the Central Advisory Board of Education, was estimated at Rs. 312.60 crore per annum. Deducting the estimated income from fees etc. the net cost per annum was estimated to be Rs. 277.60 crore. This included Rs. 200.00 crore for basic (primary and middle) education; Rs. 50 crore for high school education; Rs. 6.70 crore for university education and Rs. 8 crore for technical and art education. These estimates related to India under British control. The requirements of Indian states were excluded from the calculations. The Board estimated that the proposed modifications would become effective in a period of 40 years.

Criticism of the Educational Policy and Reactions of the Government thereon

Although the national policy enunciated by the Central Advisory Board of Education was quite comprehensive and all embracing, it met with severe criticism from academics, administrators and political leaders. Some of the points made by the critics and the reaction of the Government thereto are briefly discussed:

1. It was felt that the Wardha Scheme of Basic Education, accepted by the Board was fundamentally different from the earlier version. It was clarified that so far as educational policy and principles were concerned, there was no divergence between the two schemes. The Board's scheme, however, did not agree with the Wardha Scheme on two counts: (i) that the cost of education can be met, wholly or largely, by the sale of articles produced by the children; and (ii) it was not correct to assume that the education system would produce accomplished craftsmen whose products would have the same market value as those of the skilled craftsman.
2. While the Board's objective was to lay down certain general principles, which could be regarded as valid and axiomatic so far as the establishment of an efficient system of public education in any democratic state was concerned, it should in no way circumscribe the freedom of provincial governments to implement these principles in the way best suited to the requirements of an independent India.
3. It was pointed out that the Report dealt cursorily with the all important subject of education of the girls and women. It was clarified that the Board had recommended that whatever was required for boys and men was also

required for girls and women. This may even apply to technical education. The Board recognized that, if there was to be real acceleration in social progress, it would come only through educated mothers.

4. The Board had adopted the principle that instruction upto the end of the high school should be given in the mother tongue of the pupil. In multi-lingual areas, it would add to the difficulty and cost of school organisation. This was, however, unavoidable unless and until Hindustani or some other single language became not merely the lingua franca but the actual mother tongue of all Indians. The Board also recommended extension of the same principle to higher stages of education.
5. It was felt that there was no point in including English in the curriculum of basic schools in which the great majority of Indians would complete their education. It was not desirable to make children at this stage learn three languages viz. their mother tongue, Indian lingua-franca and English. The position would, however, be different for children of above average ability who, it was hoped, will fill the places in high schools and universities of the future. They should not only know English but should have a real mastery in it. They could attain this mastery during the high school course of six years, provided the subject is well taught. A substantial contribution could be made towards the solution of the language problem, if the Roman script was generally accepted.
6. The annual cost worked out by the Board was placed at about Rs. 300 crore. Some of the people described it as "fantastic", "idealistic", "astronomical", and quite beyond the capacity of a poor country like India. This was considered to be defeatist in effect if not in intention. It was hoped that it will not deter genuine reformers from facing the facts.

The policy recommended by the CABE also earned the ire of the critics on the ground that "it takes a long (period) and costs too much." The Report itself admitted that with the implementation of the proposals, India would reach the 1939 educational standard of Great Britain in a period of not less than 40 years! The reason for this inordinately delayed development, according to the Board, was the near impossibility of getting well qualified and trained teachers with matriculation followed by two years of professional training. This was, however, not a very valid reason for prolonging the period of achievement of the national objective, since to this day, some of the states are compelled to appoint less qualified and less trained teachers. The appointment of para teachers in some states is a pointer towards meeting an emergency situation in an unorthodox manner.

With regard to cost, the determining factor according to the Board was again the teacher. If the Board's proposed employment of teachers was reasonable, about 70 per cent of the future education budget was pre-determined. Economies that are possible elsewhere would not materially affect the total.

Universal Primary Education

The most controversial of the Board's proposal was that compulsory Basic (primary and middle) Education could be introduced only by stages, with progression being from area to area and not from age to age. Thus, the provincial governments, instead of introducing compulsory education in their areas (with the hope that, as the finances permit, it would be able to raise the school leaving age gradually until the full period of eight years of compulsory schooling is achieved) would begin by choosing areas of economic size and providing in them a complete and integrated system of primary, middle and high schools and also institutions offering further education, unless an adequate supply of teachers is available outside the area in question. It is only by increasing the facilities for higher education, along with the development of basic education, that doors of opportunity could be opened for children of outstanding ability. Merely concentrating on primary education and literacy would debar children of above-normal ability from getting good education and, in the process, India would not be able to compete in the world markets.

To Sum-up

It should be noted that for the first time in the history of Indian education, a comprehensive policy of educational development was formulated. In fact, it could be considered as the first ever exercise in educational planning, although the first five year plan was launched in 1951 - four years after India attained freedom and seven years after the Board set out its policy of educational development.

The policy envisaged not only the expansion of various stages of education but also suggested a phased programme of achievement of targets laid down for various sectors. Further, education being a transferred subject, care was taken that the provincial governments were given the freedom to work out a programme of educational development best suited to the conditions in their areas. They were also advised to formulate their programmes of development keeping in view the availability of teaching personnel and other infrastructure facilities.

At this stage, one should be amused to find that the total annual cost of the entire programme i.e. Rs. 300 crore was considered as 'fantastic' and 'idealistic', thinking that the present (2009-10) annual cost of Indian education runs into an astronomical figure: (about Rs. 2,40,000.00 crore). It should, however, not be forgotten that in 1951 i.e. four years after India's independence, the total annual expenditure on Indian education was Rs.114 crore - Central and states; and plan and non-plan expenditure taken together. Considered in that context, the proposed expenditure of about Rs. three hundred crore per annum mainly on primary education was rather ambitious.

The CABE's scheme was also bold enough to adopt the main principles of the Wardha Scheme of education, although with some modifications. It was recognised that education, through some activity, would provide the best mode of learning. The Board also stressed that for the success of the scheme, properly trained teachers would be the sine-qua-non component. It was rightly stressed that the scheme of basic education could not be self supporting; if the government wanted good education, it ought to be prepared to pay for it.

Another important recommendation made by the Board was the abolition of the intermediate stage with first year to be transferred to schools and the other year to the university. The Board also suggested the introduction of two streams at the school stage - academic and technical. This was in a way precursor to the establishment of multi-purpose schools that adorned the academic stage of Indian education for some time.

It was also suggested that the minimum duration of a university degree should be three years. This recommendation was subsequently endorsed by the Education Commission (1964-66), and adopted by the Government of India. The Board can also be credited with the suggestion of setting up of the University Grants Commission on the pattern of the British University Grants Committee.

About languages, the Board took a very realistic view. It suggested that upto the end of the high school stage, education should be given in the mother tongue of the child. In multi-lingual areas, however, it would add to the difficulty of implementation and lead to enhancement in the cost of education. This was, however, unavoidable until some common language was thought of and accepted as the medium of instruction. This suggestion could be extended to higher education also. It would, however, create difficulties. It would, therefore, be necessary to prepare the ground and till a satisfactory state was reached, it would be unwise to change English as the medium at the university level. It was, however, considered to be undesirable to include English in the curriculum of basic schools. Apart from the paucity of competent teachers, children of the age of 14 could hardly master English along with two other languages.

To Conclude

This was, in a nutshell, the plan of educational development presented to India, when the country was on the threshold of political emancipation from the colonial rule. The three years that elapsed between the presentation of the Plan (1944) and the dawn of freedom (1947) were marked by large scale communal rioting, resulting into wanton killing of innocent people - men, women and children-who were brutally murdered by frenzied mobs on both sides of the artificial border drawn by the wily British. It would, however, be utterly unjust and unwarranted to conclude that the plan worked out by the Central Advisory Board of Education was an aborted attempt. The great merits of the proposed plan were: it looked at education development in a comprehensive manner, encompassing the entire education spectrum; it emphasized the need of education from the point of view of its relevance for national development, particularly primary schooling which would remain for years to come the only education that most children would receive; and in a way, it visualized many problems of educational development which will need addressing. The Plan, in spite of its shortcomings, did form the basis of future educational planning, which was initiated soon after the attainment of independence. It was the first systematic and, in many cases, a realistic attempt to work out a comprehensive programme of educational development for the country.

References

1. Charles Grant: Observations on the State of Society Among the Asiatic Subjects of Great Britain With Respect of Morals and on the Means of Improving it, London, 1813, pp. 60-61.
2. *Ibid.*, p. 39.
3. Ghosh, Suresh Chandra: A History of Events in Modern India, Hyderabad 2009, p. 14.
4. Charles Grant; op. cit.
5. Calcutta University Commission (1917-19) p. 39.
6. Public Letter from the court of Directors to the Governor General in Council dated 3rd June, 1814; Appendix to Report from Common's Select Committee - 1 Public - 16th August, 1832: pp. 329-31.
7. Quoted from Charles Grant, op. cit.
8. Despatch of 1854 to 1868, A Collection of Despatch from the Home Government on the subject of the Education in India; p. 1.
9. Despatch of 1854, op. cit. p. 15.
10. Calcutta University Commission, *Ibid,* pp. 39-40.
11. Despatch of 1854, op. cit. p. 25
12. *Lord Curzon in India, 1898-1905*, Macmillan and Co., London, 1906, pp. 27-56.
13. Thomas Raleigh, Lord Curzon's in India, Vol. II, op. cit. - Educational Conference, Simla, 20 September, 1905 pp. 64-79.
14. *Ibid.*, p. 72.
15. *Ibid.*, pp. 44-45.
16. *Ibid.*, p. 72.
17. *Ibid.*, p. 34.
18. *Ibid.*, pp. 34-35.
19. *Ibid.*, p. 42.
20. The Indian Universities Commission, 1902, p. 1.
21. *Ibid.*, pp. 16-17.
22. *Ibid.*, p. 18.
23. *Ibid.*, p. 18.
24. *Ibid.*, p. 72.
25. As reported in the Indian Statutory Commission, Report, 1929.
26. Chapter 7.
27. The Indian Statutory Commission, 1929, p. 16.

28. See A. Biswas et. al; *Development of Education in India*; Concept Publishing Company; 1986, pp. 40-41.
29. Progress of Education in India, p. 2.
30. *Ibid.*, p. 2.
31. *Ibid.* p. 3 (The impact of Non-cooperation Movement launched by Gandhiji has been dealt with in detail separately).
32. Indian Education in 1920-21, Bureau of Education, India, Calcutta, 1922, p. 3.
33. For details, see Chapter 5.
34. Quinquennial, Report, 1927-32, p. 4.
35. Education in India, 1932-37, pp. 2-3.
36. The main architect of drafting the scheme was John Sargent, the then Educational Commissioner to the Government of India.
37. Educational Development in India; Report by the Central Advisory Board of Education, 1944, p. 1.
38. CABE, 1944 *Ibid.*, p. 2.

2

Educational Development–Over All

'Education', according to Dr. F.W. Thomas, an Indologist of repute, is not exotic for India. There is no country, where the love of learning had so early an origin or has exercised so lasting and powerful an influence. From the simple poets of the Vedic age to the Bengali philosopher of the present day, there has been an uninterrupted succession of teachers and scholars. The immense literature, which this long period has produced, is thoroughly penetrated with the scholastic spirit; and the same spirit has left a deep impression on the social conditions of the people among whom that literature was produced".[1]

Further, "the ancient Hindu theory of Education is contained along with general principles of philosophy, politics and morality in the comprehensive volume of the Sacred Law, the Institutes of Manu. Though Hindu education has always been essentially local, we should naturally be led to imagine, even were we not credibly informed, that different teachers and seats of learning acquired and lost great reputations; that under monarchs of varying temperament, knowledge was alternately patronised and eclipsed in camps and cities. But there was one permanent, and on the whole, beneficent influence, universally present, which secured or rescued the study of literature from utter annihilation. I mean the authority of the Brahman caste. It was this spiritual authority that India owed the preservation of its culture at whatever value it may be estimated, through long periods of darkness, which history has not yet succeeded in penetrating."[2]

The Islamic learning introduced mainly by the Mughal conquerors also made formidable contribution to the different areas of Indian education. It was during the Mughal period that Urdu became the repository of the Hindu-Muslim culture. The vast treasure of literature in this language is an eloquent testimony to the richness of this language and its popular appeal.

The State of Education in India

We shall discuss the progress of education during the British rule under the following periods:

Part I – Upto the end of the Nineteenth Century

Part II – During first half of the Twentieth century i.e. upto 1947.

PART-I

Progress upto the end of the Nineteenth Century

Before discussing the progress of education up to the end of the nineteenth century, it may be useful to have a bird's eye view of the population and the area under the control of the British Government.

Area and Population

The British Empire in India had two distinct divisions: the provinces under the direct control of the British Government and the native states, which were ruled by the Indian princes – the Rajas and the Nawabs – but under the suzerainty of the British Government. The total area which had been surveyed was 17,61,000 square miles with a population of 294 million in 1901. The progress discussed in this part relates mainly to the provinces under direct British control.

Major Developments

The major developments during the period under review can be discussed under the following heads:

(i) Progress of education upto and subsequent to the Despatches of 1854 and 1859.

(ii) Setting up of universities in the three Presidency towns (1857).

(iii) The aftermath of the natural calamities during the last decade of the Nineteenth Century.

(iv) Progress of education upto and subsequent to the Despatches of 1854 and 1859.

Period upto 1854

The East India Company, which assumed the mantle of the ruling power in India, was set up in 1600 as a trading organisation. The early settlers were mainly traders with commerce being their mainstay. They did not undertake any educational activity for the first one hundred years. The Charter Act of 1698 required the company to maintain priests and schools in its garrisons, which were primarily meant for the children of the soldiers and other staff. By 1756, with the grant of Diwani, the Company became a ruling power. Even then, education was hardly considered as part of its administrative responsibilities.

Sporadic Efforts

For the first one hundred and fifty years, there were sporadic efforts on the part of some officers of the company to set up educational institutions. It was in no way a part of the policy of the East India Company during the first two generations of domination in Bengal, to impose a Western or English system of education upon its Indian subjects. Warren Hastings, a dominating figure of the early part of the period, entertained a genuine admiration for the laws and literature of India. It was his policy that "if the British power was to be lasting, it must become an Indian power and that its greatest gifts would be the gifts of order and justice, under which the indigenous culture might revive and flourish."[3]

In pursuance of these sentiments, Warren Hastings, established in 1782, and thereafter maintained, the Calcutta Madrassa for the study of Arabic and Persian. Nine years later, in 1791, Jonathan Duncan, the Resident of Banaras, founded a Sanskrit College, designed to cultivate the literature and religion of the Hindus. In 1792, the Boras of Surat built Arabic colleges for the Muhammadans. A portion of the funds established by the Peshwas for the support of Pandits was utilised by the Commissioner of Deccan to set up a college for Hindu learning at Poona. The Calcutta Vidyalaya was founded in 1871 by private efforts for education in English for children of higher castes. The foundation of the Calcutta Sanskrit College was, however, opposed by Raja Ram Mohan Roy who considered this development as a retrograde step. A number of institutions for imparting western knowledge through English also came into being during this period. They included: the Baptist College at Serampur (1818); Bishop's College (1820), for the education of Christian students; the Wilson College (1834) in Bombay; the Christian College (1837) at Negapatam in Madras; and the London Missionary Society's institutions (1838) founded in Calcutta. They were followed by the establishment of Government Colleges. In 1841, the Madras University was started at first as a high school, which is now the Presidency College. At Bombay, the Elphinstone College was also started.

William Adam, a missionary, who was appointed Government Commissioner of Education in 1835, founded a number of schools in India. Burdwan, an educationally advanced district in Bengal, contained 931 schools. The schools, however, lacked proper accommodation. Teachers were poor and ignorant, and were paid out of the fees or in presents. "The use of printed books was unknown. The compositions taught contained a low standard of morality. As to the discipline, the school was a place of terror. The methods of punishing an offender were abominable."[4] There were no indigenous schools for girls.

Charter Act of 1813

The first systematic attempt to provide education to the natives of India was made by including the following regulations in the Charter Act of 1813. It said: that a sum of not less than one lakh of rupees each year shall be set apart and applied to the founding and maintaining of colleges, schools, public lectures and other institutions for the revival and improvement of literature and encouragement of the learned natives of India and for the production and promotion of a knowledge of sciences among the inhabitants of the British territories in India. In 1814, the Board of Directors clarified that the money allocated for education was not meant for building new colleges but for improving those already in existence; to concentrate expenditure on some particular city (and they named Banaras) to confer marks of distinction on natives.

It may be mentioned that for ten years ending 1823, no action was taken. It was only in 1823 that a Committee of Public Instruction was set up charged with the disposal of the yearly sum of one lakh of rupees and all institutions in the Presidency were placed under its authority. Although the grant for education was increased from Rs. one lakh to Rs. ten lakh per annum, it was only in 1835 that Lord Macaulay was able to make the government decide about the manner in which the annual grant was to be spent.

Despatches of 1854 and 1859

Education was finally accepted as the responsibility of the colonial administration through the two Despatches from the Board of Directors of the East India Company in England. As already stated, the Despatch of 1854 patronisingly declared that it was their most sacred duty to be the means of conferring upon the natives of India, those moral and material blessings, which flow from the general diffusion of useful knowledge and which India may, under Providence derive from her connection with England. The Despatch commended to the special attention of the Government of India, the improvement and wider extension of education, both English and vernacular, and prescribed the means of attainment of these objects by (1) the constitution of a separate department of administration of education; (2) the setting up of universities at the Presidency towns on the model of the London University (of affiliating type); (3) the establishment of institutions for training teachers for all classes of schools; (4) the maintenance of the existing government colleges and high schools and the increase of their number, where necessary; (5) the establishment of new middle schools; (6) the increased attention to vernacular schools, for indigenous and elementary education; and (7) the introduction of a system of grant-in-aid. The Despatch, while taking cognizance of the success of many distinguished Indian scholars and paying tribute to the ancient Indian languages, termed them as inadequate foundation for any of general scheme of Indian education. It, therefore, emphatically declared that the education, "which we desire to see extended in India is that which has, for its objects, the diffusion of the improved arts, science, philosophy and literature of Europe; in short European knowledge".[5]

The modus operandi of the system of grant-in-aid has been explained in chapter 4. Briefly, it may be stated that government grant-in-aid was to be based on observance of perfect religious neutrality. Aid was to be given so far as the requirements of each particular district as compared with the other districts and the funds at the disposal of the government may render it possible to all schools imparting a good secular education, provided they were under adequate local management and were subject to government inspection and that fees, however small, were charged in them. Grants were to be given for specific objects and their amount and continuance were to depend on the periodical reports of government inspectors. No government colleges or schools were to be founded where a sufficient number of institutions capable, with the aid of the government, of meeting the local demand for education existed; but new schools and colleges were to be established and temporarily maintained, where there was little or no prospect of adequate local effort coming forth to meet local requirements.

The Despatch of 1859

The Despatch of 1859 reviewed the progress made under the earlier Despatch. It reiterated and confirmed the course to be adopted for promoting elementary education. While it recorded with satisfaction that the system of grant-in-aid had been freely accepted by private schools, both English and Anglo vernacular, the native community had failed to cooperate with the Government in promoting elementary vernacular education. The soliciting of contribution from the people was declared inexpedient and doubts were expressed as to the suitability of the grant-in-aid system as hitherto in force, for the supply of vernacular education to the masses of population. Such vernacular education should, it was suggested, be provided by the direct instrumentality of the officers of government on the basis of some of the plans already in operation for the improvement of indigenous schools, or by any modification of those plans, which may suit the circumstances of different provinces. The expediency of imposing a special rate on land for the provision of elementary education was also commended for careful consideration of the government.

Progress of Education

Authentic information is not available about the progress of education during the period upto 1859. There were, however, two studies – one conducted by Elphinston about Bombay, which revealed that in 1823, in the British territories of Bombay for a population of 46,81,735, there were 1705 schools in which 35,143 scholars were receiving education; 25 schools having 1315 scholars being maintained by government and 1680 village schools with 33,838 scholars. According to another study by Munro, only one in eight boys of proper age were receiving instruction. Curiously enough, it did not include a single female scholar.

In January 1835, Mr. Adam was appointed by Lord Bentinck to investigate the state of education in Bihar and Bengal. The general results arrived at from these investigations were:

"In a population of 77,89,152, there were 3555 schools with 41,247 scholars; in a population of 692,270, there were 2414 children being taught at home, a number which would represent in case of a population of 77,89,152 about 28000; of the adult male population, on the average about 5.55 per cent could read and write. On the whole, about 7.8 per cent of children of the schoo' age were being taught at school and over 5.2 per cent at home, giving a total percentage of 13."[6]

It would appear that the percentage of children getting institutional and/or home based instruction in Bombay, Bihar and Bengal was almost the same, i.e., 13 per cent of the age group.

The Despatch of 1859, also gave some unsatisfactory information; it was defective in classification. It was also not for the same years. For example, the information was for the years 1854-55 for North Western Provinces, and 1856-57 for Bombay, Bengal and Madras. Similarly, in the returns for North Western Provinces, in respect of schools attached to colleges the numb · of students was included in those enrolled in colleges. Similar inaccuracies were found in the information relating to other Provinces.

Subject to these limitations, Table 1 gives some idea of the number of students attending various types of government institutions, (excluding females).

Table 1: Number of Students in 1854-55

Province	*Colleges*	*Superior* Schools*	*Inferior* Schools*
Bengal	654	6071	7097
N.W. Provinces	1370	550	6588
Madras	290	1332	1759

The definition of 'inferior' schools was that they had vernacular as medium of instruction while the so called 'superior' schools had English as the medium.

Emphasis on Elementary Education

In the light of the recommendations made in the Despatches of 1854 and 1859, emphasis was to be given to the expansion of elementary education. The Royal Commission on Decentralisation (1870-71) proposed that the efforts of the local bodies should be confined entirely to primary schools, Emphasis was also laid on devolution of educational functions to rural boards, sub-district boards and Panchayats; the grant of reasonable latitude to sub-district boards to determine the curricula; the maintenance by local bodies of their own inspecting staffs in addition to the government inspectorate; and the abrogation of rules requiring these bodies to devote specific percentage of their revenues to education.

The following is a brief review of the progress in various stages of education during the period 1854-1882.

(I) School Education

(a) *Primary Schools*

In 1854-56, the Board of Education handed over to the new Department of Education at Calcutta 13,000 pupils, from the government of North Western Province; 24,000 pupils; from the Board of Education, Bombay 21,400 and from Madras 4,500 pupils. In addition, about 70,000 children were receiving education in Missionary schools. This number increased to 6,63,915 children in 13,637 state schools in 1881-82. There were also 11,41,844 children in 57,841 aided schools, 2,55,782 children in 83,416 public elementary schools – making a total of about 20 lakh pupils.

This enormous increase in enrolment was on account of two methods generally employed by the provincial governments. One followed in Bengal and Assam aimed at bringing the indigenous schools into more or less loose connection with the Department. The other, followed in the remaining provinces, involved a system of rates and cesses. Under the former method, there was little place for local management, but under the latter, the local boards were an essential feature though their powers varied considerably; being greatest in Bombay and very inconsiderable under the northern governments.

(b) *Secondary Schools*

In 1854-55, there were 107 schools, which could be called secondary schools. Of these 73 belonged to Bengal – 47 government anglo vernacular schools, 26 'Harding Vernacular schools' and the remaining 34 set up by Lord Harding in 1844. By 1881-82, the number had increased to 378, 116 departmental, 174 aided and 88 unaided. The total number of scholars was 204,294 in 1870-71 and 2,14,077 in 1881-82. If the pupils in elementary sections are excluded, the total would be 1,50,000.

(II) University Education

(a) *Universities*

An important development during this period was the setting up of universities in the Presidency towns of Bombay, Calcutta and Madras in 1857. To work out the blueprint of universities, a Committee under the Chairmanship of James William Colville was appointed on 26th January 1855 on the orders of the Court of Directors[7]. The Court had desired that the universities be established to encourage a regular and liberal course of Education by conferring Academical Degrees as evidence of attainment in the different branches of Arts and Sciences and by adding marks of honour for those who desire to compete for honorary distinction. The court also said that the form, government and functions of the London University are the best adapted to the wants of India and may be followed with advantage although some variation will be necessary in points of detail.

The main recommendations of the Colville Committee, which were approved by the Government, were:

1. The universities at the three Presidency towns be established forthwith;
2. There should be an examination for entrance to the universities;
3. Mathematics upto a certain stage or the elements of logics as treated in the works of one or other standard units might be prescribed as subjects upon which the knowledge of the candidates be strictly tested; and
4. The proceedings of the senate of the universities should be reported to the Government of India and all byelaws and regulations should receive the sanction of the Government.

   As a temporary measure, the Governor General of India was to be the Chancellor of the University of Calcutta; and the Governors of Madras and Bombay, were to act as Chancellors of the universities of Madras and Bombay.

(b) The Colleges

In 1857, there were 22 Arts colleges and one college each for engineering and medicine. The former consisted of 13 state managed institutions and nine managed by Missionary societies. By 1882, the total number of colleges increased to 59. The number of students was 5400 of whom nearly 2000 were attending 20 aided colleges, 700 were in unaided institutes and 2700 were attending 30 state managed colleges. The students were charged fees, which varied between Rs. one and Rs. eight per month.

(ii) Towards the Close of the Nineteenth Century

At the close of the nineteenth century, India suffered natural calamities like Bubonic Plague that claimed over 8 lakh lives during 1896 and 1902. It was followed by an earthquake of a very severe magnitude that visited the eastern region of India in 1897, devastating cities like Shillong and its surrounding areas. To make matters worse, the Gulf of Bengal was hit by a cyclone between 21st and 24th of October, 1897 causing 50,000 deaths.[8]

The Progress of Education

The calamities that occurred during the period 1891-92 to 1901-02 played havoc with the progress of education in some provinces, particularly during the period 1891-1896. The position, however, improved in the subsequent quinquennium ending 1901-02. Table 2 illustrates[9]: (p. 57)

The unsatisfactory features disclosed in the table are attributable to plague and famine. In Bombay, however, the increase in the number of pupils was less than one per cent in the decade; the first five years had shown a growth of about 10 per cent, when the plague and the resulting panic caused disorganisation, which was shared by all classes of schools and colleges. The fall in the number of pupils occurred mostly in primary schools. It occurred in most of the native states of the Bombay province except in Baroda state, where education was most efficient. Similar reduction occurred in Punjab, United Provinces and Bengal. During the decade, however, there was an increase of 4.6 per cent in the number of schools and 11.2 per cent in the number of pupils. In case, the private institutions are excluded, the overall increase would be 16 per cent in 1901-02 as compared with that in 1891-92.

The progress was, however, uneven. Female pupils constituted only about 2 per cent of the relevant age group. The lowest per cent of females was in the Punjab (including North West Frontier Province) being 0.6 per cent of the relevant age group. Males constituted 22.3 per cent of their age group in 1901-02.

The slow rate in the growth of primary education was also on account of the fact that the methods of instruction were faulty; in spite of the advice of the Education Commission (1881-82) that primary education should be in vernaculars, this course was not followed. Secondly, primary education had shared the disadvantage caused by an undue extension of the system of examinations. Further, notwithstanding the governments' insistence that larger proportion of expenditure should be devoted to primary education, it was not done.

Table 2: Schools and Enrolment

Name of the Province	1891-92		1896-97		1901-02		Increase/Decrease per cent in the last Five Years		Increase/Decrease per cent in Ten Years 1891-1902	
	Schools	Pupils	Schools	Pupils	Schools	Pupils	Schools	Pupils	Schools	Pupils
Madras	23,204	693,985	26,872	822,853	26,490	861,479	-1.4	+ 4.7	+ 14.2	+ 24.1
Bombay	12,272	634,438	12,934	672,705	12,251	639,868	-5.3	-4.9	-0.2	+0.9
Bengal	67,824	1,531,965	67,847	1,674,775	61,790	1,667,254	-8.9	-0.4	-8.9	+8.9
United Provinces	10,862	282,570	12,506	352,972	14,358	452,517	+14.0	+28.3	+32.2	+60.2
Punjab					{6,853}	{248,123}	-6.3	+3.3	-15.3	+5.6
NWFP	9,408	260,227	8,507	265,922	{1,118	26,581}				
Central Provinces	1,988	117,483	2,524	149,507	2,562	142,558	+1.5	-4.5	+28.4	+21.4
Burma	12,007	196,028	15,820	255,137	18,283	316,156	+15.6	+24.0	+52.3	+61.3
Assam	2,800	83,638	3,534	103,541	3,426	108,020	-3.0	+4.0	+22.4	+29.2
Coorg	104	5,004	120	5,115	99	4,758	-17.5	-7.0	-4.8	-4.9
Berar	1,322	51,483	1,361	54,343	11,50	53,379	-15.5	-1.8	-13.0	+3.7
Total	1,41,791	38,56,821	152,025	43,56,870	1,48,30	45,20,693	-2.4	+3.8	+4.6	+17.3

Secondary Education

There was considerable progress in secondary education as would appear from Table 3:

Table 3: Secondary Schools and Enrolment

1891-92		*1896-97*		*1900-01*		*Increase or decrease of pupils in the secondary stages in the last 10 years*
Secondary Schools	*Pupils*	*Secondary Schools*	*Pupils*	*Secondary Schools*	*Pupils*	
4872	4,73,294	5281	5,37,819	5477	5,89,427	+ 24.5

In spite of the recommendation made by the Education Commission (1882) that the upper classes of the high schools should have two divisions; one leading to the entrance examination of the universities and the other to be of a more practical character, preparing students for commercial or non-literary character, not all the provinces moved in that direction.

Collegiate Education

The number of universities remained five throughout the decade. The number of colleges increased from 136 in 1891-92 to 192 in 1901-02. Correspondingly, the student enrolment went up from 16,110 to 23,029 during the same period indicating a percentage increase of 44.6.

About the quality of higher education, the Universities Commission (1902) did not agree with the sweeping condemnation of the university system. According to the Commission, many of the colleges commanded the services of devoted and able teachers; and that the students as a class did not lack either the natural talent or industry.[10]

Technical Education

There was sizeable increase during the period 1891-1902 in the number of technical institutions. From 302 in 1891-92, their number increased to 853 in 1902 and the enrolment increased from 16,753 to 29470, during the same period.[11]

Female Enrolment

The growth of female education was marred by indifference, want of schools, inadequacy of trained teachers and lack of earnest efforts on the part of authorities. The number of girls in educational institutions rose from 3,07,388 in 1891-92 to a modest 3,93,597 in 1901-02. The enrolment was only 2.3 per cent of the relevant age group as against 20 per cent for boys. The lowest enrolment of girls enrolled in schools in relation to their age group was 16 per cent in United Province, only 0.38 per cent in North-West Frontier Province and 0.87 per cent in Punjab.

Progress of Education in the Provinces

Table 4 indicates the overall progress of education in regard to institutions as also enrolment in different provinces over the period 1891-92 to 1901-02.

Table 4 : Institutions/Pupils in Recognised Institutions

Province	*Institutions*				*Pupils*			
	1891-92	*1896-97*	*1901-02*	*Percentage increase/ decrease over 10 years*	*1891-92*	*1896-97*	*1901-02*	*Percentage increase/ decrease over 10 years*
Madras	28,204	20,872	28,490	+14.2	6,93,985	8,22,853	9,61,479	+24.1
Bombay	12,272	12,034	10,251	-0.2	6,34,438	6,72,705	6,30,908	+0.9
Bengal	67,824	67,847	61,780	8.9	15,31,965	16,74,775	16,87,254	+8.9
United Provinces	10,862	12,506	14,368	+32.2	2,83,570	3,52,972	4,32,517	+60.2
Punjab NWFP	9,408	8,507	7,780	-15.3	2,60,227	2,65,972	2,74,704	+5.6
Central Province	1,988	2,524	2,562	+28.4	1,17,483	1,49,507	1,42,558	+21.4
Burma	12,007	15,820	18,282	+52.3	1,96,028	2,55,137	3,16,156	+61.3
Assam	2,800	3,534	3,426	+22.4	83,638	1,03,541	1,08,020	+22.2
Coorg	104	120	99	-4.8	5,004	5,115	4,758	-4.9
Berar	1,322	1,361	1,150	-12.0	31,483	54,343	53,370	+3.7
Total	**1,41,701**	**1,52,025**	**1,48,380**	**+4.6**	**38,56,821**	**43,56,870**	**45,20,693**	**+11.2**

(*Source*: Progress of Education in India 1901-02, pp. 306-307).

While there was an overall increase in the number of institutions (4.6 per cent) as also in enrolment (11.2 per cent) over a period 10 years, some of the provinces like Bombay, Bengal, Punjab and North Western Frontier Province and Berar showed substantial decline in the decade 1891-92 to 1901-02. This unsatisfactory situation, according to official sources, was attributed to plague and famine, which ravaged certain parts of the country. In Bombay, where increase in the number of pupils was less than one per cent in the decade, the first four years had shown a growth of 10 per cent, when the plague and the resulting panic caused disruption which was shared by all classes of schools and colleges. During the famine, the fall in the number of pupils occurred mostly in primary schools in Bombay. In Madras, the number declined partly due to the epidemics and partly due to the more stringent application of the rules of recognition. In Punjab, there was an increase in private institutions and a decline in the number of government managed institutions. On the whole, however, there has been increase of 4.6 per cent in the case of institutions and 11.2 per cent in the enrolment.[12]

The data given in the table should be used with caution. In no way can they be compared with the position in independent India. The provinces indicated in the table are not comparable with the states carved out after the country became independent. The provinces do not include Indian states, which were almost semi-independent units and which were ruled by Indian princes – Rajas, Nawabs and other rulers. The concern for education in them was not uniform. Moreover, some of the provinces included areas, which no longer form part of the present day states. Some of the provinces have been bifurcated/excluded as a result of the partition of the country. Further, Burma, which has been included in the table, was no longer a part of India even before the partition of the country.

To Conclude

In conclusion it may be stated that the East India Company did not pay any attention to the education of the Indians during the first two centuries of its rule. Even when, in the early years of the nineteenth century, it was realized that the Company had some responsibility for the education of the natives, there were controversies about the manner in which the government assistance was to be utilised. The progress of education in the nineteenth century was, therefore, not of much consequence. However, in fairness to the Company, it may be stated that upto the mid nineteenth century and beyond, two important steps were initiated. One was the introduction of the system of grant-in-aid which has stood the test of time till this day. The other was emphasis on elementary education as also on the imparting of education through vernaculars. Although not much achievement was registered on these counts, yet the fact that these two priority areas were identified at the early stages of the British rule could be considered as steps in the right direction.

PART-II

Educational Development under the Colonial Rule (1901-1947)

The progress of Indian education during the first half of the twentieth century will be discussed under the following heads:

1. Progress of overall education during the period including a discussion of some specific problems that affected progress of educational development.
2. Sectoral Programmes –
   - (a) School Education:
     - (i) Elementary Education
     - (ii) Secondary Education
   - (b) Adult Education
   - (c) University Education

A Clarification

At the outset, it needs to be stated that there are wide variations in the data presented in this and subsequent chapters, which deal with sectoral progress. This is primarily due to differences in the nomenclature of different stages of education at different periods. For example, in initial stages, primary education was inclusive of middle school education. At some stage, middle schools became a part of high schools and the data about enrolment, number of institutions etc., was presented accordingly. Similarly, university education was post-secondary education but the duration of this stage of education varied from 4 years to 6 years. This depended upon whether the intermediate stage was a part of the university system; a separate entity or a constituent of secondary education. Further, in the initial stages, compilation of statistical information about education was not a regular feature. As a consequence, there was ad-hocism about the collection of information. For example, various committees/government documents would collect data about specific stages of education in order to substantiate their analysis/findings/recommendations. This ad-hocism would very often lead to incorrect/misleading information. Another problem was that in the initial stages, information was collected through school inspectors in different provinces without the use of some standardised form of data collection. This would result in the collection of information depending on the understanding of the school inspector about the various aspects of educational system, which itself was undergoing changes from time to time.

An over view of the state of Indian education during the first half of the twentieth century reveals the following rends:

(a) Top Heavy Education

Indian education, right from the beginning, has been top heavy. This is in spite of the fact that all through the period, expansion of primary education has been emphasised. In actual fact, however, primary education was not able to secure its rightful place as revealed in the analysis of sector-wise progress. In terms of mass education, India has been far behind some of the advanced countries as would be evident from Table 5.

Table 5: Comparison of percentage coverage of the elementary and secondary stages – India and some developed countries in 1914[13]

Country	*Percentage of the population enrolled in schools*	
	Elementary Education	*Secondary Education*
United States	19.87	1.502
England and Wales	16.52	0.620
German Empire	16.30	0.988
France	13.90	0.32
Japan	13.07	NA

Ceylon	8.94	0.354
Rumania	8.21	NA
Russia	3.77	NA
Brazil	2.61	NA
India	2.38	0.486[14]

The figures for university education are also significant. Paulson has given the data about the number of students attending universities in Germany and in countries of similar conditions as about 0.05 per cent (1914-15). This has been held by some to be an understatement and the figure for that country appears to be 0.093 per cent; for England and Wales 0.054 per cent; for France 0.106 per cent; for Italy; 0.063 per cent; for the Netherlands 0.066 per cent; for the United States 0.218 and for Japan 0.014 per cent. The percentage of those under university education to the population in Bengal Presidency was 0.05 equal to Paulson's figures for the U.K. in 1912 and if the female population in Bengal is excluded, it would be 0.097[15].

Thus, while the lower masses in India were largely illiterate, the middle class, which is the class that mainly patronizes institutions of higher education, was at least numerically educated to a pitch equal to that attained in countries, whose social and economic conditions are more highly developed.

(a) Predominance of Literary Education

A second feature which partly accounts for the first is the predominance of literary courses, which are ordinarily available to Indian students. The following table gives a comparative picture of pupils at different types of institutions in India and Japan:

Table 6: Type of Institutions

Types of Institutions	*Percentage of pupils in different types of institutions to the total number of pupils*	
	Japan1914-15	*India1916-17*
Universities	0.11	0.70
High Schools	0.16	7.29
Middle Schools	1.65	4.49
Primary Schools	87.77	77.45
Institutions for Training	0.37	0.24
Technical Schools	6.52	0.27

This comparison is, not wholly accurate and must be used with caution. But, howsoever rough the figures, it decisively proves that higher education in India has a predominant place and that the development of special vocational schools is abysmally low. "The inference that could be drawn is that the genius of the country is speculative rather than practical. The literary courses lead to government employment and are a necessary preliminary to the study and practice of the law.

They adapt themselves to the traditional methods of teaching and to the highly developed memorizing faculty, which characterises so many Indian students. Technical and industrial courses entail physical exertion (though this is by no means irksome to all) and offer a less easy or less lucrative career. But the greatest deterrent is the slow growth of industries and the shyness of capital in supporting them. Were industrial employment assured; students would readily come forward and technological institutions would fill and multiply".[16]

Progress of Education (1901)

Before analysing the progress of Indian education, it may be stated that no reliable data are available about the sectoral progress of Indian education during the first year of the twentieth century. The paucity of information has been attributed to the insufficiency of the inspecting staff, who was expected to collect the requisite information from the educational institutions. Notwithstanding this inadequacy, an attempt has been made to give a glimpse of the state of Indian education in the first year of the twentieth century. We shall start with Primary Education.

Primary Education

In 1901, out of more than 18 million boys, who ought to have been in schools, only a little more than one sixth were receiving primary education. There were wide variations among the provinces. For example, in Punjab and the United Provinces, out of 100 boys eligible for going to schools, only eight or nine boys were actually in schools.[17]

Secondary Education

The number of secondary schools rose from 3916 in the last twenty years (1881 to 1901) to 5493 and that of the pupils from 2,14,077 to 5,58,378. It has been reported that in all provinces, there was eagerness among parents to send their sons to English schools and the provision of a high school was the common object of liberality among all sections of the community.

It was also noticed that the courses of study in secondary schools were too literary in character. In fact, high school courses at the secondary stage were exclusively preparatory to the university entrance examinations. It was felt that attempts were needed to vocationalise these courses.

University Education

In 1857, three universities were established at Calcutta, Bombay and Madras. By the end of the nineteenth century, two more universities were set up, making a total of 5 in 1901. All these universities were modelled on the London University, which, subsequently, enlarged its scope of functioning. Indian universities, however, remained predominantly examining bodies for a long time.

In 1901-02, the number of students in Arts colleges was 16,971, which works out to 9 students out of 10,000 of the age group. It is interesting to note that bulk of these students (14,650) were Hindus; 1,259 Mohammadans, 175

Europeans, 450 native Christians and the rest 437 were Buddhists, Parsis and others. The number of female students was merely 177, i.e., 0.01 per cent of the age group.

Technical Education

The engineering colleges at Roorkee, Sibpur and Madras and the College of Sciences at Poona, the technical institute at Bombay, the Engineering College at Jabalpur provided training for government services as engineers, mechanics, electricians, overseers, surveyors, revenue officers or teachers in schools and for employment in railways workshops, cotton mills and mines.

Schools of Art

There were four schools of art in British India; one each at Madras, Bombay, Calcutta and Lahore. The aim of these schools was to encourage Indian Art and Art industries.

Industrial Schools

Industrial schools were entrusted with the responsibility to train artisans or foremen and to further develop those local industries which were capable of expansion by the application of improved methods and implements. The total number of such schools was 129 in 1901 – not very adequate for the needs of the industries at that time.

Agricultural Education

For a country, where more than two thirds of the population subsisted on agriculture, the urge for agricultural education was inadequate. There were colleges at Poona and Saidapet in Madras teaching a three year course in agriculture. In United Provinces, there was a college at Kanpur with a two years course for the training of subordinate revenue officers. At Nagpur a school with a two year course gave good practical education. Bengal's College of Engineering at Sibpur offered a two year course in Agriculture.

Teacher Training Colleges

There were training colleges for teachers at Madras, Kurseong, Allahabad, Lahore and Jabalpur. These institutions were, however, in no way, adequate to meet the burgeoning requirements of trained teachers for the entire country. Similarly, there were training schools for primary school teachers.

This was the educational scenario in the first year of the twentieth century. From the point of view of providing educational facilities of various types, the array of institutions, presented in the foregoing paragraphs, does not appear to offer a very encouraging situation. It should, however, be admitted that a beginning had been made to provide all types of educational facilities to various sections of the Indian population. It was an edifice that later on developed into a gigantic educational complex, which is producing, among others, professional, scientific and technical manpower of the highest calibre, who can compete with the best in the world.

We shall now discuss the overall progress of education in selected years about which adequate data are available.

1906-07

The following table indicates the number of various types of educational institutions and enrolment therein during 1906-07. (See Next Page)

It would appear that out of a total student enrolment of 53,88,632 in 1906-07, school education including privately run institutions accounted for 45,92,508, which works out to 85.23 per cent of the total enrolments. The female students were 6,45,028, which was 11.97 per cent of the total enrolment. Further, there were 182 colleges including professional colleges out of a total of 1,62,528 institutions. Out of this the total number of institutions of the school level was 1,56,253, which works out to about 96 per cent of the total. The number of institutions exclusively for girls was merely 12,440, which works out to 7.6 per cent of the total.

1911-12

There was marked development in education in terms of institutions and scholars. The total number of primary schools under the Government was 1,21,578 with 49,88,142 pupils. Out of this the number of institutions for females was 12,886, i.e., 10.6 per cent of the total. The number of female pupils stood at 7,85,581, which works out to 1.6 per cent of the total. Further, there were 74,970 female pupils in the privately run elementary schools. This works out to 0.15 per cent of the total enrolment of 5,96,796. It would therefore appear that the female enrolment was abysmally lower than that of the boys.

At the secondary stage, the number of schools for girls was 496, which was 0.086 per cent of the total number of institutions (6370) at the secondary level.

At the university stage, there were 186 colleges out of which only 10 colleges were exclusively for girls. The number of students was 36,248, out of which those pursuing Arts courses, was 28,196.

It could be concluded that in terms of number of institutions as well as enrolment, girls lagged far behind that of boys.

Table 7: Public Institutions – 1906-07

	Public Institutions								*Private*			
	Arts Colleges	*Professional Colleges*	*Secondary Schools*	*Primary Schools*	*Total*	*Training*	*All others*	*Total*	*Advanced*	*Elementary*	*Total*	*Grand Total*
Males	128	43	5314	102947	108261	314	1870	110655	3676	38757	39433	150088
Females	8	3	504	9983	10548	63	70	10681	11	1748	1759	12440
Total	136	46	5818	112930	118809	377	1940	12326	3687	37505	41192	162528
Scholars												
Males	18758	6137	55205	342461 8	4076723	7760	55454	4164832	59432	51930	578772	574360
Females	160	113	6127	513248	574485	1420	3470	579448	1360	67020	68380	64028
Total	18918	6250	61332	4651208	4651208	9180	58924	47,44,280	60792	583360	647152	5388632

Source: H.W. Orange, Progress of Education in India, 1906-07, Calcutta, 1909.

Important Developments

An analysis of the educational scenario existing during the first decade of the twentieth century highlights three important developments: the rapid growth of demand for English education, the gradual acceptance of the responsibility towards Indian education by the government and the tardy recognition of the importance of elementary education as against higher education. In view of the very slow progress of elementary education, Gopal Krishan Gokhale introduced, in March, 1910, a bill for making it permissible for municipal and district boards to introduce free and compulsory education in their areas. The bill was however, thrown out of the Legislative Council by opposition from overwhelming majority of British officials.[18]

Another important development was the commencement of systematic surveys of each province of the distribution and expansion of school education. The task was, however, beset with difficulties, particularly due to the non-availability of correct maps, especially because the course of rivers was changing the complexion of the landscape.

1917-1922

The period was marked by acute economic distress, high prices and political unrest following the disastrous First World War. According to Richey, "the long continuance of the war brought depression in its train. The cost of education rose with the price of food and clothing and school materials. Money was scarce. Employment proved hard or impossible to get. The spirit of hope was discouraged and as the line wavered, the politicians struck..."[19]

"The Non-Cooperation Movement, which started in December, 1920 succeeded in crippling some schools beyond hope of recovery; in disorganising the work of others for six months or a year and in ruining the career of many promising scholars. At the Nagpur session of the Indian National Congress, a resolution was passed declaring boycott of all schools recognised by the government. This started a movement, which spread in successive waves over the whole of India..."[20]

According to government sources, the Movement hardly affected primary and middle schools; there was, however, a fall of 23 per cent approximately, i.e., of 45,000 students in enrolment of high schools. "Girls' schools have as yet little significance in the life of the people and this obscurity has been of service to them in saving them from sharing, except in a very minor degree, in the attack made on those for boys."[21]

The progress made during the period is illustrated in the table below:

Table 8: Institutions and Scholars (1917-22)

Type of Institutions	*Institutions*			*Scholars*		
	1917	*1922*	*Increase or Decrease*	*1917*	*1922*	*Increase or Decrease*
Arts Colleges	134	167	(+)33	47135	45933	(-)1202
Professional Colleges	61	64	(+)3	11504	13662	(+)2158
Secondary Schools	7004	8918	(+)1914	1107141	1240124	(+)142983
Primary Schools	142203	160070	(+)17867	5818730	6310400	(+)507670
Special Schools	4861	4011	(-)850	143604	132706	(-)10898

It appears that in spite of the adverse political factors, there was sizeable increase in the number of institutions and in enrolments, with the exception of special schools. While all categories of institutions and enrolment in them showed an increase, the number of special and unrecognised schools declined.

There was, however, a marginal decline in the number of scholars in Arts colleges, and special schools and curiously enough, in unrecognised institutions. The overall increase in enrolment was 10 per cent.

The increase in the number of secondary schools was mainly due to the reclassification of primary schools with the smaller schools with four classes being retained as primary schools and larger schools with six classes being renamed as lower middle (secondary schools).

The number of universities doubled. There was a tendency to set up smaller universities like that in Punjab and Madras, because the older universities had become unwieldy.

Further, in pursuance of the recommendations made by the Calcutta University Commission, there was an accent on establishing unitary teaching universities and reorganisation of the existing universities into teaching institutions. Another important development was the general introduction of vernaculars as medium of instruction and emphasis on vocational education. There were, however, difficulties in making vocational courses popular among students.

1922-27

The period under review followed the constitutional reforms of January, 1921, which made radical changes in the control of education in British India. As already stated, the World War impacted educational development in many ways. The cuts in budgetary allotments gave rise to the abandonment of certain schemes or curtailment of their budgetary allotment. At the central level, the Inchcape Committee[22] suggested drastic cuts in the expenditure, which resulted in the abolition of the Central Advisory Board of Education, the Bureau of Education, the possible sacking of the Educational Commissioner and even the proposed closing of the Delhi University, which had just been brought into being.

There were also State Retrenchment Committees, which suggested budgetary cuts as also abandonment of certain important schemes of educational development. In spite of these factors the period witnessed considerable expansion at all stages of education as would be apparent from Table 9.

Table 9 : Institutions and Scholars (1922–27)

Type of Institutions	*Institutions*			*Scholars*		
	1922	*1927*	*Increase or Decrease*	*1922*	*1927*	*Increase or Decrease*
Universities	12	14	(+)2	-	7053	-
Arts Colleges	167	232	(+)65	44929	64256	(+)19327
Professional Colleges	64	77	(+)13	13062	17616	(+)4654
Secondary Schools	8967*	11338	(+)2371	1230824	1837627	(+)606803
Primary Schools	160676	180954	(+)20278	6310400	8256760	(+)1946360
Special Schools	4011	10639	(+)6628	132706	328604	(+)195898

1932-37

The economic depression gradually ebbed out during the quinquennium under review. There was reduction in the cuts imposed at the end of the previous quinquennium (1927-32) from 3.5 per cent to two per cent. By 1932-33, the cut was removed altogether.

Dissatisfaction with the System

An outcome of the depression was the emergence of a widespread dissatisfaction with the education system. The main cause of the dissatisfaction was that it was not practical enough, not in consonance with the child's environment and experience and not adequately related to the needs of one's later life. This aspect was particularly related to secondary education, which was considered too academic and not diversified. It was felt that secondary education accentuated the drift of unsuitable students to higher literary education. There was large wastage at the primary education stage which retarded the attainment of literacy.

The third Conference of Indian Universities held in March, 1934 suggested readjustment of the prevailing system in schools in such a way that a large number of pupils at the secondary stage are enrolled in vocational courses and diverted towards occupations. A committee under the chairmanship of P.N. Sapru was formed to investigate the question of unemployment among educated young men. The state governments also appointed similar committees to make educational system related to employment. There seemed to be general agreement that the outstanding need was to place the present educational system, admittedly top-heavy, on a really firm and stable basis.

There was continued development of education at all levels as would be evident from Table 10.

Table 10: Total Number of Institutions (Recognised and Unrecognised) and Pupils

	1922	*1927*	*1932*	*1937*
Institutions	2,08,106	2,46,264	2,57,792	2,55,709
Increase(+)	—	+38,158	+11,528	-2,083
Decrease(-)				
Pupils	83,51,350	11,15,74,96	1,27,66,537	1,41,46,038
Increase(+)	—	+27,76,146	+16,09,041	+13,79,501
Decrease(-)				

Source: Progress of Education for various quinquenniums.

It would appear that throughout the years under review, there was an increase in the number of students although during 1932-37, there was a perceptible down slide in the number of institutions. An analysis of the year-wise position of institutions reveals that there was a gradual decrease of number of institutions between 1926-27 and 1931-32. There was a further decline by 2,445, in the number of institutions between 1931-32 and 1932-33. Since then, the number of institutions almost stabilised itself till 1936-37. It may also be stated that besides the government recognised institutions, there were 36,920 unrecognised institutions with 7,11,656 students and both the number of institutions and the enrolments were on the increase.

The Last Quinquennium (1942-47)

Table 11: Institutions and Enrolment

	1941-42	*1946-47*
Institutions	2,09,914	2,03,873
Increase(+)/Decrease(-)	—	-6041
Enrolment	1,54,41,177	1,77,50,263
Increase(+)/Decrease(-)	—	+23,09,086

It would appear from Table 11 that although there was a decline in the number of recognised institutions – by 6041 – there was a sizeable increase in enrolment (23,09,086). In addition there were 18,139 unrecognised institutions in 1941-42; their number decreased to 14292 in 1946-47. It might have been due to uncertainty created by the political turmoil that preceded the independence of the country and the large scale riots that led to migration of the minorities from the newly created states of India and Pakistan.

The progress of education institution-wise is given in the Table 12 below:

Table 12 : Progress of Educational Institutions

Institutions	*1941-42*	*1942-43*	*1945-46*	*1946-47*	*Increase (+) Decrease (-)*
1. Universities	15	15	16	17	(+)2
2. Arts and Science Colleges	209	219	265	297	(+)88
3. Intermediate Colleges	129	135	189	199	(+)70
4. High Schools	4035	4164	4949	5297	(+)1262
5. Middle Schools	11162	11227	12120	12843	(+)1681
6. Primary Schools	181968	176034	167841	172661	(-)9037
7. Engineering Colleges	9	10	12	16	(+)7
8. Training Colleges	31	35	38	42	(+)11
9. Other Professional Colleges	53	56	73	82	(+)29
10. Engineering & Technical Schools	670	636	654	665	(-)5
11. Training Schools	612	587	588	650	(+)38
12. Other Special Schools	11021	10,557	9255	11104	(+) 83
13. Total	209914	203675	196000	203873	(-) 6041
14. Unrecognised Schools	18139	15682	15564	14292	(-) 3847

Source: Progress of Education for various quinquenniums.

It would be seen that there was a decline of 6041 institutions between 1941-42 and 1946-47. Most of this was due to the decline in the number of primary schools and engineering and technological institutions. There was also a reduction in the number of unrecognised schools, to the extent of 3847 during the five year period.

It may be mentioned that the period under analysis (1941-47) was the most troubled period, when politics and not education was in ascendance. It was during this period that communal divide was at its height and internecine killings were the order of the day. It was really a miracle that the decline in educational institutions was within manageable limits. The number of unrecognised institutions, however, declined substantially.

The position about enrolment in various institutions is given in the table below:

Table 13: Enrolment in Institutions by Type of Education

Institutions	*In Recognised Institutions*				*Increase*
	1941-42	*1942-43*	*1945-46*	*1946-47*	*(+)Decrease(-)*
1. Universities	12,532	11,433	15,693	16,148	(+)3,616
2. Arts and Science Colleges (including Intermediate colleges and others	1,32,129	1,23,904	1,75,509	196,158	(+)64,029
3. High School	1,33,5948	13,39,846	19,79,546	21,93,493	(+)8,59,548
4. Middle Schools	1,45,0841	13,92,931	16,20,000	17,81,300	(+)3,30,459
5. Primary Schools	1,20,18726	1,15,94,358	1,21,03,203	1,30,26,248	(+)10,07,522

6. Engineering and Technical Colleges	3,009	3,180	4,780	5,162	(+)2,153
7. Training Colleges	2,504	2,600	2,550	3,095	(+)591
8. Other Professional Colleges	21,612	18,960	31,489	35,880	(+)14,268
9. Engineering and Technical Schools	37,189	23,475	35,619	36,048	(-)1,141
10. Training Schools	32,121	31,389	31,383	38,772	(+) 6.651
12. Other Special Schools	4,09,098	3,68,301	3,62,589	4,24,071	(+) 14,971
13. Total	1,54,55,708	1,49,10,377	1,63,62,371	1,77,56375	(+) 23,09,086
14. Unrecognised Schools	5,32,010	5,54,699	4,67,007	4,36,521	(-) 55,489

During the last quinquennium, before India attained political freedom, there was substantial increase in enrolment in all institutions with the exception of engineering and technical schools. This is in marked contrast to the number of institutions, which showed a reduction of 6041 over the period under review. It is also noteworthy that, in the quinquennium, the number of unrecognised institutions and the enrolment therein suffered a setback – the largest being in enrolment which plummeted to 4,96,521 resulting in a reduction of 55,489 over the period under review.

To Sum-Up

As already stated, the data in regard to educational development in the early years of the first half of the twentieth century is somewhat unreliable, inadequate and also incomparable because of the changing complexion of different stages of education. It has also been pointed out that, in the earlier years, primary education was of four years duration. At a later stage, middle classes were added to it to make it elementary education. Similarly, secondary education would consist of either two years of high school or of four years inclusive of two years of the middle school. This also applied to what is called higher/university education.

Subject to these limitations, one could sum up the progress of education as follows:

(a) There was considerable expansion of education in the first half of the twentieth century.

(b) Taking the institutions first. In 1901, there were 97,100 primary schools, 5493 secondary schools and five universities. By 1947, the number of primary schools rose to 1,72,661 (annual growth rate of about three per cent); the number of secondary schools rose to 18140 (annual growth rate of about seven per cent). The number of universities which was five rose to 19 by 1947.

There was considerable increase in enrolment also. It was estimated that against about 30 lakh in 1901, the enrolment rose to one crore and seventy seven lakh – a little less than a six fold increase.

Grey Areas

In spite of these achievements, there were quite a few grey areas in the development of education. For example, in spite of continued emphasis on primary education, the coverage of the age group 6-11 was 40 per cent even in 1951, i.e., four years after independence. Further, there were wide disparities among the provinces in regard to the coverage of the age group. There were also large scale gender disparities that have continued till the present times.

It is also worth noting that education was largely literary in character. There was hardly any emphasis on vocationalisation of education. The total number of engineering and technical schools was 665 in 1947. Vocationalisation of general education, as is understood now, was conspicuous by its absence. Further, in a country like India, where agriculture is the mainstay of the general population, agricultural education, was very inadequately provided at the school and college stages.

The period under review witnessed a series of natural calamities and political turmoil. The beginning of the century was marked by natural calamities – plague, famine, earthquakes and cyclone. During the middle of the first half of the twentieth century, there was the world war in which India, as a part of the colonial empire, was made to participate. At the end of the war, India had to face the brutish might of the victorious Britain, hell-bent on crushing its defiant subjects, who had pledged to throw away the yoke of centuries old slavery. This resulted in large scale use of force on the part of the alien administration leading to, among others, Non-cooperation Movement, which impacted adversely the progress of Indian education.

To meet the stupendous expenditure of the war, there were budgetary cuts propelled by the Retrenchment Committees at the Centre and states. A number of schemes for the development and improvement of Indian education had to be dropped/curtailed.

Positive Achievements

It would be unjust to say that the period under review was devoid of any positive achievements. The following developments are worth mentioning:

Firstly, though delayed, there was general acceptance by the Government of India of its responsibility for financing and developing Indian education, either through direct investment in the sector or by providing financial assistance to private organisations. The grant-in-aid system introduced in the mid nineteenth century is still an important factor in Indian education.

Secondly, there was continued emphasis on providing primary education in spite of the rejection of the bills moved in the Legislative Council to make primary education free and compulsory.

Thirdly, though not directly related to education, the Department of Archaeological Survey of India was set up in 1861 to identify and maintain archaeological sites. This department has continuously undertaken research in the ancient monuments and has been responsible for preserving the cultural heritage of India.

Fourthly, besides establishing universities of a general type, three specialised institutions were set up during the early years of the twentieth century. One was the Agricultural Research Institute at Pusa set up in Bengal in 1905. The Institute was later re-christened as Central College of Agriculture, which was charged with responsibility of carrying out experimental research; education and demonstration agriculture. The college was subsequently shifted to Delhi and renamed Pusa Institute of Agricultural Research.

The second was the establishment of Institute of Science in 1909 at Bangalore, which received an initial grant of Rs. 30 lakh from Jamsetji Tata, besides by the government. The Institute has developed into a prestigious world class institution.

The third institution: the School of Oriental Studies was set up in 1916 to carry out research in Indian history and culture.

Fifthly, there was genuine effort by the government to improve university education. The reorganisation of university education with emphasis on setting up of unitary teaching universities, as against affiliating institutions as suggested by the Calcutta University Commission (1917-19) is a classic example of the government's concern about improving university education.

Sixthly, with the transfer of Indian education to the Indian Ministries under Dyarchy, Indian educationists/political leaders also started taking interest in reforming education. The Wardha Scheme of Basic Education, worked out with the blessings of Mahatma Gandhi, was an important step towards bringing about radical reforms in the Indian educational system. Although, the scheme as such was not pursued, the basic concept of making education practice-oriented still holds good.

Seventhly, regardless of the motives behind Macaulay's emphasis on English and Western Sciences in Indian education and notwithstanding his tirade against the Indians, their religious beliefs and his contempt for classical languages, India has benefited from the introduction of English as a medium of instruction at the higher education stages. The domination of Indian professionals, scientists and men of letters in the world markets is an eloquent testimony to the wisdom of the Government of India to accept Macaulay's interpretation of the Board of Directors' Directive.

Eighthly, the period also saw the introduction of reforms in the administrative system of education at the advisory and implementation levels. Among the advisory bodies, the pre-eminent position goes to the creation of the Central Advisory Board of Education in 1921. For data collection, the Government set up the Bureau of Education. Further, in order to keep the Government of India informed about the educational development in the country as a whole and to advise the provinces about educational matters, the post of Education Commissioner was created and retained in spite of adverse recommendations of the Inchcape Committee.

The Government of India also created the all India service in education – IES- at par with the Indian Civil Services (ICS). This service was meant to give an all India perspective to educational administration, teaching and research. With the onset of political emancipation, the all India service in education was allowed to fade out. It was, however, felt that the all India service in education was an important instrument in enabling officials with all India experience and outlook to bring to bear their wider expertise in solving local educational problems and thus accelerating the pace of educational development, particularly, in the educationally backward states, whose number is not insignificant in India.

It may be pointed out that the Education Commission (1964-66) had recommended the recreation of the All India Service in Education as an agency for educational administration and planning besides teaching and research. It was also suggested that it should consist of persons who have teaching experience, with the possibility of the educational administrator returning to teaching and the teacher going over to administration at least on expiration of a tenure assignment. The proposal, however, could not be implemented because of stiff resistance from the state governments, who do not want any interference from the Central Government in a subject which is predominantly a state responsibility, notwithstanding its being a concurrent subject in the Indian Constitution.

Lastly, at the fag end of the British rule, an effort was made to initiate educational planning with particular reference to the introduction of free and compulsory elementary education. The Central Advisory Board of Education, in its report, popularly known as Sargent Committee Report worked out the scheme of introducing universal elementary education during the next 40 years. It also calculated the cost of the programme. In spite of the scheme being subjected to criticism by the political parties, educationists and the press, the scheme deserves to be considered as the first ever attempt to work out the details of the programme including the targets to be achieved, the phasing of the programme and its total cost.

The Report also recommended the setting up of a body to oversee the progress of university education and to provide financial assistance for their development. The body was to be on the pattern of the British University Grants Committee (which has now been renamed as Universities Funding Council). The present University Grants Commission has been set up on the basis of the recommendations of the Sargent Committee Report.

References

1. The Report of the Indian Statutory Commission, 1929, p. 9.
2. Selections from Educational Records.
3. The Calcutta University Commission, 1919, p. 31.
4. Progress of Education in India, 1907-12, Government of India p. 3.
5. Despatch of 1854, p. 2.
6. Selections from Educational Records, op.cit. pp. 4-5.
7. For details, see chapters 3 and 8.
8. The damage caused by these natural calamities has been described in a separate chapter.
9. Progress of Education in India 1901-02, p. 307.
10. For details, see Chapters 3 and 8.
11. The Indian Universities Commission, 1902.
12. Progress of Education in India, 1901-02, pp. 306-07.
13. H. Sharp: Progress of Education in India, 1912-17 Seventh Quinquennial Review, Calcutta, 1918, pp. 4-5.
14. This applies to primary schools, to the primary stage of secondary schools, which, if reckoned, would bring the percentage to 2.63. If the percentage of males enrolled in primary schools to the male population were taken, it would rise to 3.83 and similarly with the addition of primary pupils not in primary schools, it would reach 4.25.
15. Quoted by H. Sharp, *Ibid.* p. 5.
16. H. Sharp, *Ibid.*, p. 6.
17. Indian Educational Policy, Resolution of the Govt. of India in Home Department, Nos. 199-211 dated 11th March, 1904.
18. It has been discussed in detail in a separate chapter.
19. J.A. Richey, Progress of Education in India, 1917-22; p. 2.
20. The Non-cooperation Movement and its impact on education has been discussed in Chapter 5.
21. *Ibid.* p. 8.
22. We have discussed the implications of the Central Retrenchment Committee in a separate section in 'Significant Events that Impacted Education, (Chapter 5).

3

Progress of Various Sectors of Education

In the previous chapter, an overall analysis of the state of Indian education during almost two centuries of the colonial rule has been attempted. In this chapter, it is intended to highlight the salient features of the educational system on a micro-level basis. The discussion will centre around the sectoral programmes encompassing elementary, secondary and higher education. It may, however, be clarified that the various sectors which will be taken up for discussion do not constitute a water-tight compartment. For example, primary education may be of four or five years duration or may, at some stage include middle school education. The same holds good for secondary and higher education. The determining factor will be the patterns of Government's policy, which would be changing from time to time.

This chapter has been broadly divided into two sections:

(i) School Education consisting of Elementary and Secondary Education. It will also include Adult Education.

(ii) Higher Education, which includes General and Technical Education.

SECTION-1

School Education

(a) *Elementary Education*

Pessimistic Situation

In the previous chapter, it has been stated that the position of Indian education at the time, when the Board of Directors of the East India Company sent their first Despatch (1854), was not very encouraging. Out of the then population of over two hundred and forty million, there were more than 18 million of boys, who ought to have been in schools, but only a little more than one sixth were actually receiving primary education. The census of 1901, found that only one in ten of the male population and only seven in a thousand of female population were literate. These figures showed the vast illiterate population who had to be provided with schooling facilities.

This state of affairs made the Government of India to realise that primary education had hitherto received insufficient attention and an inadequate share of public funds. It was also conceded that it (primary education) had a strong claim on the sympathy both of the Central Government and of local governments and should be made a leading charge upon provincial revenues and that in those provinces, where it was in backward condition, its encouragement should be a primary obligation[1].

The Despatch of 1854 also stated:

"Our attention should now be directed to a consideration, if possible, still more important, and one which has been hitherto, we are bound to admit, much neglected, namely, how useful and practical knowledge, suited to every station in life, may be best conveyed to the great mass of people, who are utterly incapable of obtaining any education worthy of name by their own unaided efforts, and we desire to see that active measures of the Government, more especially directed, for the future of this object, for the attainment of which we are ready to sanction a considerable increase of expenditure." [2]

Five years later, the Despatch of 1859 reviewed the progress of education and stressed the need for expanding primary education. It also suggested the levy of a special rate on land to provide adequate finances for the expansion of vernacular education. Unfortunately, far greater interest was taken for the promotion of secondary education than of primary education.[3]

The Indian Education Commission 1882-83 reiterated the significance of primary education in order to spread education among the masses. It made elaborate recommendations which were generally on the lines of the County Council Act of England with regard to its policy, objectives, curriculum, methods of teaching, teacher training, finance and administration, etc. It recommended:

(i) That primary education be declared that part of the whole system of Public Instruction, which possesses an almost exclusive claim on local funds set apart for education and a large claim on provincial revenues.

(ii) That curriculum should be made according to local needs and its practical aspects properly emphasised.

(iii) That mother tongue should be the medium of instruction.

(iv) That both municipal and local boards keep a separate school fund.

The Commission also recommended that primary education should be regarded as an end in itself and not necessarily a portion of institution leading up to the university. For this purpose, the standards were to be revised with a view to the introduction of practical subjects such as native arithmetic, mensuration and elements of physical education. The indigenous schools were to be everywhere recognised, encouraged and gradually improved. Special attention was to be paid to backward districts. As to finances, primary education should have an almost exclusive claim on local and larger claim on provincial funds.

Position at the Beginning of the Twentieth Century

The beginning of the twentieth century witnessed a perceptible downfall in primary education when compared to the last quinquennium of the Nineteenth century. This happened mainly because of natural calamities which have been discussed in an earlier section. In the period 1887-88 to 1891-92, the number of boys at primary stage increased by 2,75,000 and in the next five years by 3,61,000. During the first quinquennium of the nineteenth century (1902-1907), it remained practically stationery. Bombay lost 55,000 and Bengal 19,000 boys of primary schools stage and the United Provinces' gain of 74,000 was the only considerable increase. As already stated, the period under review witnessed a series of multi-faceted misfortunes: two severe famines and a widespread epidemic of plague, which caused havoc among the populace and disorganised the administration and educational systems.

Progress of School Education

1907-1912[4]

The next quinquennium of 1907-12, however, recorded an increase in the number of pupils. From 53,88,632 pupils in 1907, the number rose to 67,80,721 - nearly 26 per cent larger as compared to the earlier period (including Burma). The increase was large, but compared to the population, it was insignificant. The table below gives province-wise school enrolment[5]:

Table 1: Province-wise Enrolment

Province	*Pupils at Schools*		*(Figures in thousands) Percentage increase*	*Percentage of the total population*
	(1907)	(1912)		
Madras	1007	1280	27.1	3.1
Bombay	721	923	28.0	3.4
Bengal	1269	1610	26.9	2.9
United Provinces	606	712	17.5	1.5
Punjab	300	381	27.0	1.9
Eastern Bengal and Assam	816	1075	31.7	3.1
Central Province and Berar	232	313	32.1	2.0
Coorg	5	7	40.0	3.9

Source: Sixth Quinquennial Review, 1914, Vol. I.

It would appear that the maximum coverage of the age group was 3.4 per cent in Bombay followed by Eastern Bengal and Assam and Madras (3.1 per cent each). Considering that 15 per cent of the relevant age group should have been at school, the position in various provinces and India as a whole seems very dismal.

A redeeming feature of the not so encouraging a situation, however, was that the "quinquennium witnessed a remarkable realisation on the part of almost all classes of the growing importance of education. The movement in favour of denominational universities, the prominence which educational problems now assume on the platform and the press, the debates in the Imperial and local legislative councils and the introduction of a private bill for compulsory education – all these were considered to be symptoms pointing in the same direction. The growing numbers indicated incontestable proof of enhanced demand."[6] The government of Bombay aptly remarked that the history of the period indicated "the presence among the people themselves of a growing disposition favourable to the reception of higher education ideals and aspirations."[7]

Compulsory and Free Education and Problems of the Future

As already stated, this period witnessed great enthusiasm for expansion of primary education. In 1910, Gokhale introduced, in the Imperial Legislative Council, a well thought out bill intended to make permissible the introduction of compulsory education in municipal or board areas. The proposal was that before compulsion could be introduced, a certain percentage of children of the area must already be at school; the local authority must use its discretion in asking for the application of the provision in their areas, keeping in view the various provisions of the Bill. The Bill, however, did not meet official acceptance and was thrown out by an overwhelming majority (38 against 13).[8]

The proposal of introducing free and compulsory education at the primary stage, however, did not die. It was introduced several times in the Imperial and local legislative councils. But it was not till the close of the quinquennium that the suggestion received support. The Hon'ble Mr. Patel then introduced a bill, the provisions of which resembled those of Mr. Gokhale. It was to be applicable to municipalities in the Bombay Presidency other than Bombay city. The bill was passed into a law. Once the lead was taken, others followed and private bills of a similar nature (but excluding also the local board areas) were introduced. They, however, met a lukewarm reception at the hands of the local bodies. The Punjab Report observed the apathy shown by many municipalities towards elementary education. The Delhi Report contained the following passage:

"It is doubtful, if there is much wide-spread feeling in favour of compulsory education; the growing interest in education has not persuaded the classes, who need the services of their children as wage earners and these are very numerous… until the general sense of the community has strengthened or the pitch of adult wages improved, compulsory education certainly could not be made universal".[9]

Retarding Factors

The reasons assigned for failure to send children to school were generally the conservatism of the agriculturists; their disinclination to spare children from the fields, the non-utility of curriculum, the inefficiency of schools and the parents' financial burden involved in the payment of fees.

The official circles, felt that there was no doubt that the first impediment existed, but it was losing its hold and there was demand for new schools in rural areas. The objection was considered to have been exaggerated since small children could not do any work of value. It was also doubtful if any change in the curriculum would have a noticeable effect on school attendance. Indeed the parents looked mainly for instruction in three R's, and in the time at disposal, in school there was but small opportunity to teach more. About the question of fees, it was thought that the rate was so low and exemptions so numerous that probably very little loss would be incurred with their abolition. In fact, conservatism and inefficiency of the school were considered as the two main retarding factors.

Free Education

Demands for compulsion are ordinarily and naturally coupled with demand for free education. The fees paid in primary schools for Indian boys during the early twentieth century averaged 14.7 annas per pupil per annum. In Assam and NWFP, primary education was free. The Bombay Report said that primary education was particularly free for girls and the most backward classes. According to the Central Provinces, under the then prevalent fee system, nothing was likely to be gained by free education and that only one such demand emanated from a local body. The obvious reply to it was that our rules made it impossible for anyone to be deprived of primary education on grounds of poverty. Those who pay, but have no use for education, will not be converted by the remission of 12 annas a year.

While there is some force in the argument that the level of fees was so low that it would not have ordinarily impeded the entry of young children to schools, yet the fact of making some payment to a school for a kind of education that did not equip the child to meet the diverse situations of life does lessen the willingness of the parents to commit their children to school. This factor, coupled with depriving parents of child's labour, for whatever it was worth, would certainly have been a retarding factor.

Girls' Education

The government also felt concerned about slow progress in education of girls. The Government of India's view was conveyed in a letter[10] from the Department of Education, dated 1st July 1911 addressed to governments of Madras, Bengal, etc. Some excerpts:

1. "According to last returns, out of a female population of more than 119 millions, only 8,30,000 are at schools and of the total direct expenditure upon education in India, only 11 per cent represents expenditure upon the education for girls. In the last five years, however, there has been an increase of 2,00,000 in the number of girl scholars and a demand for female education may be expected to grow rapidly in many parts of India.
2. "The Government of India thinks it very desirable to anticipate this demand by being ready with schemes which will meet it. These schemes will conveniently take the form of a 10 year programme for:

(i) the expansion of girls' education by means of the allocation of educational funds – whether disbursed to for the maintenance of Board's schools;

(ii) the improvement of facilities for the training of mistresses;

(iii) the amelioration of the conditions of service in the cases of mistresses and members of the inspecting staff such as granting of free quarters of a suitable kind, of carriage allowance and of special facilities during journeys etc. While unable to commit themselves to any promise regarding the allotment of Imperial funds for these purposes, the Government of India would be glad, in connection with the preparation of a working plan for the financing of education generally, to be furnished with the schemes which the governments of Madras, Bombay and Bengal, etc. may have already on hand, expanded, where necessary to a ten year working plan. An estimate of the cost is likewise requested with a statement as to how much of the additional cost can be found from Provincial revenues".[11]

How much progress was achieved by this letter is not known. It, however, highlights the awareness on the part of the Government of India to accelerate the pace of girls' education.

Progress of Education – Primary Education – 1917-1937

There was a sizeable increase in the number of primary schools and pupils during 1917-27. While the number of schools increased from 1,42,203 in 1917 to 1,60,070 in 1922, enrolment increased from 58,18,730 to 82,56,760 during the same period. In the case of special schools, there was a substantial diminution. The number of institutions declined by 850 i.e. from 4861 in 1917 to 4011 in 1922 and the number of students decreased from 143,604 to 1,32,706 during the period. In the next quinquennium, however there was some improvement; the number of schools more than doubled i.e. from 4,011 to 10639. Similar improvement occurred in enrolment also. Further, there was marked improvement in enrolment of girls. From 16.61 per cent of the total enrolment in 1917, it rose to 17.5 per cent of the total enrolment in 1927. According to the Hartog Committee, this increase occurred because of the slow but steady break down of the obstacles that stood in the way of the spread of education. It was also noted that isolation of rural areas and the difficulties imposed by distance on the extension of education were gradually being lessened by the building of new roads and railways and by the provision of motor services, which are linking up even remote villages with the mainstreams of life and activity. The age of marriage was gradually rising and there were powerful movements on foot to raise the age of consent and to mitigate the rigour of the system of *purdah*.

Further, "...the attention given to it by legislative councils is both a symptom and evidence of this recognition. The transfer of the Department of Education to popular control, as represented by a Minister, has both increased the public interest in it and made it more sensitive to the currents of public need and public opinion. ...Communities, which had for long been educationally backward like the Muhammadan community, have awakened to the need and possibilities of education for their children. The movement has spread to the depressed classes and even to the tribal aboriginals and has stirred a much larger proportion of the people than before to demand education as a right".[12]

The Hartog Committee also Stated:

"...there has been a great awakening to the need for improvement both in the quality of education provided and in the conditions, which determine the working of the educational institutions. In many provinces, comprehensive measures of reform, whether by way of legislation or otherwise, are under consideration and steps have been taken to deal with unsatisfactory features of the system. New agencies of local or institutional control have been established. A new type of the university organisation has been created; facilities for professional and technical education have been extended and made more varied; the methods of training teachers in some provinces have been over-hauled and made more effective; the pay and conditions of services of teachers have been improved; curricula have been recast and widened and unrecognised schools have been drawn up into the public system".[13]

This was the somewhat encouraging picture of primary education during the decade ending 1927. The momentum, however, could not be sustained. According to reports: "economic distress far exceeding in magnitude and intensity even that experienced in post war years has intervened, expenditure has been cut down in all directions, the pace of expansion has been retarded, political life has been disturbed, communal bitterness has been accentuated".[14]

At the primary stage of education, there was increase in the number of pupils from 91,20,438 in 1927 to 1,14,65,700 in 1937. At the middle stage, the corresponding figures were, 7,13,939 and 11,42,254, respectively. The increase was, however, 13,07,522 between 1927-32 and 10,37,729 between 1932-37. This means that the pace of progress was somewhat slow between the quinquennium 1932-37 as against the period 1927-32.

Ineffectiveness of the Educational System

The Hartog Committee, which reviewed the measures and manner of educational progress during the period 1928 onwards, was very pessimistic about the waste and ineffectiveness of the educational system. The Committee said:

"...In this primary system, which from our point of view should be designed to produce literacy and the capacity to exercise an intelligent vote, the waste is appalling. So far as we can judge, the vast increase in numbers in primary schools produces no commensurate increase in literacy for only a small proportion of those who are at primary stage reach class IV in which the attainment of literacy may be expected. In one province, despite a very large increase in primary schools, pupils who reached class IV, were actually less by 30,000 in 1927 than it was ten years previously...

"The wastage in the case of girls is even more serious than in the case of boys. The disparity in education and literacy between women and men, far from decreasing is actually increasing. The disparity between the wealthier part of the country and poorer parts tends to increase".[15]

There were quite a few other problems that afflicted the primary stage of education. The Report for Bengal province said:

"The number of schools has increased, largely as a result of individual initiatives and there are about twice the number of primary schools as are actually necessary... schools of a very low grade, schools with only one teacher, teachers without a living wage, teachers without proper training, schools under no adequate control, schools with no effective inspection – these are the problems we have to face..."[16]

Another problem that was highlighted was the movement for substituting for the village school a variety of schools intended for the benefit of particular communities. "We are now reaching a stage, when each village wants a primary school, a *maktab* and a *pathshala*. In addition, it is claimed that even at the lower primary stage, separate schools are necessary for girls and also in many places, separate schools for the children of depressed classes. Thus, in the poorest provinces (Bihar and Orissa), we are asked to provide five primary schools for each village."[17]

Last Decade – 1937-1947

In the last decade of the period under study (1937-47), there was a steady decline in the number of institutions at the primary stage, both for boys and girls in some of the provinces. From a total of 1,89,601 for both boys and girls in 1937-38, the number of institutions plummeted to 1,72,661 indicating a decline of about 17,000 institutions.

Contrariwise, there was substantial increase in enrolment at the primary stage. In 1937-38, it increased from 1,05,16,353 (90,29,887 boys and 14,84,466 girls) to 1,30,26,248 (1,14,24,402 boys and 16,01,846 girls) in 1946-47 indicating a growth rate of 12.40 per cent during the ten year period. The growth rate of girls enrolment was a little higher than that of boys – 12.7 per cent for boys and 13.83 per cent for girls. This was a hopeful sign considering the not so encouraging growth rate for girl's education in the earlier period. Much leeway, however, needed to be made for promoting the education of girls, considering the fact that in 1937-38, girls constituted almost 14 per cent of the total enrolment, which declined to 12.4 in 1946-47.

Wastage

Further, there was substantial wastage in terms of pupils not completing their four year course of primary education. In 1936-37, 76 per cent of the pupils dropped out midway. By 1946-47, however, the wastage was reduced to 65 per cent – still a significant figure. The wastage was much higher in the case of girls – 73 per cent in 1946-47 against 61 per cent for boys. The main causes of wastage were identified as the incidence of child labour, especially in respect of those belonging to labouring and agricultural classes; inadequate supply of teachers, ineffective teaching and supervision, admissions to schools throughout the year, irregular attendance; and faulty administration by local bodies.

Various steps were taken to reduce wastage. These included introduction of compulsion, coupled with free education in some areas; appointment of attendance officers to draw up lists of out of school children and inducing them to attend educational institutions etc. However, due to economic difficulties, the general public was not quite convinced of the value of education. Even threats of punishment failed to work "as punishment is problematic and loss of children's earnings is immediate and tangible. Besides enforcement of punishment on a sufficiently large scale, is beset with obvious difficulties."[18]

Middle Stage

There were two types of middle schools: Vernacular (without English) and Anglo-Vernacular (with English). The former were mainly in rural areas. Table 2 below indicates the progress of schools as also enrolment in them:

Table 2: Number of Middle Schools and Enrolment

1937-38				*1946-47*				*Percentage increase over ten years*			
Vernacular Middle School		*English Middle School*		*Vernacular Middle School*		*English Middle School*		*Vernacular Middle School*		*English Middle School*	
Schools	Enrolment	Schools	Enrolment	Schools	Enrolment	Schools	Enrolment	Schools	Enrolment	Schools	Enrolment
5326	7,32,885	45635	32,102	5911	8,80,862	6,932	9,00,481	10.98	20.19	5.19	69.23

It is evident that in terms of number of schools as also enrolment, the English middle schools registered faster progress.

Province-wise Position

Table 3 indicates province-wise position of the various types of middle schools and their enrolment over the quinquennium 1937-38 to 1946-47.

Table 3: Statistics of Middle Schools

Province	*1937-38*				*1946-47*			
	Vernacular Middle School		*English Middle Schools*		*Vernacular Middle Schools*		*English Middle Schools*	
	Schools	*Enrolment*	*Schools*	*Enrolment*	*Schools*	*Enrolment*	*Schools*	*Enrolment*
Assam	248	38,711	285	27,228	353	48,672	511	47,885
Bengal	44	3,737	1,968	2,04,1[illegible]5	14	1,460	2,752	3,14,915
Bihar	96	11,934	731	1,00,412	59	8,318	1,483	1,94,186
Bombay	00	00	362	25,501	00	00	626	46,508
C.P. and Berar	423	78,370	251	36,084	443	84,583	344	67,896
Madras	00	00	201	33,419	00	00	254	48,830
N.W.F.P.	214	28,647	21	5,394	226	33,029	46	13,834
Orissa	66	8,354	127	3,143	58	6,596	215	21,985

Punjab	3,105	4,15,799	231	51,670	3,100	4,89,010	201	62,038
Sind	00	00	130	7,239	00	00	164	11,738
United Provinces	1,067	1,38,760	189	24,059	1,583	1,97,083	267	50,758
Ajmer-Merwara	18	1,218	12	1,238	29	1,782	9	1,493
Baluchistan	00	00	4	667	00	00	8	1,670
Bangalore	7	2,275	6	1,550	10	3,670	6	926
Delhi	37	4,881	26	6,736	36	6,659	30	11,438

It would be seen that Punjab had the largest number of vernacular middle schools both in 1937-38 (3105) and in 1946-47 (3100). This was followed by United Provinces – 1067 in 1937-38 and 1583 in 1946-47. In all other provinces, the number of vernacular schools was less than 500, with Bangalore having the lowest number of schools; being 7 in 1937-38 and 10 in 1946-47. In the case of English vernacular schools, Bengal topped the list having 1968 in 1937-38 and 2,752 in 1946-47. This could be because of the continued insistence of reformers like Raja Ram Mohan Roy, who stressed the introduction of English education rather than the establishment of schools teaching vernaculars. The availability of government jobs and possibility of admissions to institutions of higher education could also be the factors responsible for the growing demand for English schools.

To Sum-Up

We have reviewed the progress of elementary education in the first half of the twentieth century. It has been seen that, in spite of a number of socio-economic and financial problems, facilities for education expanded in terms of educational institutions. There were, however, substantial disparities among the provinces in regard to the availability of educational facilities as also the coverage of the relevant age-group. The attempts to introduce bills in the Legislative Council to introduce free and compulsory education were vehemently opposed by officials, who constituted a majority in the Council. Even the demand for providing free education at the primary stage was vetoed on flimsy grounds of fees being already very low. It was not realised that a parent, who is already unwilling to admit his child to schools would be much more reluctant to do so if he was asked to pay, even though the amount may be very low.

The gender disparity in the utilisation of educational facilities was visible all through the period. The comparative figures for boys and girls enrolment are not available for the entire period. It has been mentioned that in 1917, girls constituted only 17 per cent of enrolment at the primary stage. This percentage was reduced to about 12 in 1946-47. Undoubtedly, there were a number of socio-economic factors that hampered the progress of girls' education. It is doubtful, if the Government of India or the provincial governments initiated any significant measures to accelerate the progress of girls' education. There was, however, a communication from the Government of India dated 1st July 1911 to the provincial governments to work out plans for accelerating the progress of female education and to prepare schemes for a ten year period for allocation of resources for the maintenance of Boards' funds and subsidies to aided schools. It was also suggested that service conditions of teachers and the inspecting staff need to be improved. The Government of India also provided financial assistance for carrying out these programmes.

No mention has been made about the action taken by the Government of India and the provincial governments on the implementation of the proposals and their impact on the progress of female education.

The problem of wastage at the primary education stage was highlighted and the socio-economic causes responsible for the large wastage identified. But not much seems to have been done to reduce the extent of the wastage that has been eating into the vitals of the education system till this day!

(a) Secondary Education

The expansion of secondary education during the twentieth century has been analysed on a uinquennial/decennial basis, subject to the availability of data. We shall start with the analysis relating to this sector of education for the period 1902-07.

(a) 1902-07

As in the case of elementary education, there was, during the twentieth century, a marked expansion of schools with English as one of the subjects at the secondary stage. The quinquennium, 1902-07 registered substantial increase in the enrolment of boys; the number of boys at secondary stage of English schools increased by over 49,000 as compared to less than 18,000 during the previous quinquennium. There was, however, a downslide in the number of vernacular secondary schools. Against an increase of 4,000 of such schools during the quinquennium, 1891-92 to 1896-97, the number dwindled by nearly 500 during the period under review.

(b) 1907-12

During the quinquennium, the government reiterated its policy to utilise private efforts to the full in the extension of secondary education. As a consequence, there was a kind of moratorium on the setting up of government secondary schools.

In 1912, government schools numbered only 271 and their enrolment was 74,689. Table 4 indicates the number of schools:

Table 4: Secondary Schools in Enrolment (1912)

Managed by	*Schools*	*Percentage of the total*	*Pupils*	*Percentage of the total*
Government	271	7.6	74,689	11.5
Local Bodies	358	10.1	65,062	9.9
Native States	161	4.5	17,547	2.7
Private Agencies	2,770	77.8	4,96,306	75.9
Total	3,560	100.0	6,53,604	100.0

It would be seen that private schools accounted for more than three-fourths of the total number of secondary schools and enrolment in them.

(a) 1912-17

The total number of institutions for boys and girls, inclusive of primary schools, rose from 6,370 in 1911-12 to 7693 in 1916-17 and that of pupils in them from 9,24,370 to 11,86,335 or by 28.3 per cent. The enrolment in high and middle English schools increased from 7,02,566 to 9,24,770 or by 31.6 per cent.

The advance was most rapid in Assam, Burma and the N.W.F.P. The popularity of secondary education was the greatest in Bengal, which accounted for 35.8 per cent of all secondary schools and 35 per cent of all secondary school pupils in India.

The reasons for progress were twofold:

"First a strong sentiment is growing in favour of professions, which are deemed respectable and which provide a more or less sedentary life. Secondly, great economic changes have been at work. Easier communications etc. have rendered profitable the production of marketable crops than cereals. Wealth has increased among the cultivators and the lower classes. Consequently, the cost of living has risen. Meantime, the wages of the great bulk of professional classes have not increased. The movement, therefore, which has enriched the cultivators and made it profitable further to aspire to an education and a career for their children for which they would previously not have dreamed of, has forced a larger number of middle classes to seek their livelihood through education and the employment, which it brings."[19]

Expenditure on Secondary Education

It would be of interest to examine whether the policy of the government to encourage private effort in setting up and maintaining educational institutions resulted in larger private investment in education. Table 5 below indicates the percentage contribution by government and its agencies vis-a-vis the private and philanthropic organisations.

Table 5: Expenditure on Secondary Education

Sources from which	*Amount Contributed (in Rupees)*		*Percentage in Total*	
	1911-12	*1916-17*	*1911-12*	*1916-17*
Provincial fund	42,81,105	71,71,709	20.6	22.3
Local Fund	11,38,265	18,38,358	5.5	5.7
Municipal Funds	7,43,946	10,70,671	3.6	3.4
Fees	1,05,25,878	1,67,46,922	50.6	52.3
Endowments	NA	14,20,092	NA	4.4
Subscription	40,99,531	36,81,340	19.7	11.9

(inclusive of local and municipal funds)

It would be seen that the government contribution, inclusive of local boards increased from 29.7 per cent in 1911-12 to 31.4 per cent in 1916-17. The private contribution downslided from 19.7 per cent to 16.3 per cent during the corresponding period. The fee contribution, however, increased by about two per cent from 50.6 to 52.3 per cent during the period under review. This is mainly because the average annual fee for a pupil in English secondary school for Indian boys rose from Rs.14.1 to Rs.17.6. It was Rs. 24.5 in a government school, and Rs. 4.7, 17.3 and 16.4 in a board or municipal and aided or unaided school respectively.

The average annual cost of a secondary school (inclusive of all types) was Rs. 4150 and of a pupil Rs. 27.6. The comparable figures for secondary English schools for boys were: English secondary schools Rs. 28.9 in 1916-17 as against Rs. 24.9 in 1911-12. In a government English school, education of an Indian boy cost Rs. 49; in a board or municipal school Rs. 24; in an aided school Rs. 28 and in an unaided school Rs. 21. The effect on the quality of education in various types of schools on account of cost differentials can be easily surmised.

1917-1922

Table 6 indicates the progress of secondary education during the quinquennium 1917-1922.

Table 6 : Progress of Secondary Education: 1916-17 and 1921-22

Year	*High Schools*		*Middle Schools (English)*		*Middle Schools (Vernacular)*		*All Secondary Schools*	
	Schools	*Scholars*	*Schools*	*Scholars*	*Schools*	*Scholars*	*Schools*	*Scholars*
1916-17	1,584	5,47,569	2,906	3,28,766	2,514	2,30,806	7,004	11,07,141
1921-22	2,248	5,84,910	3,056	2,98,172	3,614	3,57,042	8,918	12,40,124
Increase Decrease	664	37,341	150	30,594	100	1,26,236	914	1,32,983
Percentage (+)(-)	+14.20	+1068	+1.05	-9.31	+14.37	+15.47	+12.73	+11.20

It would be seen that, except in the case of middle schools (English), in which there was a reduction in the number of scholars to the extent of nine per cent during the quinquennium 1916-17 to 1921-22, there was marked expansion in the number of educational institutions at the middle and secondary levels. The overall Percentage increase was higher in the case of schools (12.73) than in the case of scholars (11.20).

Muted Demand for Vernacular Education

According to Richey, "In secondary education, the most noteworthy development has been the more general introduction of vernacular education and growing demand for vocational education. The use of vernacular as the medium of instruction has been supported by both the publicists on sentimental or patriotic grounds and by teachers on educational grounds since it is natural that a child should receive his early instruction in his mother tongue. When English education was first introduced into India, it was never intended that it should replace the vernaculars or the ordinary medium of instruction....

Further, it was also hoped that when vernaculars are introduced, the teachers would enrich the vernaculars by translating European literature....

There is little incentive for Indian scholars to translate European books of learning into the vernaculars. The dearth of vernacular literature due to lack of reading public is a serious handicap to the encouragement of literacy among the masses – for after all only 22,89,188 men and 2,38,162 women are literate in English."[20]

Vocational Education

During the period under review there was an insistent demand for vocational training. This was thought to be indicative of the desire for employment rather than for education. It was felt that there was need for a movement for adapting secondary education to the needs of young persons of the age group 12 to 18. It was also considered necessary that before introducing a subject of vocational education, the possibility of any opening for the boys, who undergo such training to practise such vocation profitably, should be explored. Introducing vocational subjects in the general schools, however, met with little success. It is because of the lack of opportunity for the scholars to use their skills. Further, there is disinclination to enter anything in the nature of a blind alley.

The second obstacle was the reluctance on the part of students to decide early their future careers. This can be illustrated from the recent experience of introducing agricultural education. Agriculture is the most important industry in India and there is no question of the products of agricultural institutions not finding any outlet for themselves. And yet they prefer government jobs rather than practising their expertise in the field. Special agricultural schools also have failed to attract a good number of students – that also not of adequate quality. The most successful experiment is introducing agricultural education in the ordinary curriculum in rural schools.

The problem of lack of interest in vocational education continues even to this day even though nearly 90 years have passed since some effort was made in this direction. According to the latest reports, only about five per cent of higher secondary school students opt for vocation based education[21]. This is in spite of the fact that the government has been insisting that besides providing for specialized short-term and long-term vocational courses, the general education courses should have vocational components both at the school and college stages.

1927-37

Table 7 below indicates the number of secondary schools of all types for boys and their enrolment in British India.

Table 7 : Secondary Schools for Boys

Year	*High Schools*		*Middle Schools (English)*		*Middle Schools (Vernacular)*		*All Secondary Schools*	
	Schools	*Pupils*	*Schools*	*Pupils*	*Schools*	*Pupils*	*Schools*	*Pupils*
1926-27	2,444	7,44,444	3,201	3,49,233	4,728	6,21,984	10,373	17,15,661
1931-32	2,801	8,73,802	3,875	4,13,770	5,894	8,05,918	12,570	20,93,490
1936-37	3,242	10,22,580	4,123	4,60,717	5,609	7,38,570	12,975	22,21,867
Increase between								
1927-32	357 (11.50)	1,29,358 (11.74)	674 (10.64)	64,537 (8.98)	1,166 (12.47	1,83,934 (12.96)	2,197 (12.11)	3,77,829 (12.20)
1932-37	+441 (11.57)	148,778 (11.70)	248 (10.64)	+46,947 (11.13)	-285- (4.84)	-67,348 (-8.36)	+405 (3.22)	+128,377 (10.57)

(Figures in parentheses indicate Percentages)

While there was an increase of 2,197 secondary schools with an additional enrolment of 3,77,829 pupils during the previous quinquennium, the period under review witnessed a rise of 405 schools and 1,28,377 pupils only. These figures indicate that the tide of expansion had slowed down. This may have been due largely to economic factors. The Madras Report contained some interesting observations on this point:

"The slow rate of progress may be partly accounted for by the continuance of economic depression and the growing volume of educated unemployment during the quinquennium under report. A further explanation may, perhaps, be found in the predominantly literary character of secondary education, the demand for which seems to be fast reaching the stage of inelasticity. It is also possible that a sort of saturation point has been reached."[22]

Expenditure

Table 8 indicates the sources of expenditure on secondary education for the years 1921-22 to 1936-37.

Table 8: Expenditure on Secondary Schools for Boys

Year	*Expenditure From*				*Total*
	Govt. Funds	*Board Funds*	*Fees*	*Other Sources*	*Expenditure*
1921-22	1,39,54,026	38,87,479	1,77,34,627	66,41,316	4,22,17,448
Percentages	33.05	9.21	42.01	15.73	100.00
1926-27	1,93,38,209	57,25,549	2,43,04,498	80,86,064	5,74,54,320
Percentages	33.66	9.57	42.30	14.07	100.00
1931-32	2,34,99,407	81,45,108	2,97,13,108	84,15,917	6,97,73,540
Percentages	33.68	11.68	42.58	12.06	100.00
1936-37	2,37,35,062	90,33,789	3,39,36,672	81,50,696	7,48,56,219
Percentages	31.71	12.07	45.34	10.88	100.00
Increase between					
1922-27	53,84,183	18,38,070	65,69,871	14,44,748	1,52,36,872
1927-32	41,16,198	24,19,559	54,08,610	3,29,853	1,22,74,220
1932-37	2,35,655	8,88,681	42,23,564	-2,65,221	50,82,679

Source: Progress of Education in India for various years.

In a period experiencing financial stress, it appears surprising that there was substantial increase in the total expenditure, of about Rs. three crore for secondary school education for boys during the fifteen year period 1922-1937. In proportionate terms, the largest increase was in the case of fees – from 42.01per cent, it went up to 45.44 per cent during the period under review. Even in absolute terms, the contribution from fees was the largest exceeding the contribution from the Government sources.

The average annual cost per pupil in Anglo-vernacular schools was Rs. 42.3. The average annual fee for British India remained stationary since the last quinquennium, being Rs. 22.2 in Anglo-vernacular secondary school and Rs.1.4 in vernacular secondary schools.

1937-47

(a) Schools

There was some increase in the number of high schools during the decennium 1937-47. While in 1937-38, the number of high schools was 3,416 (3018 for boys and 308 for girls), the total number increased to 5,298 (4,573 for boys and 725 for girls) in 1946-47 indicating a percentage increase of 55.09. The bulk of increase was however, in respect of boys' schools (1555) against for girls (417).

(b) Enrolment

There was a sizeable increase in enrolment at the high school level during the period under review. The number of students increased from 11,17,901 to 21,94,030 indicating a percentage increase of 86.09 per cent. This was mainly due to the increase in the number of boys from 10,09,331 to 19,61,894 (94.37 per cent). The increase in the number of girls was also quite sizeable; from 1,08,660 to 2,32,136 indicating a percentage increase of 113.64 per cent.

Expenditure

There was marked increase in expenditure on high school education during the period 1937-47. From Rs. 5,62,70,679 in 1937-38, the expenditure more than doubled to Rs. 12,22,59,471 in 1946-47 indicating an increase of 110 per cent. There was a marked difference in expenditure on boys' and girls' education. In 1937-38, the expenditure on girls' education was about 21 per cent of expenditure on boys' education. By 1947, the percentage of expenditure on girls' education decreased to 18.

Table 9 indicates the state-wise expenditure on boys and girls during the period under review.

Table 9: Expenditure on High Schools

	Province	*1937-38*		*1946-47*	
		Boys	*Girls*	*Boys*	*Girls*
1.	Assam	1165489	189984	2556368	458904
2.	Bengal	12278434	2152418	26281950*	3610790*
3.	Bihar	2517964	241481	5031323	515900
4.	Bombay	6033266	1581427	16462112	3602835
5.	C.P. and Berar	1080467	118809	1851350	307189
6.	Madras	8105519	1437780	18879068	3718208
7.	North-West F.P.	756719	54876	1362996	172031
8.	Orissa	558839	63306	1111564	119227
9.	Punjab	6405461	914785	14861750*	2521235*
10.	Sind	1085321	253513	2405216	726383
11.	United Provinces	6190746	1021957	9194806	2199179
12.	Ajmer-Merwara	307751	55173	790729	166042
13.	Baluchistan	177929	30034	272423	78420
14.	Bangalore	227494	142825	357854	283980
15.	Coorg	63383	15031	189277	25707
16.	Delhi	538360	136667	1108683	512801
19.	**GRAND TOTAL**	**56270679**		**122259471**	

* *Estimated figures.*

Average Annual Cost

The following table indicates the average annual cost for boys and girls in schools maintained by Government and private managements.

Table 10: Average Annual Cost per Pupil (Rupees)

Schools Managed by	*1937-38*		*1941-42*		*1946-47*	
	Boys	*Girls*	*Boys*	*Girls*	*Boys*	*Girls*
1. Government	13.7	15.2	12.8	15.6	24.5	25.7
2. Dist. Board and Municipal	9.9	13.6	9.1	13.5	14.9	23.3
3. Private	4.9	5.9	5.2	16.5	11.2	12.4
4. All Schools	7.6	9.4	7.6	10.3	13.5	18.7

Source: Progress of Education in India, 1937-47, p. 67.

To Sum-up

1. There was significant expansion in enrolment as well as number of secondary schools during the first half of the twentieth century. During the quinquennium ending 1912, there were 3,560 secondary schools out of which government schools accounted for only 271, i.e., 7.6 per cent of the total. The private bodies administered 2,770 schools i.e. about 78 per cent of the total. This number almost doubled itself to 5,298 (4573 for boys and only 725 for girls) in 1947.

2. There was marked increase in enrolment at the secondary stage. From 6,53,604 in 1912, the enrolment increased more than three fold i.e. 21,94,030 in 1947.
3. Similar increase occurred in expenditure on secondary education. From Rs.117 lakh in 1907, the expenditure increased to Rs.166(1/3) lakh by 1912. It further increased to Rs. 562.71 lakh in 1937-38 and further to Rs.12,22.59 lakh by 1947. Thus while the enrolment increased more than threefold, the expenditure on secondary schools went up to 7.5 times of the figure in 1912.
4. There was large disparity in the enrolment among boys and girls. In spite of a considerable increase in the enrolment of girls, i.e., from 1,08,660 to 2,32,136 during the period 1937-47, the percentage of girls in secondary schools in 1937 was 9.2 of the total enrolment. It increased to 10.2 per cent by 1947. It is also noteworthy that the average annual cost per student was higher in the case of girls schools than that of the boys. (Table 10)
5. In the context of the policy of the government to withdraw from direct involvement in establishing secondary schools and institutions of higher education, there was reduction in the proportional contribution from the government over the years. While in 1921-22, the government provided about 33 per cent of the expenditure on the establishment and maintenance of secondary schools, in 1921-22, the percentage declined to about 32 in 1936-37. By 1949-50, however, the Government's contribution (excluding Local Board's) had gone up to 37.9 per cent of the total expenditure. The student fees and other sources were the major contributors – 56.3 per cent of the total expenditure.

(C) Adult Education

Progress, Problems and Perspectives

It has been said: "Education does not end with schooling but is a life-long process. The adult today has a need for understanding of the rapidly changing world and the growing complexities of society. Even those who have had the most sophisticated education must continue to learn; the alternative is obsolescence".[23] The need for life-long education is as imperative today as it was during the Colonial rule or even earlier. It was, however, not given the requisite priority in the initial stages of the British Raj. In fact it took a very long time for the Government to recognize the need for giving their Indian subjects rudiments of a systematic education. As already stated, earlier attempts under the East India Company were sporadic and based on individual perceptions. They were, at the initial stages, aimed at the revival of the Indian learning. With that end in view, the first institution to be set up was the Calcutta Madrassa by Warren Hastings in 1781. This was followed by the establishment of the Sanskrit College at Banaras with the consent of Lord Cornwallis in 1792. Some other institutions founded by some philanthropists followed.

It was only in 1813 that the company set aside an amount of Rs. one lakh for the furtherance of education of the natives. The utilization of the amount available for education was, however, embroiled in a controversy between what have been euphemistically called the 'Orientalists' and the 'Anglicists'.

It took another 22 years to resolve the problem in 1835 on the basis of the forceful plea made by Lord Macaulay that the government should spend the earmarked amount for the promotion of Western system of education. In these circumstances, any attempt at promoting mass education was a distant dream.

There was, however, an attempt at bolstering female education. The work was taken up by missionary societies in the three Presidencies of Bengal, Madras and Bombay. The movement was supported by David Hare and Raja Ram Mohan Roy. In 1824, Lady Amherst agreed to be the patron of a society for female education in Calcutta and surrounding areas. A girls' school was established in Calcutta in 1849 by J.E. Drinkwater Bethune, Legal Member of the Legislative Council, who persuaded Lord Dalhousie to accept his views. This was a turning point in the history of female education.

The next significant step in the history of Indian education was marked by the Parliamentary enquiry into the condition of India. It was the first serious and sympathetic consideration by the British Parliament, among other things, of the state of Indian education. The recorded evidence formed the basis of the Despatch by Charles Wood, the president of the Board of Directors of the East India Company, which was the first step towards promoting education among the Indians. Upto that time, the company had regarded a direct involvement in promoting mass education an impossibility. They thought that 'the only means of educating the masses was by educating the literary class, which was comparatively small and letting education 'filter down' through it, the attempt generally, known as the (Downward) 'Filtration Theory'.[24]

The Wood's Despatch (1854) reversed the policy of the 'Downward Filtration'. It declared that education had to be the responsibility of the State. The Indian Education Commission (1882), which was appointed by the government of India to inquire into the working of the then prevailing system of public instruction and to the further extension of that system on a popular basis did not make any specific recommendation for encouraging post-school adult education except suggesting the encouragement of night schools wherever practicable. The Commission, however, recommended the encouragement of indigenous education by encouraging school masters of such schools to undergo training and to bring their relatives and probable successors under regular training. It was also suggested that such schools should be given free play and adequate financial assistance for development.

The Commission, however, made specific recommendations for developing primary education. According to the Commission, primary education should be regarded as the instruction of the masses through the vernaculars in such subjects as will best fit them for their participation in life and be not necessarily regarded as a portion of instruction leading to university. Further, "while every branch of education can jointly claim the fostering care of State, it is desirable, in the present circumstances of the country, to declare the elementary education of the masses, its provision, extension and improvement, to be that part of the educational system to which strenuous efforts of the state should now be directed in a still larger measure than heretofore".[25]

It would thus be seen that the Government of India did not take any responsibility for encouraging post-primary adult education. In fact, according to the thinking at that time, government efforts were to be directed towards expanding and nurturing the regular institutions education, particularly at the initial stages with the hope that in course of time, Indians would achieve a level of education, which would be practical, besides being an instrument for the all round development of the individuals' personality.

Keeping this policy framework in view, it was not surprising that no effort was made to provide post-school education for those who were unable to take advantage of institutional training at the appropriate age level and were a part of the swelling ranks of the illiterates. In fact, the government was unaware of the dismal literacy level of Indian population. The only information available through the much belated census of 1911 was that 3.22 per cent of the population was under instruction. Further, the number of male pupils rose from 4.47 per cent of the male population to 5.31 per cent. One can surmise the low level of general literacy of those times.[26]

The Quinquennial Review of Education for 1922-27 gave a very dim view of the out-reach of primary and adult education. It said that, there was no outstanding development in the field of primary education during the decade. According to the progress report there was undoubtedly satisfactory increase in the number of pupils reading in primary schools but the figures for the number of pupils of school going age still to be provided for is distressingly large and the problem of mass education is complicated by the necessity of providing schools for thousands of isolated villages which cannot, knowing the low density of the population, be satisfactorily served by central or common schools. The total approximate number of boys of school going age in British India is 1,77,90,000 (14 per cent of the total male population) while the total number of male scholars in educational institutions of all kinds in 1926-27 was approximately 87,78,000; the Percentage of male scholars to the total number of males of school going age thus being only 49.4. Low as the Percentage is in relation to the total number of scholars still to be provided for, it represents a great improvement, when compared with the figures for the previous Quinquennial. In 1922, the Percentage was 36.0 and in 1917, 34.6 ...."[27]

The Report also stated that: "compulsory education has introduced a sufficiently large number of urban and rural areas to have considerable effect on the total attendance at schools and though the number of areas in which compulsion has been introduced is still very small and though strict compulsion cannot yet be enforced, in most of these areas, the experiments which have been undertaken have provided valuable experiences which will undoubtedly enable larger measure of compulsion to be introduced in future years. In nearly all provinces, a change has taken place in the general outlook on the position and functions of the primary school and notable endeavours have been made during the quinquennium to make the village schools house a guiding force in the life of the village and its surrounding and to adapt the curricula in training schools and in primary schools to the special needs of the rural community...."[28]

Enrolment in Educational Institutions

It would be seen that till the end of the twenties of the last century, no specific efforts were made to provide for out of school education to those who had not been fortunate enough to partake of the facilities provided by regular educational institutions. According to the census of 1921, it was found that the total population of India was 27,17,80,151 composed of 14,00,75,258 (51.54) males and 13,17,04,893 (48.46) females. Table 11 below gives the Percentage of total population, gender-wise, receiving instruction in all kinds of institutions for five years 1917, 1922, 1927, 1932 and.1937.

Table 11: Percentage of total population receiving instruction in all institutions by sexes (in %)

Sex	*Year*				
	1917	*1922*	*1927*	*1932*	*1937*
Males	5.31	5.49	7.33	7.33	7.86
Females	1.03	1.18	1.53	1.89	2.38
Total	3.22	3.39	4.51	4.70	5.20

Source: Progress of Education in India for different years.

It would be seen that while females constituted about 48 per cent of the total population, in 1921 there was very large disparity in their utilization of educational facilities. Although the ratio was one female against 5 males during 1917, 1922 and 1927; it deceased to 1:3.8 in 1932 and 1:3.3 in 1937. The disparity, however, still remained sizeable.

Province-wise Disparities

There were large disparities among the provinces in regard to the Percentage of total population receiving instruction in educational institutions. Table 12 below indicates the position:

Table 12: Percentage of total population receiving instructions in all types of institutions (recognised and unrecognised) by Provinces

Sl. No.	*Name of the Provinces*	*Year* 1917	1922	1927	1932	1937
1.	Madras	4.01	4.3	5.96	6.25	7.20
2.	Bombay	3.96	5.0	5.95	5.11	7.46
3.	Bengal	4.22	4.0	5.02	5.55	6.39
4.	United Provinces	1.91	2.3	2.97	3.13	3.40
5.	Punjab	2.43	3.0	5.71	5.16	5.51
6.	Bihar and Orissa	2.45	2.40	3.26	2.90	3.56
7.	Central Provinces and Berar	2.32	2.40	2.86	2.96	3.22
8.	Assam	3.48	2.80	3.70	4.32	5.30
9.	North West Frontier Provinces	2.11	2.30	3.00	3.60	4.10

Source: Progress of Education in India, for different quinquennia.

While there was an increase in the percentages in respect of almost all the provinces, four provinces (Bombay 7.46 per cent), Madras (7.20 per cent), Bengal (6.39 per cent), Punjab (5.51 per cent) had the largest percentages of their population in educational institutions. Central Provinces had the dubious distinction of being the lowest utilizer of educational facilities in terms of the percentages of their overall population being in educational institutions.

By 1937-38, adult education seems to have got its rightful place in the educational system. A Committee appointed by the Central Advisory Board of Education had emphasized that literacy was not the sole criterion and end of adult education. It was intended to lead to further education. By this time, education through correspondence was also recognised as an important means of providing education, which would be available to the seekers of knowledge transcending the time and space barriers. Even as it is, the number of institutions for adults continued to increase. Table 13 denotes the sharp rise in the number and enrolment of adult schools.

Table 13: No. of Adult Schools and their Enrolments

Adult Education	*1937-38*		*1946-47*	
	Schools	*Enrolment*	*Schools*	*Enrolment*
For Men	1,532	44,623	5,722	171445
For Women	15	983	371	7719
Total	1,547	45,606	6,093	1,79,164

There was almost four times increase in the number of adult schools and a little less than four times increase in the overall enrolment. The gender-wise disparity in the number and enrolment, however, was too obvious to be brushed aside.

Province-wise Position

The province-wise position of adult education is indicated in Table 14 as follows:

Table 14: Progress of Adult Education (1937-38)

Province Schools	*No. of Adult Schools*		*Enrolment in (in Rs.)*		*Expenditure on School (in Rs.)*	
	Men	*Women*	*Men*	*Women*	*Men*	*Women*
Assam	3	—	146	—	813	—
Bengal	703	—	19,659	—	31,862	—
Bihar	—	13	—	—	—	—
Bombay	204	2	7,513	608	1,28,537	15,263
C.P. and Berar	60	—	2,036	375	5,859	4,793
Madras	4	—	258	—	2,504	—
Orissa	2	—	127	—	459	—
Punjab	153	—	3,892	—	11,345	—
Sindh	24	—	605	—	6,035	—
United Province	350	—	9,885	—	36,322	—
Ajmer Merwara	12	—	233	—	1,583	—
Delhi	17	—	269	—	3,054	—
Total	**1,532**	**15**	**44,723**	**983**	**2,28,373**	**20,056**

Source: Progress of Education in India, 1937-47, p. 147.

Table 15: Progress of Adult Education (1946-47)

Province	*No. of Adult Schools*		*Enrolment in Schools*		*Expenditure on School (in Rs.)*	
	Men	*Women*	*Men*	*Women*	*Men*	*Women*
Assam	580	45	13,390	903	37,428	2,207
Bengal*	447	—	23,433	—	1,08,818	—
Bihar	N.A.	N.A.	N.A.	N.A.	N.A.	N.A.
Bombay	2,740	281	71,006	5,601	2,69,047	54,937
C.P. and Berar	17	1	721	200	6,545	6,502
Madras	9	—	400	0	4,591	0
Punjab*	96	3	3,002	45	12,2292	240
Sindh	—	—	—	0	—	0
United Province	1,825	41	59,347	970	5,74,247	9,707
Ajmer Merwara	1	—	20	—	102	—
Baluchistan	—	—	—	—	—	—
Bangalore	—	—	—	—	—	—
Coorg	—	—	—	—	—	—
Delhi	7	—	126	—	437	—
Total	**5,722**	**371**	**1,71,445**	**7,719**	**10,06,444**	**73,593**

Source: Progress of Education in India, 1937-47, p. 147.

Note: * Estimated figures.

It would appear that during the decennium 1937 and 1947, there was almost four-fold increase in the number of adult schools; the schools for women, however, increased by 25 times. Similarly, the overall enrolment also increased almost four times and the women's enrolment increased eight times. There was sizeable increase in the expenditure on adult education, which increased almost four times.

Having said this, it is difficult to vouchsafe for the adequacy of schools, their enrolment and the expenditure incurred thereon. In a country with crores of illiterates, the provision of facilities for the education of 1.80 lakh is not significant by any standard. Similarly, to spend about Rs. 5.7 per year on the education of each adult in 1937-38 rising marginally to about Rs. 6 per adult 10 years later, notwithstanding the escalating inflation, is also not a very satisfying phenomenon. Obviously, the process of educating adults as also the quantum of expenditure thereon needed to be stepped up considerably to meet the burgeoning requirements of this important sector of education.

SECTION-2

Higher Education

1857 is remembered, among other things, for two important developments: It was the year when the first war of India's independence was fought – "the first anti-colonial mass movement against the aggression of imperialist policies demonstrated in course of the first half of the 19th Century."[29] The bloody confrontation impelled the British Government to take control of the administration of the country. The rule of the 'Honourable' East India Company came to an abrupt and dishonourable end.

1857 also witnessed the setting up of three universities – one each in the Presidency towns of Calcutta, Bombay and Madras. Till that year, there were no universities in this large country except for a few colleges, giving instruction mostly in Sanskrit and Arabic languages.

The task of preparing scheme for establishment of the university was started long before the political turmoil had engulfed the country. The Committee, which was appointed on 26th January, 1855, submitted its report in August, 1855. It made detailed recommendations about the system of examination for entrance and award of degrees and honours in the several branches of Arts, Medicine, Law and Civil Engineering. The Committee also suggested that the proceedings of the senates of several universities should be subject to the control of a central authority so that general uniformity was ensured and that, at each Presidency town, the same degree of requirement, in every branch of knowledge, should entitle its professor to the same kind of academic distinction and honour.

In founding the universities at Calcutta, Bombay and Madras, the Government of India adopted the model of the University of London, which was at that time basically an examining body. In due course, however, the London University ceased to be a merely examining institution and became a teaching university. In India also, it was realised that "...a system which provides merely for examining students in those subjects in which their aptitude directs them, and does not at the same time compel them to study those subjects systematically under first rate instruction, tends inevitably to accentuate certain characteristic defects of the Indian intellect – the development of the memory out of all proportions to the other faculties of the mind, the incapacity to observe and appreciate facts and the taste for metaphysical and technical distinctions..."[30]

Reforms in University Education

In view of these considerations, the Government of India sought to introduce reforms in the constitution and management of universities. Notable among these were:

1. The Senate of the universities, which have outgrown in size should be reconstituted to facilitate their functioning;
2. The position and powers of the syndicates should be defined and regulated. This would include reduction in the number of ex-officio fellows;
3. Power will be conferred on universities to make suitable provision for university teaching;
4. Colleges will be liable to systematic inspection. A college applying for affiliation will be required to satisfy the university about the adequacy of teaching staff, courses of instruction and buildings and equipment. It will also have to provide evidence that it has adequate financial resources.
5. Colleges already affiliated will be regularly inspected and will have to show that they comply with the conditions on which the privilege of affiliation is granted.

In spite of the realisation that teaching should be an integral part of the universities, the Government of India took 30 years to establish the first teaching university. (Allahabad, 1887).

Impetus to Technical Education

Another development that took place and is worth mentioning in the closing years of the nineteenth century is the impetus given to technical education.

Emphasis was laid on the expansion of industries and especially in those areas in which the native capital may be invested. Technical education directed towards the preparation of manpower for this purpose was emphasised. It was felt that besides providing for high grade technical education institutions, training in technical schools should also be encouraged. To achieve this, assistance in the form of scholarships to selected students was provided. Provision was also made for encouraging commercial and agricultural education.

Development of Higher Education

There was some expansion of higher education during the Nineteenth Century. The number of universities increased from three in 1857 to five by the end of the century. While the number of Arts Colleges increased from 100 in 1891-92 to

141 by 1901-02; professional colleges increased from 32 to 46 during the same period.

There was marginal increase in the number of oriental colleges – from 4 to 5. The number of students also increased from 16,110 in 1891-92 to 23,291 in 1901-02. This included 503 students in oriental colleges and 5338 in technical colleges. There was, however, considerable wastage at various stages of education. For example, the percentage of students passing the matriculation examination was 36.8. The same was the case with the examinations at the higher education stage. The number of candidates coming out successfully from various examinations in Bombay University was: MA – 12 succeeded out of 33 candidates who appeared in the examination (36 per cent). In BA, 238 were successful out of 384 (61.98 per cent).

Higher Education in the Twentieth Century

Policy Paradigms

At the beginning of the twentieth century, Lord Curzon took over as Governor General of India. As already stated, in an Educational Conference convened by him at Simla, he spoke about the need for evolving a realistic policy relating to the development of education, including higher education. In a candid admission, he said that "there was an element of misdirection, for which he would not hold Government of India free from blame". He admitted that "education of Indian people was as much a duty of the Central Government as the policing of our cities or the taxation of our people. Indeed more so, for whereas these duties can be safely delegated to subordinate hands, the Government can never abrogate its personal responsibility for the living welfare of the multitudes that have been committed to its care.[31]

About higher education, Curzon was equally forceful. He referred to the fundamental contrast, both of character and conception, between Indian and British university systems. According to him, "Oxford and Cambridge are incorporated institutions which constitute and are embodied in the corporate while the Indian university has no corporate existence."[32]

He also suggested that "higher education ought not be run either by politicians or by amateurs. It is a sincere service of human life and conduct in which we must give a fair hearing and a reasonable chance to professor."[33]

Indian Universities Commission (1902)

In 1902, the Government of India constituted the Indian Universities Commission to 'inquire into the conditions and prospects of the universities established in British India; to consider and report upon any proposal which have been, or may be made for improving their constitution and working and recommend such measures as may tend to elevate the standard of university teaching and advancement of learning.'

The Commission recommended the reorganisation of university administration; a much more and systematic administration of colleges by the universities and the imposition of more exacting conditions of affiliation; the abolition of the second grade colleges; much closer attention to the conditions under which students live and work, the assumption of teaching functions by the universities within defined limits; the fixing of fees in such a manner that it does not tempt a poor student of low ability to join colleges and substantial change in the curricula and in the methods of examination.

The Commission also made a general statement about the quality of college education in India. It stated, "Having visited considerable number of these institutions (colleges), we are not disposed to confirm the sweeping criticism, which has sometimes been passed upon our university system. Many of the colleges command the services of able and devoted teachers and we do not consider the students as a class to be wanting either in natural talent or in industry. In comparing our graduates with those of other universities, it must be remembered that Indian student often enters his college course at an age when boys of other countries are still at school. We must also remember that Indian universities are of comparatively recent foundation and that resources of our universities and colleges are very small when compared with vast endowments of England and America and vast sums placed by the governments of other countries at the disposal of their universities... At the same time we must admit that the acquirements of Indian graduates are in many cases inadequate and superficial... After the allowance is made, it is most unsatisfactory to be told that Indian B.A. not infrequently lacks the general training which he requires to fit him for the business of life or for a further course of study."[34]

A perusal of the above statement would indicate that the quality of higher education at the close of the nineteenth century represented a phenomenon of lights and shades. While the Commission eulogised the ability and devotion of the teachers as also the natural talent and industriousness of students, it lamented the immaturity of Indian students to acquire knowledge and skills as compared to more mature students in universities in advanced countries.

It may be stated that the proposal for enhancing the age for entry to universities was also made by, among others, the Calcutta University Commission (1917-19). For its actual implementation, however, India had to wait for about 64 years after the Indian Universities Commission (1902) addressed this issue. This was effected on the basis of the recommendations made by the Education Commission (1964-66) to that effect. The Commission had referred to the proposal of the University Education Commission (1948-49) that students should be admitted to the university after the completion of twelve years of study and that the first degree course should be of three year duration.[35]

The Indian Universities Commission (1902) also talked about the scarcity of resources for higher education as being a cause for low standards of Indian institutions of higher education. The comment of the Commission is relevant even now. The successive Indian governments, though swearing by the effectiveness of education in accelerating the pace of socio-economic development and cultural regeneration, have failed to provide adequate resources for education as a whole as also for higher education. For example, an analysis of the allocations made for educational development in the successive five year plans reveals that in spite of the recommendation made by the Education Commission (1964-66) that 6 per cent of the Gross National Product (GNP) be earmarked for education, it has not been possible, even after the lapse of half a century, to provide more than about 4 per cent of the GNP for education. Further, expenditure on higher education as a percentage of expenditure on all sectors had decreased from 2.70 in 1990-91 to 2.20 in 2004-05. It has also been reckoned that the overall expenditure on higher education, as percentage of GNP, which was 0.77 in 1990-91 decreased to 0.66 in 2004-05. Same position emerges when the share of higher education in the total development expenditure on education is considered.[36]

Indian Reaction

The recommendations made by the Indian Universities Commission fell far short of the expectations of the Indians. In a forceful criticism, organisations and individuals brought out the fallacies and short-sightedness of the Commission's recommendations. It was pointed out that the implementation of the Commission's recommendations will lead the social, intellectual and moral conditions in India to miserable depths. Another organisation was of the opinion that the Commission's recommendations, taken as a while, will deal a blow to the progress of education in India.

We give below excerpts from the views expressed by some of the organisations/ individuals about the Commission's recommendations:

(a) The Mahajan Sabha of the Trichinopalli (Madras Province) in a representation dated 16th November 1902, endorsing the view of the Commission that "efficiency should not be sacrificed to cheapness" hoped "that the rules to be finalised by the government and the university in regard to affiliation and disaffiliation of the first grade colleges will not be so stringent and exacting as to make the existence and development of such colleges impossible and the scales of fees will not be so heavy as to shut out the poor and deserving students from the benefits of higher education."[37]

(b) S. Kailash Iyer in an article which appeared in *Madras Standard* of 25th October, 1902 was of the opinion that the Commission's recommendations about the constitution of the senate, the abolition of second grade colleges and raising of fees have thrown into shade 'the most vital question: the curricula of studies...' Further, the question "what happens to India if the recommendations of the Universities Commission were adopted has been more than once asked in your columns and those of your contemporaries. It has been answered again and again with sufficient clearness; and the miserable depth to which the social, intellectual and social conditions will go down has been pointed out with sufficient stress and emphasis..."[38]

(c) The Mohamadan Associations at Chitoor in North District in a Resolution passed in December, 1902 requested the Viceroy to withhold the sanction of the Commission's report because, according to them, the carrying out of the Commission's recommendations and suggestions will result in immense disabilities for the Mohamadans. The Resolution, inter-alia, said: "Resolved that the meeting is of the opinion that the recommendations and suggestions of the Universities Commission, taken as a whole, are such as to deal a dead blow to the progress of education in general and of the Mohamadan's community in particular and that a respectful protest be sent to the Viceroy that effect be not given to the same."[39]

(d) In another Resolution[40] passed at a public meeting at Nrottampur District Backergange, held on 30th September, 1902, respectfully but strongly disapproved of the recommendation about abolishing the second grade colleges. The meeting also disapproved of the recommendation regarding fixing the minimum rate of fees. The meeting also rejected recommendations on:

(i) separate buildings and management and establishing central law colleges;
(ii) abolishing existing law classes;
(iii) raising the standard of matriculation examination and multiplicity of examinations;
(iv) the constitution of senates and syndicates; and
(v) enforcing discipline.

(e) The inhabitants of Banaras in a public meeting held in December, 1902 termed as unsound the "principle avowedly adopted by the Universities Commission viz. that a small number of young men should receive a sound liberal education rather than a large number should be passed through an inadequate course of instruction leading to a depreciated degree." They were of the view that every person should be given the utmost facility for reaching the highest stage in education that his circumstances allow.

The Memorialists also stated that the recommendations of the Commission are likely to hamper all students generally and the poor students in particular; because of:

(i) The definition of the local limits of the universities;
(ii) Higher fees to be levied and that aided and unaided institutions should be given full liberty to determine the fees;
(iii) The rules of affiliation and disaffiliation to be decided by one single person, howsoever high official he may be;
(iv) The proposal to close down second grade colleges;
(v) The recognition of unaided schools to rest with the Education Department, rather than the university;
(vi) Avoiding rigidity and disallowing students of one province from studying in another.

(f) In a Resolution, the *Malayala Evvajana Sabha*, Madras, a reference was made to "a great heart burning and feeling of sympathy, both in the hearts of Indians and Anglo-Indians as well," that the Report of the Commission has created. The Resolution was bold enough to say that the Report was full of fallacious reasons and arguments and aims to strike a very heavy disastrous blow at the very root of university education in India, the privilege of which we, the poor Indians enjoy. It dubbed as uncalled for and unwarranted the recommendations of the Commission that the tuition fees "must not be fixed so low as to tempt a poor of ordinary ability to follow the university courses, which is not his real interest to follow."[41]

It may be stated that the views expressed by the Indian educationists and organisations, 'submitted with utmost humility and profound respect to the Viceroy' were cold-shouldered by the British bureaucracy. They were simply acknowledged with thanks; the usual way of disposing off the unsolicited and unwanted cases. There is no record of any action taken about the various recommendations/ suggestions made by the memorialists.

Indian Universities Act (1904)

In utter disregard of the protests by Indians, the Indian Universities Act was passed in 1904. The Act, stipulated, among other things, that universities should make provision for the promotion of study and research; to appoint adequately qualified faculty; to set up university libraries and undertake teaching functions. The Government control over universities was increased manifold in that the Government could veto the regulations framed by the senates. The Act also extended university control over colleges. The universities were required to maintain proper control over colleges. The government also assumed the power to determine the territorial limits of the university as also to decide about the affiliation of the colleges. The colleges were required to satisfy the university and the government that the teaching staff was adequate; was under the management of a regularly constituted governing body and that the buildings and equipment as also their financial resources were adequate. In sum, the Government assumed sweeping powers to control universities.

Overall Assessment

Higher education in India, according to the government, presented three general characteristics: It was secular, it was utilitarian (not practical) and it was conducted in English. Courses of study were framed with a view to facility and fairness of examination and lacking in those elements, which go to make up what does not tell in an answer paper – character, practical adaptability and reasoning power. The text books were also not always chosen with a consideration for the environment and the mental plane of either the teacher or the taught. There was an outcry that the courses are literary and that a practical bent is needed in high school and also in the shape of technological institutions... the desire for a broader basis of instruction is slowly crystallising; and probably few will gainsay it, especially when the existence of higher institutions finds its justification no longer only in the public servants, but also in the wider outlets of professional activity and culture..."[42]

In order to achieve the objectives laid down above, the Government of India decided that teaching faculties be developed at the seats of existing universities and corporate life encouraged in order to promote higher study and to create an atmosphere from which students will imbibe good social, moral and intellectual influences. The government also sanctioned grants for developing good libraries. Universities were also freed of giving recognition to schools, which would be performed by the local governments.

Institutions

In 1911-12, there were 187 colleges, which included 123 arts colleges, 17 colleges of oriental studies and 47 professional colleges out of which Law with 22 colleges topped the list. This was followed by 12 Teacher training colleges and the rest were: Medicine 4, Engineering 4, Agriculture and Veterinary Sciences 3.

The total number of students enrolled at the higher education stage was 36,284 out of which the predominant number was of students of Arts courses – 28,196. The number of students in oriental studies was merely 1452. 3036 students were studying Law; Medicine-1396 and Engineering-1187. Balance of 1017 was shared by Teaching, Agriculture and Veterinary Sciences.

Compared with the present enrolment of 136.42 lakhs, (2009-10) at the higher education stage, the number in 1912 looks quite microscopic. It has, however, to be remembered that the period under study was the beginning of the 20th century, when the educational system in India was in its infancy. It is also worth mentioning that the university system had become a multi-faculty enterprise and there were arrangements for the teaching of subjects as diverse as law, teacher education, agriculture and veterinary sciences, etc.

Government of India's Resolution (1913)

Education got a boost by the declaration of His Majesty, the King-Emperor. While replying to the address of the Calcutta University on the 6th of January, 1912, he stated:

"It is my wish that there may be spread over the land a network of schools and colleges, from which will go forth loyal and manly and useful citizens, able to hold their own in industries and agriculture and all the vocations of life... It is through education that my wish will be fulfilled and the cause of education in India will ever be very close to my heart."[43]

This spurred the Government of India to have a relook at the educational system. The government's views were expressed in the Resolution of 1913, in which it was admitted that the deficiencies in the educational system were largely because of want of funds. In order to remedy the situation, government grants to private institutions were doubled.

The Resolution made suggestions about developing, remoulding/ reforming institutions of professional education in order to make them potent instruments of imparting practical work oriented education. Technical institutions were, however, no longer to be run on commercial lines. Education in technical schools was to be supplemented by practical training in workshops, where the application of new processes were to be demonstrated.

About university education, the Resolution made the following recommendations:

1. At present, there are 5 universities with 186 colleges of various types affiliated to them. It is necessary to restrict area over which the affiliating universities will have control by securing in the first instance a separate university for each of the leading provinces. Simultaneously, teaching facilities will be developed at the seats of existing universities and corporate life encouraged.
2. The power of granting affiliation for examining school students will be passed on to the local governments.
3. Research was no longer a sort of intellectual luxury, or elegant accomplishment as was 'scholarship' in the past. "It is the nerve centre of modern education, an organic necessity for the training of those, where influence in gradually widening circles must permeate the whole system of higher education, if it is to rise to western standards."[44] In view of this, adequate provision for research facilities cannot be postponed.

1917-22

The period 1917-22 was marked by the Non-Cooperation Movement, which originated in 1920 pursuant to a Resolution passed by the Indian National Congress, which, according to the Government, "succeeded in crippling some schools beyond hope of recovery, in disorganising the work of others for six months or a year and in ruining the career of many prominent scholars."[45]

During the period, three important developments took place: the submission of the Calcutta University Commission's Report under the Chairmanship of Sir Michael Sadler (1917-19); the setting up of the Central Advisory Board of Education in 1921; and the transfer of Indian education to the charge of Indian Ministers under the Government of India Act. We have discussed the setting up of the Central Advisory Board of Education and the Bureau of Education in a separate chapter. We shall discuss briefly the situation arising out of the transfer of Education to Indian Ministries as also the recommendations made by the Calcutta University Commission.

Transfer of Education

Theoretically, all education was transferred to democratically elected Indian Ministries. No single Minister in any province was, however, made responsible for all types of education. European education was taken out of the purview of the Indian Ministers and placed under the charge of a Member of the Legislative Council; his tenure in office was not dependent on the support of the Legislature. Similarly, technical education was put under the charge of another Minister, university education was placed under the Governor of the province, who was the chancellor of the universities. This arrangement, however, met with severe criticism. It was felt that this type of split - organisation would never achieve the overall objectives of education, which necessitates a coordinated approach. Education was a unified whole and its planning, administration and maintenance needed well thought out policy parameters and not a divided and quite often conflicting administrative system. It may also be mentioned that the transfer of education took place at a time of acute financial stress and political turbulence and therefore many of the reforms that the Indian Ministers would have contemplated could not be carried out. In spite of all these handicaps, the transfer of some parts of education to Indian Ministers was a step in the right direction.

Calcutta University Commission (1917-19)

The Calcutta University Commission, although concerned with only one university, made a comprehensive review of the entire gamut of Indian education and made suggestions which were relevant to the entire university system available at that time. We describe below the main observations/ recommendations of the Commission:

Defects of the University System

The Commission identified the following problems facing university education:

(a) The number of students that the university has to cater to is too large to be efficiently dealt with by a single university.

(b) The undergraduate courses are almost entirely self-contained and, in many cases, widely scattered in institutions; generally meagrely staffed and equipped to do justice to their students; some of them wholly, and most of them mainly, are dependent upon the fees paid by students – a source of income wholly inadequate for the purpose.

(c) The courses of instruction are predominantly literary in character and too little varied to suit various needs.

(d) Majority of teachers are under paid and have no legal security of tenure and no freedom in their work.

(e) The relations between government and the university are of an unsatisfactory kind, involving much detailed government intervention, which cannot be satisfactorily exercised and which undermine the sense of responsibility of the university.

(f) Despite consistent efforts and large expenditure during recent years, the conditions under which many of the students live are such as must be deleterious to their health, morals and work. Further, there is lack of that corporate spirit, which constitutes one of the most effective factors in university life.

(g) Owing to the practice, which has been followed ever since the foundation of Indian universities, of treating university qualifications as the sole formal credentials for public employment – a practice which has been insensibly

> extended to even minor clerkships – too many students think of their university courses not as a thing worth pursuing for itself, or as a training for life, but simply as a means of obtaining entry to careers for which, in many cases, no university training ought to be required.[46]

It would be pertinent to mention that the shortcomings listed out by the Commission pertained to the university system as a whole and not only to the Calcutta University. Some of the deficiencies have transcended the time and space barriers and exist even in the present university education system.

Improvements Suggested

Based on these observations, the Commission made detailed suggestions for improving the system. The suggestions cover the entire spectrum of education and, therefore, need to be mentioned in detail.

1. *The Relation between Government and the University*

The government provides guidance and control to university system because:

(a) the provincial universities of India were all established by government action; and they were established partly in order that they might exercise, on behalf of the government, certain functions of regulation and control over colleges and schools within their allotted areas;

(b) the Government supplies, other than the income from fees of students, bulk of funds required for the conduct of university work, for institution and examination;

(c) the character and requirements of the teaching institutions which prepare students for university examinations are in the main determined by the government, not only because the government approves the conditions of affiliation of colleges, and is the final authority for the decision of all applications for affiliation, but still more because government defines the staff and equipment and actually provides the teachers, retaining them under its most direct orders for several of the most important colleges; professional and general.

(d) the government provides subsidies for secondary education and through its provincial departments of public instruction, supplies the only existing mechanism of inspection, both for secondary and for primary education; and

(e) a very powerful factor in the influence exercised by the Government over university system arises from the fact that a large proportion of the students, who undertake courses, do so in the hope of obtaining admission to government service, for which even in humbler branches, a university degree or success in a lower university examination is for Indian candidates a required qualification.[47]

It is thus, in theory, an extremely close control which is exercised by government, directly and indirectly, over the working of the university system.

2. *Affiliating Universities*

Much criticism has been made against affiliating universities: their divorce from teaching, their reliance on formal and external examinations, the vast area of the jurisdiction, their lack of control on teaching in affiliated colleges, the almost inevitable lowering of standards of teaching and examination, etc.

According to the Commission, all these factors resulted into the universities becoming "over-burdened, indeed broken by the weight of rapidly increasing number of students, many of them unsuited for university work and also by a rapid increase in the number of colleges, many of which did not command the financial support for maintaining high standards."[48] The Commission strongly recommended the setting up of unitary teaching universities rather than merely affiliating institutions.

It may be recalled that the problem of the over burdened affiliating universities was recognised as early as 1913 when the Government of India, in a Resolution, pointed out the dangers inherent in the unrestricted expansion of affiliating universities and suggested that it was necessary to limit their area and also to create new teaching and residential universities. It is interesting to note that the first departure in this direction was made in the case of Banaras Hindu University, a University which grew out of the Central Hindu College at Banaras.[49]

The Commission also recommended that the control of the government should be greatly reduced and that the general public should have considerable influence on the broad policy of the university. Academic matters should be placed in the hands of bodies truly representative of the teachers.

Control over Affiliated Colleges

Efforts were made to tighten the control of universities over affiliated colleges by strengthening the conditions of affiliation and by prescribing the right of inspection.

Reorganisation of Higher Secondary Education

The Commission recommended that "the work now done in the intermediate classes of the university should be transferred to institutions of a new type, to be known as intermediate colleges to be organised and conducted according to the methods appropriate for school work, to be distributed over every part of Bengal and to be placed under the same general direction as the higher English schools. This change is necessary not only for providing more adequate preparation for university work for those of the students in intermediate classes, who will proceed to degree courses; it is still more necessary to meet the needs of those, who will go no further than the intermediate stage and who require more carefully differentiated courses of study than are now offered to them. It is necessary as the best practical means of relieving the congestion caused by the crowding of young and immature students to mitigate the evils and changes, which result from this..."[50]

To Sum-Up

The Commission recommended:

(i) The stage of admission to the university should be (approximately) that of the present intermediate stage instead of the present matriculation level.

(ii) The responsibility of providing education at the intermediate stage should be transferred from the universities to new institutions known as intermediate colleges, some of which should be attached to selected high schools, while others should be organised as distinct institutions.

(iii) There should be two secondary school examinations: the first approximately corresponding to the matriculation to be taken at the end of the high school stage at the normal age of 16, or in special cases at the age of 15, and to be known as high school examination; and the second approximately corresponding to the present intermediate, but much more varied in its range, to be taken at the end of the intermediate college course, at the normal age of 18, and to be known as Intermediate college examination. Success in the examination should constitute the normal test of admission to university courses.

(iv) Establishment of a Board of Secondary Education: The division and clash of responsibilities between the Government and its Department of Public Instruction on the one hand, and the university on the other, which has introduced so much confusion should be brought to an end by government establishing a Board of Secondary and Intermediate education, upon which the universities, industrial, commercial, professional and agricultural organisations as also the Hindu and Mussalman committees should all be effectively represented. This Board must exercise the functions of inspection, aid and recognition, in regard to the English high schools, which are at present divided between the Department and the university and it would exercise these functions not only in regard to high schools, but in regard to the proposed new intermediate colleges. It would be the duty of the Board to administer (subject to government audit and approval), the funds which government found it possible to devote to these ends, and to advise government as to the needs of these branches of education.

The Board should conduct both the examinations at the end of high school course and at the end of the intermediate course...[51]

(v) While the fees might be kept very low for students, who had done well in admission examination – for example, obtained a first class or mark of distinction either in the high school examination or at the intermediate stage; a higher fee might be charged from those who had not done so well in the admission examination. It argued that this will reduce the number of those weaker students, who constitute the greatest difficulty of the teacher and who would be, in most cases, better advised to pursue another kind of career...[52]

We have given in details the observations/suggestions of the Calcutta University Commission because they are comprehensive in nature and quite a few of them are relevant even at the present times. For example, the Commission identified deficiencies like the predominantly literary character of the university courses; the unnecessary intervention by the government in university affairs; treating university qualifications as passport to government jobs; the predominance of affiliating universities, which have no control over teaching in colleges etc.

Among the suggestions for improving university system, mention may be made of tightening of universities control over affiliated colleges; drastically reducing the control of the government over universities and the association of the general public with policy formulation of the universities.

The Commission made a controversial recommendation about student fees. It suggested that differential fees should be levied based on the level of achievement of students – higher fees for those who were not upto the mark. It may be recalled that the Universities' Commission (1902) had made an almost similar recommendation that the tuition fees must not be fixed so low as to tempt a poor student of 'ordinary' ability to join university courses. The Indian organisations were of the opinion that this recommendation was uncalled for and unwarranted. Knowing that the examination system lacks objectivity and does not grade students accurately, the recommendation about levying fees on a differential basis does not appear to be sound.

It may be mentioned that in the post-independence period a suggestion of levying of differential fees has been mooted based on the basis of economic criterion; those, who are economically well off, to pay higher fees and the weaker sections to pay lower fees or even be exempted from payment of fees. The proposal is still at a discussion stage.

Although not concerned with lower levels of education, the Commission made two important recommendations about secondary education. One was that the age of admission to university should be after the intermediate stage corresponding to the present higher secondary stage and that the present intermediate stage should be transferred to the school. Further, a Board of Secondary Education should be set up to take care of the high school and intermediate stages. Further, the students who were not suitable for higher studies may be directed towards vocational courses.

It would appear that all these recommendations were a pre-cursor to the reorganisation of secondary and university education envisaged by the three Commissions appointed by the government of free India: the University Education Commission (1948-49); the Secondary Education Commission (1952-53) and the Education Commission (1964-66).

1922-27

The Hartog Committee, which was constituted to review the means and manner of educational progress covered by the political reforms inaugurated in 1921, stated about university education:

"...many of the universities and colleges showed marked improvement in their methods of teaching and in the amount of original work, which they have produced and, in some of them, there is undoubtedly better training for corporate life than formerly. But the theory that a university exists mainly, if not solely, to pass students through examinations still finds too large acceptance in India and we wish that there were more signs that the universities regarded the training of broad minded, talented and self reliant citizens as one of their primary functions. They have been hampered in their work by being overcrowded with students, who are not fitted by capacity for university education and of whom many would be far more likely to succeed in other careers."[53]

About unitary teaching universities, the Committee felt that a unitary university, with swollen numbers, faces greater complications than of even the larger colleges of India. Unitary universities have rarely risen through the annihilation of colleges, but they have either originated as such or have developed from a single college, which formed part of another university and remained so until it gathered sufficient strength and support to stand alone. In such cases, collegiate traditions, far from having been stifled, have ripened...[54]

It is open to question, however, whether "in other places, the benefits gained by improved organisation, have not been outweighed by the loss of college traditions which these unitary universities have eclipsed."[55]

To solve this vexed problem, it would be better to set up a federal type of university in which the university and its colleges (particularly those in close proximity) would be bound together in a close cooperative union.

1932-37

There was considerable expansion in the number of university level institutions and student enrolment. The number of universities increased to 18 with a student enrolment of 1,28,623, which was more than double than the enrolment of 61,225 in 1917. The number of arts colleges was 272 against 243 in 1931-32. Their enrolment increased from 72,314 to 86,407 during the same period.

A notable development during this period was a Conference of Indian Universities, convened in March, 1934. The Conference suggested a radical readjustment of the present system in schools in such a way that a large number of pupils are directed at completion of the secondary courses either to occupations or to separate vocational institutions. The same view was expressed by the Punjab University Committee, which suggested complete overhauling of the school system, which was considered important for improving university education. The government of United Province, in a resolution emphasised the reorganisation of secondary education and said that "the value of university education is impaired by the presence in universities of a large number of students, who are unfit for higher literary or scientific education; that these students cannot hope to obtain employment which would justify the expense of their education and the only feasible remedy is to divert them to practical pursuits in the pre-university stage."[56]

The provincial governments appointed committees to consider the incidence and causation of unemployment among educated persons. There was general agreement that the outstanding need was to view the entire system of education in its present state, admittedly top heavy in the perspective of other measures, particularly the need for a determined attack on the problems of universal elementary education. This would have to be done on the basis of resources available and the local conditions, which would need to be translated into implementable programmes of action.

1937-47

There was some expansion in university education. By the time, India attained freedom, there were 21 universities, out of which only 3 were affiliating, 10 were affiliating and teaching and the other 8 teaching institutions. The number of arts and science colleges increased from 272 in 1937-38 to 420 in 1946-47. The number of colleges catering exclusively to females was 32 in 1937-38 and 50 in 1946-47.

The enrolment in the universities increased from 1,65,422 (inclusive of 14,435 women) in 1941-42 to 2,41,369 (including 24,466 women) in 1946-47. The largest enrolment (41,005) was recorded by the Calcutta University to be followed by the Bombay University (36,565) and Punjab (31,933) in 1946-47. The largest enrolment of women was however recorded by the Bombay University followed by the Madras University (4,468). Calcutta University, though topped in the total enrolment, was at the third position in regard to the number of women students (4003).

To Conclude

We may conclude by stating that higher education could be said to have been ushered in by the setting up of the three universities – Calcutta, Madras and Bombay in 1857. During the next 90 years till 1947, when India attained freedom, there was considerable progress in university education in terms of institutions, student enrolment and expenditure. In spite of the fact that, at least theoretically, the Government of India was committed to give priority to elementary education, higher education had a multi-dimensional expansion as well as structural reorganisation. This was based on the recommendations made by two important Commissions – the Universities Commission of 1902 and Calcutta University Commission of 1917. In between the Auxiliary Committee of the Indian Statutory

Commission known as the Hartog Committee (1929) and the Abbot Wood Committee (1936-37) made recommendations about the reorganisation of the educational system including university education. We shall discuss the state of affairs in the university sector in the post-independence period in a separate chapter.

References

1. Indian Education Policy; Progress of Education in India 1897-98 – 1901-02, Calcutta, 1904, pp. 462-63.
2. The Indian Education Commission, 1882-83, p. 24.
3. Brief survey of Indian Education Policy down to the Reforms, Indian Statutory Commission, 1929 p. 13.
4. Sixth Quinquennial Review, Vol. I, 1914.
5. Excludes Burma.
6. Progress of Education in India; 1907-12, Volume-I; Sixth Quinquennial Review, 1914, p.18.
7. *Ibid.*, p. 19.
8. This has been discussed fully in chapter 7.
9. *Ibid.*, p. 20.
10. Letter dated 1st July, 1911 from H. Sharp Joint Secretary, Government of India to Government of Madras etc. (proceedings).
11. *Ibid.*
12. Indian Statutory Commission, Interim Report Review of Growth of Education in British India by Auxiliary Committee appointed by the Commission, London, 1929, p. 31.
13. *Ibid.*, pp. 31-32.
14. Progress of Education in India; 10th Quinquennial Report, p. 1.
15. Hartog Committee, the Auxiliary Committee of the Indian Statutory Commission, 1928, pp. 345-46.
16. Quoted in the Progress of Education in India, 1927-32, pp. 4-5.
17. Bihar and Orissa, Report, p. 62.
18. Progress of Education in India, 1937-37, p. 57.
19. H. Sharp, Progress of Education in India, Seventh Quinquennial Review, 1912-17, p. 85.
20. J.A. Richey: Progress of Education in India, 1917-22, pp. 19-20.
21. Eleventh Five Year Plan, Planning Commission, p. 27 (Education Chapter).
22. *Source:* Progress of Education in India, 1927-37, pp. 11-12.
23. Education Commission (1964-66), p. 422.
24. Report of the Indian Statutory Commission, 1929, Interim Report, p.12.
25. *Ibid.*, p. 14.
26. The general literacy level, according to the 1911 Census, was less than 10 per cent. The female literacy was almost non-existent.
27. Progress of Education in India, 1922-27.
28. *Ibid.*, pp. 13-14.
29. Biswamoy Pati, Historians and Historiography, Situating 1857; published in the *Economic and Political Weekly*; May 12, 2007, pp. 1688-89.
30. Progress of Education in India; 1897-98 – 1901-02 Volume I, Calcutta, 1904, p. 167.

31. Lord Curzon in India (1898-1905), Macmillan and Co. Ltd., London, 1906, Vol. II, pp. 33-34.
32. *Ibid.*, p. 34.
33. *Ibid.*, p. 42.
34. Quoted from Progress of Education in India, 1901-02; statement Exhibiting the Moral and Material Progress of Conditions of India during 1901-02 and Nine Preceding years; p. 315.
35. Education Commission (1964-66); Ministry of Education, Govt. of India, p. 28.
36. For details see J.L. Azad: Financing and Management of Higher Education in India, the Role of the Private Sector, Gyan Publishing House 2008, pp. 42-43; 46.
37. Home (Education) Department, Proceeding No. 27-28, Dec. 1902.
38. *Ibid.*, Proceedings No. 78, Part B, December, 1902.
39. Home (Education) Department, Branch B, Proceedings 31/32 – December 1902.
40. Home (Education) Department, Part-B, Proceedings No. 80-81, October, 1902.
41. Home-Education Department, Part-B, Proceedings No.13-14, December 1902.
42. Progress of Education in India, 1907-12, Evolution of Policy; pp. 11-12.
43. Quoted as a part of the Educational Policy of the Government of India; Progress of Education in India, 1907-12, p. 1.
44. Proceedings of the Department of Education, 1912, p. 37.
45. Progress of Education in India, 1917-22, p. 2.
46. Calcutta University Commission, pp. 302-304.
47. Calcutta University Commission, pp. 223-25.
48. Calcutta University Commission, 1917-1919, p. 58.
49. According to latest information available, it was Allahabad University set up in 1887, which became a teaching university. Banaras Hindu University was set up in 1916.
50. Calcutta University Commission, *op.cit.*, p. 95.
51. *Ibid.*, p. 220.
52. *Ibid.*, p. 7.
53. Quoted in Progress of Education in India, 1927-32, p. 4.
54. *Ibid.* p. 76 and 80.
55. *Ibid.* p. 76 and 80.
56. Progress of Education in India, 1932-37, p. 2.

4

Financing Indian Education

This chapter has been divided into two sections. Section-1 discusses the policy framework evolved by the British Government to finance Indian education. The various types of grants-in-aid systems introduced by the Government of India and the provincial governments have been discussed in details. The impact of the government grant-in-aid on the progress of institutions under various managements has also been analysed.

Section-2 provides an analytical study of the magnitude of financial investment in education; the income and expenditure of various types of institutions with respect to different stages of education; the sources of finance – over all and stage wise and the break up between Direct and Indirect expenditure. An attempt has also been made to assess the relationship between the capacity of the various provinces in terms of the revenue available to them and the quantum of resources provided for educational development.

Section-1

POLICY ABOUT FINANCING OF EDUCATION

The Emergence of the Grant-in-aid System

It has been mentioned that for more than a century of the British rule in India, the alien government did not pay any attention to the education of the people inhabiting the vast landscape of this country. The colonisers were more interested in expanding their territories and strengthening their suzerainty over the hapless population than providing them facilities for any kind of education. It was as late as in 1813, more than two centuries after the East India Company was set up, that the Government of India received a Directive from the Board of Directors of the East India Company to spend an amount of Rs. one lakh per annum for "the revival and promotion of literature and encouragement of learned natives of India." Even this paltry amount remained blocked because of the controversy that erupted over the manner in which the amount should be spent. It was only in 1835 that Lord Macaulay, in his minute (2nd February, 1835) vigorously pleaded for the introduction of European education and English, based on utterly biased and unsubstantiated arguments, arising out of his disdain for anything that was euphemistically called as oriental. Indian education was forced to discard the centuries old system of education – the bête-noire of His Lordship and to adopt the western system of education, with English as the medium through which it had to provide, apart from being a subject.

In less than two decades, the British Government in India realized that it was beyond their financial capabilities to provide for education of their subjects and therefore they should seek the support of the wealthier classes of Indians for providing education of the masses. This was ordained in the Despatch of 1854, which was described as a "bold, farseeing and statesman like document".[1] The "Despatch pointed out that" the educational system in India should not entirely depend upon the direct efforts of the Government. It recognised that there was an increased desire on the part of the native population not only in the neighbourhood of the great centres of European civilisation but also in remote districts, for the means of obtaining a better education, as we have evidence in many instances of their readiness to give a practical shape of their anxiety in this respect by coming forward with liberal pecuniary contribution. Throughout all ages, learned Hindoos and Mohamedens have devoted themselves to teaching with little other remuneration than a bare subsistence and munificent bequests have frequently been made for the permanent endorsement of educational institutions. At the same time, societies of Christians have guided the natives of India in the way of religious truth and to instruct uncivilised races... by the diffusion of informed knowledge, thus contributing to the spread of that education, which it is our object to promote[2].

Introducing System of Grant-in-aid

The Despatch[3] reaffirmed Government's intention to introduce the system of grant-in-aid based on entire abstinence from interference with religious instructions supported in schools. Further, aid was to be given (so far as the requirements of each particular district, as compared with other) and the funds at the disposal of the Government, would render it possible to all schools, imparting a good secular education provided that they were under adequate local management... and provided also that their managers consented that the school would be subject to Government inspection and agree to any modification, which may be laid down for the regulation of such grants relating to the charging of fees from students.

Another important point raised in the Despatch was that, an entirely gratuitous education valued far less by those who receive it than one for which some payment, however small, was made and that payment induced a more regular attendance and greater exertion on the part of the pupils and for that reason as well as because school fees themselves insignificant, as they may be in each individual instance, would in the aggregate when applied to support of a better class of masters, become of very considerable importance. The Despatch desired that grant-in-aid should, as a general principle, be made to such schools only (with the exception of normal schools) as require some fee, however small, from their scholars.

The other suggestions were:

1. The augmentation of salaries of teachers would be the most important object of grant-in-aid; and
2. The continuance of aid will depend upon the periodical reports of inspectors who will, among other things, ascertain whether secular knowledge is imparted in schools. The Government will adopt the principle of perfect religious neutrality in giving grant-in-aid to schools.

The Despatch also outlined the policy of the government:

(i) To improve the existing schools and increase their number;

(ii) The ruling power should remain aloof from all questions of religion;

(iii) The scheme of instruction to be introduced was one which should culminate in the acquisition of literature and science essentially foreign. The government therefore admitted that to imbue a vast and ignorant population with a general desire for knowledge and to take advantage of that desire, when excited to improve the means for diffusing education amongst them, must be a work of many years. This admission was followed by an announcement that as a government, they could do no more than direct the efforts of the people and aid them wherever they appeared to require most assistance.

Policy of Withdrawal from Direct Involvement in Education

The Despatch looked forward to the time, when any general system of education entirely provided by the government might be discontinued with the gradual advance of the system of grant-in-aid and when many of the existing government institutions, especially those of higher order, might be safely closed or transferred to the management of local bodies under the control of and aided by the State.[4]

The policy of government's intention to withdraw itself from direct involvement in providing education to the masses was reiterated in government's instruction to the Indian Education Commission (1882). While advising the Commission that it should keep in mind the great importance which the government attached to the subject of primary education in terms of the objectives contemplated by the Despatch of 1854, the government, in a long winding treatise, said:

"While this is the main object to which the inquiries of the Commission should be directed, the Governor General in Council desires to impress upon it at the same time the fact that it is not possible for the government to find sufficient funds to meet the full requirements of the country in the matter of primary education, if their requirements are to be judged by any European standard. The resources at the disposal of the Government of India, whether Imperial, provincial or local one, and must long remain, extremely limited in amount and result in not only that progress must necessarily be gradual but that, if satisfactory progress is to be made at all, every available private agency must be called into action to relieve and assist the public funds in connection with every branch of the Public Instruction. It was in view of the impossibility of Government alone doing all that must be done to provide adequate means for the education of the Natives of India that the grant-in-aid system was elaborated and developed by the Despatch of 1854, and it is to the wider extension of this system, especially in high and middle education, that the Government looks to set free funds, which may then be made applicable to the promotion of education of the masses.... The resources of the Government ought, as remarked by the Secretary of State in Despatch No.13 of 25th April 1864, to be so applied as to assist those who cannot be expected to help themselves and the richer classes of the people should gradually be induced to provide for their own education".[5]

According to the Education Commission (1882-83) the relation of the state to private effort, as indicated in the Despatch of 1854, could be summed up as follows:

The state undertook:

1. To give pecuniary assistance as th grant-in-aid system to efficient schools and colleges;
2. To direct their efforts and offer them counsel and advice;
3. To encourage and reward the desire for learning in various ways, but chiefly by the establishment of universities;
4. To take measures for providing a due supply of teachers, and for making the profession of teaching honourable and respected.

The most important and far ready stipulation was, however, the introduction of grant-in-aid system.

The Despatch of 1859

The Despatch of 1859 endorsed the policy of providing pecuniary assistance to educational institutions. It pointed out:

"While the system had been readily accepted by schools of higher education, it had been unsuccessful in its affiliation to those of a lower class. Local support was difficult to get by way of subscriptions, which was a main condition of grant. Hence, it was felt that vernacular education should be provided rather by the direct instrumentality of the officers of the Government according to some of the plans in operation in Bengal for the improvement of indigenous schools or in the North Western Provinces for the establishment of circle schools, or by such modification of these schemes as might commend itself to the several local government as best suited to the circumstances of different localities..."[6]

The necessity of requiring the wealthier classes to contribute to the cost of their education and thus to make government schools more self-supporting than before, was reiterated in 1861 (Despatch No.14, dated 8th April, 1861) with reference to the levy of fees in high schools, when it was declared to be impossible, even if desirable, that the state should bear the whole expense of education, in so densely populated a country as India.

Necessity of Encouraging Private Efforts – Limitation of the Policy of Withdrawal

The Secretary of State in Despatch No. 6, dated 16th May, 1892, stated that in such withdrawal, attention must necessarily be given to local circumstances and that the government were unwilling that a government institution should be given up in any place, where the inhabitants show a marked desire that it should be maintained, or where there is a manifest disinclination, on the part of people, to send their children to private schools of neighbourhood.

Systems of Grant-in-aid

In the 1860s, the following five grants-in-aid systems were in vogue in various provinces:

(i) The system of salary grant;
(ii) The system known as payment by results;
(iii) The combined system, giving small salary grants and additional payment by results;
(iv) The Bengal or fixed period system, which was applied on a very limited scale, based on expenditure and modified by results and;
(v) The capitation grants system, which was applied on a limited scale.

The salary grant system was peculiar to Madras and the combined system almost so, though in a few districts of Bengal and generally in Assam; a mixed system of small stipend, combined with payment after examination, was applied to primary schools. The system of payment by results obtained in Madras for majority of the schools that provided elementary institutions and in Bombay to nearly all institutions of every class.

A discussion of the various systems of grants based on the points made by the Education Commission (1882-83) follows:

The Salary Grants System

Advantages:

(i) It tends to ensure efficiency by inducing the managers to employ teachers who have proved by success in an examination that they have acquired certain amount of knowledge and some fitness for imparting it to others;
(ii) The system gives freedom to managers to choose their textbooks and all other points in the internal economy of the school; and
(iii) The schools have the fullest scope for free development.

Disadvantages:

(i) School would be content with mediocrity, since no pecuniary advantage depended upon excellence of any kind;

(ii) Teachers may be shown as getting higher salaries only on paper and not in actuality.

The Results System

The students were examined by school inspectors and fixed payments made for each pupil, who has attained a certain measure of efficiency.

Advantages:

(i) It enables the inspectors to gauge the attainment of pupils and to apply praise or blame with a firmness, otherwise decision is impossible under any system that pays less attention to the examination of individual pupils; and

(ii) It ensures that the state aid is never wasted.

Disadvantages:

(i) Proverbial uncertainty of the examination results can do havoc to the financial system. The standard demanded by inspectors varies and therefore the quantum of grant would be affected;

(ii) It tends to give most aid to managers, who can influence and least to those who need it most. Unless modified, it gives no aid to a school at starting, when difficulties are naturally the greatest;

(iii) It tends to create antagonism between managers and school inspectors and also between managers and the Department as a whole;

(iv) It requires a large inspecting agency, though its disadvantage counts for little when it is applied to elementary schools;

(v) The chief disadvantage was its making examinations the main objective of the pupils and teachers and thus tending to give entirely false views to the meaning and purpose of education. Examinations then must be under any system but they need not be made the pivot on which it turns.

The System of "Fixed Period Grant"

Known as "Bengal System". grant is settled for a term of years – in Bengal generally five – and the amount is determined by a conjunct view of all the circumstances and wants of the institution aided. The points taken into consideration in fixing the grants were: the strength and expense of the teaching staff and establishment, the accommodation, the probable efficiency and pecuniary resources and the situation of the school whether in populous, prosperous and advanced districts, where considerable fees may be levied, or in a less progressive locality, where the amount raised in fees must for a time be small. It was provided that the grant would in no case exceed income of the school from other sources.

Advantages:

The greatest advantage was its simplicity and elasticity. No elaborate code was necessary.

Disadvantages:

(i) False accounts can be presented;
(ii) It is arbitrary in character. Under it, the power of the Department in giving or refusing aid is scarcely subject to any practical limitation;
(iii) It gives little security for the efficiency of teachers and has no strong tendency to improve their quality as years pass by.

The System of Capitation Grants on the Average Monthly Attendance

This system was applied in Bengal to some girls' schools. The rate was 4 *annas* per head, but the total grant was not to exceed Rs.ten *per mensem*. The system was in force for those girls' schools, which were attached to boys' schools and in which teachers employed in the latter instructed the girls at special hours in addition to their ordinary duties.

The Education Commission (1882-83) made the following recommendations for remodelling this system of grant-in-aid:

(i) With the object of rendering assistance to schools in the form best suited to the circumstances of each province, and thus calling forth the largest amount of local cooperation, the grant-in-aid scales be revised by the local government in concert with the managers of schools and that, in this revision, the rules be so defined as to avoid any ambiguity as to the amount and duration of the aid to which an institution would be entitled, the condition of grants for buildings, apparatus and furniture being clearly stated...
(ii) While the existing state institutions of higher order should be maintained in complete efficiency, wherever they were needed, the improvement and extension of privately managed institutions be the principal care of the Department...
(iii) As a general principle, the grant-in-aid should depend:
  (a) On locality, i.e., larger proportionate grants to be given to schools in backward districts;
  (b) On the class of institutions, i.e., larger proportionate grants given to those in which a large amount of self support cannot be expected, e.g., girls' schools and schools for lower castes and backward races.

General principles to regulate the amount of grant-in-aid:

(a) That no grant be given to an institution which has become self supporting by means of fees, and which needs no further development to meet the wants of the locality.
(b) That as a general rule, this minimum rate of aid be given only to girls' schools, primary schools and normal schools.

Explaining further the Commission stated:

(a) Aid should cease when no longer needed, and that it should be given liberally when really required.

(b) About withdrawal of the state from the direct provision as management of education especially of higher education, it was suggested that the policy of withdrawal had already been implemented. The reasons were the success and popularity of the government institutions, which naturally made the Department anxious to retain them and the difficulty of finding suitable agencies able and willing to accept the transfer, without detriment to education in the locality concerned.

(c) With regard to future action, two strongly opposed lines of arguments were followed. On the one hand, it was urged that the very success of the advanced institutions supported directly by the State was a reason for maintaining them; that the people regarded the maintenance of such institutions as an important part of the duty of the State representing the community, which cannot justifiably be neglected or shifted to other shoulders; that the example of many civilised communities in favour of the management of advanced education by the state; that this duty is carried out in India at a cost, which bears insignificant proportion to the whole expenditure upon education, and still more insignificant, when compared with the whole resources of the state; that as a rule, there are no agencies to whom such institutions can be safely transferred. It was also felt that any withdrawal of the state from higher education would throw it into the hands of the Missionary organisations, the chief advocates of a change, which would cause disinterest and apprehension in the great mass of the native community.

On the other hand, it was argued that if education is to be adequate, it must be national in a wider sense than is implied in mere state management, and must be managed in a great measure by the people themselves... that as a matter of course, the people will not exert themselves to supply their educational wants so long as it is understood that government is ready to undertake the task.

(d) The Commission expressed the view that in some provinces at present and in others in course of time, native private effort with proper aid and supervision can take the place of departmental effort in, at any rate, secondary institutions and that the withdrawal of the department be not carried out too suddenly or on too large a scale... At the same time, it was thought that withdrawal of direct departmental agency should not take place in favour of missionary bodies, and that institutions of the higher order should not be transferred to missionary management.

(e) That in order to evoke and stimulate local cooperation in the transfer to private management of government institutions for collegiate or secondary instruction, aid at specially liberal rates be offered for a term of years, whenever necessary to any local body willing to undertake the management of any such institutions under adequate guarantees of permanence and efficiency.

(f) That the fact that any school raises more than 60 per cent of its entire expenditure from fees be taken as affording a presumption that the transfer of such school to local management can be safely effected.

(g) Those that might be transferred with advantage, as a measure promising useful political results, to bodies of native gentlemen, provided the new managers give satisfactory guarantees that the college will be maintained (i) permanently (ii) in full efficiency (iii) in such a way as to make it adequate for all the wants of the community.

J.A. Richey summed up the system in the Quinquennial Report, 1917-22, thus:

The system adopted in different provinces for the assessment and distribution of grants in aided schools falls into three categories:

(a) Systems which limit the grant either to the proportion of the approved expenditure or by making it bear a fixed ratio to the sum provided by the managers from other sources including fees. The determining support factor in this case is the amount of local support accorded to each school.

(b) Systems which limit the grant to a standard scale of expenditure laid down by Government for each type of school as sufficient to maintain it in a state of efficiency. The grant under these systems is assessed by deducting from the cost of standard scale of income from fees at fixed rates. The determining factor in this case is the standard of expenditure prescribed by government for each type of school.[7]

It would be seen that a comprehensive system of grant-in-aid was worked out in order to stimulate, among other things, private participation in the field of education. For this purpose, the measures for attracting private entrepreneurship were also put into place with the proviso that the quality of education and its quantitative expansion should not be compromised. It may be recalled that in 1881-82, the average annual cost per student stood at about Rs. 355, which was shared by the Government and private sources (including fees) on a 60-40 per cent basis. Table 1 explains:

Table 1: Percentage Contributed by Government and Private Sources – 1881-82 (Figures in Percentages)

(i) Public Funds	59.69
(ii) Fees	23.50
(iii) Other Sources	16.81
Total	100.00

Problems Galore

It may, be stated that the grant-in-aid system, so meticulously worked out, developed quite a few problems. Within a quarter of a century, it was reported that in the case of primary schools, the grant-in-aid system has generally broken down. It was initiated and maintained in the case of secondary education, not because its results were in any way better than those of government schools, but by reasons of its cheapness and the devolution of authority it permitted to local endeavour which, it was expected, would supervise these institutions. It was also pointed out that the weak point in the system was the fact that its underlying idea, the subvention of local organised effort, had not always been kept in mind. Few secondary schools were endowed, and the absence of endowment made them too dependent on fee collection and obliged them to have in mind not so much an ideal of education as the demand of the pupils and their parents. Again, these schools, which were not on the aided list, were insufficiently controlled.[8]

It is difficult to ascertain the growth of total grants given to educational institutions. In proportionate terms, however, the quantum of grants to the total educational expenditure showed a perceptible decline. For example in 1870-71, the total grant assigned to institutions was Rs. 14,01,155, which rose to Rs.18,50,489 in 1881-82. In percentage terms, however, the grant-in-aid fell from 18.70 to 18.17 during the corresponding period. The increase in the amount of grant was mainly in the case of primary schools i.e. from Rs. 3½ lakh to Rs. 11½ lakh. This increase had been at the cost of secondary schools and had resulted into the closing down of many schools under private management. Thus, the actual implementation of the grant-in-aid system had retarded the growth of secondary education, notwithstanding the avowed intention of the Despatches of 1854 and 1859 to ensure a balanced growth of the educational system.

The System Reviewed

The system of grant-in-aid to educational institutions was again reviewed in 1922-23 by the Indian Retrenchment Committee under Lord Inchcape[9], which suggested, among others, far reaching changes in the administrative set up of the Education Department. About the Grant-in-Aid system, prevailing at that time, the Committee made the following observations:

System of Grants: The basis of government grants to schools and colleges in different administrations varies considerably. In some cases, they are based upon the rules in force in neighbouring provinces and, in other cases, they are assessed on the total expenditure of individual schools, on a fixed capitation allowances or on the difference between income and expenditure etc.

In the North West Frontier and Delhi Provinces, grants are of three kinds:

(i) **Capital Grants:** These grants are made usually on the pound per pound principle to the manager of private institutions for the erection and extension of school buildings and the purchase of school furniture.

(ii) **Direct Maintenance Grants to Colleges:** These grants are usually determined in each case after consideration of the special condition of the colleges and in some cases government may subsidise a college to avoid the necessity of opening a government college.

(iii) **Direct Maintenance Grants to Secondary Schools:** In the North West Frontier Province, the grants represent the amount necessary to raise the income from fees and other sources to the minimum needed for maintaining efficiency. Supplementary and additional grants are given to encourage the managers to improve their staff and pay them well. A standard minimum scale of staff and salaries is laid down for each class of schools, and the amount of grant is based on the difference between what the income of the school would be from fees charged at full government rates and the cost of the staff, if paid in accordance with standard rates. If the managers pay their teachers more than the standard rates of pay, Government meets half of the cost of the additional pay. The cost of maintenance of any building and any deficit arising from any reduction in the rates of fees below the Government scale has to be met from private or local sources.

In Delhi, the grants to each school consist of a capitation grant based on the average attendance of students and a staff grant to teachers holding certificates granted by the Department. The total grant may not exceed three fourths of the excess of expenditure on tuition over income from fees. The cost of tuition, however, includes not only the cost of the staff, but also petty repairs to buildings.

(iv) **Grants to Local Bodies for Maintenance of Primary and Vernacular Schools:** Primary and vernacular education was financed partly from local funds and partly from Government grants. In the NWFP, 25 per cent of each District Board's income is devoted to education and all additional sums required for opening new schools, the enhancement of teachers' salaries, the provision of additional teachers etc. are paid by government. The grants to municipalities for primary education are said to be fixed in accordance with their needs after consideration of their financial circumstances. In Delhi, the basis of assessment of grants was the salaries of the teachers. Government paid two thirds of the salaries of trained or qualified teachers in vernacular, middle and primary schools and half the salaries paid to unqualified teachers. It also paid half the expenditure on the upkeep of primary school buildings. These arrangements applied both to municipal and district board schools.

(v) **Committee's Criticism of the Grant-in-Aid System:** The Inchcape Committee described the then prevalent system under which grants were made as unsatisfactory, uneconomical and prejudicial into the best interest of the country. In their opinion, the most primary need was the extension of primary education facilities to the greatest possible number and it was evident that the then existing policy did not fulfil this fundamental requirement. The Committee were informed that probably not more than 20 per cent of the children of school going age in the minor Administrations were attending school; therefore, a large increase in expenditure was inevitable. In these circumstances, there was, in Committee's opinion, no justification for allocating to primary education only 36.6 per cent of the funds available for education in minor Administrations. The Committee recommended that in the present financial situation in the country, *the grants for higher education should be curtailed and fixed at a lump sum for each administration for the next five years; any additional expenditure being met by fees, increased grants from District Boards, municipalities and private contributions.* (emphasis added)

(vi) The Committee felt strongly about the necessity for increasing facilities for primary education and, therefore, did not recommend any reduction in the amount granted for the purpose, but they recommended that, in future, grants should be made on a capitation basis for each school; fixed up on the average daily attendance of pupils and the number of teachers necessary to maintain a recognised standard of staffing, which they thought should be fixed at not more than one teacher for 25 pupils, rising in five years to one teacher per 30 pupils. The Committee recognised that this may not be possible in every case, when the number of pupils was not obtainable.

The following is the summary of the Committees' specific recommendations:

(1) The whole educational policy be revised with the present system of grants being modified to secure that such funds as were available are applied for the extension of primary education.

(2) Grants for secondary and higher education be curtailed and fixed at a lump sum for each Administration for the next five years; any additional expenditure required being met from increasing fees, increased grants from local bodies and private contributions.

(3) As already stated, grants for primary education be fixed, as far as possible, on the basis of an average of one teacher per 25 pupils rising to one teacher per 30 pupils within five years.

To Sum Up

The grant-in-aid system was introduced in order to absolve the government of its full responsibility of providing education to the teeming millions of this country. It was also hoped that the contribution from private sources (including fees) would increase. In order to find out how far these two objectives were achieved, we have analysed the quantum of contribution made by private sources in terms of financial inputs as well as setting up of institutions. The data are available on a decennial basis for the period 1881-82 to 1937-47 (Annexures A to F).

Table 2 indicates the financial contribution from various sources to educational programmes for the period 1881-82 to 1946-47.

Table 2 : Source-wise Financial Contribution for Education

(Figures in percentages)

Sources	*1881-82*	*1891-92*	*1901-02*	*1911-12*	*1921-22*	*1931-32*	*1941-42*	*1946-47*
1. Government (including Local Bodies)	59.69	52.00	44.00	51.57	62.56	61.95	58.49	59.60
2. Fees	23.50	29.00	32.00	27.87	20.68	22.90	27.69	26.40
3. Other Sources	16.81	19.00	24.00	20.56	16.76	15.15	13.82	14.00
TOTAL	100.00	100.00	100.00	100.00	100.00	100.00	100.00	100.00

It would be seen that except for 1891-92, 1901-02 and 1911-12, the government expenditure has been in the realm of about 60 per cent of the total expenditure. The fees contributed between 21 per cent (the lowest in 1921-22) to 32 per cent in 1901-02. The contribution from private sources has fluctuated from 13.82 per cent (the lowest in 1941-42) to 24 per cent (the highest) in 1901-02. Thus the assumption that over time, there will be an increase in the contribution from private sources has not been validated.

Institutions

Table 3 indicates the percentage of institutions according to the managements over time.

Table 3 : Percentage of Institution According to Management (1891–1947)

Management	*1891-92*	*1901-02*	*1911-12*	*1921-22*	*1931-32*	*1941-42*	*1946-47*
Government (including Local Bodies)	20.71	21.62	77.36	83.27	32.16	46.16	53.75
Private	79.29	78.38	22.64	16.73	67.84	53.84	46.25
TOTAL	**100.00**	**100.00**	**100.00**	**100.00**	**100.00**	**100.00**	**100.00**

It would appear that there was a steep decline in the percentage of institutions under private management; from about 79 per cent in 1891-92 to about 23 per cent in 1911-12 and to about 17 per cent in 1921-22. This was due, according to government sources, to economic depression arising out of the First World War (1914-18) and political unrest. According to J.A. Richey, the long continuance of war brought depression in its train. The cost of education rose with the price of food and clothing and school material. Richey explained further on: "it was only after the meeting of the Indian National Congress in Nagpur in December 1920 that the campaign non-cooperation (movement) was launched, which succeeded in crippling some schools beyond hope of recovery, in disorganising the work of others for six months or a year and in ruining the sources of many promising schools... It was an appeal to the student community to break away from the control of government and government control is represented to students by the authorities, who direct their studies. A large number of students, who responded to the appeal, did so under the impression that they were, in some obscure way, serving their country..."[10]

From 1931-32 (which recorded the lowest percentage of government administered institutions) onwards there was a marked upsurge in the proportion of government administered institutions, which rose to about 54 per cent of the total numbers of institutions. It may also be noted that there was no correlation between the percentages of government investment in education and institutions managed by the government.

For example in 1901-02, the government contribution was about 44 per cent; the percentage of government administered institutions was very low, about 22 per cent. In 1921-22, the government investment was around 63 per cent of the total expenditure, the percentage of institutions managed by the government was high, being 83.(Percentages) (As shown in Tables 2 and 3).

Table 4 shows the comparison between 1891–92 and 1901–02 of the source-wise contribution for Education and Break-up of public funds.

Annexure A

Table 4 : Break-up of Public Funds and Source-wise Contribution for Education (1891-92 and 1901-02)

Source	*1891-92*	*1901-02*
Provincial Revenues	29.00	25.00
Local Funds	18.00	15.00
Municipal Funds	05.00	04.00
Total Public Funds	**52.00**	**44.00**
Fees	29.00	32.00
All other sources	19.00	24.00
Sub Total	**48.00**	**56.00**
Total	100.00	100.00
Total Expenditure (£)	20,34,642.00	26,79,278.00

Table 5 : Break-up of Total Expenditure on Educatin (1891-92 and 1901-02)

Management	*1891-92*	*Percentage*	*1901-02*	*Percentage*
Government Institutions	1,397	1.36	1,078	1.02
Local Bodies	17,634	17.20	18,080	17.16
Native States	2,218	2.16	3,630	3.44
Private Management				
Aided	60,478	58.88	62,922	59.71
Unaided	21,017	20.40	19,671	18.67
Total	1,02,744	100.00	1,05,381	100.00

Annexure B

Table 6 : Source-Amount and Percentage of Public (Private Funds during British India Rule)

Source	*Amount (Rs.)*	*Percentage*
Municipal Revenues	2,69,58,808.00	34.31
Local Funds	1,05,80,114.00	13.46
Municipal Funds	29,84,150.00	3.80
Total Public Funds	4,05,23,072.00	51.57
Fees	2,19,08,646.00	27.87
Other Sources	1,61,60,887.00	20.56
Total Private	3,80,69,533.00	48.43
Grand Total	7,85,92,605.00	100.00

Table 7 : Institutions by Management (British India) 1911-1947

Management	*No. of Institutes*	*Percentage*
1911-12 Public (Government) Institutions	1,36,332	77.36
Private Institutions	39,893	22.64
Total	1,76,225	100.00

Annexure C

Table 8: Sources of Expenditure 1921-22

Management	*Amount (Rs.)*	*Percentage*
Government Funds	9,02,30,028.00	49.10
Board Funds	2,47,31,150.00	13.46
Fees	3,80,08,648.00	20.68
Other sources	3,07,83,143.00	16.76
Total	**18,37,52,969.00**	**100.00**

Table 9: Institutios by Management (British India) 1921-22

Management	*No. of Institutes*	*Percentage*
Public (Government) Institutions	1,73,299	83.27
Private Institutions	34,807	16.73
Total	**2,08,106**	**100.00**

Annexure D

Table 10: Sources of Expenditure 1921-22

Sources	*Expenditure (Rs.)*	*Percentage*
Government	12,46,03,905.00	45.83
Local Boards	4,38,18,535.00	16.12
Total Government	16,84,22,440.00	61.95
Aided	6,22,69,534.00	22.90
Unaided	4,11,64,648.00	15.15
Total Private	10,34,34,182.00	38.05
Grand Total	**27,18,56,622.00**	**100.00**

Table 11: Institutions by Management (British India) 1931-32

Management	*No. of Institutes*	*Percentage*
Public Institutions Government	4,261.00	1.65
Board	78,641.00	30.51
Total Government	82,902.00	32.16

Private		
Aided	1,24,159.00	48.16
Unaided	50,731.00	19.68
Total Private	1,74,890.00	67.94
Grand Total	**2,57,792.00**	**100.00**

Annexure E

Table 12: Sources of Expenditure 1941-42

Sources	*Expenditure (Rs.)*	*Percentage*
Government Funds	13,51,72,784.00	43.81
District Board Funds	(2.63.26.553.00)	
Municipal Board Funds	(1.89.85.175.0)	
(+)	4,53,11,728.00	14.68
Fees	8,54,57,945.00	27.69
Other Sources	4,26,37,286.00	13.82
Total	30,85,79,743.00	100.00

Table 13: Institutions by Management (British India) 1941-42

Management	*No. of Institutions*	*Percentage*
Government	6,878	3.27
District Boards	90,032	42.89
Total Government	**96,910**	**46.16**
Aided	1,00,761	48.01
Unaided	12,243	5.83
Total Private	**1,13,004**	**53.84**
Grand Total	**2,09,914**	**100.00**

Annexure F

Table 14: Sources of Expenditure 1946-47

Sources	*Expenditure (Rs.)*	*Percentage*
Government Funds	25,95,89,051.00	45.03
District Board Funds	**(5.18.67.224.00)**	
Municipal Funds	**(3.21.53.830.0)**	
(+)	8,40,21,054.00	14.57

Fees	15,22,22,448.00	26.43
Endowments	8,07,80,874.00	14.00
Grand Total	57,66,13,427.00	100.00

Table 15: Institutions by Management (British India) (1946-47)

Management	*No. of Institutions*	*Percentage*
Government	6,821.00	3.34
District Boards	1,02,775.00	50.41
Total Government	1,09,596.00	53.75
Aided	83,739.00	41.08
Unaided	10,538.00	5.17
Total Private	94,277.00	46.25
Grand Total	2,03,873.00	100.00

Section-2

FINANCING INDIAN EDUCATION

An Analytical Study

The East India Company was set up in 1600 AD to undertake trade with the sprawling market in India. The first two hundred years may be said to have been characterised by general apathy towards education of the *natives.* In fact, the initial attempts by the Company to educate the Indian people were primarily directed towards proselytisation[11]! It was only in 1757, when the British Raj could be said to have been established in India, after the British forces won the battle of Plassey. With the Treaty of Allahabad in 1765, the Diwani of Bengal, Bihar and Orissa and the right to administer these provinces and collecting revenue was given to the British conquerors. Even after that about 50 years had to elapse, that colonial rulers paid some grudging attention to education of the Indians, who were forcibly brought under their hegemony. Till then, Indian education was imparted in the traditional way. "The advent of the British rule in India found Indian systems of education of great antiquity existing among both Hindus and Muhammadans; in each case closely bound up with their religious institutions. To give and receive instruction was enjoined by the sacred books of the Brahamans... Schools for learning were formed in centres containing considerable high caste populations, where Pundits gave instruction in Sanskrit grammar, logic, philosophy and law. For the lower classes, village schools were scattered over the country in which a rudimentary education was given to the children of traders, petty land holders and well to do cultivators. The higher education of the Muhammadans was in the hands of men of learning, who devoted themselves to the instruction of youth. Schools were attached to mosques and shrines and supported by state grants in cash or land or by private liberality."[12]

Analysis of Educational Finance

We shall analyse the problems and procedures of educational finance under the British rule in two parts:

In **Part-1** analysis will be made of the policies, procedures and quantum of financing Indian education during the period 1765-1900. In 1765, East India Company was given the right of collecting revenues in respect of some provinces, heralding the onset of British rule in India. The Company was divested of its power in 1857 in the aftermath of the first war of Indian independence. Thereafter, the British Government assumed direct control of Indian administration. Educational finance also became an important component of its responsibilities.

Part-2 contains an analysis of the problems and procedures of educational finance for the first half of the twentieth century. In this part, an attempt has been made to discuss the quantum of investment in education in view of the policy paradigms brought out by the central government from time to time. The emerging contours of educational finance in the context of inter-sectoral priorities, sources of finance, average annual cost per scholar for different stages of education, gender disparities as observed in the allocation of resources, etc. have been scrutinised. The relationship between the 'capacity' of the provinces in terms of their total revenue receipts and their willingness to spend on education, have also been statistically analysed. In this analysis, Karl Pearson's method of Rank Correction (R) has been used.

PART-I

As already stated, the East India Company was not enthusiastic about providing resources for the education of the people of India in the first two centuries of its rule. There were, however, some sporadic efforts, to set up educational institutions at selected places. For example, on a petition presented to Lord Warren Hastings, (1781) by a 'considerable number of Mussalmans of credit and learning to establish a Madrassa or college, Hastings recommended to the Board of Directors of the East India Company a more adequate and permanent endowment. The cost of land and buildings of the Institution was to be about Rs. 57,745 and the running expenses were Rs. 625 per month.[13]

Similarly, J. Duncan, Resident, Benares in his letter dated First January 1792 to the Earl of Cornwallis, Governor General in Council suggested: "Having in view to the surplus revenue expected to be derived from the Permanent Settlement (as reported in my address of the 25th November, 1789) and the instructions thereon passed by your Lordship in Council in February last to transmit for the consideration of government my sentiments regarding its appropriation reflected frequently on the subject, it appeared to me that a part of these funds could not be applied to more general advantage or with more local propriety than by the institution of a Hindoo College or academy for the preservation and cultivation of the Laws, Literature and Religion of that Nation, at this centre of their faith and the common resort of all their tribe."[14]

The proposal was agreed to by the Governor General. In his letter dated 13th January 1792, he said interalia: "The expenditure is to be limited to Rs.10,000 for the current year and to Rs. 20,000 from the next year in case the surplus collections will be adequate to the payment of the account, otherwise you have to restrict the expense to the sum authorised to be disbursed in the current (1792) year".[15]

In 1816, David Hare, an English watchmaker, joined hands with Raja Ram Mohan Roy and formed a Committee of Indians and Englishmen, among whose members was included the Chief Justice, Sir Edward Hyde and raised a fund for establishing a school and college of western learning. Thus was formed the Hindu College in 1817, which transformed itself to the present day Presidency College and the Hindu School. A Hindu College was also set up in Poona in 1821.

The Missionary societies helped in organising education for girls in the three Presidencies of Bengal, Bombay and Madras. The movement was supported by David Hare and Raja Ram Mohan Roy. J.E. Drinkwater Bethune established a Girls' school in Calcutta in 1849. Superintendence of native female education became the responsibility of the Bengal Council of Education.

Dismal State of Education

The position about education in 1831 was, however, quite dismal. According to the General Committee of Public Instruction, the total number of institutions under its control was 14 with 3,490 pupils. The total receipts for the year were Rs. 2,54,994 and the expenditure was Rs. 2,63,994. The main beneficiaries were Hugli Madrasa (Rs. 37,350) Calcutta Madrasa (Rs. 34,800), Banaras College (Rs. 35,600) Sanskrit College (Rs.30,000), Anglo Indian College (Rs. 2 6,244) and Delhi College (Rs. 16,800).

Government Moves Haltingly

As already stated, in 1813, provision was made for giving regular assistance to education. The Charter Act of 1813 empowered the Governor General in Council to direct that one lakh of rupees in each year should be set apart and applied to the revival and improvement of literature and the encouragement of the learned natives of India and for the introduction and formation of a knowledge of sciences among the inhabitants of the British territories of India. In spite of the specific directive of the Charter Act of 1813, nothing substantial happened for the next 10 years except providing encouragement to private educational institutions and societies by giving some monetary assistance. Rather, a controversy ensued over the manner in which the amount provided by the Company should be spent. It was in 1835 that Lord Macaulay, through his extremely provocative Minute, prevailed on the Government to provide assistance for western education; to extend English education by "the establishment of government schools and colleges and by strengthening indigenous schools; while missionary efforts continued to play an important part in providing educational progress."[16]

Expenditure on Institutions Prior to 1835

Information on the expenditure on education as also the number of institutions and students in educational institutions prior to 1835 is very scanty. As stated above, according to the General Committee of Public Instructions, which submitted its first report in December, 1831, it appeared that the total number of institutions under its control was 14 with 3,490 pupils. Further, the total educational receipts for the year were Rs. 2,75,047 and the total expenditure Rs. 2,54,994. The following table gives details of expenditure on various institutions existing at that time[17]:

Table 16 : Expenditure and Receipts about various Institutions, 1831

Expenditure				*Receipts*	
		Pupils	*Cost Per Annum (Rupees)*		*(Rupees)*
1.	Calcutta Madrassa and	80	30000	Annual Grant	100000
	English Department	100	4800	Calcutta Madrassa	30000
2.	Sanskrit College	160	30000	Sanskrit College	25000
3.	Anglo Indian College	400	26244	Banaras College	20000
4.	Hugli Madrassa	—	37350	Agra College	16000
5.	Chinsurah School	1,050	7200	Interest General Fund	30622
6.	Bhagalpur School	77	3600	Interest General Banaras	6374
7.	Banaras College and	160]	35600	Interest General Agra	9701
		40]		Interest General Hugli	37350
8.	Allahabad School	100	1200		
9.	Jaunpur College	100	1000		
10.	Sagar School	398	1200		
11.	Cawnpur School	145	4800		
12.	Agra College	180	16000		
13.	Ajmer School	91	3600		
14.	Delhi College and	309	16800		
	English Department	100	9600		
	Total Pupils	**3,490**	**228994**		

Add charges for		15000		
Printing Books		5000		
Donations, Prizes		3000		
and Committees' Office		6000		
Total		**254994**	**Grand Total**	**275047**

To account for the very large average annual cost in institutions designed to give oriental teaching, it may be explained that bulk of the students received stipend of Rs. 5 or Rs. 8 a month, whereas in schools, where English or vernaculars were taught, most of the pupils paid fees. The contrast had an important bearing on controversy between the rival advocates of European and Asiatic literature."[18]

Educational Finance[19]- An Analytical Study

No authentic information is available about the manner in which the Government of India and the provincial governments financed Indian education till the close of the nineteenth century. We have, therefore, discussed the various aspects of finance of education in two parts: Part-1— 1886-87 to 1901-02 and Part-2— 1901-02 to 1947.

PART-I

At the outset, it needs to be stated that it would not be correct to compare the financial investment in the nineteenth century with that of the present times. The Purchasing Power Parity (PPP) is fundamentally different from country to country and from period to period in the same country. Further, geographical and political boundaries of the provinces, about which some information is available, are not the same as the states/provinces which were carved out/annexed during the British regime in the nineteenth century. Further, one province (Burma), which was a part of India, is no longer so.

Total Expenditure

Without going into the vast differential in the PPP, it may be stated that during the years under study, the total expenditure on education during 1886-87 was Rs. 2,52,42,000, which increased to Rs. 2,99,60,000 by 1891-92, to Rs. 3,54,45,000 by 1896-97 and to Rs. 4,01,21,000 by 1901-02. The average annual increase during the period under review was 2.8 per cent. The expenditure on education increased somewhat faster than the increase in the population. In 1891-92, the expenditure per thousand of population averaged Rs. 131. By 1901-02, it had reached a figure of Rs.167.

Province-wise Expenditure

Table 17 indicates the Province-wise expenditure during the period under review - 1886-87 to 1901-02:

Bengal had the highest expenditure on education in all the years under study. It was closely followed by Madras and Bombay. United Province and Punjab ranked 4 and 5. Leaving aside Burma, the Central Provinces, Assam and Berar ranked 6, 7 and 8. Coorg was the last in the hierarchy.

Expenditure Per Thousand of Population

The position of provinces underwent a radical change when they were ranked in terms of educational expenditure per thousand of the population. Bengal, which was spending the largest amount of expenditure on education both in 1886-87 and 1901-02, ranked No. 6 in both the years in terms of expenditure per thousand of population. Madras and Bombay maintained their position. The most neglected were the larger provinces: United Provinces and the Central Provinces. Although it may not be correct to say that these two provinces were exactly the same as Uttar Pradesh and Madhya Pradesh of the present times, yet it is more than a coincidence that these states are still backward in terms of educational development as also the quantum of investment in education. They still have the dubious distinction of being dubbed as *Bimaru* (sick) states. Table 18 explains.

It would appear that in terms of the three parameters - quantum of expenditure, expenditure per thousand of population and the cost per student, the provinces have not been able to maintain their respective positions (Tables 17,18 and 19). For example, Punjab, which ranked 5 in terms of expenditure, ranked 7 in relation to expenditure per thousand of population and was No.1 in terms of cost per student. Similarly, Bengal, which ranked 1 in terms of quantum of expenditure ranked 6 and 7 in relation to expenditure per thousand of population and cost per pupil, respectively.

It would be hazardous to draw any definite conclusions based on the preceding analysis of the financial data. One could, however, infer that there was no well thought out policy relating to the allocation of resources for education during the last 15 years of the nineteenth century. Perhaps the power of persuasion of the provincial authorities with officials at the helm of affairs in the central finance departments was the most important determining factor.

Objects of Expenditure

The analysis of expenditure by objects has been attempted in two ways: (a) Total expenditure by objects; and (b) Direct expenditure by objects.

Table 17 : Total Expenditure by Province

(Figure in thousands of Rs.)

Province	*1886-87*	*Percentage of the total/Rank*	*1891-92*	*Percentage the total/Rank*	*1896-97*	*Percentage of the total/Rank*	*1901-02*	*Percentage of the total/Rank*
Madras	45,63	18.08 (3)	58,76	19.61 (3)	66,87	18.85 (3)	79,32	19.78 (2)
Bombay	49,96	19.80 (2)	62,81	20.91 (2)	75,73	21.35 (2)	77,96	19.44 (3)
Bengal	78,87	31.23 (1)	93,53	31.21 (1)	1,09,69	30.94 (1)	1,22,50	30.54 (1)
United Provinces	28,68	11.37 (4)	33,53	11.29 (4)	36,40	10.25 (4)	45,60	11.37 (4)
Punjab	22,57	8.94 (5)	26,70	8.91 (5)	30,73	8.65 (5)	32,54	8.11 (5)
NWFP	00	00	00	00	00	00	1,53	0.38 (10)
Central Province	9,38	3.71 (6)	10,96	3.65 (6)	13,03	3.67 (6)	17,96	4.47 (6)
Burma	8,19	3.24 (7)	3,04	1.01 (9)	10,53	2.97 (7)	11,11	2.76 (7)
Assam	4,57	1.81 (8)	5,18	1.72 (7)	6,51	1.83 (8)	7,63	1.90 (8)
Berar	4,21	1.66 (9)	4,70	1.56 (8)	4,55	1.28 (9)	4,66	1.16 (9)
Coorg	36	0.14 (10)	39	0.13 (10)	41	0.11 (10)	40	0.09 (11)
Total	**25242**	**100.00**	**29960**	**100.00**	**35445**	**100.00**	**40121**	**100.00**

Source: R. Nathan, Progress of Education in India; 1897-98; Vol. I, Calcutta, 1904. **Note:** Figures in parentheses indicate ranks.

Table 18 : Total Expenditure per Thousand of Population (in Rupees)

Province	*1891-92*	*Rank*	*1901-02*	*Rank*
Madras	165	3	208	3
Bombay	210	2	306	1
Bengal	128	6	160	6
United Provinces	71	9	95	9
Punjab [N.W.F.P.]	128	6	152	7
Central Province	144	5	194	4
Burma	67	10	94	10
Assam	95	8	131	8
Berar	162	4	169	5
Coorg	225	1	221	2
Average	131	—	167	—

Source: Progress of Ecucation for relevant years.

The position further changes when the provinces are ranked in terms of cost per pupil. The following table explains:

Table 19 : Cost Per Pupil (1901)

Sl. No.	*Province*	*Rupees*	*Annas*	*Paise*
1.	Punjab	12	10	11
2.	Bombay	11	6	0
3.	North West Frontier	9	12	5
4.	Burma	8	3	4
5.	Madras	8	3	3
6.	Berar	7	5	1
7.	Bengal	6	8	6
8.	Central Provinces	6	2	9
9.	Assam	5	12	8

Source: Progress of Education for relevant years.

Total Expenditure by Objects[20]

Table 20 indicates the total expenditure on various sectors of education.

Table 20 : Total Expenditure by Institutions - 1901

Sl. No.	*Object*	*Total Expenditure (Figures in 000)*	*Percentage of the Total*	*Expenditure from Public Funds (Figures in 000)*	*Percentage of the Total*
1.	Arts College	2,601	6.48	952	5.34
2.	Professional Colleges	1,198	2.98	881	4.94
3.	Secondary Schools	12,684	31.61	3,276	18.40
4.	Primary Schools	11,876	29.60	6,050	33.97
5.	Special Schools	2,279	5.68	1,515	8.50
6.	University Charges	773	1.93	9	0.05
7.	Buildings & Equipment	2,573	6.42	1,529	8.58
8.	Direction and Inspection	2,545	6.34	2,450	13.75
9.	Scholarships	912	2.27	635	3.56
10.	Miscellaneous	2,681	6.69	519	2.91
	Total	**40,122**	**100.00**	**17,816**	**100.00**

As would appear, bulk of the expenditure (about 67 per cent of the total) was incurred on school education. The colleges including "university charges" accounted for only 11 per cent of the total expenditure. Scholarships got a measly 2 per cent. Administrative charges, buildings and equipment accounted for about 6 per cent each. This would indicate that in allocations of resources, greater priority was given to school education; collegiate education appeared to be in a nascent stage.

Expenditure from Public Funds

The position somewhat changed when considered in terms of the Government contribution for various sectors of education. Arts colleges, which accounted for about 6.5 per cent of the total expenditure, received only about 5 per cent of the government contribution. University charges had the barest minimum of government contribution (0.05 per cent of the total government expenditure). Similarly, school education (primary and secondary schools) which accounted for about 67 per cent of the total expenditure had to be content with only 52 per cent of the government munificence. There was, however, substantial increase in government expenditure on Direction and Inspection indicating that the government tightened its control on the educational institutions. There was substantial increase in the expenditure on Buildings and Equipment by government. The average annual expenditure on buildings and special equipment by governments was, however, a pittance: Punjab schools averaged Rs. 70 per annum, followed by North West Frontier Province, Rs.59; United Provinces Rs. 51; Bombay Rs. 46 and Central Provinces Rs. 31. Bengal and Assam were the lowest beneficiaries of government grant; being Rs.13 and Rs.10, respectively.[21]

(a) Direct Expenditure by Objects

The same position holds good when Direct Expenditure is analysed by objects. Arts and professional colleges accounted for 11.92 per cent in 1891-92 and 12.40 per cent in 1901-02. The school sector (primary and secondary) accounted for 80.98 per cent in 1891-92 and 80.16 per cent in 1901-02. If special schools are also added, schools accounted for about 90 per cent of the Direct Expenditure in both years. Table 21 explains:

Table 21 : Direct Expenditure by Objects

Sl. No.	*Institutions*	*1891-92*	*Percentage of the total*	*1901-02*	*Percentage of the total*
1.	Arts Colleges	2,044	8.48	2,601	8.49
2.	Professional Colleges	829	3.44	1,198	3.91
3.	Secondary Schools	9,896	41.08	12,684	41.40
4.	Primary Schools	9,614	39.90	11,876	38.76
5.	Special Schools	1,740	7.10	2,279	7.44
	Total	**24,123**	**100.00**	**30,638**	**100.00**

(b) Indirect Expenditure by Periods

Table 22 indicates the indirect expenditure in different years:

Table 22 : Indirect Expenditure by Periods

Sl. No.	*Objects of Expenditure*	*1891-92*	*Per cent*	*1896-97*	*Per cent*	*1901-02*	*Per cent*
1.	Buildings and Equipment	2182	33.96	2370	31.58	2573	27.13
2.	University	473	7.36	671	8.93	773	8.15
3.	Direction and Inspection	2250	35.01	2437	32.47	2545	26.83
4.	Scholarships	727	11.31	798	10.63	912	9.62
5.	Miscellaneous	794	12.36	1230	16.39	2681	28.27
	Total	6426	100.00	7506	100.00	9484	100.00

There is proportionate reduction in the expenditure on buildings, Direction and Inspection and scholarships during the period 1891-92 and 1901-02. The expenditure on miscellaneous items increased more than three times. The expenditure on university also showed a marginal increase.

It is also worth noting that there was substantial increase in the indirect expenditure as compared to the direct expenditure. While the indirect expenditure was 21 per cent of the total expenditure in 1891-92, it rose to about 24 per cent in 1901-02. This indicates that there was recognition of the need for enhancing the expenditure on infrastructure.Table 23 indicates the position about average annual cost per student for the year 1901-02:

Table 23 : Average Annual Cost per Student in Different Institutions

Sl. No.	*Institution*	*Average Annual Cost in Rs.*	
		1891-92	*1901-02*
1.	Arts College	162.0	149.1
2.	Professional Colleges	253.3	233.9
3.	Secondary Schools	21.0	21.0
4.	Primary Schools	3.6	3.9
5.	Training Schools	130.9	131.3
6.	Special Schools	65.1	53.8

It may be noted that compared to 1891-92, the average cost of educating a pupil in Arts College fell by about Rs.13 and in a professional college by about Rs. 20, while the average cost of education in a primary school rose by almost Rs. 0.3 in1901-020. The cost in special schools also plummeted by about Rs.12.

Expenditure by Sources

As already stated, the Government of India, in view of various Despatches from the Imperial Government, had decided to encourage private philanthropy to meet bulk of educational expenditure. It would, therefore, be interesting to see the extent to which private sources contributed in providing resources for education. Table 24 explains:

Table 24 : Expenditure by Sources

(In thousands of Rupees)

Sl. No.	*Sources*	*1891-92 Total*	*1891-92 Percentage*	*1901-02 Total*	*1901-02 Percentage*
1.	Provincial Revenues	8946	29.29	10391	25.90
2.	Local Funds	5395	17.65	5887	14.67
3.	Municipal Funds	1410	4.60	1558	3.88
4.	Native State Revenues	773	2.23	1289	3.21
	Total	**16524**	**54.07**	**19195**	**47.66**
	Private Sources				
1.	Fees	8855	29.00	12688	31.61
2.	Other Sources	5183	16.93	8328	20.73
	Total	**14038**	**45.93**	**21016**	**52.34**
	Grand Total	**30520**	**100.00**	**40121**	**100.00**

It would appear that over a ten year period, the contribution from government and semi-government organisations declined from about 54 per cent in 1891-92 to about 48 per cent in 1901-02, while the contribution from private sources, including student fees, increased from 46 to 52 per cent. Bulk of the increase was in the case of private sources, although contribution from student fees also rose by 2 percentage points.

About fees, the position was as follows:

In primary schools, the yield from fees was relatively a small portion of the total expenditure; the bulk of peasantry could not be expected to pay much by way of school fees and where Board schools existed, the contribution of agriculturists towards the local rates were regarded, in whole or in part, as a substitute for the payment of fees. In secondary schools and colleges, the government encouraged levy of adequate fees; the state schools set the standard and the privately managed schools were expected to follow at a reasonable distance.

Province-wise Position

The position of various provinces in relation to relative contribution from public and private sources has been considered in two ways: (1) Public and private contribution in terms of the total contribution from these sources; and (2) The relative contribution from public and private sources separately for each province.

The following may be noted:

1. The source-wise contributions in various provinces varies significantly. For example, Bombay received the largest contribution from public revenues (about 25 per cent) and ranked 1 but contribution from private sources was less than 15 per cent of the overall contribution from that source. Similarly, Bengal received the largest contribution (about 40 per cent) from private sources, while its position about public sources was almost half of the private contribution. Madras also contributed about 23 per cent out of the overall private contribution, while the contribution from public sources was about 16 per cent.

Table 25 sums up the position in 1901-02:

Table 25 : Expenditure by Source, and Province

(Figures in thousands of Rupees)

Sl. No.	*1901-02*					*Ratio between Public and Private Sources*		
							Percentages	
	Province	*Public**	*Percentage to the total*	*Private++*	*Percentage to the total*	*Total*	*Public*	*Private*
1.	Madras	3152	16.40	4780	22.75	7932	39.74	60.26
2.	Bombay	4739	24.80	3057	14.55	7706	61.50	38.50
3.	Bengal	3878	20.30	8372	39.85	12250	31.66	68.34
4.	United Provinces	2629	13.76	1931	9.19	4561	57.64	42.36

5.	Punjab	1792	9.38	1462	6.95	3254	61.12	38.88
6.	N.W. Frontier	90	0.48	63	0.30	153	58.82	41.18
7.	Burma	1201	6.28	595	2.83	1796	66.87	33.13
8.	Central Provinces	788	4.13	322	1.53	1110	70.99	29.01
9.	Assam	464	2.43	299	1.42	763	59.26	40.74
10.	Berar	345	1.81	121	0.57	466	74.03	25.97
11.	Coorg	27	0.14	13	0.06	40	67.50	32.50
	Total	**19105**	**100.00**	**21015**	**100.00**	**401,21**	**47.61**	**52.38**

*Includes government Resources, Native States Resources.
++Includes Fees and other Sources.

2. In regard to ratios between the public and private sources among the major states, Bombay retains its position of eminence having contributed about 62 per cent from public sources. This is closely followed by Punjab (61.12 per cent from public sources). Curiously, Central Provinces also received the highest contribution from public sources. Bengal and Madras seem to be mainly depending upon philanthropy of private benefactors with 68 and 60 per cent respectively of their overall expenditure coming from private sources.

Educational Expenditure as Percentage of Total State Expenditure

The position about the percentage of educational expenditure in relation to total expenditure is given in the following table:

Table 26 : Percentage of Educational Expenditure on Total State Expenditure (1901-02)

(Percentages)

Sl.No.	*Provinces*	*Provincial*	*Municipal*	*Local*	*Total*
1.	Madras	7.4	14.3	10.3	8.9
2.	Bombay	6.3	53.6	8.1	10.0
3.	Bengal	7.0	25.1	1.5	8.0
4.	United Provinces	3.3	22.8	6.0	6.8
5.	Punjab	5.4	23.3	14.1	8.9
6.	Burma	3.0	16.2	7.6	4.1
7.	Central Provinces	4.8	71.1	16.5	8.8
8.	Assam	3.2	35.1	8.6	6.6
	Total	**5.3**	**25.3**	**7.0**	**7.8**

It would be seen that the older provinces - Bombay, Madras, Central Provinces, Punjab and Bengal - retained their pre-eminent position in regard to the percentage of Educational Expenditure to Total Expenditure. The position, however, changed when viewed from the point of view of Provincial expenditure. In this respect, the United Provinces, Central Provinces and Assam went much down in hierarchy.

To Conclude

The following conclusions can be drawn from the above analysis relating to financing of Indian education during the period ending with the Nineteenth century.

1. For the first two hundred years of the British rule, there was no effort on the part of the British government in India to provide any financial assistance for the education of the natives. There were, however, sporadic efforts by the individual rulers and a few enlightened Englishmen, motivated by their Indian counterparts, who established some institutions.
2. In 1813, a sum of Rs. One lakh was provided by the East India Company's Board of Directors for the revival and improvement of literature and encouragement of the learned natives of India and promotion of knowledge of sciences. Because of the ambiguity of the objectives stipulated in the Charter Act and, possibly, the half heartedness of the authorities who were charged with implementing the programme, there was no progress in achieving the target laid down by the company. Instead, there was controversy about the manner in which the objective was to be achieved. The matter was resolved by the government decision to promote English education and Western sciences as forcefully argued by Lord Macaulay, the then Legal Member of the Government General's Executive Council.
3. Some information is available about the quantum of expenditure prior to 1835, when the controversy was resolved. The expenditure in 1831 was about Rs. 2.55 lakh on 14 institutions supported by the Government. The Government provided Rs. 2.75 lakh as grants to various institutions. This included the stipends paid to students of oriental colleges amounting to Rs. 5 to Rs. 8 per month per student.
4. The total expenditure during 1886-87 was Rs. 2.52 crores, which increased to Rs.4.01 crore by the turn of the Century.
5. Considered province-wise, the largest expenditure on education was incurred by Bengal-the then seat of British administration, followed by Madras and Bombay. In terms of expenditure per thousand of population, however, Bengal ranked No. 6, while Madras and Bombay maintained their position. The same position emerged when the provinces were ranked in terms of average annual cost per pupil.

It may, therefore, be concluded that there was no definite, well thought out, policy about the allocation of resources for educational programmes for different provinces. A possible reason could be that the persuasive power of the provincial authorities and their contiguity to the decision making authorities could have been the more important deciding factors than the educational needs of the people.

6. Consistent with the policy laid down in the Despatches of 1854 and 1859, the bulk of expenditure was incurred on school education. Collegiate education was accorded lower priority. The same position emerged when the sectoral allocations in term of direct expenditure were analysed. The school sector was allocated about 88 per cent of the total direct expenditure. The position remained the same when average annual cost per student was analysed. Both in arts and professional colleges, there was a downslide in the cost per student in arts colleges and professional colleges, while there was a slight upsurge in the cost per student in primary and training schools.
7. It is also worth noting that there was substantial increase in the 'indirect' expenditure as compared to direct expenditure. Although there was proportionate decline in the expenditure on buildings, direction and inspection and scholarships, the expenditure on miscellaneous items more than doubled itself.
8. In pursuant to the declared policy of the government that it should absolve itself from establishing institutions and should encourage private participation in educational development, there was a down-sliding of percentage contribution from the government. From about 54 per cent in 1891-92 it came down to about 48 per cent in 1901-02. Fees and other private sources increased from about 46 per cent to 52 per cent. The fees in primary schools were, however, nominal.
9. There were wide differences between public and private contribution in respect of various provinces. Among the major provinces, Punjab and Bombay accounted for the largest percentage of government contribution i.e. about 61 per cent of the total expenditure. Curiously, Bengal, the seat of administration, could muster only about 32 per cent of public contribution.

To Sum Up

An analysis of the overall provincial and sectoral expenditure and the changing sources of finance leads up to confirm our tentative finding that the power of persuasion and not any well thought out policy of allocation of resources among various sections was the determining factor. It may not be far-fetched to conclude that a somewhat reluctant administration resorted to 'ad-hocism' rather than basing their decisions on a well thought out policy in this regard.

PART II

Financing Indian Education 1901-1947

The financing of Indian education during the first quarter of the twentieth century was based on the educational policy of the Government of India as enunciated in the Resolution of the Government of India in the Department of Education dated the 21st of February 1913. The Resolution itself mandated from the principles bearing on education in their wider aspects and under modern conditions, which were discussed at threc important conferences of experts and representatives of non-officials. The salient features of the Policy were:

1. In the forefront of that Policy, the Government of India's objective was the formation of the character of scholars and undergraduates under tuition. This was to be achieved by providing better educational conditions which were expected to accelerate social reform, spread female education and secure better teachers. Emphasis was also to be placed on personal hygiene of students.
2. The steady raising of standard of existing institutions would need adequate emphasis.
3. The scheme of primary and secondary education for the average scholars should steadily be diverted to more practical ends, e.g., by means of manual training, gardening, outdoor observations, practical teaching of geography, school excursions, etc. The provision should also be made for higher levels of work without having to go abroad.
4. For promoting research, good libraries, laboratories, systematic collaboration among the professors were considered to be essential pre-requisites.
5. Primary education had a predominant claim on public funds. There should be a large expansion of lower primary education, teaching the three R's with drawing, knowledge of the village map, nature study and physical exercises. Upper primary schools should be established at suitable places. The teacher pupil ratio should be between 30 and 40.
6. Education of girls should be: (a) practical (b) should pay attention to hygiene and surroundings of social life and (c) should employ female teachers.
7. At the secondary stage, private enterprise should be encouraged. To improve existing government secondary schools, trained graduate teachers should be employed; hostel facilities should be provided and manual training and improving science teaching should be emphasized.
8. The output of training colleges, technical schools and colleges should be expanded. Agriculture and veterinary science education should be promoted.
9. With regard to university education, the government recognised that the conditions were far from satisfactory. The five universities, existing at that time, were mainly affiliating institutions. It was considered necessary to set up federal type of universities as also to develop teaching facilities of the existing universities. Further, preliminary recognition of schools should be

given by local governments and not the universities. Emphasis was also to be laid on the training of teachers for both primary and secondary schools.

10. Lastly, the Government of India also desired that grants to oriental colleges should be given so as to enable them to secure better teachers. Further, scholarships to students should be given to pursue their education to the highest point.

It would appear that besides laying emphasis on formation of character and personal hygiene, which are amorphous in connotation and cannot be subjected to any statistical scrutiny, the Government of India laid emphasis on the following aspects which had financial implications:

(i) Raising of quality of existing institutions;
(ii) Expansion of primary education, particularly promoting girls' education;
(iii) Giving practical orientation to school education; and
(iv) Setting-up of teaching universities.

In the backdrop of these broad guidelines, we shall examine the various contours of financing of Indian education during the first half of the twentieth century.

Analysis of Expenditure

The first decade of the twentieth century did not show any enthusiasm on the part of the Imperial government to provide financial assistance for education. In fact, during the period 1907-08 to 1910-11, no grants were given to provinces. The only exceptions were a grant of Rs.10,000 per year to Punjab for the maintenance of European training classes at Sanawar and Rs. 10,000 for the Calcutta University for the establishment of Minto Professorship of Economics.

It was only after the creation of the Departments of Education in 1910-11 that a non-recurring grant of Rs. 93 lakh was distributed. That was followed by a grant of Rs. 50 lakh per year for popular education together with a further grant of Rs.10 lakh a year for university and secondary education from 1912-13. In the next year, recurring grant of Rs. 55 lakh was given for different forms of education, along with a small non-recurring grant of Rs. 0.95 lakh. In 1914-15, a non-recurring grant of Rs. 9 lakh was made for any educational purposes selected by the local governments. This was supplemented by a non-recurring grant of Rs.10 lakh for the construction of hostels by the University of Calcutta.

Phase I

1901-02 to 1921-22

The educational expenditure will be examined in terms of 'Objects' in Table 27 as follows:

Table 27 : Expenditure by Objects for the Year 1901-02 to 1921-22

Objects of Expenditure	*1901-02* Amount (in 000)	Percentage	*1911-12* Amount (in 000)	Percentage	*1921-22* Amount (in 000)	Percentage
(a) Direct						
Arts Colleges	2601	6.48	4799	6.1C	11042	6.20
Professional Colleges	1198	2.98	2253	2.86	5978	3.48
Secondary Schools	12684	31.63	20788	26.45	48727	28.55
Primary Schools	11876	29.59	20726	26.37	56908	33.10
Special Schools	2279	5.68	5375	6.85	13701	7.97
Total (a)	30638	76.36	53941	68.63	136356	79.30
(b) Indirect						
Buildings and equipment	2573	6.43	9730	12.40	1976	1.15
University	773	1.92	1587	2.01	7341	4.29
Direction	392	0.97	689	0.87	1399	0.80
Inspection	2153	5.36	4086	5.19	7936	4.61
Scholarships	912	2.27	1340	1.71	3176	1.83
Miscellaneous	2681	6.69	7219	9.18	13784	8.02
Total (b)	**9484**	**23.64**	**24651**	**31.37**	**35612**	**20.76**
Grand Total (a + b)	**40122**	**100.00**	**78592**	**100.00**	**171968**	**100.00**

Source: Progress Reports for various years.

This 'liberal' policy, made possible by favourable financial conditions, could not continue for long. The War of 1914-18, forced the governments to curtail their expenditure. The local governments were prohibited from drawing freely from the unspent balance of their Imperial grants. It was only in 1916-17 that a recurring grant of Rs. 30 lakh was provided for the training of teachers. A recurring grant of Rs. 30 lakh was also made available for primary education and an equal amount of Rs. 30 lakh was earmarked for agriculture, commercial and technical education.

We shall now analyse various facets of educational finance in two phases covering the period 1901-02 to 1921-22 in the first phase and the expenditure incurred between 1921-22 to 1946-47 in the second phase.

The following conclusions can be derived from the above table:

(i) There was sizeable increase in the total expenditure on education. From about Rs. 4 crore in 1901-02, to about Rs. 8 crore in 1911-12 and to about Rs. 17 crore in 1921-22.

(ii) In spite of the fact that in 1916-17, 4.3 per cent of public revenue was spent on education, a figure which compares favourably with the percentage spent by other countries, the total expenditure from all sources represented an abysmally low figure of Rs. 0.46 per head of the population and expenditure from public sources only Rs. 0.25 per head.

(iii) In 1901-02, direct expenditure (teachers' salaries, consumables etc.) accounted for more than three fourths of the total expenditure; the percentage decreased to 68.63 in 1911-12 but increased to about 79 per cent by 1921-22. This would seem to indicate that buildings, direction and inspection received lesser priority during the period.

(iv) The percentage of expenditure on primary education, which was expected to get higher priority, as indicated by the government, decreased from about 30 per cent of the total direct expenditure to about 26 per cent in 1911-12. The percentage, however, increased to 33 per cent by 1921-22 indicating that the government attempted to be in consonance with their oft declared policy.

(v) It has been reckoned that India occupied a very low position in terms of per capita expenditure on education, when compared to some advanced countries. For example, "the incidence of expenditure on education per head of population came to Rs. 12.81 in Scotland, Rs. 10.08 in England and Wales; Rs. 7.68 in Germany, Rs. 3.27 in France, Rs. 1.35 in British Honduras, Rs. 1.17 in Jamaica, Rs. 0.276 in Ceylon and Rs. 0.105 in British India[22]. Even when allowance is made for the difference in purchasing power of money, the amounts spent on education were insignificant.

(vi) The paucity of resources for primary education during the first two decades of the twentieth century had an adverse impact on the progress, particularly in the case of girls' education. In spite of the fact that the total number of pupils, including those in the primary classes of secondary schools in 1916-17 was 67,48,01 equivalent to 2.8 per cent of the total population - only 0.95 per cent of the female population was enrolled in schools against 4.5 per cent of males.

(vii) University education, though in a nascent stage, was given higher priority; arts colleges and universities received 8.4 per cent of the total expenditure in 1901-02. The percentage rose to more than 11 in 1921-22.

The government recognized the irregularity of the Imperial grants being given to the provinces and the waste that occurred in the process. According to the government:

"It is sometimes asserted that the Imperial assignments for education have largely been wasted. The system under which large sums of money are made available at irregular intervals and not as part of an orderly financial programme may conduce on the one hand to discontinuity of policy or on the other to spasmodic and hence reckless expenditure. Schemes which accommodate themselves to the amount of the allocation may not be ready. The ultimate cost of the programme may far exceed the sum available and uncertainty regarding the future may deter a local government upon a scheme the first instalment of which will involve subsequent enhanced expenditure, which they have no certainty of being in a position to meet. The danger of waste is particularly present in the case of non-recurring grants."[23]

Having said all this, the Report claims that the Imperial grants have not been wasted and they have been of inestimable value in remedying the old and recognized defects. This 'miracle' has been achieved by providing large sums to the local bodies, which have been able to raise the salaries of their teachers, the easiest way to spend money!

Expenditure by Sources

The main sources of finance for institutions of various types were provincial revenues, local funds, municipal funds and native state funds. Among the private sources, mention may be made of fees and donations from private philanthropy. For the first two decades of the twentieth century, the source-wise contribution is given in the table below:

Table 28 : Expenditure by Sources and Period

(Rs. in thousands)

Name of the Source	*1901-02*	*Percentage*	*1911-12*	*Percentage*	*1921-22*	*Percentage*
(a) Public Sources						
Provincial revenues	10391	25.89	20958	28.86	90230	49.12
Local funds	5887	14.68	10584	14.58	24731	13.46
Municipal funds	1538	3.84	2074	4.11	—	—
Native state revenues	1289	3.21	—	—	—	—
Total (a)	**19105**	**47.62**	**34516**	**47.55**	**114961**	**62.58**
(b) Private Sources						
Fees	12688	31.63	21909	30.19	38008	20.69
Other sources	8328	20.75	16161	22.26	30733	16.73
Total (b)	**21016**	**52.38**	**38070**	**52.45**	**68741**	**37.42**
Grand Total (a + b)	**40121**	**100.00**	**72586**	**100.00**	**183702**	**100.00**

Source: Progress reports for various years.

It would be seen in Table 28 that:

(a) Among the contribution from public sources, the main source of finance was the grants from the government including from local and municipal funds. The percentage of government contribution increased from about 48 in 1901-02 to about 63 in 1921-22. There was, however, sharp reduction in relative contribution from local and municipal funds; from about 18 per cent in 1901-02 to about 13 per cent in 1921-22. The contribution from private sources declined from about 52 per cent to 37 per cent during the period.

Table 29 : Source-wise Expenditure on Different Stages of Education, 1921-22

Stages of Education	*Source-wise Expenditure*				*Total Expenditure*
	Government Funds	*Boards*	*Fees*	*Other Sources*	
	23399	**11469**	**4632**	**3848**	**43348**
Primary Schools for boys	(53.9)	(26.5)	(10.7)	(8.9)	(100.00)
	13954	3887	17735	6641	42217
Secondary Schools	(33.1)	(9.2)	(42.0)	(15.7)	(100.00)
	7155	47	6288	5156	18646
University/Arts Colleges	**(38.5)**	**(–)**	**(33.7)**	**(27.8)**	**(100.00)**

(Figures in parentheses denote percentages)

Source: Progress of Education in India, 1916-22.

(b) The main reduction in the sources related to fees; the percentage plummeted from about 32 per cent to about 21 per cent. The decline in 'other sources', which comprised donations and private philanthropy, was marginal, i.e., from about 21 per cent to about 17 per cent.

From the above table it is seen that the government and local boards met about 80 per cent of the expenditure on primary schools. Secondary schools received about 42 per cent of the government munificence while universities had to be content with about 38 per cent of the government subsidy. This was in consonance with the declared policy of the government of giving higher priority to primary education in the allocation of resources by the government.

Dependence on Fees

The secondary and university sectors depended largely on fees and other sources. The average fee paid by a student in an arts college was Rs. 82.50 (1921-22) while the total cost to the government was Rs. 107.50 per student. This figure differed from province to province. For example, in the United Provinces, the annual cost of educating a student in a state administered college was Rs. 652 against Rs. 356 in an aided college. According to the government, the large difference in per student expenditure between government and private colleges was because of the higher quality of education provided in the former.

In primary schools, fees and other sources accounted for about 20 per cent of the total expenditure. The average annual expenditure on primary schools had risen from Rs. 203 to Rs. 315. This however, does not mean that the quality of education had improved. The increase in cost was mainly due to inflation as also the increase in teacher costs. The teacher who was available for Rs.14 per mensem before the war now required to be paid Rs.20 per month, in order to make both ends meet! The cost of educating a boy in a primary school which had risen from three *annas* (about 18 paise) to about 5 *annas* (30 paise) in the last forty years, had further risen to about eight annas (50 paise).

Expenditure in Provinces

Table 30 indicate the percentage of expenditure on education as also the total revenues in different provinces:

Table 30: Expenditure on education as percentage to total revenues in1921-22

Sl. No.	*Name of the Province**	*Population (in 000)*	*Revenue (in Rs.)*	*Rank*	*Educational Expenditure (figures in thousands)*	*Per capita educational expenditure*	*Rank*	*Percentage of educational Expenditure to Revenues*	*Rank*
1.	Madras	42319	117489	2	14252	0.33	6	12.4	6
2.	Bombay	19358	131073	1	17125	0.88	1	13.4	4
3.	Bengal	46695	83244	4	11877	0.25	9	14.3	3
4.	United Provinces	45376	100155	3	15141	0.33	6	15.1	2
5.	Punjab	20685	70969	5	8711	0.42	4	12.3	7
6.	Bihar and Orissa	34002	44262	7	5337	0.16	10	12.1	8
7.	Central Provinces and Berar	13913	47188	6	5308	0.38	5	11.4	10
8.	Assam	7606	18153	8	2314	0.30	8	12.7	5
9.	North West Frontier Provinces	2251	6286	10	1213	0.54	3	19.3	1
10.	Minor Administrations	1670	10854	9	1254	0.75	2	11.8	9
	Total	203885	629673		82593	0.41		13.1	

Relationship between the Provincial Revenues and Educational Expenditure

It would be interesting to measure the extent of relationship between expenditure on education in various provinces with, among others, the provincial revenues. For this purpose the data were subjected to Karl Pearson's method of

Rank Correlation. The following formula was used to measure the co-efficient of correlation (R).

$$R = 1 - \frac{6\Sigma D^2}{N^2 - N}$$

The following results are worth noting:

(a) Correlation between per capita expenditure on education and percentage of expenditure on education to provincial revenues: R = 0.357.
(b) Correlation between provincial revenues and percentage of educational expenditure to revenues: R = 0.162.
(c) Correlation between per capita revenues and per capita expenditure on education R = 0.25.

It may be concluded that there is no significant correlation between the per capita expenditure on education with the quantum of provincial revenues as also between the percentage of expenditure of revenues available in the provinces indicating that the effort on education was not necessarily dependent on the capacity to fund it. Further, the correlation between per capita revenues and per capita expenditure on education was almost negative. All the variables appear to be independent of each other. In other words, provinces were spending on education without taking into account their capacity to spend. For example, Bombay which ranked number one in regard to the size of revenues available to the province and again ranked number one in regard to the per capita expenditure on education, ranked number four in terms of percentage of educational expenditure to its revenues. Similarly, Central Provinces and Berar ranked number six in terms of the quantum of available revenues and five in terms of per capita expenditure on education ranked number ten as regards the percentage of expenditure to the size of the revenues. In fine, adhocism and not any planned system seems to have prevailed in the allocation and utilization of resources for education.

Impact of the First World War on Educational Finance

We shall conclude this portion by giving a glimpse of the adverse effect of the First World War on Indian education, particularly on the availability of financial resources for education. It may be recalled that the War was fought between two imperialist powers which, blinded by the brutal force at their command, intended to grab as much of the World's resources as they could. India, being a British Colony, had to bear the burnt of the man-made scourge, which devastated the socio-economic fabric of the entire world and decimated its cultural moorings.

The World War impacted the educational system of India very adversely. It led to the curtailment of educational budgets and abandonment of schemes of educational development. There was a large scale rise in prices, which resulted in the withdrawal of considerable number of scholars, whose parents were unable to keep their children in schools. The worst effected was primary education, in which the attendance decreased considerably. The rise in prices also necessitated a general revision of teachers' salaries, which accounted for bulk of the funds which were available for educational expansion. The cost of educating a scholar increased substantially during the quinquennium 1916-1922. Table 31 explains:

Table 31 : Average Annual Cost Per Scholar in Recognised Institutions (in Rs.)

Year	*General Education*			*Special Education*			
	Arts College	*Secondary Schools*	*Primary Schools*	*Professional Colleges*	*Training Schools*	*Other Schools*	*Total*
1916-17	152	28	5	318	157	38	11
1921-22	241	40	8	436	212	77	18
Increase per head	+89	+ 12	+3	+ 118	+55	+39	+7

Source: Progress of Education in India, 1917-22, p. 14.

The war also impelled the government of India as well as provincial governments to appoint 'Retrenchment Committees'. The members of most of these Committees were oblivious of the needs of the educational system, its significance in the acceleration of the process of socio-economic development and cultural regeneration. They recommended far reaching changes in the educational system; abandonment of a large number of schemes of qualitative and quantitative development of education; closing down of certain institutions and abolition of a few important posts/organisations, which were vital to the sustenance of the Indian education. It took decades for Indian education to come out of their sinister grip.

Phase II – 1922-47

The period under review coincided with the Constitutional Reforms under which control of education, with a few crucial exceptions, was passed on to Indian ministers. The period also witnessed the end of the severe economic distress caused by the prolonged War between the British imperialism and the German expansionism.

Mahatma Gandhi launched the 'Non-Cooperation Movement' which had far reaching consequences for education. Further, the curtailment in educational expenditure initiated by the Retrenchment Committees[24] appointed by the government of India and the provincial governments continued unabated.

In the back drop of these developments, we shall discuss the progress of educational expenditure during the period 1931-47.

Inter-sectoral Priorities

Table 32 below indicates allocation of resources for various sectors of education for the period 1931-32, 1941-42 and 1946-47:

Table 32 : The Expenditure on Education by Objects

(Figures in thousands)

Name of the Objects	*1931-32*		*1941-42*		*1946-47*	
	Expenditure	*Percentage*	*Expenditure*	*Percentage*	*Expenditure*	*Percentage*
(a) Direct Expenses						
Arts colleges	16622	6.14	24123	7.86	43915	7.62
Professional colleges	8138	3.00	13269	4.33	27492	4.77
Secondary schools	81300	29.94	65063	21.22	123174	21.36
Primary schools	81260	29.92	122665	40.01	232882	40.39
Training schools/colleges	5595	2.06	5109	1.67	11302	1.96
Other special schools	13000	4.79	8328	2.72	14523	2.52
Universities	13208	4.87	13642	4.45	22977	3.98
Total (a)	219163	80.72	252199	82.26	476265	82.60
(b) Indirect Expenses						
Direction	1720	0.63	11578	3.78	18238	3.16
Inspection	9688	3.57	*	*	*	
Buildings	18197	6.70	15658	5.11	28453	4.93
Miscellaneous	22766	8.38	27144	8.85	53657	9.31
Total (b)	52371	19.28	54380	17.74	100348	17.40
Grand Total (a + b)	**271534**	**100.0**	**308579**	**100.0**	**576613**	**100.0**

Source: Quinquennial Progress Reports, various years. *Included under Direction.

The following may be noted:

1. There was sizeable increase in the overall expenditure on education; from about Rs. 27.15 crore in 1931-32, the expenditure rose to more than double i.e. Rs. 57.66 crore in 1946-47. Much of the increase was accounted for by school education which increased from about Rs. 18.1 crore in 1931-32 to Rs. 38.17 crore in 1947. Within the school education sector, primary education received bulk of the increase; from Rs. 8 crore in 1931-32, the expenditure went up to about Rs. 23 crores. This was in consonance with the declared policy of the government of India to accord higher priority to primary education.
2. The percentage of expenditure on Direct objects, went up by about 2 percentage points; from about 81 per cent in 1931-32 to 83 per cent in 1946-47. This shows that items like teachers' salaries, repair of buildings and provision of equipment and consumables were given a somewhat preferential treatment.
3. There was considerable increase in expenditure on primary education; from about 30 per cent of the total expenditure in 1931-32 it went up to about 40 per cent in 1946-47. Correspondingly, the percentage of expenditure on

secondary education declined from about 30 per cent in 1931-32 to about 21 per cent in 1946-47. As already stated, the increase in primary education was in consonance with the policy of the government of giving primary education a higher priority in the allocation of resources and secondary and university education to be left mainly to private enterprise subject, however, to some government assistance under the grant-in-aid system.

4. There was some increase in the expenditure on girls' education as against boys' education. For example, while the expenditure on institutions for boys increased from Rs. 20.45 crore in 1926-27 to Rs. 22.01 crore in 1931-32, for girls' institutions the increase was from 2.98 crore to 3.65 crores during the same period. This meant that while the expenditure on girls' institutions was 12.01 per cent of the total expenditure in 1926-27, it went up to 13.42 per cent of the total expenditure in 1931-32. The substantial disparity between the expenditure on boys and girls institutions, however, remained.
5. Curiously enough, there was an increase in the expenditure on university and higher education, which rose from about 14 per cent to 16 per cent. This was, however, mainly due to the increase in the percentage of expenditure on professional colleges. There was a significant down slide in the percentage of expenditure on universities; from about 5 per cent to 4 per cent.

Gender Disparities

The inequitable distribution of expenditure for boys and girls institutions was highlighted in respect of different provinces. It was reported:

"It would be unreasonable to expect that during a period of acute financial stringency, the necessary funds could be provided in a moment of time, but even the modest additional funds, which were actually available have not been equitably distributed between boys and girls education and that little efforts have been made to correct the disproportion in expenditure between the sexes.

"For example, whereas in the United Provinces, expenditure on boys education rose by Rs. 32 lakh during the quinquennium (1927-32), that on girls education, rose by only Rs. 4 lakh. In Bihar, an increase of expenditure of Rs. 87,000 on girls' instruction compares very unfavourably with that of Rs. 11 lakh on boys' institutions. The figures convey the awkward impression that in time of financial stringency the first item to be thrown over board is that of girls education."

Further, "a pleasing exception to this attitude of neglect is in Madras, whose annual expenditure on girls' education rose by Rs. 24 lakh during the quinquennium. The additional expenditure on boys' education, however, amounted to Rs. 64 lakh so even, in this province, the disproportion is being accentuated.[25]

The next highest additional expenditure was in Punjab, where the amount reached Rs. 9 lakh in girls institutions as against an increased expenditure of Rs. 45 lakh for boys institutions".[26]

The Bengal Report was much more forthright. It lamented:

"When we consider the history of women's education, there is reason to be disquieted at the haphazard manner in which it is developing. The history of men's education should have been fruitful of warnings at least, but those warnings have been unheeded and women's education is following the same ill-advised, disordered path. The truth is that it has not yet received sufficient attention; it has been regarded as of secondary importance; incidental not vital. In the province, which has the largest female population and the largest number of women's institutions, there is no woman as yet on the headquarters staff to plan and control. At present, if women's education is expanding, it is expanding as the result of impulses from below, not from above. The income from fees in all women's institutions together has risen from Rs. 11(1/2) lakh to Rs. 14(1/2) lakh, but the contribution from provincial revenues to this most important and potentially fruitful of all creative public duties has actually decreased. It is to be hoped that this apathy and lack of policy will soon be replaced by some wise, well planned comprehensive scheme buttressed by adequate financial support".[27]

Expenditure by Sources and Periods

The following table indicates the overall expenditure on education by sources for different years:

Table 33 : Expenditure by Sources and Periods

(Figures in thousands)

Name of the Objects	*1931-32*		*1941-42*		*1946-47*	
	Expenditure	*Percentage*	*Expenditure*	*Percentage*	*Expenditure*	*Percentage*
Public						
Provincial Revenues	124600	45.83	135173	43.80	259589	45.04
Local funds	43819	16.12	26327	8.53	51867	8.99
Municipal funds	—	—	18985	6.15	32154	5.57
Native state funds	—	—	—	—	—	—
Total (a)	168419	61.95	180485	58.48	343610	59.60
Private						
Fees	62270	22.91	85459	27.69	152222	26.39
Other sources	41168	15.14	42637	13.82	80781	14.01
Total (b)	103438	38.05	128095	41.42	233003	40.40
Grand Total (a + b)	**271857**	**100.0**	**308580**	**100.0**	**576613**	**100.0**

It would be noted that:

1. The bulk of expenditure was provided by the government and local boards. But there was a down-slide in the government contribution over the years. While in 1931-32, the contribution from the government was about 62 per cent of total expenditure, it decreased to about 58 per cent in 1941-42; and rose to about 60 per cent in 1946-47.

2. Correspondingly, the contribution from private sources including fees, increased from about 38 per cent to 42 per cent in 1941-42 to go down to 40 per cent in 1946-47. The bulk of the increase was in respect of student fees which went up from about 23 per cent to about 28 per cent in 194142 to go down to 26 per cent in 1946-47.

Source-wise Expenditure on Institutions for Males and Females

It is interesting to analyse the source wise expenditure for institutions exclusively for males and females. Table 34 indicate the position for 1937.

Table 34 : Expenditure on Institutions by Sources in 1937

Name of the Objects	*Expenditure (in Rs.)*	*Percentage of Expenditure from*				*Average Cost Per Scholar**		
		Government Fund	*Local Fund*	*Fees*	*Other Sources*	*Rs.*	*A.*	*P.*
Institutions for males								
(a) Arts colleges	1,62,37,207	37.7	0.2	48.6	13.5	197	4	0
(b) Professional colleges	74,38,848	61.1	2.1	30.7	6.1	357	13	9
(c) High schools	5,31,37,619	29.9	5.4	53.8	11.8	49	8	9
(d) Middle schools	2,41,53,194	37.3	26.1	27.5	9.1	20	2	3
(e) Primary schools	6,98,00,051	49.4	34.5	6.5	9.6	7	11	5
(f) Special schools	1,46,76,118	58.4	5.2	15.8	20.6	56	15	3
Total	18,54,43,037	42.3	18.4	28.1	11.2	15	14	10
Institutions for females								
(a) Arts colleges	7,17,594	49.3	0.8	32.3	17.8	327	6	10
(b) Professional colleges	3,53,417	82.5	—	12.7	4.8	803	0	10
(c) High schools	89,50,405	38.5	2.0	37.7	21.5	79	3	0
(d) Middle schools	45,69,658	40.6	15.4	16.7	27.3	27	13	8
(e) Primary schools	1,39,79,988	42.3	39.1	4.1	14.5	9	5	8
(f) Special schools	26,48,833	63.4	2.4	5.8	28.4	137	3	1
Total	3,12,19,895	43.5	20.5	16.5	19.5	17	6	9
Indirect Expenditure								
(a) Direction and Inspection	1,17,11,885	90.9	9.0	—	0.1	—	—	—
(b) Universities	1,43,83,507	37.8	—	43.4	18.8	—	—	—
(c) Board of secondary and Intermediate education	4,35,905	13.4		86.3	0.03			
(d) Miscellaneous	3,73,75,145	33.9	12.8	19.1	24.2	—	—	—
Total	6,39,06,442	45.1	9.1	21.5	24.3			
Grand Total	**28,05,09,374**	**43.1**	**16.5**	**25.3**	**15.1**			

Note: * = In the pre-independence period, cost was expressed in Rs. Annas and Paises. A Rupee was equivalent to 16 Annas and one Anna was equal to 4 paise. Thus a rupee was equal to 64 paise.

The following may be stated in regard to the above tables.

1. On an average, the government was providing larger funds for institutions for females (43.5 per cent) than the institutions for males (42.3 per cent).

This was in contrast to the position that existed in 1927-32 (see Gender Disparities).

2. Professional colleges, both for males and females, were the largest beneficiaries of government munificence, the percentage being about 61 for institutions for males and 82.5 for institutions for females.
3. Primary schools (including middle schools) also received large subsistence from the government. The expenditure was 66 per cent for institutions for males and about 83 per cent for institutions for females. This was, as already stated, in consonance with the government's declared policy of promoting elementary education.
4. Local bodies played a very minor role in financing educational programmes except in the case of primary education for which they provided 61 per cent of the over all expenditure for males and about 56 per cent for educational institutions for females.
5. Fees played a minor role in financing primary education both for males and females. In the case of middle schools, however, 27.5 per cent of the expenditure for institutions for males and 16.7 per cent of expenditure for females was met by fees. Such a large percentage of fee contribution must have been a great deterrent for education at this stage of school sector.

Expenditure by Provinces

In order to find out the extent of relationship between the total provincial revenues and expenditure on education from government sources, the percentage of expenditure in education from government to total provincial revenues was calculated for the years 1931-32 and 1936-37. The percentages were ranked and Rank Correlation Coefficients was calculated by Karl Pearsons' method.

Table 35 indicates the percentage for the two years under study:

Table 35: Percentage of Expenditure on Education to Total Provincial Revenues

Name of the Provinces	*1931-32*		*1936-37*	
	Percentage	*R1*	*Percentage*	*R2*
Madras	15.74	3	15.8	3
Bombay	12.42	5	13.0	6
Bengal	13.13	4	12.0	7
United Provinces	16.89	1	16.8	2
Punjab	15.89	2	15.1	4
Bihar and Orissa (average)	10.26	8	14.9	5
Central Provinces and Berar	10.41	7	10.0	9
Assam 11.04	6	10.7	8	
North West Frontier	5.20	10	11.7	7
Smaller Administrations (average) (Delhi, Ajmer, Marware and Baluchistan etc.)	9.26	9	19.6	1

R (0.36) is insignificant, indicating that there is no significant correlation between the provincial revenues and the expenditure on education. Both of them operate independently of each other. This is in consonance with the position arrived at earlier in relation to the similar data calculated for the years 1921-22.

To Conclude

We have waded through the labyrinthine pathways of educational finance during the period when India became a British Colony. It was seen that in the initial stages, the British authorities were not very enthusiastic about providing any financial support for the education of the Indians, whom they had subjugated. It was only in 1813 that the ruling East India Company set side a sum of Rs. 1 lakh for the education of the natives. Even this insignificant amount resulted into a fierce controversy which was resolved after twenty two years in 1835, with the acceptance by the Governor General of the policy set out in Lord Macaulay's brilliantly drafted, but palpably arrogant, Minute of 2nd February 1835. By the turn of the 19th Century, an amount of Rs. 4 crore was being spent on education of teeming millions numbering about 24 crore.

The onset of the 20th Century saw an awakening of the British authorities towards the education of Indians. It was Lord Curzon (1901-05), who took some interest in Indian education. Since then, there had been sizeable increase in the overall educational budgets of the Imperial and provincial governments. Besides, there were also non-official attempts to expand educational facilities particularly at the primary education level. They were, perhaps, too far ahead of the time. The Bill to provide free and compulsory education to children introduced by Gopal Krishan Gokhale in 1910 in the Legislative Council was thrown out because of the stiff opposition of the British bureaucracy who had the majority in the Council. The bills introduced subsequently by other Indians met the same fate.

The period 1900-1947 was, not uneventful. It witnessed attempts at systematization of the programmes of qualitative improvement and quantitative expansion of Indian education in terms of policy statement issued by the British authorities in 1913. The period was however, marred by two World Wars and prolonged economic depression with the consequent squeeze on educational budgets which thwarted educational progress.

The later part of the 20th Century also witnessed prolonged political unrest leading to the Non-Cooperation Movement and defiance of the British autocracy, which impacted educational development very adversely. Indian nationalism demanded complete freedom from British suzerainty, which was met with brutal force by the British authorities. This period was besmeared with the blood of innocent Indians, who demanded their right to live with dignity. The massacre at Jalianwala Bagh is an eloquent testimony to the arrogance of the British authorities, who had the temerity to declare publicly that they wanted Indians to have a taste of the ferocity of the British might. The brutalities remained unabated and thousands of Indians were incarcerated and hanged without trial.

As a sop to estranged Indians, Constitutional Reforms like Dyarchy (1919) and Provincial Autonomy (1935) were introduced. But the demand for complete freedom of the country from British hegemony remained non-negotiable.

At last the British government realized the futility of holding under its control a country, which was in perpetual rebellion. It decided to leave the country but only after partitioning it into two parts. The thoughtless vivisection of the country led to the unorganised exchange of population in which millions were displaced from their hearths and homes and innumerable lives were lost.

All through this period, educational development and financing took a back seat!

The salient points made in the analysis of financing of Indian education are summarised below:

1. There was sizeable increase in the expenditure on education during the first half of the 20th Century (1901-1947); from an insignificant Rs. 4 crore in 1901-02, the expenditure increased to about Rs. 58 crore in 1946-47 indicating over 14 times increase. During this period, the total enrolment increased from about 45 lakh to about 183 lakh i.e. about 4 times. It is, however, difficult to vouchsafe the adequacy of funds for education in the period under review. Much of the expenditure would have been counter balanced by the inflation that overtook the Indian economy particularly in the aftermath of the First World War.
2. The per capita expenditure, on education, rose from Rs. 0.105 in 1916-17, to Rs. 1.4 in 1946-47. As already stated the bulk of the increase was counter balanced by the inflation that affected Indian economy, particularly because of the two wars that devastated the Indian economic system. The post-War period led to drastic curtailment of budgets and abandonment of schemes of educational development. The large scale rise in prices also led to withdrawal of students from schools, particularly at the primary stage of education. The cost of education skyrocketed.
3. In spite of the fact that government policy was to promote primary education, it did not get requisite priority during the first decade. At the beginning of the 20th century, primary education received about 30 per cent of the total expenditure on education. The percentage decreased to about 26 in 1911-22. It was only in the forties that the expenditure on primary education increased to about 40 per cent of the total. Correspondingly, the expenditure on university education including Arts colleges increased from about 8 per cent of the total expenditure in 1901-02 to about 10 per cent by 1921-22; it further increased to about 11 per cent in 1946-47. The brunt of the reduced outlays was borne by secondary education, which declined from about 32 per cent of the total expenditure in 1901-02 to about 30 per cent in 1931-32 and further decreasing to about 21 per cent in 1941-42 and

1946-47. This seemed to be the result of the declared policy of the government that secondary education should be left largely to private enterprise while the government would provide financial assistance for its qualitative development through a system of grants-in-aid.

4. The main source of finance for education has been the Imperial and provincial grants including the contribution from local bodies. In 1901-02, the government provided about 47 per cent of the total resources for education. The contribution increased to about 62 per cent by 1921-22 but decreased to about 60 per cent by 1946-47. The second major source of income for education was student fees which was 31 per cent of the total income in 1901-02 and about 26 per cent in 1946-47. The 'other sources' plummeted from about 22 per cent in 1901-02 to about 17 per cent in 1921-22 and further to about 14 per cent in 1946-47.
5. In spite of the government - both Imperial and provincial- being the main source of educational finance, the inputs from the government, especially the provincial governments were ad-hoc in nature and unplanned. In order to find out the extent of relationship between the 'capacity' of the government as reflected in the size of the revenues available to them and their 'willingness' as indicated by the actual expenditure incurred on education, Rank Correlations by Karl Pearson's method were calculated. The correlation between per capita expenditure on education and percentage of educational expenditure to provincial revenues was insignificant. The same was the case of correlation between provincial revenues and percentage of educational expenditure to provincial revenues.
6. There was iniquitous expenditure on education for boys and girls; the sufferer generally being institutions for girls. The position, however, improved from 1937 onwards.

References

1. Calcutta University Commission, 1917-19, p. 39.
2. Selections from Educational Records, p. 378.
3. Despatch of 1854, as reported in the Indian Education Commission (1882-83) pp. 22-23.
4. *Ibid.*, p. 352.
5. The Indian Education Commission 1882-83, op. cit, p. 355.
6. The Indian Education Commission 1882-83, op. cit, p. 355.
7. Progress of Education in India, 1917-22; p. 108.
8. As reported in the Quinquennial Progress Report, 1907-12, Department of Education, Government of India; pp. 84-85.
9. Report of the Indian Retrenchment Committee, 1922-23, Calcutta, 1928.
10. *Ibid.*, p. 3.
11. In a despatch of 1659, the Court of Directors had declared their earnest desire, by all possible means, to propagate the gospel. Missionaries were allowed to embark on their ships. (Selections from Educational Records (Part I, 1781-

1839, p. 7). It was only after the Battle of Plassey (1757), on the assumption of wider powers by the Company, that the policy was reversed and strict religious neutrality was declared in regard to educational matters.

12. Indian Educational Policy: Resolution of the Government of India in the Home Department; Nos. 199-211, Calcutta dated 11th March 1904. p. 457.
13. H. Sharp; Selections from Educational Records, *ibid.*
14. *Ibid.*, p. 10.
15. *Ibid.*, p. 457.
16. *Ibid.*, p. 458.
17. Arthur Howell, op. cit., p. 21.
18. Arthur Howell, op. cit., p. 22.
19. The data about finance was obtained from the following sources:
    (a) Progress of Education Vols. I and II for various years;
    (b) Indian Educational Policy: Resolution of the Government of India in the Home Department No.199-211 dated Calcutta, the 11th March, 1904.
20. R. Nathan, Progress of Education in India 1897-98 to 1901-02, Calcutta, 1904, p. 447.
21. Progress of Education India; op. cit., p. 449.
22. Report of the Commissioner of Education, Washington for the year ended June 30, 1916, p. 668, Quoted in Progress of Education in India, 1911-16.
23. Progress of Education; 1911-16, p. 16.
24. The havoc caused by the Central Government's Retrenchment Committee has been discussed in a separate chapter.
25. Progress Education in India, 1927-32, pp. 169-70.
26. *Ibid.*, p. 168.
27. Bengal Report, pp. 77-78 quoted in Progress of Education in India, 1927-32, pp. 169-70.

5

Significant Events that Impacted Education

The British government decided to terminate its suzerainty in 1947. Thus, only a period of about 90 years – 1854 to 1947 was available to the colonial administration to organise the educational system in the country. During this period, five major events occurred that affected the progress of education. The first was the war of India's independence that erupted in 1857. It had very little impact on the progress of education because it was short lived and confined to a few areas/ regions in the country. The second event was the onset of the natural calamities like bubonic plague, cyclone and earthquake that visited this country in the closing years of the nineteenth century and spread death and devastation in certain parts. The third major event that almost halted the progress of education and gave rise to a number of problems was the First World War between two imperialist powers – Britain and Germany– hell bent upon imposing their supremacy over the world. The war was followed by acute economic depression that befell the country in 1914 and lasted till almost the mid-twenties of the twentieth century.

The fourth major event was the Non-Cooperation Movement launched by the Indian National Congress in the early twenties to protest the high handedness of the British rulers.

The fifth major event that impacted education was the Constitutional reforms that, among other things, divided the administrative departments of the Provinces into Reserved and Transferred subjects. Education became a transferred subject under Indian Ministers elected by the people, while the control of the reserved subjects was retained by the British administrators.

A discussion about the events and their impact on the educational system follows.

1. The First War of India's Independence, 1857

The first war of India's independence, euphemistically called by the British the 'Sepoy Mutiny' was caused by various factors. The foremost among them was the belief among the Indians that the British were bent on converting them to Christianity. The Act XXXI of 1850, which enabled the converts to Christianity to inherit property, aroused the fear about the evangelical intentions of the Company. Further, provision had been made for Christian bishops/ministers to have access to schools and the Bible was placed in every school and library. The policy of introducing non-religious, secular education affirmed by the Court of Directors and various Governor Generals was ridiculed by the evangelists. In 1839, Dr. Duff denounced Lord Aukland's minute (1836) as "remarkable above all for its education without religion; its plans without a Providence, its ethics without God."[1] The Doctrine of Lapse which denied the childless princes to adopt a successor also confirmed this belief. Further, the British Officers were very rude and arrogant towards the natives. The British judges were also partial – they hardly convicted the Europeans. The immediate cause, however, was the introduction of the new Enfield rifle cartridges, which were heavily greased with animal fat. The news spread among the soldiers that the grease was a mix of cow's as well pig's fat – abhorrent to Hindus and Muslims alike.[1]

Mangal Pande was the first native soldier to trigger the revolt. He shot at his sergeant and subsequently wounded the British Adjutant on 29th March, 1857. The revolt of the native soldiers spread to Meerut on 29th of April, 1857. The mutineers of Meerut reached Delhi on 11th of May, 1857 and declared Bahadur Shah Zafar as the King. The rebellion spread to Kanpur, where it was joined by Nana Sahib, who proclaimed himself as the Peshwa. The other freedom fighters, who participated in the war of independence, were Rani Laxmi Bai of Jhansi, Tantia Tope, Jawala Prasad, Azimullah Khan, Kunwar Singh of Arrah in Bihar, Begum of Awadh – (Hazarat Mahal), and a number of others who challenged the might of the British empire.

It is not intended to give a blow by blow account of the various phases of the struggle for India's independence. Suffice it to say that enough blood was shed on both sides. Unfortunately, the unmitigated zeal to fight for India's freedom from foreign subjugation, even at the cost of one's life, could not sustain the struggle for long. Lack of organisation and leadership also played their sinister role in reaching this unfortunate end.

The reprisals by the British soldiers were extremely brutal, inhuman and horrific. No Indian soldiers were left alive after their positions were over-run. The male members in the entire villages, which were suspected to be the abodes of the rebellious elements, were hanged without the modicum of any trial. According to Macaulay, in Peshawar 'forty men were blown off at once from the mouths of cannon – their heads, arms flying in all directions.'[2] The reluctant Mughal King, Bahadur Shah Zafar, was arrested. His four elder sons were killed in cold blood and their heads were brought in a platter to be presented to their father. Later on the King was deported to Rangoon (now Yangon) in a very humiliating condition.

The dethroned king suffered untold atrocities, humiliation, indignities and deprivations at the hands of his captors. Being a poet, he expressed his anguish in a poem, which is full of pathos, disappointments and utter helplessness. Rendered in English, it would read like this:

"I cannot reconcile myself to this deserted place;
"Who has been able to set store with this transitory world?
"Tell my aspirations to go somewhere else;
"They have no place in my tormented soul;
And then the heart rending cry of anguish :
"How much unfortunate is Zafar that for his grave;
"He could not get two yards of land in the vicinity of his beloveds."[3]

Thus ended the story of the first war of India's independence. India had to wait for ninety years to attain its most coveted goal of political emancipation from the British masters.

The Aftermath of the War and its Impact on the Educational System

There is no particular mention of the impact of the war of India's independence on the educational system of India. Perhaps, the period when parts of India were up in arms was too short to have any positive or negative impact on Indian education.

The turmoil however, caused fundamental changes in the administrative system of the country. The ageing East India Company was dismembered and the administration of the country was taken over by the British Crown. Thus the war of India's independence gave rise to the termination of a private company which had presided over the fortunes of the Indian people for about 110 years. This, among other things, led to the acceleration of the process of educational development.

2. The Scourge of Natural Calamities

The death and devastation through natural calamities happened to hapless Indians in the closing years of the 19th century. In 1876-78, India experienced the 'Great Famine' in which 6 to 10 million people are reported to have died. In 1892, various parts of India were recovering from the effects of scarcity, which though not declared as famine, caused severe distress in parts of Madras and the Deccan. A deficient monsoon in 1895 and the failure of the winter rains, caused serious deficiency in the crops and by the end of May, 1896, more than a quarter million persons were in receipt of relief to satisfy their pangs of hunger. It was in the Allahabad Division of the United Provinces, known as Bundelkhand, that famine first made its appearance. In the Indian famine of 1899-1900, the loss of human life is estimated to have been around 1.25 million in British India alone, of whom a quarter million belonged to native states. Out of the total number of deaths, about 2.3 lakh died of cholera and small pox brought about by famine conditions.[4] Recent research, including the work of Mike Davis and Amartya Sen attribute most of the effects of these famines to the British Policy of neglect.[5]

Bubonic Plague

Bubonic plague broke out in Bombay in 1896. It spread to most provinces. The total number of deaths from the first outbreak up to March, 1902 were reported to be 8,20,000. They were, however, half of the actual deaths since many of the deaths in the provinces were not reported. The epidemic paralysed industries. It spread from Bombay to Karachi by sea and to Sukkar and other principal towns of Sind. The plague occurred mainly in district towns in almost all the provinces of the country.

To make matters worse, an earthquake of exceptional severity visited Assam and north-eastern portion of Bengal. According to the Geological Survey of India, "at about quarter past five in the afternoon of 12th June, 1897, there burst on the western portion of Assam, an earthquake, which for violence and extent, has not been surpassed by any of which we have historical record. Lasting about two and a half minutes, it had not eased at Shillong before an area of 1,50,000 square miles had been laid in ruins; all means of communication disrupted, the hills rent and cast down in landslips and the plains fissured and riddled with vents, from which sand and water poured in most astounding quantities, and ten minutes had not elapsed from the time when Shillong was laid in ruins before about one and three quarter million of square miles had felt a shock, which was everywhere recognised as one quite out of the common."[6]

Because of the hour at which the shocks occurred, the loss of life was relatively small. The most noteworthy damage included the destruction of bridges, railway lines and of crops. The damage to river banks led to the exceptionally serious floods in lower Assam.

Another calamity that visited the Gulf of Bengal was the cyclone which occurred between 21st and 24th October, 1897, particularly, in Chittagong. It is estimated that this calamity caused 50,000 deaths. This was followed by another cyclone that occurred in 1902 in Dacca.

These calamities played havoc with the progress of education, particularly during the period 1891-1896. There was reduction in the number of schools and pupils; largely in the provinces affected by these natural calamities. For example, in Bombay Presidency, there was a reduction of 5.3 per cent and 4.9 per cent in the number of schools and pupils respectively. In Assam, the percentage reduction in schools during the period under review was 5, although the enrolment increased by 4 per cent. The largest decline in the number of schools was in Bengal (about

9 per cent) and in student enrolment (about 4 per cent). We have given a detailed account of the loss suffered by the educational system in a separate chapter.

3. The First World War and its Aftermath

The First World War resulted in severe economic distress. Financial stringency made the curtailment of education budgets inevitable. This led to the non-introduction of new schemes of educational development; some of the important schemes were postponed. In some cases even the normal budgets had to be considerably reduced. A Retrenchment Committee was appointed at the Centre. The same process was repeated in the provinces. We shall first take up the Retrenchment Committee appointed by the Government of India and the confusion caused by its recommendations on the education system.

(i) Retrenchment Committee

The Central Government's Retrenchment Committee under Lord Inchcape made far reaching recommendations, relating to the curtailment of the Central Government's expenditure on education in areas directly controlled by it; these recommendations were, unfortunately, accepted. Even some of the bizarre recommendations were agreed to. The recommendations included, among others, the following:

(i) Amalgamation of the Department of Education and Health with that of Revenue and Agriculture – an unusual combination;

(ii) Abolition of the post of Education Commissioner with the Government of India. While the Government of India did not abolish the post, they attached additional responsibilities to it and kept in abeyance the creation of separate posts of Superintendents of Education for Delhi and Ajmer-Merware. The Education Commissioner had to hold the additional charge of the duties of the Superintendent of Education, Delhi and Ajmer-Merware. It is obvious that the management under which a single officer was entrusted with many responsibilities of a diverse nature-specialist, advisory, administrative and executive – must have been necessarily very unsatisfactory. The Education Commissioner with the Government of India, who combined the offices of Superintendent of Education in Delhi and Ajmer-Merware, with other duties, had little time to do more than paying a flying visit to Ajmer in the course of a year. Further, this officer in his capacity as Superintendent of Education submitted proposals to the local administration, who, in turn, submitted them to the Government of India. At that stage, these proposals had to be examined by the same officer in his capacity as Education Commissioner with the Government of India. "A system with the above accumulation of defects is not, and clearly cannot be, in the interests of educational administration..."[7]

The Inchcape Committee's other recommendation in respect of educational retrenchment which needed reconsideration were: (i) closing down of the University of Delhi and (ii) the abolition of the Central Advisory Board of Education and the

Bureau of Education. We shall discuss these seemingly thoughtless recommendations in detail.

(ii) Closing Down the Delhi University

The importance of improving the facilities for higher education in the then Imperial City of Delhi was recognised as early as 1912, when the new capital was founded. The original proposal was for the establishment of a Government College, which would eventually develop into a university. For various reasons, no college could be established. The Calcutta University Commission (1917-19) pleaded for the decentralisation of higher education and the establishment of unitary teaching and residential universities at important educational centres. The acceptance of this policy, so far as the University of Punjab was concerned, was expected to result in the centralisation of university teaching at Lahore and the relegation to the background of the Delhi Colleges, which would have been isolated from the life and activities of the University. In December, 1919, the Chief Commissioner of Delhi invited the representatives of the three colleges in Delhi and certain officials of the Education Department of the Government of India to a conference for discussing the lines on which a university might be established.

The conference resolved:

(i) that a unitary teaching university should be established at Delhi;

(ii) that the university, which was to consist of a central block of buildings including lecture rooms; laboratories, library, etc. for university work, should be surrounded by halls and hostels to be built by colleges; and that

(iii) instruction in the existing colleges should provide intermediate stage of education and teaching beyond that stage should be transferred to the new university.

It appears that the representatives of the colleges, who were present at the conference of 1919 did not fully realise the implications of the expression: "unitary teaching and residential university". Their considered views are embodied in the following resolution passed unanimously at a meeting of the college representatives in June, 1921:

1. The establishment in Delhi of an independent examining university, with inter-collegiate lectures as a general rule and university teaching in special subjects, is early desired.
2. The primary condition asked for was that at least two thirds of the controlling body of the university should be representatives of the colleges.
3. This body should be given statutory powers to determine the date of move to a new site and of separation of the intermediate classes from the University, the agreement of all three colleges being necessary on these two questions.
4. The colleges also thought that for the present, separation of the intermediate stage from B.A. classes was impracticable; at any rate until the neighbouring universities had effected such separation.

Government of India's Memorandum

The Government of India's Memorandum in December 1921, gave the general outlines of the University:

"The existing colleges in Delhi city would become intermediate colleges. Government would erect University buildings including laboratories, lecture halls, etc. on the Raisina site at the cost of Rs. 34 lakhs (inclusive of furniture). The total eventual recurring cost would be about Rs. 2 lakhs a year rising gradually to Rs. 4 lakhs against which fees may be reckoned at Rs. 30,000 per annum. The existing institutions would build their own halls.

It was proposed to commence work with the existing colleges. The colleges insisted that the term unitary should be interpreted liberally and the colleges should be associated directly in the teaching work of the university. The joint Committee, to which the Delhi University bill was referred for consideration merely made provision under sub-section 7 of the Act for the gradual adoption of the colleges to the organisation of the university of the type contemplated.

The University Starts Functioning

The Delhi University started functioning with two faculties – a faculty of arts and a faculty of sciences and three recognised colleges teaching up to degree standard. It also instituted faculty of Law and recognised four intermediate colleges. The total number of scholars was 1215 against 603 in 1921.

It appears that at the initial stages, there was very little enthusiasm about the setting up of a unitary type of university at Delhi. The existing three colleges strongly objected to the proposal to destroy their identity and individuality, and in particular to the proposed separation of intermediate classes from the university. It was felt that "Delhi cannot, at any rate for another generation, supply either the academic material or financial resources for the development of university of this type. In these circumstances, the possible solution of the present difficulties would be the abolition of the university."[8]

The Inchcape Committee Recommendations

In the backdrop of these developments, the Inchcape Committee, which had been formed to suggest measures for economy in government expenditure, recommended sweeping changes in the educational set up at the central level, not all of which were based on a well thought out policy of educational development in India. As already stated, these recommendations included the abolition of the recently created Central Advisory Board of Education and the Central Board of Education as also the post of the Education Commissioner to the Government of India.

About Delhi University, the Committee ordained

"We understand, there is no lack of facilities of university education in Northern India and consider that the present financial conditions do not justify the *formation* (emphasis added) of a new university."

Academia React

The Committee was blissfully ignorant of the fact that the university at Delhi had already come into existence. Quite naturally this caused utmost consternation in the academic circles in Delhi, leading to the submission of a Memorandum dated 5th March 1923 to the Government of India by the then vice-chancellor of the University (H.S. Gour) and the three principals of the then existing colleges: F.F. Mark (St. Stephens); N.V. Thadani (Hindu College) and Kedar Nath (Ramjas College).

The Memorandum said

1. There is complete misapprehension on the part of the Committee (Retrenchment Committee). It has taken for granted that the Delhi University is yet to be formed. It has overlooked that the University has already been formed and is functioning.
2. Delhi University Act was passed on 5th March 1922. It was brought into force on 1st of May of that year. Necessary Statutes, Rules etc. have been framed.
3. The three Arts colleges with 750 undergraduates were disaffiliated from the University of Punjab and they became the constituent colleges of the Delhi University.
4. The University can be abolished only by repealing the Act of the Imperial Legislature.
5. It will cause a serious setback for higher education started under its auspices.
6. Every provincial capital has a university of its own. Nagpur is the only exception.
7. The Retrenchment Committee seems to be unaware that the Sadler Commission had recommended the setting up of a unitary university (in Delhi).

And Finally

A dig on the all powerful Inchcape Committee:

"The composition of the Inchcape Committee will show that with the exception of Mr. Purshotam Das Thakur Das, there was not a single university man upon it. The Commercial magnates, who formed the Committee, with due deference to their position, were not the best judges of the necessity and utility of university education".

The Memorandum was considered by the Legislative Department of the Government of India, which expressed the view:

"The University cannot be put an end to without a repealing Act. Also that by mere repeal of the Act, the three Delhi colleges, now included in the University will not automatically be restored to Punjab University. They will have to seek re-affiliation." The Department advised that the University should be continued in its present position.

The matter was submitted to the Assembly which voted the Delhi University's budget demand. The Assembly did not take cognisance of the recommendation made by the Retrenchment Committee about the new university.

The Grand Finale

The last actor in the melodrama initiated by the obnoxious recommendation of an ill-informed Committee was no less than Lord Reading, the then Viceroy of India who, in his convocation address, delivered in 1926, eulogised the upcoming university in these words:

"What I hope, and what I believe you all hope, to see in Delhi is an university of which not only Delhi but India as a whole may be justly proud..."

And the University has earnestly endeavoured to live up to that expectation during the last 92 years of its existence!

(ii) Abolition of the Central Advisory Board of Education and the Bureau of Education

In its enthusiasm for economy in government expenditure in the context of economic depression arising out of the First World War, the Retrenchment Committee (henceforth called the Committee) recommended, among others, the abolition of the Central Advisory Board of Education and the Bureau of Education. The relevant recommendation of the Inchcape Committee was:

"In view of the essential modification of the position of the Central Government vis-à-vis the provinces under the Reforms Scheme in respect of education and medical administration, which are now transferred subjects on which the Government of India exercises a very limited control, we do not consider that there is any justification for the retention of the Education Commissioner, the Bureau of Education or the Central Advisory Board of Education (CABE) costing about Rs.1,00,000 or indeed the continuation of the Department as a separate entity."[9] The CABE and the Bureau of Education were abolished forthwith by the Government of India which seemed to be looking for some ways of economising the Government expenditure.

About seven years later, the Auxiliary Committee of the Indian Statutory Commission (Hartog Committee, 1929) strongly recommended that the CABE should be re-established. Their main reason for this suggestion was somewhat curious, viz. that the Central Government is "concerned directly with the educational qualifications of the electorate for the Legislatures". The Statutory Commission endorsed this view on the more general ground that a CABE would be a valuable means of providing information and advice to the provincial administrations and 'helping to make everywhere available the results of experiments and practices in educational methods and organisation.'

The proposal of the Statutory Commission was reinforced by the Joint Select Committee, which recommended that some machinery should be set up at the headquarters of the Central Government to coordinate the activities of the local governments in connection with certain principal subjects including education.

On the recommendations of the Finance Department, the proposal was sent to the local governments in January, 1931. The proposal had a mixed response from the provincial governments. In spite of this, the Executive Council, in June, 1933, decided that the question should be sympathetically considered, "if financial situation permits". The question was again brought before the Council in January, 1934, but it was decided that the proposal could not be proceeded with on account of prevailing financial stringency.

In view of the recommendations of the Indian Statutory Commission and its Auxiliary Committee on the growth of education in India, the Government of India accepted the proposal of reviving the CABE and of attaching to it a Bureau of Education. In their report, the Joint Parliamentary Committee emphasised the need for a central organisation to facilitate the collection of data and information and generally to help in co-ordinating the provincial activities in subjects such as education. The Committee also suggested that such an organisation should be in existence, at least in skeleton form, when the new constitution begins to function.

Non-official opinion in the Indian Legislatures, as well outside it, also demanded establishment of the CABE. The All India Educational Conference held at Delhi in December, 1934 passed a Resolution for the reconstitution of such a body. Many provincial governments were in the process of reconstructing their educational systems. It was felt that the existence of an all India organisation such as the CABE was needed to help them in formulating their schemes of development and nurturing their plans. The idea got a boost from an unexpected quarter. The International Committee on intellectual Cooperation of the League of Nations also pressed the Government of India for the establishment of a National Committee on Intellectual Cooperation and the formation of a National Centre of Information for India. The Committee expressed the view that the CABE, when established, would be in a position to undertake the functions of such an organisation.

It was also stated that the Finance Department had agreed to the establishment of the CABE. The approximate cost of the proposal was worked out to be Rs. 32,000 per annum.

The proposal was circulated to the members of the Legislative Council on 11th January, 1935. It was agreed to by all members except – J.W. Bhore and N.N. Sircar. Bhore, Member Convener who, while not objecting to the proposal, protested against the procedure adopted for the consideration of the proposal. His objection was that all new proposals for expenditure "should be viewed as a whole so that all Departments might have a fair chance of putting forward suggestions pertaining to their own departments and that finally an agreed list should be drawn up in order of urgency and importance." This view was endorsed by F. Noyace, another member of the Council. He, however, supported the proposal. The other member (N.N. Sircar), who disagreed with the proposal, doubted whether the proposal would be of any practical benefit.[9]

The proposal was approved by the Viceroy on 18th January, 1935. It may be mentioned that the proposal for revival of the CABE was initially worked out by A.H. Mechanize, the officiating Education Commissioner on 18th October, 1930. It was finally approved on 18th January, 1935, after a period of 5 years.

The matter was referred to the Standing Finance Committee on 1st February, 1935. The Committee approved the proposal relating to the revival of the CABE with an annual expenditure of Rs. 30,000. Curiously enough, three Indian members of the Committee (Pandit Govind Ballabh Pant, Mr. Shiv Kishna Sinha and Mr. T.S. Avinashlingam) dissented on the ground that they were unable to accept a proposal, which was based, to some extent, on a recommendation made in the report of the Joint Parliamentary Committee. Thus the CABE, which was set up in 1915 and abolished in 1922-23 was revived in 1935. The Board, in its first meeting held in December, 1935, resolved that the Bureau of Education, which was also abolished on the recommendation of the Inchcape Committee, should be revived. The recommendation was accepted by the Government of India and the Bureau was revived with Secretary of the CABE being the curator of the Bureau.

(iii) Abolition of the Post of Education Commissioner with the Government of India

As already stated, among the recommendations made by the Inchcape Committee, one was about the abolition of the post of Education Commissioner to the Government of India. In this context the Finance Department sent a note to the Education Department of the Finance Department which, inter alia, stated that the post of the Education Commissioner was created because "the extensive tours of the former Director General of Education have fulfilled a useful purpose in increasing the appreciation by the Government of India of difficulties faced by the provincial governments in diffusing information and assisting local officers by suggestions based on a wider range of experience than they themselves could command."[10] It was stated that under the clear cut distribution of responsibility between the Central and the provincial governments under the Reforms, such considerations no longer applied, if indeed they were not consistent with real provincial autonomy as now understood. In any case, in the face of existing financial stringency, the Finance Department argued that the Central Government can no longer afford to maintain an expensive establishment to advise provincial ministers on education on issues which were not the concern of the Government of India.

The principal arguments for and against the continuation of the post of Educational Commissioner were:

1. The Education Commissioner advises the Central Government in regard to examination for imperial services;
2. He conducts certain examinations;
3. He travels and discusses problems with ministers and finds out what is happening in the provinces;

4. He collects educational statistics and issues annual and Quinquennial Reports;
5. He is Chairman of the CABE.

According to the Inchcape Committee, the functions under the Central Government do not justify his continuance. As regards provincial functions, the altered position under the Reforms makes it difficult to justify its existence.

The Department of Education insisted that the post should be retained. It was also suggested that the general interests of education in India are advanced by the coordination effected by the Education Commissioner. The case was circulated among members of the Viceroy's Council.

Voting Analysis

The view that the Government of a vast country cannot get on without an expert advice in educational matters, was supported by two members: Mohammad Shafi and B.N. Sarma. Four members, W.H. Vincent, T.B. Sapru, C.A. Innes and Rawlinson, disagreed with it. Contrariwise, they supported the view of W.H. Hailey, an officer in the Government of India, who in his note dated 29th September 1927 stated: "Education is conducted in provinces and they have their expert advisers... I must again repeat that we cannot expect the provinces to believe that we are managing their affairs economically, so long as we continue to employ officers to advise us on subjects which are entirely controlled by them and on which, as far as I know, they have not asked for the benefit of our advice".[11]

The matter was resolved by retaining the post of Education Commissioner by reallocation of work in the Imperial Secretariat and assigning more work to him by way of economising expenditure. The argument was like this:

"... The Retrenchment Committee also recommended the abolition of the appointment of Education Commissioner and in this case again we are of opinion that under the changed conditions brought about by the Reforms, there is not sufficient work to justify the employment of a whole time officer. We do, however, require expert advice from time to time, on educational matters, especially in connection with University legislation and we propose to retain, for the present, the services of the Education Commissioner, but to effect economy, as an experiment for one year, by putting him in-charge of the duties of the Superintendent of Education in areas of Ajmer and Delhi, thus saving the pay of the latter appointment, which will be held in abeyance. We are abolishing the Central Advisory Board, as recommended by the Retrenchment Committee and are foregoing all separate expenditure on the Bureau of Education so that the net cost of the Education Commissioner will be reduced by Rs. 19,000 per annum..." The Resolution was approved by the then Viceroy Lord Reading and 7 members of the Viceroys' Council.

4. The Non-Cooperation Movement (1920-21)

After victory in the First World War (1914-18), British Government in India seems to have gone berserk; instead of acceding to the popular demand of sharing power with the people, who had contributed substantially to the furtherance of the war effort both in men and material – and were expecting political quid-pro-quo – the British Government in India adopted a policy of repression, suppressing brutally the movement for national emancipation. The draconian Rowlatt Act was enforced in 1919 to silence the national demand for independence. This was followed by the mindless blood bath at Jalianwala Bagh in Amritsar on 13th April, 1919 in which innocent men, women and children were massacred to satisfy the whims of an arrogant army officer, General Dyer. The execution of Bhagat Singh, Raj Guru and Sukhdev on the bank of river Sutlej severely wounded the conscience of the nation. To gag expression of national sentiment, martial law was enforced under which a large number of Indians were summarily incarcerated. The British authorities, with their Indian cronies, subjected the general populace to inhuman brutalities. The ill-conceived Montagu–Chelmsford (Montford) Reforms, which introduced Dyarchy in the administrative system failed to satisfy the Indian demand for Home Rule. Coincidentally, the severe terms of the Sevres Treaty with Turkey after the war antagonished Indian Muslims and they started the *Khilafat* Movement, with which Gandhiji agreed to cooperate in order to give popular dimension to the anti-government sentiments.

In the backdrop of these developments, Indian National Congress, under the leadership of Gandhiji, resolved at its Calcutta session in 1920[12] to launch the Non-cooperation Movement, requiring passive resistance against all government activities; the refusal of the Indians to participate in any government launched programme, not to perform official duties; rejection of official *Darbars;* surrender of honorary certificates and titles, which were given to British loyalists (the whole 'army' of Sirs, *Khan Bhadurs, Rai Bahadurs, Shams-ul-ulemas, Maha Mahopadhyayas* etc.). The Movement also emphasized promotion of *swadeshi* (home-made) goods and boycott of foreign goods, particularly textiles; to boycott British courts and to set up indigenous arbitration centres to settle disputes.

On the positive side, Indians were expected to wear hand woven *khadi* and to observe truth and non-violence in day-to-day dealings. They were also expected to join Congress and to follow the leadership of Mahatma Gandhi. The Muslims, as a part of the *Khilafat* Movement, also joined in the Non-cooperation Movement.

To the bewilderment of the British Government, Mohammad Ali of famous Ali brothers gave a call to the Muslims to desert the British army. He was instantly arrested.

Boycott of Educational Institutions

An important component of the Movement was the boycott of the government managed and assisted educational institutions – schools, colleges and universities. It is reported that, in the first month of the Movement, 9000 students left schools and colleges and joined more than 800 national institutions that were set up by non-official organisations. The educational boycott was particularly successful in Bengal under the leadership of Chittaranjan Das and Subhash Chandra Bose. Most of the colleges in that province were closed on 31st March 1921 to coincide with Gandhiji's arrival in Calcutta. At that time there were 33 Arts colleges for men and 3 for women with 19,788 students, against 21,557 students of the previous year. Gandhiji's arrival in Calcutta, gave a spurt to the Non-cooperation

Movement. There was significant reduction in the number of students in the Chittagong College.[13] There was substantial decline in the number of students in high schools, which lost 26,222 students. In Middle English 10,215 students and in middle vernacular schools, 1718 boycotted their institutions.

Punjab also responded to the call for educational boycott under the leadership of Lala Lajpat Rai. Bombay, U.P., Bihar, Orissa and Assam were also active, though Madras remained lukewarm. The Movement also gave rise to the establishment of national institutions of which the most prominent were Jamia Millia University, Delhi; and the National Colleges at Lahore and Calcutta. Kashi Vidyapith, Tilak Maharashtra Vidyapith, Gujarat Vidyapith and several other institutions were set up. C.R. Das opened on 15th April, 1921, a National Medical Institute at Calcutta, which had three branches, of Allopathy, Ayurvedic and Homeopathy. It admitted 323 students from various parts of India.

As a result of the Khilafat agitation, a strike took place in Calcutta, and Chittagong Madrasa. After the students' conference at Nagpur, a demand was made by students of many colleges in Calcutta that all institutions should be nationalised. Except for professional colleges many colleges were closed. Even the prestigious Presidency College of Calcutta was closed. "The picketing of colleges and schools was carried to such a length that the entrance to the examination hall was blocked against the ingress of the law candidates by rows of supine students. Only the most determined of the examinees ventured to cross the barricade."[14]

The Official Version[15]

The government termed the Movement as an attack on the educational system of the country which came in waves, which were not simultaneous in all provinces. It was, however, admitted that non-cooperation alone was responsible during the year for a substantial, though not alarming, reduction in the enrolment of high and middle anglo-vernacular schools. As regards colleges and anglo-vernacular schools, while some provinces of Madras and the United Provinces and the Punjab reported recovery of the situation, before the end of the year, others e.g. Bengal, Bihar and Orissa. Burma and Central Provinces recorded comparatively severe losses at its close. According to the Vice-Chancellor of the Calcutta University, more than 47,000 pupils or 23 per cent of the total number had disappeared from high schools between July 1920 and July, 1921 and up to the 1st March, 1921, a fall of 42 per cent in the enrolment of the first and third year classes (not classes preparing for examinations) of arts colleges.

A number of institutions – 'national' schools and colleges according to the government statement, came into existence and they attracted a large number of students. "No estimate can be framed of their numbers and their financial position at present since their attitude towards the government makes the comprehensive collection of statistics impossible. Though the numbers are undoubtedly small in relation to recognised institutions and pupils, and though the financial position of many is precarious, it is too early to expect to accept, as yet, the views expressed in some provincial reports that they are ephemeral...".[16]

With the development of 'national' institutions also came the withdrawal of recognised institutions from all forms of government control and aid. According to the government: "...There is no marked fall in the number of institutions under any head except English middle schools, where the fall is possible due to changes in the classification of schools. Very strong influence has been brought to bear on many larger institutions under predominantly Indian management, which depend mainly on fee income. Even primary schools in villages as well as towns have not been immune from attacks in some provinces e.g. Burma and the Central provinces. Local bodies have not escaped infection and three municipalities in Bombay province have refused government grants for their schools in the hope that this will mean freedom from all forms of government control or inspection...".[17]

Further, "though privately managed institutions have on the whole resisted the attack with some success, some of them have financially suffered heavy loss and their very existence has for this reason been jeopardised. In colleges, there has been no such fall since fees are usually levied for the term or year in advance. But in unaided colleges, where such a procedure is less general, there has been a fall in fee income, while the receipts from this source in unaided schools have fallen more than 12 per cent. Such institutions can least bear a sudden strain on their finances and there can be no doubt that the assault on privately managed institutions has in its financial results postponed the surely needed improvement of teachers' salaries and thereby set back the educational clock. The vice-chancellor of the Calcutta University estimated a total loss of examination fee income of Rs. 2,73,000 and if this estimate is approximately correct, the financial position of this great educational body must be gravely effected."[18]

Effect on Students

According to government report, all classes of students were affected and among those who responded to pressure are those whom colleges could best afford to lose as well as those whose departure caused no regret. It admitted that there was something in the movement that appealed to most diverse type of mind. The call to 'national' service and self sacrifice found a quick response among the best, unintelligible to those who do not realise the emotional background of student life and the absence of a strong sense of humour. While older men have been seeing visions, the young men are dreaming dreams. Imagination has been fired and a spiritual "uplift" initiated. Something that had long been wanting in our college life had been supplied. To another class of temperament, the situation presented possibilities of romance and adventure that irradiated a colourless existence. Picketing and processions were as irresistible to such minds as bump supper and a 'rag' to Oxford undergraduate. Others became for the first time conscious that they were wasting time over a kind of education not suited to their needs and leading them at its best to an office stool. It is greatly to the credit of the staff that their feelings, so natural in themselves but affording such excellent material for unscrupulous agitators, found expression comparatively seldom violent or offensive action and that judgment was so often suspended and scope left for reflection. Credit is also due to parents as has specially been recorded in the Punjab report..."[19]

The government assessment was that, the Movement had adversely effected the student discipline and almost every province reports an increase in strikes and serious offences... Concentration on studies had been greatly impeded and if the examination results show generally for India as a whole no deterioration, it is mainly because so many of the worst students had left and because in the examination going classes, prudential motives had, as a rule, prevailed.

In spite of the extensive nature of the Movement, India, according to the British authorities emerged 'triumphantly' from the ordeal and even 'the hottest heads, involved in the Movement, realised that the 'golden age promised them as a result of national institutions was but a fantasy, since the charkha spinning plus Urdu or Hindi teaching institutions refused to materialise..."[20] The government also realised that there was profound dissatisfaction with the then prevailing educational system. It was felt that the objectives of Indian education needed restatement. It was stressed that if the function of education is the adaptation of the future citizen to his environment, then the content of education must change in harmony with changes in that environment. The "political and economic conditions of India have been undergoing change and the national school movement can at least claim that it lent strength to the advocates of educational reforms."[21]

The agitation also created a strong opinion in favour of practical and vocational education, which arose, largely from the knowledge that in present day conditions, the prospects of employment which await the average products of the literary type of education, are somewhat drab, and from a belief that practically or vocationally trained men will more easily fit into the economic structure, and thus may be more valuable members of the society.

And finally the Government realised that "in addition to the explicit demand for more extensive and intensive training for professions and vocations other than the legal and clerical, there was widespread demand for fuller recognition of Indian culture and aspirations, for fuller treatment of what India had contributed and may contribute to civilisation and for a more direct call to national services. With this combined a desire for more attention to vernacular languages and literature and a protest against English as a medium of instructions so far as it was inconsistent with such attention. But this demand implied no repetition of what the West could contribute and no assignment of a less important place to the study of English."[22]

In sum, the Movement spurred the government to realise that there was an urgent need for reforming the educational system in order to enable it to meet the changing requirements of the time. It also forced the government to take cognizance of the genuineness of the popular demand for administrative and political reforms rather than depending on brutal force to silence the voice of the Indian subjects.

The Movement also kindled among Indians, the blazing fire of revolt against the British imperialism. It produced a large number of freedom fighters, nation builders and selfless workers, imbued with an uncanny zeal to work for the country. Notable among them were Subhash Chandra Bose, Dr. Zakir Husain, Lala Lajpat Rai and Acharya Narender Dev. Besides Lal Bahadur Shastri, a product of Kashi Vidya Peeth, S.C. Bose Principal of the National College of Calcutta, Dr. Saifuddin Kichlu, Dr. Rajindra Prasad, Pandit Moti Lal Nehru are the illustrious examples of those, who were intimately associated with the Movement.

Movement Suspended

There was considerable pressure on Gandhiji to start civil disobedience movement. He gave an ultimatum to the British but it did not cut any ice with the government. This forced Gandhiji to start a civil disobedience movement in Bardoli Taluqa of Surat district of Gujarat. This was the famous salt *satyagraha*. Unfortunately, a great tragedy occurred, which drastically changed the course of events. A mob, 3000 strong, killed 25 policemen and one inspector at *chauri chaura*. This deadly incident shocked Mahatma Gandhi – the apostle of peace – who had pledged to keep the movement free from any kind of violence. He suspended the Non-cooperation Movement, much to the dismay of the other senior Congress leaders. Thus on 12th February, 1922 ended India's battle for *swaraj* (political emancipation). The war, however, raged on till the British were forced to relinquish their Indian empire on 15th August, 1947.

5. Political Reforms[23]

The Montague-Chelmsford Reforms (1919), reaffirmed the principle of communal representation set out by the infamous Minto-Morley Reforms (1909), which ultimately led to the vivisection of the country. These reforms, though offered Indian representatives opportunity to exercise legislative power, were extremely limited in outreach. They were in fact, a half-hearted attempt to share power with the Indian subjects while making it sure that the British interests were firmly secured. They were, in the words of Annie Besant "unworthy of England to give and India to accept."

We shall discuss the implications of this political 'benefaction' so far as it impacted Indian education.

Position before the Reforms

Prior to the introduction of Reforms, the Government of India exercised general supervision and control over education throughout British India. The government issued circulars and Resolutions of educational conferences for the benefit of local governments. Higher education opportunities were under their control and schemes involving legislation or large expenditure on education had to come up to them for consideration. The finances of India were then centralised and it was possible for the Government of India to encourage educational advance on the lines, which it favoured by means of Imperial grants for particular objects from their surplus revenues. A few scholarships to enable students to pursue further studies outside India were also awarded by the Government of India. Subject to the general control exercised by the Government of India over educational policy and finance, provincial governments were wholly responsible for the administration of local educational institutions and for the development of their educational systems. They were thus free to adopt different policies concerning the control and finance of secondary education, and the introduction of free, compulsory primary education.

The Education Commissioner with the Government of India acted as an expert adviser to Government in all educational matters. He was in touch with all educational activities. He was also in-charge of Bureau of Education... He had no formal relations with local governments, but he was free to correspond with the provincial Directors of Public Instruction.

Policy after the Reforms

1. With the introduction of Reforms in January 1921, education became a 'provincial transferred subject', with a few exceptions e.g. European Education, the Aligarh and Banaras Universities, the Chief's Colleges and certain military education institutions.
   The effect of provincialisation of education was chiefly financial. It was no longer possible for the Government of India to influence educational policy by making Imperial grants for education or by giving state scholarships. It also ceased to exercise any general control or supervision over education in the Governor's provinces. In every province, the Minister for Education, who was nominated by the Governor of the province from among the elected members of the local legislative council, was responsible for the educational policy of the province – that responsibility being one not to the Government of India, but to the electorate of the province. The Government of India was, therefore, not able to influence or interfere with that policy. They were rarely consulted by the local governments in purely educational matters. As a general rule, it may be stated that Ministers did not like to have advice thrust upon them; they wished to be left alone in the framing of their educational policies.
2. The CABE and Bureau of Education constituted in 1920 were disbanded in 1923 as a measure of economy.[24]
3. The Government of India held occasional conferences of Educational Administrators for exchange of ideas.

Although the reforms were considered somewhat advantageous to the cause of education, it was felt that there was the danger of excessive and exaggerated form of provincialisation in education, which, if not checked, would result in disastrous consequences. There was also the danger of serious and extravagant overlapping between the several provinces, particularly in the field of education. It was, therefore, felt that there was need for a central body to coordinate the programmes of education in India. It was also felt that the Central Government has well defined role which, if not performed, would be disastrous for the educational system of the country. The Hartog Committee showed concern about it. The Committee expressed the view that they could not accept the view that the Central Government should be relieved of all responsibilities for the attainment of universal primary education. In regard to finance, the Central Government should devise means, whereby those provincial governments, which were not in a position to meet the cost of developing compulsory primary education, should be provided assistance from the Central exchequer.

In retrospect, the Reforms were a precursor to the complete transfer of education to elected ministers under the Government of India Act, 1935. Even the Constitution of independent India has limited the role of the Central Government in some designated areas of education.

References

1. Selections from Educational Records; op. cit., p. 59.
2. Trevelyan, Sir George Otto, 1876: The Life and Letters of Lord Macaulay; Oxford University Press (second volume), p. 359.
3. The last Mughal King, Bahadur Shah Zafar, was buried unceremoniously at an unknown place in Rangoon in Burma (now Myanmar).
4. H. Coldwell Lispitt; Lord Curzon in India, 1898-1903; pp. 53-56.
5. Quoted in British Raj – Wikipedia, the free encyclopedia; p. 55.
6. Statement Exhibiting the Moral and Material Progress of India during the year 1901-02 and the nine preceding years, Government of India, p. 14.
7. Quinquennial Review on Education in Ajmer-Merware as quoted in 'Progress of Education in India', 1922-27, p. 19.
8. Report of the Delhi University Inquiry Committee.
9. Based on Notes, Serial Nos. 1-9 and K.W. (File No. 2-1/35-E, (*Source:* The National Archives of India, New Delhi).
10. Proceedings No. 22 (Deposit) October, 1922, Note in the Finance Department on the Expenditure on the Education Commissioner and the curator of the Bureau of Education.
11. Proceeding No. 210-238 (B) E.O. Dec. 1927.
12. The Resolution was reaffirmed at the Nagpur session of the Congress in December, 1920.
13. Nand Kishore Singh, 1922, Mahatma Gandhi and Non-Cooperation Movement, p. 108.
14. Based on the Progress of Education in India, 1917-22, Bureau of Education.
15. Based on the Progress of Education in India, 1917-22, Bureau of Education.
16. *Ibid.*, p. 3.
17. *Ibid.*, p. 3.
18. *Ibid.*, p. 4.

19. *Ibid.*, pp. 3-4.
20. *Ibid.*, p. 7.
21. *Ibid.*, p. 9.
22. *Ibid.*, p. 10.
23. Notes in File No. 28, Ministry of Education, March, 1929 (National Archives of India).
24. As stated earlier, the CABE was revived in 1935 after lot of dilly-dallying by the Departments of the Government of India.

Important Personalities Who Attempted to Alter The Course of Education during the British Rule

In the previous chapter, we have discussed the significant events that impacted education during the Colonial rule. In the following chapters, we shall examine critically the role of some individuals – both British and Indian – who attempted to bring about a change in the system of Indian education. While during the almost two centuries of British rule, a very large number of persons impacted Indian education, only a few very prominent persons, who left their mark on the educational scene, have been selected for discussion.

These individuals may be roughly categorized into

1. ***The Proponents of Modern English Education*** *who advocated the introduction of European literature and sciences through the medium of English language, instead of the indigenous languages like Sanskrit, Arabic and Persian. The pioneer in this category was Raja Ram Mohan Roy. The two persons, who were instrumental in giving a concrete shape to the idea, were Lord Babington Macaulay and Lord William Bentinck, notwithstanding their covert evangelical zeal.*
2. ***The Crusaders of Mass Education*** *includes persons, who took the cause of providing free and compulsory education to children at the primary stage. The most important persons in this category include Gopal Krishan Gokhale and some other members of the Imperial Legislative Council like Mazhar-ul Haque, B.N. Sarma etc.*
3. ***Protagonists of Indian Education*** *includes persons, who attempted to provide modern scientific education in the context of India's cultural moorings. This category includes Swami Dayanand, Jamshetji Tata, Pandit Madan Mohan Malaviya, Sir Syed Ahmed Khan, Rabindra Nath Tagore, Mohan Das Karam Chand Gandhi and Zakir Hussain.*

6

Proponents of Modern English Education

(i) Raja Ram Mohan Roy (1772-1833)

Ram Mohan Roy belonged to a rich Bengali family. As a student, he studied Persian, Arabic and Sanskrit languages. He studied English language in Banaras. In 1803, he published his first book: '*Tohfat-ul-Muwahiddin*' in which he criticised idol worship and declared that all religions had full faith in one God. In 1815, he founded the 'Atmiya Sabha' which discussed the basic principles of Hinduism. He believed in 'Advaita', which advocated the unity of individual and universal soul. According to him, human reason was the first standard of the truth of any doctrine. He believed that the philosophy of Vedanta was based on reason.

As a social reformer, he rejected discrimination in the caste system. He fought against the inhuman custom of *Sati*; the horrific practice of burning of widows with the dead bodies of their husbands. He believed in the equality of sexes. He was against child marriages, which were rampant in Bengal in those times.

Ram Mohan Roy was an ardent supporter of modern education through English. He was against the setting up of colleges in oriental languages. In a letter dated 11th December 1823[1], addressed to William Pitt, the then Prime Minister of England and Lord Amherst, the Governor General of British territories in India, he wrote: "The establishment of a new Sangscrit (Sanskrit) school in Calcutta evinces the laudable desire of the Government to improve the natives of India by education – a blessing for which they must be grateful..." He further stated:

"When this Seminary of learning was proposed, we understood that the Government in England had ordered a considerable sum of money to be annually devoted to the instruction of its Indian subjects. We were filled with sanguine hopes that this sum would be laid in employing European gentlemen of talents and education to instruct the natives of India in Mathematics, Natural Philosophy, Chemistry, Anatomy and other useful sciences, which the natives of Europe have carried to a degree of perfection; that has raised them above the inhabitants of the parts of the world."

"We now find that the government are establishing a Sangscrit school under Hindoo Pundits to impart such knowledge as is already current in India. This seminary (similar in character to those, which existed in Europe before the time of

Lord Bacon) can only be expected to lead the minds of youth with grammatical niceties and metaphysical distinctions of little or no practical use to the possessors or to society. The pupils will thus acquire what was known two thousand years ago, with the addition of vain and empty subtleties since produced by speculative men such as is already commonly taught in all parts of India."

Continuing his argument

"The Sangscrit language, so difficult that almost a life time is required for its perfect acquisition, is well known to have been for ages a lamentable check on the diffusion of knowledge and the learning concealed under this almost impervious veil, is far from sufficient to reward the labour of acquiring it. But if it were thought necessary to perpetuate this language for the sake of the valuable information it contains, this might be much more easily accomplished by other means than the establishment of a new Sangscrit college..."

"From these considerations, as the sum set apart for the instruction of the Natives of India was intended by the government in England, for the improvement of its Indian subjects, I beg leave to state, with due deference to your Lordship's exalted situation, that if the Plan now adopted be followed, it will completely defeat the object proposed; since no improvement can be expected from inducing young men to consume a dozen of years of the most valuable period of their lives, in acquiring the niceties of the *Byakurun* or Sangscrit grammar..."

Ram Mohan Roy concluded his submission by reminding the government that "if it had been intended to keep the British nation ignorant of real knowledge, the Baconian philosophy would not have been allowed to displace the system of schoolmen, which was the best calculated to perpetuate ignorance. In the same manner, the Sangscrit system of education would be best calculated to keep this country in darkness, if such had been the policy of British Legislature. But as the improvement of the native population is the object of the Government, it will consequently promote a more liberal and enlightened system of instruction, embracing mathematics, natural philosophy, chemistry and anatomy with useful sciences, which may be accomplished with the sum proposed by employing a few gentlemen of talents and learning educated in Europe and providing a college furnished with the necessary books, instruments and other apparatus..."

It may be pointed out that, while stressing the need for the teaching of sciences through English medium, the redoubtable Raja was rather harsh on Sanskrit language. His contention that 'teaching of Sanskrit would keep the country in darkness' and that "Sanskrit has exercised a lamentable check on the diffusion of knowledge of ages" was an unnecessary denigration of this language which has been aptly described as the mother of all languages. He could have promoted the cause of English language without being so aggressively hostile to this ancient language.

Even the British bureaucracy did not take kindly to Ram Mohan Roy's thesis. J.H. Harington, the President of the General Committee on Public Instruction, appointed by the government in 1823 was of the opinion that "had the views taken in the letter been even less accurate, the Committee would still consider it entitled to no reply, as it had disingenuously assumed a character to which it has no pretension. The application to government against the cultivation of Hindu literature and in favour of the substitution of the European tuition is made profoundly on their part and on the behalf of the natives of India. But it bears the signature of one individual alone, whose opinions are well known to be hostile to those entertained by almost all his countrymen. The letter of Ram Mohan Roy does not express the opinion of any portion of the natives of India and its assertion to that effect is a dereliction of truth, which conceals the claim of its author to respectful consideration."[2]

In fairness to Ram Mohan Roy, it may be stated that in his unmitigated zeal for the introduction of European literature and sciences, he, perhaps exceeded his mandate. Basically, he was not against the revival of the Indian languages and literature. His Vedanta College and his translation from Vedanta showed that he was eager to continue his linkages with the historical past. The following quotation from his works would indicate his appreciation of the ancient Indian heritage:

"If by the 'Ray of Intelligence' for which the Christian says we are indebted to the English, he means the introduction of useful mechanical arts, I am ready to express my assent and also my gratitude, but with respect to science, literature or religion, I do not acknowledge that we are placed under any obligation. For, by a reference to history, it may be proved that the world was indebted to our ancestors for the first dawn of knowledge, which sprang up in the East and thanks to Goddess of Wisdom, we still have a philosophical and copious language of our own which distinguished us from other nations, who cannot express scientific or abstract ideas without borrowing the language of the foreigners."[3]

Sir Jagdish Chandra Bose, an eminent scientist, eulogized Raja Ram Mohan Roy in these words:

"Ram Mohan did not belong to any narrow sect nor did he entertain any theoretic bias. He liberalised all beliefs and foresaw the importance of absolute freedom in all fields of inquiry. It was owing to his influence that the scientific advance of modern India has been rendered possible."[4]

In spite of the forceful pleading of Ram Mohan Roy for the introduction of modern sciences, it took Government of India more than two decades – two years after the expiry of Raja Ram Mohan Roy – to delineate the policy of promoting sciences with English medium in educational institutions in India. His advocacy of the introduction of English and modern sciences in the education system is, however, a standing monument to his sagacity and farsightedness in suggesting a course of action, which has facilitated India to attain a predominant position in the

English speaking world and has enabled Indian professionals to compete successfully in the highly competitive world markets. Being a person of great eminence and influence, his advocacy of western learning through the medium of English facilitated their adoption by the elite who in many ways influenced the thought and behaviour of influential persons in the society.

(ii) Thomas Babington Macaulay (1800-1859)

Lord Macaulay, a poet, essayist, historian, a Whig politician, graduated from Trinity College, Cambridge University. At the age of 26, he was called to the bar but showed more interest in politics than in a legal career. In 1830, he became a Member of Parliament. He became the first Law Member of the Governor General's Council in British India in 1834 and remained in that position till 1838. It was as Law Member that he persuaded the Government to adopt English as medium of instruction in India rather than the classical languages: Sanskrit and Persian. He also drew up the Indian penal Code, which is still in force in a modified form in India as also in some of the adjoining countries. After retirement from India, he wrote his famous work: '*The History of England from the Accession of James the Second*', which, among others, described the Glorious Revolution of 1688. His writings were, criticised for their one-sidedness and complacency. Karl Marx referred to him as a 'systematic falsifier of history'. A number of other scholars also criticised his interpretation of the British History.

On his arrival in India, Macaulay's first reaction was as of Alice in a Wonderland! In his own words: "But to be in such a land! The dark faces with white turbans and flowing robes; the trees not our trees, the very smell of atmosphere that of a hot house and the architecture as strange as the vegetation."

One can imagine that the disdain of His Lordship to anything Indian would be reflected in his attitude towards Indian culture, civilization and education.

It was left to T.B. Macaulay to give a concrete shape to the sentiments expressed by Ram Mohan Roy to introduce modern European education with English as the medium in India. It was the aggressive advocacy of Macaulay, which made the Government, led by Lord William Bentinck at that time, enforce the proposal to introduce knowledge of sciences and western literature among the Indians. While pleading his case, Macaulay berated the Indian civilization, culture and religions, condemned the languages and literature of Sanskrit and Arabic and ridiculed the existing educational institutions of the Hindus and the Muslims. He even threatened to resign from the official position that he occupied in case his proposal was not accepted.

Regardless of the underlying motivation of the great crusader for the English language and literature – which was patently evangelical – it may be stated that Macaulay's insistence on European education has proved to be a boon for India. It has enabled India to occupy a coveted place in the English speaking world. It has enabled our scientists and social scientists to compete successfully in the world markets. It has opened up vistas of knowledge and research for Indians, who have made their mark in the academic and professional fields, all the world over.

The Circumstances Prevailing at that Time

In order to understand the full implications of Lord Macaulay's insistence on the promotion of European language and literature, it would be necessary to give a brief account of the circumstances prevailing at that time as also the manner in which Macaulay argued and won his case.

It started with the East India Company Act, which had stipulated in 1813 that a sum of Rs. One lakh would be spent annually on the education of the Indians. The Act stated: "It shall be lawful for the Governor General in Council to direct that out of any surplus, which may remain of the rents, revenues and profits arising from the said territorial acquisitions, after defraying the expenses of the military, civil and commercial establishments, and paying the interests of the debt, in manner hereinafter provided, a sum of not less than one lakh of rupees in each year shall be set apart and applied to the revival and improvement of literature and the encouragement of the learned natives of India, and *for the introduction and promotion of a knowledge of the sciences among the inhabitants of the British territories in India...*"[5] (emphasis added).

It would appear that the first major Directive relating to Indian education was couched in such an unnecessarily legalistic phraseology and hedged with so many provisos that for two decades not much was done to implement it. It had not specified the manner in which the amount was to be spent and the priorities that had to be kept in view in distributing the amount of Rs. one lakh per annum. It had clubbed together the task of revival and improvement of (Indian) 'literature' and the encouragement of learned natives' with 'promotion of (western) sciences' – both seemingly irreconcilable concepts. As a consequence, it gave rise to a fierce controversy between what subsequently came to be called the 'Anglicists' and the 'Orientalists'. The situation has been aptly described by Trevelyan – Macaulay's biographer – in these words:

"...that moment was the very turning point of her (India's) progress. All educational action had been at a stand still for some time back on account of an irreconcilable difference of opinion in the Committee of Public Instruction which was divided five[6] against five on either side of a controversy – vital, inevitable, admitting of neither postponement, nor compromise, and conducted by both parties with a pertinacity and warmth that was nothing honourable to those concerned. Half of the members were for maintaining and extending the old scheme of encouraging oriental learning by stipends paid to students in Sanskrit, Persian and Arabic, and by liberal grants for the publication of works in those languages. The other half were in favour of teaching the elements of knowledge in the vernacular tongues and the higher branches in English. On his arrival, Macaulay was appointed President of the Committee but he declined to take any active part in its proceedings until the Government had finally pronounced on the question at issue. Later in January, 1835, the advocates of the two systems than whom ten abler men could not be found in the service, laid their opinion before the Supreme Council and on the second of February, Macaulay, as a member of that Council, produced a Minute in which he adopted and defended the views of the English section in the Committee."[7]

Similar views were expressed by the Sub-Committee of the Calcutta Madrasa which, in a resolution, said that the time had arrived for encouraging more openly and decidedly the study of English in the Madrassa. This was, however, criticised by H T Prinsep, a secretary in the Government, who in his note dated 9th July, 1834 said that this measure was hasty and indiscreet, as preventing the funds of an endowment from the purpose to which they were specifically assigned and as involving nothing less than a breach of trust.

The Controversy Rages

In the backdrop of these developments, we will elaborately examine the various facets of the controversy that engulfed the Government over the manner in which the amount of Rs. one lakh may be spent and which virtually stalled any action that could have been taken.

The Dramatis Personae

The two principal contenders in the controversy were H.T. Prinsep ad T.B. Macaulay. Both, although poles apart in status and views, took very rigid and even uncompromising stand. The Minute dated 2nd February 1835 recorded by Macaulay, which, according to Howell, was distinguished by the 'brilliance of style, the profuse illustration and incisive logic peculiar to the author' concluded with a threat that the writer would resign, if the present system was permitted to remain unchanged. Prinsep was equally adamant. In his note dated 15th February 1835, he reaffirmed, "I remain not only unshaken, but confirmed in my opinion on the general question_ _ _ _ I do not retract the substance of a simple proposition, I have advanced". Ironically, the Indians, whose future was at stake, were hardly in the reckoning, with the exception of Raja Ram Mohan Roy whose views have already been quoted.

The points made by the two contenders are summarised below:

T.B. Macaulay

Before elaborating the points made by Macaulay in his much debated Minute dated 2nd February 1835 – 22 years after the Company sanctioned Rs. one lakh for the education of the subjects of the British Indian empire – it may be pointed out that regardless of the validity or otherwise of his arguments, his whole approach seemed to be based on arrogance and racial superiority peculiar to the then rulers of India. In his contempt for Indian culture, religion, customs and habits, Macaulay seems to have been influenced by Charles Grant – the great crusader of Christianity, who had a pathological aversion for the ancient Hindu *Dharma*, scriptures, traditions and beliefs. Grant, as has been stated elsewhere, vehemently believed that the only way to perpetuate the Company's rule and to bring about a radical transformation in the religious, moral and social modes of the *heathens* (emphasis added) was to expose them to the dazzling brilliance of Christianity to dart the guilty holes of their conscience and to make them a part of the civilised (read western) world.

Macaulay confessed that he had no knowledge of either Sanskrit or Arabic. His whole knowledge of the literature in Sanskrit and Arabic was based on his reading of the translations of the most 'celebrated Arabic and Sanskrit works, (which he did not identify) and conversations with men distinguished by their proficiency in the Eastern tongues. In spite of this glaring handicap, he claimed that he had formed a correct estimate of their value! Based on his self-confessed lack of knowledge, he had the audacity to conclude that he had not come across an orientalist, who could deny that, "a single shelf of a good European library was worth the *whole native literature of India and Arabia*" (emphasis added). This was followed by another brash statement about the intrinsic superiority of the western literature which he claimed was fully admitted by the members of the Committee (of Public Instruction), who supported the oriental plan of education.[8]

Following his aggressive view point – which appeared to be a precursor to the infamous '*Apartheid*' in another British Colony – he stated that he had never met any orientalist, who ventured to maintain that the Arabic and Sanskrit poetry could be compared to that of the great European nations. Further he believed that "all the historical information which has been collected from all the books written in the Sanskrit language (he spared Arabic language) is less valuable than what may be found in most paltry abridgments used at preparatory schools in England".

At another place, he declared, "What the government spends on Arabic and Sanskrit colleges is not merely a dead loss to the cause of truth; it is bounty money paid to raise up champions of error. It goes to form a nest not merely of helpless place hunters but of bigots prompted alike by passion and by interest to raise a cry against every useful scheme of education."

Continuing his tirade against Arabic and Sanskrit literature, which in his view was of little intrinsic value, he questioned the policy of the government to promote its study because that literature "inculcates the most serious errors on the most important subject; is a course hardly reconcilable with reason, with morality or even with that neutrality which ought, we all agree, to be sacredly preserved. It is confessed that a language is barren of useful knowledge. We are to teach it because it is fruitful of monstrous superstitions. We are to teach false history, false astronomy, false medicine, because we find them in company with a false religion. We abstain and I trust shall always abstain from giving any public encouragement to those who are engaged in the work of converting the natives to Christianity. And while we act thus, can we reasonably or decently bribe men out of the revenue of the State to waste their youth in learning how they are to purify themselves after touching an ass, or what text of the Vedas they are to repeat to expiate the crime of killing a goat?"[9]

In view of his claim to the superiority of western knowledge and languages, Macaulay forcefully argued that whether when it is in our power to teach this language (English), we shall teach in a language in which, by universal confession, there are no books on any subject, which deserve to be compared to our own. "Whether when we can teach European science, we shall teach system which, by universal confession, whenever they differ from those of Europe, differ for the worse and whether when we can patronise sound philosophy and true history, we shall countenance at the public expense, medical doctrines, which would disgrace an English farrier; astronomy which would move laughter in girls at an English learning school; history, abounding with kings thirty feet high and reigns thirty thousand years long and Geography made of seas of treacle and seas of butter".[10]

Curiously enough, this denunciation emanated from a person who, by self-confession, did not know a word of the languages that he had chosen to ridicule so viciously!

Coming to the substantive question, His Lordship averred that the amount of Rs. one lakh, set apart by the Company, should be spent not only on reviving literature in India but also for the introduction and promoting a knowledge of the sciences among the inhabitants of the British territories – "words which are alone sufficient to authorise all changes for which I contend." He concluded that "there was not a single word in any public instrument from which it can be inferred that the Indian government even intended to give any pledge of promoting the present system, or even considered the destination of these funds as of unalterably fixed. These funds can be used in promoting learning in India in any way, which would be thought most advisable."[11] Macaulay hoped that with the introduction of western learning through the medium of English, it would be possible to develop in India, "a class of persons, Indian in blood and colour but English in tastes, morals and intellect."[12]

H.T. Prinsep

In his Memorandum dated 15th February, 1835, H.T. Prinsep, a Secretary in the government, attempted to give a point by point reply to Macaulay's highly biased and arrogant stipulations about the learning imparted in the oriental institutions as also the manner in which the amount of Rs. one lakh sanctioned for the education of the natives could be spent. We discuss below the main points made by Macaulay and the responses/reactions of Prinsep.

About the literature and languages that the government should promote, Prinsep was of the opinion that by the revival and promotion of literature and the encouragement of the learned natives, the legislature did not mean to refer to any other literature than the native literature, nor any other learned natives than such as were eminent by their proficiency in that literature.

Macaulay, in a brazen display of racial arrogance had argued, "I can by no means admit that when a nation of *high intellectual attainments* (England) (emphasis added) undertakes to superintend the education of a nation comparatively ignorant (India), the learners are absolutely to prescribe the course, which is to be taken by the teachers.....*we are not at present seeking the cooperation of the natives* (emphasis added). It would be bad enough to consult their intellectual taste at the expense of their intellectual health. But we are consulting neither. We are forcing them the mock learning, which they nauseate. This is proved by the fact that we are forced to pay our Arabic and Sanskrit students while those who learn English are willing to pay." [13]

Prinsep, however, challenged this assertion. According to him, government scholarships are available only to one fourth of the students studying these courses; these scholarships are given not as inducement to study the language but as rewards of successful study and in order to maintain the institution for the prosecution of further studies. Further, it was only in the case of English instruction that teachers were paid for their services. Contrarily, the Hindu and Muslim scholars did not ask nor were paid for their services because that was not an accepted or practised tradition.

It had also been said that – "Sanskrit and Arabic do not prepare the students for any gainful employment". In this connection, a reference was made to the ex-students of the Sanskrit college petitioning the Committee, which said: "notwithstanding such testimonials (certificates of proficiency) we have but little prospects of bettering our condition...we want means for a decent living and for our progressive improvement".

About this proposition, Prinsep argued that the frustration, which the alumni of the oriental colleges felt, did not mean that the knowledge they acquired was useless. This would require intensive research to find out the real causes of this frustration. This would also necessitate continuously to give them education that they desire and giving them instruction to improve prospects of their employment.

Macaulay had also suggested that the books in Arabic and Sanskrit had no purchasers. The Law Commission is preparing a code and as soon as that is promulgated, the Shastras and Hedaya will be useless to a Moonsiff (Judge). It would be absurd to educate young men in these books.

Prinsep countered this assertion by saying that the prices of the books have been exorbitant and the getup of the books is not attractive. Further, there is no proof that there is no taste for reading these books among the natives. Prinsep also said that Macaulay gives only half the story as he forgets to mention the thriving business of printing in Persian and Arabic literature almost to the same degree as that of English Press.

Macaulay summed up his Minute by stressing that he would at once stop the printing of Arabic and Sanskrit books and abolish the Madrasa and Sanskrit College at Calcutta. In case these are retained, no stipend should be given to the students. People should be allowed to take their own decision about joining the institutions selected by them rather than be bribed to learn what they have no desire to know.

The arrogance, the wanton display of racial superiority and the tendency to draw conclusions based on scanty knowledge culminated into a threat which Macaulay chose to deliver to the authorities: "if the decision of His Lordship in Council should be such as I anticipate, I shall enter on the performance of my duties with the greatest zeal and alacrity. If, on the other hand, it be the opinion of the government that the present system ought to remain unchanged, I beg that I may be permitted to retire from the Chair of the Committee."[14] At this stage, His Lordship seems to have become far more aggressive and vituperative, He said: "We have at present no right to the respectable name of the Board of Public Instruction. We are a Board for wasting the public money for printing books, which are of less value than the paper on which they are printed while it was blank; for giving artificial encouragement to absurd history, absurd metaphysics, and absurd theology – for raising up a breed of scholars, who find their scholarships an encumbrance and blemish, who live on the public while they are receiving their education and whose education is so utterly useless to them, when they have received it; they must either starve or live on the public all the rest of their lives. Entertaining these opinions, I am naturally desirous to decline all share in the responsibility of a body which, unless it alters its whole mode of proceedings, I must consider, not merely as useless, but as positively noxious."[15]

It may be stated that all this happened about two centuries back, when the East India Company was trying to spread its tentacles in the vast terrain of India. It was the first policy issue relating to education that confronted the rulers and it is no wonder that it took almost two decades to arrive at a decision of sorts. It may also be stated that the exponents of the two systems of education were not of equal rank. Macaulay was a member of the Governor General's Council and Prinsep was a Secretary in the Board of Public Instruction. One should, however, admire the courage of a subordinate official to take cudgels with a superior official, particularly of Macaulay's temperament. It may also be noted that in this whole dialogue, the Indians, who were to be the most affected, were not at all consulted except that they were subjected to unwanted ridicule, derogatory remarks and sustained humiliation.

Very little attention was paid to Prinsep's observations and the Governor General (Lord Bentinck) in an undated note gave his "entire concurrence to the sentiments expressed in this (Macaulay's) Minute". (See Annexure-I)

It is interesting to recall the great dismay experienced by Prinsep at the manner in which he was treated by his immediate bosses – Lord Macaulay and the Governor General Lord Bentinck. In a note dated 20th May, 1835, he expressed his anguish in the following words:

"The mind of the public of Calcutta was immediately in a ferment (over the proposal to abolish the Madrasa and Sanskrit College). In three days, a petition was got up signed by no less than 30,000 people on behalf of the Madrasa and another by the Hindus from the Sanskrit College. T.B. Macaulay took into his head that this agitation was excited and even got up by me. He called the Head of the Madrasa to ask him whether he had obtained the knowledge that the Madrasa was to be closed. The Hafez replied in the negative."[16]

Further: "Lord William Bentinck would not even allow me to place my Memorandum on record. He said that it was quite an abuse that secretaries should take upon themselves to write Memorandums; that it was enough for the Court of Directors to see what the members of the Council chose to place on record; that *what the secretaries wrote was nothing unless adopted by the Government*" (emphasis added).[17]

One may question the bonafides of both the Lords – William Bentinck and T.B. Macaulay – in rushing through the controversy and arriving at a conclusion, which had long term implications for the future of the Indians and their educational system. It is noteworthy that in the mad rush for arriving at a decision, the Governor General did not consider it necessary to consult the Board of Directors, who had mandated that all important decisions should be taken in consultation with them.

Question had also been raised about the appointment of Macaulay as President of the Council. Was it because, as pointed out by Prinsep, that Lord Bentinck wanted to overawe the members of the Council of Education by Macaulay's literary reputation and position as a Whig politician to impose the preconceived ideas of the latter? It may be recalled that the Governor General gagged the dissenting voice of Prinsep, according to whom he was even suspected of having incited the agitation that erupted at the assumed closure of the Madrasa and the Sanskrit College. Another explanation that fits into the circumstances then prevailing was the evangelising zeal of the Lords for the spread of Christianity to remedy the evils of the Hindus and Muslims whom Charles Grant (1746-1823) had charged with dishonesty, fraud, mutual hatred, distrust and licentiousness.

It may be recalled that Grant, in his plan of education had commended teaching of English as a means of communication of 'superior lights' of the west to removing the Hindus' ignorance. This would, according to him, "silently undermine and subvert this (Hindu) fabric of error and lead them to adopt Christianity."[18]

Be that as it may, the controversy ended for the time being. The Resolution passed on that occasion was afterwards made a little more favourable for the old native institutions by Lord Auckland, but English has ever since been the study preferentially encouraged by the government in comparison with vernacular literature. The study of Sanskrit, Arabic and Persian was, in consequence, less cultivated than here-to-fore. But none of the old institutions was altogether abolished.

The Aftermath

The decision arrived at in favour of Macaulay's contention was, however, not the end of the story. 70 students of the Government Sanskrit College, Calcutta, in a petition dated 9th August, 1836, to Lord Auckland, the Governor General, challenged Lord Bentinck's order depriving the newly admitted students of the Sanskrit College their stipends. According to them, "this measure would be a great deterrent to the progress and interest of Sanskrit College – it is in fact indirectly abolishing the said institution and eradicating that sacred language from the Earth, for your petitioners, having none to support them in the city, cannot attend it nor acquire that proficiency, which can reform their manners and customs...."

They prayed for the conferment of the little allowance they enjoyed for that will enable them to prosecute their studies without any inconvenience and preserve the Hindoo Shastras from sinking into oblivion".[19]

Lord Auckland in his Minute dated 24th August 1836 expressed the opinion that an undiscriminating payment of allowances to students to induce them to attend a place of instruction, will be found to have been generally unsuccessful in all countries. Three years later, however, he reviewed the situation. In a note he said that "although English was to be maintained as the medium of higher instruction in European literature, philosophy and science, the existing oriental institutions were to be kept up in full efficiency and were to receive the same encouragement that might be given to students at English institutions. Vernacular institutions were to be combined with English; full choice to be allowed to student to attend whichever tuition they might individually prefer."[20]

The reverberations of the highly biased and utterly one-sided fulminations of Macaulay refused to die down with the passage of time. Almost 66 years later, Lord Curzon (1898-1905) in his address to Educational Conference lamented over the fact that the Government had not fulfilled its duty towards the expansion of primary education, and neglected vernacular languages. He said:

"Ever since the cold breath of Macaulay's rhetoric passed over the field of Indian languages and Indian text books, the elementary education of the people in their own tongue has shrivelled and pined. This, I think, has been a mistake and I say so for two reasons. In the first place, the vernaculars are the living languages of this great Continent. English is the vehicle of learning and of advancement of the small minority; but for the vast bulk, it is a foreign tongue, which they do not speak and rarely hear. If the vernaculars contained no literary models, no classics, I might not be so willing to recommend them. But we all know that in them there are enshrined famous treasures of literature and art; while even the secrets of modern knowledge are capable of being communicated thereby in an idiom and in phrases, which will be understood by millions of people, to whom our English terms and ideas will never be anything but an unintelligible jargon. My second reason is even wider in its application. What is the greatest danger in India? What is the source of suspicion, superstition, outbreaks, crimes – yes, and also of much of the aggression, discontent and suffering among the masses? It is ignorance. And what is the only antidote to ignorance? Knowledge. In proportion as we teach the masses, so shall we make their lot happier, and in proportion as they are happier, so they will become more useful members of the body politic."[21]

The bonafides of Macaulay were severely questioned by one of the Indian members of the Viceroy's Council. In a note dated 13th April, 1916, C. Sankaran Nair, said:

"The intention of Macaulay and those who cooperated with him in introducing English education in India was really to introduce Western Civilization into this country. (See Macaulay's letter to his father; Annexure-2) They wanted, if possible, to *introduce Christianity* (emphasis added). They desired to change the social, political and moral outlook of the people. To give to all Hindus, an English mind and to give all who come within its way to look at the past and at the future from the stand point of an English man was their aim. This involved the teaching of British political philosophy with its notions of freedom, rights and its ideals of an active civic life and philanthropic ideas, to displace the Indian philosophy of duty, submission, caste privilege, quietude and individual salvation."[22]

An Assessment

We have traversed a vast expanse of time – almost two centuries since Macaulay recorded his Minute based on which the Government of India resolved to promote European literature and science among the natives of India. In the meantime, India has attained freedom from foreign subjugation. It appears that the time is ripe to review and reassess the contribution of Macaulay to the cause of Indian education and its repercussions for the future development.

It would not be too far fetched to argue that, notwithstanding the racial arrogance – sheer contempt for India's culture and civilisation, unwavering hatred for classical languages and literature – both Sanskrit and Arabic and self assumed role of the exponent of Western civilisation – Macaulay deserves some compliments. Supposing he had not stood his ground to introduce Western (English) type of education, would India have advanced so much among the comity of nations? Would our scientists, men of literature, engineers and social scientists have been able to compete in the world markets? Would it have been possible for Indians to occupy vantage positions in science and technology, art and literature, medicine and life sciences all the world over as is the position at present?

According to a recently released Census, (2001) data on bilingualism and trilingualism in India, more Indians speak English than any other language, with the sole exception of Hindi. Further, English speaking persons in India out-number those in all Western Europe, not counting the United Kingdom. English speaking persons in India are more than twice the population of the United Kingdom. India with 125 million English-speaking persons ranks second after the USA (263 million). The birth place of Macaulay (UK) ranks fourth with 60 million English speaking persons. It is equivalent to Russia, which also has 60 million people speaking English.

It has also been revealed that English was the primary language for barely 2.3 lakh Indians; more than 86 per cent listed it as their second language and another 39 million as their third language (as reported in the *Times of India* dated 14th March 2010).

Shall we attribute all this progress to Macaulay, who spearheaded the cause of English and European literature and science? Can we extol his 'farsightedness' in visualising almost two centuries back about the ushering in of Globalisation with its accent on liberalisation of world's socio-economic system and India's active and significant participation in the process?

It is difficult to give a positive answer to these questions. Lord Macaulay was moved by no such altruistic motives. In his zeal for forcing the Government to accede to his proposal, he had no hesitation to debase our ancient heritage; our religion, our civilisation; to ridicule our history and denounce the classical languages and literature and to replace them by English and European literature. He was moved by the desire of producing robots of the Indian youth who would have contempt for their own religion, scriptures, way of living and thinking. They would, instead be the torch bearers of perpetuating the British Raj in India. He wanted to produce a body of loyal Indians who would sing the glory of the colonial masters, recite the English National Anthem; and take pride in writing essays on themes like, 'Invincibility of the British Empire', 'Blessings of the British Rule', etc. He was in fact a die-hard imperialist, who wanted to keep Indians in perpetual slavery – mental, physical and political.[23] If any good has come out of the policy enunciated by him, it is in spite of him and not because of him.

It needs also to be recognised that while Macaulay's Minute and the government policy to promote western knowledge through English language provided a means, their expansion depended much on the desire and effort made by the Indians. To some extent that desire is reflected in the letter sent by Raja Ram Mohan Roy to William Pitt, the British Prime Minister; though not much notice was taken of his letter.

It may, however, be conceded that the introduction of European sciences and English has motivated Indian academics, social reformers like Swami Dayanand Saraswati, Pandit Madan Mohan Malaviya, Sir Syed Ahmed Khan to provide western education in the context of Indian culture, moral values and Indian civilization. We shall discuss the contribution of some of the Indian celebrities, who were able to attune the Indian education system in such a way that western advancement in science and technology, is homogenised with the Eastern traditions and behavioural patterns. In fact, these far sighted persons were successful in Indianising English language and Literature, Sciences and Technology.

Annexure-1

The Government's Resolution[24]

It has already been mentioned that immediately after Macaulay recorded his Minute (dated 2nd February 1835) Lord William Bentinck, the Governor General, expressed his 'entire concurrence' with the sentiments expressed in Macaulay's Minute. It did not take his government long to agree to the stipulations made by Macaulay. Lord Bentinck in a Resolution of 7th March, 1835, gave it the seal of his authority. The Resolution said:

"The Governor-General of India in Council has attentively considered two letters from the Secretary to the Committee of Public Instruction, dated the 21st and 22nd January last, and the papers referred to in them.

First: His Lordship in Council is of opinion that the great object of the British Government ought to be the promotion of European literature and science among the natives of India; and that all the funds appropriated for the purpose of education would be best employed on English education alone.

Second: But it is not the intention of His Lordship in Council to abolish any College or School of native learning, while the native population shall appear to be inclined to avail themselves of the advantages which it affords, and His Lordship in Council directs that all the existing professors and students at all the institutions under the superintendence of the Committee shall continue to receive their stipends. But His Lordship in Council decidedly objects to the practice which has hitherto prevailed of supporting the students during the period of their education. He conceives that the only effect of such a system can be to give artificial encouragement to branches of learning which, in the natural course of things, would be superseded by more useful studies; and he directs that no stipend shall be given to any student that may hereafter enter at any of these institutions; and that when any professor of Oriental learning shall vacate his situation, the Committee shall report to the Government the number and state of the class in order that the Government may be able to decide upon the expediency of appointing a successor.

Third: It has come to the knowledge of the Governor-General in Council that a large sum has been expended by the Committee on the printing of Oriental works; His Lordship in Council directs that no portion of the funds shall hereafter be so employed.

Fourth: His Lordship in Council directs that all the funds which these reforms will leave at the disposal of the Committee be henceforth employed in imparting the native population a knowledge of English literature and science through the medium of the English language; and His Lordship in Council requests the Committee to submit to Government, with all expedition, a plan for the accomplishment of this purpose."

Annexure-2

Calcutta, October 12, 1836

My Dear Father,

We were extremely gratified by receiving a few days ago, a letter from you which, on the whole, gave a good account of your health and spirits.

Our English schools are flourishing wonderfully. We find it difficult, — indeed, in some places impossible, — to provide instruction for all who want it. At the single town of Hooghly, fourteen hundred boys are learning English. The effect of this education on the Hindoos is prodigious. No Hindoo, who has received an English education, ever remains sincerely attached to his religion. Some continue to profess it as a matter of policy; but many profess themselves pure Deists, and some embrace Christianity. It is my firm belief that, if our plans of education are followed up, there will not be a single idolater among the respectable classes in Bengal thirty years hence. And this will be affected without any efforts to proselytise, without the smallest interference with religious liberty; merely by the natural operation of knowledge and reflection. I heartily rejoice in the prospect.

Ever yours most affectionately

T.B. Macaulay

References

1. Quoted from Reena Chatterji; *Impact of Raja Ram Mohan Roy on Education in India*; 1983; S. Chand and Company, New Delhi 110055, pp. 209-212.
2. Resolution of General Committee of Public Instruction (January 14, 1824) Proceedings of the Committee (1823 – 1841) Vol. 5. pp. 45-46.
3. Quoted from Reena Chatterji; op. cit., p. 66.
4. *Ibid.*, p. 68.
5. H. Sharp; Selections from Educational Records *Ibid*, pp. 22.
6. This was disputed by Prinsep, who claimed that he carried with him (orientalists), the vote of majority of the Council of Education before Macaulay intervened (Extract from the T. Prinsep Diary (1835).
7. Trevelyan, Sir George Otto, 1876, The Life and Letters of Lord Macaulay, pp. 408-409.
8. H. Sharp; Selections from Educational Records, p. 5.
9. *Ibid.*
10. *Ibid.*
11. *Ibid.*
12. *Ibid.*
13. It is interesting to note that in his remarks in the margin, Macaulay had claimed to have consulted Sir E. Ryan (Law Member) Governor General's Council, about which Prinsep remarked, "He did not feel overwhelmed by this authority".
14. Macaulay's Minute, dated 2nd February, 1835.
15. *Ibid.*
16. Prinsep's Diary, National Archives.
17. *Ibid*
18. For full text of Grant's 'superior lights', a reference may be made to Chapter 1: Educational Policy.
19. H. Sharp; op. cit.
20. Indian Education Commission, 1882, p. 89.
21. Lord Curzon in India, 1898-1905, Macmillan and Co.; London, 1906, Vol. 2, p. 46.
22. C. Sankaran Nair; Note (National Archives).
23. His hidden agenda is evident from his letter to his father dated 12th October, 1835. (Annexure-2).
24. H. Sharp, Selections from Educational Records, 1920.

7

The Crusaders of Mass Education

(i) Gopal Krishan Gokhale – A Crusader for Free and Compulsory Primary Education (1866-1915)

Gopal Krishan Gokhale belonged to a middle class family. His father Krishnarao worked in a small princely state – Kagal. Gopal passed his matriculation examination at the age of 15, joined a college in Kolhapur in January 1882 and passed his B.A. in 1884 – at the age of 18. He became a teacher at Rs. 35 per month. As a teacher he had the privilege of working with Bal Gangadhar Tilak, Agrakar and Apte. Later he was associated with the Deccan Education Society.

Gokhale began his political career as secretary of the Sarvajanak Sabha. He started working under Ranade. The Sabha was, in a way precursor to the Indian National Congress. Gokhale and Tilak joined the Congress in 1889. He attended almost all the sessions of the Congress till his death in 1915. He was elected to Bombay Legislative Council in 1899 and subsequently to the Imperial Legislative Council in 1902 at the age of 36. It was as a member of the Imperial Council that he moved a Resolution on 18th March, 1910 about the introduction of free and compulsory education at the elementary education stage.

The Resolution was discussed threadbare and thrown out by British members of the Council who were in majority. We have given below, among others, a summary of the points made by the mover of the Resolution and the discussions that followed.

Introduction

At the outset, it may be stated that the Government of India was fully aware of the importance of providing educational facilities to the teeming millions of India, particularly at the primary stage. The Despatches of 1854 and 1859 and the Indian Education Commission 1882-83 had emphasised the significance of primary education and had made detailed recommendations with regard to its policy, objectives, curriculum and even methods of teaching. The problem was emphasised by Lord Curzon, in his address to Education Conference held on 20th September 1905 at Simla.

Government's Reluctance to Remedy the Situation

In the context of the statement made by Curzon, following the review of the abysmal state of affairs of Indian education, particularly of primary education as recognised in various Despatches as also by the Indian Education Commission (1882-83), one would have expected that the Government of India, as also the local governments would go out of their way to remedy the situation. The Government, however, seemed to be very reluctant to fulfil its obligation of providing educational facilities at the grass-root level and to perform its "sacred duty to confer upon the natives of India those vast moral and material blessings, which flow from the general diffusion of useful knowledge," as patronisingly declared in the Despatch of 1854 and reiterated in 1859. This is apparent from the resoluteness and stubbornness with which the well thought out resolutions for providing free and compulsory education at the primary stage were summarily rejected in the Legislative Council by its official members. We shall highlight the main features of these resolutions and the stand taken by the government representatives in this regard.

Official Apathy to Resolutions moved by Indian Members of the Legislative Council

To promote the programme of providing free and compulsory primary education, a few Indian members of the Legislative Council moved resolutions to require the government at the Central and local levels to take appropriate measures in that direction. Although not much came out of these resolutions – they were rejected mainly due to the opposition from official members – they forced the government to take some action. We shall discuss, in detail, the main elements of these resolutions, the discussion that followed and the reaction of the Government. We start with the Resolution moved by Gopal Krishan Gokhale in the Legislative Council.

A Bill for Free and Compulsory Education Introduced by Hon'ble Gopal Krishan Gokhale – Discussion in the Imperial Legislative Council

Gopal Krishan Gokhale, a member of the Imperial Legislative Council, moved a Resolution in the Council which, inter-alia, stated: "This Council recommends that a beginning should be made in the direction of making elementary education free and compulsory throughout the country and that a mixed communion of officials and non-officials be appointed at an early date to frame definite proposals." He proposed that before compulsion is introduced, a certain percentage of children must already be in schools; the local authority must use its discretion of asking for the application of the provisions to the area or any part of it, and the consent of the local government must be obtained wherever the provision came into force; primary education would become compulsory for every boy who is not under six or over ten years of age. Exemption would be permitted in particular cases and classes. No boy would be compelled to attend school and required to pay any fee, if his parents' income did not exceed Rs.10 a month; wherever compulsion was applied to boys, it might also be made applicable to girls. Fines were to be imposed on defaulting parents, after complaints made by the school attendance committee. Child employment was to be restricted. The local authority in any area to which the Act had been applied was to provide school accommodation as required by the department and for this purpose, with the sanction of the local government, levy a special rate. The local government was also to bear a share of the cost as laid down by the Government of India.

Later, Mr. Gokhale, in moving a reference of the Bill to a select committee, explained that the proportion of children already at school, needed to justify for the choice of adoption of this measure, should be 33 per cent of those of a school going age; that education, where compulsory, should be wholly free and that of the expenditure borne by the government and the local bodies should be in the proportion of two thirds and one third. He also indicated that reckoning the number of boys, who should be at school as ten per cent of the male population, it would require providing for 12½ million children, of whom four million were already receiving education. The cost of educating the remaining at Rs. 5 a head would be Rs. four and half crore, of which the government would have to provide Rs. three crores and another crore for girls. He also suggested that this reform should be carried out in ten years by raising funding by increasing customs duties from 5 to 7 per cent.

The Discussion on the Bill

In the debate on the bill held on 18th March, 1910, the Government promised that Mr. Gokhale's bill would be examined. In pursuance of this promise, H. W. Orange, the Director General of Education, in his note dated 26th April, 1910 examined the proposal. According to him:

1. In order to discuss the most important part of Mr. Gokhale's bill relating to expansion of education, the abolition of fees, and the enactment of compulsion, it would be necessary to know the financial requirements for their implementation. According to estimates prepared by the Finance Department, it would require a substantial initial sum of money and a recurring sum running by half a crore annually to five crores in ten years and that, of this sum of money, at any rate something out of the initial grant and 2½ crores of the recurring grant will be devoted to primary education.
2. The main points made by Mr. Gokhale and the reactions of Mr. Orange were:
   (i) Mr. Gokhale's first proposal was that an Act should be passed conferring powers upon local bodies to make primary education compulsory in their areas. At the present times, it is much more important to increase

facilities for education than to prepare for compulsory school attendance. It is improbable that even after 10 years, it would be possible to introduce compulsory primary education but it may be possible to introduce it in some parts. Mr. Orange had no objection to framing and submitting to the local governments by-laws requiring the attendance of children at school.

(ii) Mr. Gokhale's second proposal was that compulsion should be only for boys and not for girls. The Government of India would assent to this.

(iii) The third proposal was that period of compulsion should be between 6 and 10 years as in Japan. The Government should not limit the period to 4 years, but should offer primary education for 6 or 7 years. The child should not be exempted from education at the age of 10 years, but should go beyond it. In Baroda, according to Administrative Report, 1907-08, the orders as to compulsory school attendance applied to boys between the ages of 7-12 years and girls from 7 to 10. The Report adds that it is not intended to rest content with only three standards that have now been prescribed. According to Orange, the outside limits about introducing compulsion may be fixed at 6-13, thus leaving the local authorities the discretion to fix any period within these limits.

(iv) Mr. Gokhale's fourth proposal was that where 33 per cent of boys are actually at school, elementary education should be made compulsory for all boys in that area. *This does not seem to be a sound proposal* (emphasis added). Alternatively, it would be better to empower the local bodies to make bye laws regarding school attendance. Further, local governments may compel local bodies to make such laws.

(v) Mr. Gokhale's fifth proposal was wherever compulsory education was introduced, it should be gratuitous or parents with a monthly income of Rs. 25 should be eligible for free education for their children. According to Mr. Orange, the matter should be left to the discretion of the local governments. The Government of India should not indicate any limit of monthly income for providing free education.

(vi) Mr. Gokhale's sixth proposal was that extra cost may be divided between the government and local bodies in the proportion of two to one. Prima-facie, there was no objection to this suggestion. Mr. Orange's main doubt was whether, if by an imperial assignment, we raised provincial expenditure on education upto such a level as to effect substantial expense of primary education, whether local bodies would be able to meet so much as one third of the cost. At present, the total expenditure by municipalities upon primary schools was only Rs.13 lakhs per annum. The municipalities contain a population of 16½ million and this at 15 per cent meant a population of school age of 2½ million; say 1¼ million boys and 1¼ million girls. If it were possible for municipalities to provide instruction for them at a rough rate of Rs. 6 per head, the state funding Rs. 4 and the municipalities Rs. 2 per head, then the cost that would fall upon the municipalities would be Rs. 25 lakhs per annum for boys and Rs. 25 lakhs for girls. But he doubted whether municipalities could provide education to children so cheaply i.e. Rs. 6 per annum; for the city of Bombay spent Rs. 21.50 per head on its municipal schools and he could not pretend to offer an opinion on the elasticity of the municipal powers of self-taxation.

(vii) Mr. Gokhale's seventh proposal was that there should be now a separate Secretary for education in the Home Department and he looked forward finally to the time when a member in separate charge of education will be included in the Executive Council. This would be dealt with separately.

(viii) Mr. Gokhale's eighth proposal was that education should be now a divided head instead of being a provincial head. Underlying the technical form in which the proposal was prepared by Mr. Gokhale was the very important principle of the participation of the Government of India in responsibility for finance and control of education. It was necessary for the Finance Department to consult the Home (Education) Department in the finalisation of budget proposal for education.

(ix) Mr. Gokhale's ninth proposal was that a statement describing the progress of education from year to year should be published as was done in the case of Army services and Railway Board. This was a plausible suggestion and could be implemented.

As usual, the note by Mr. Orange passed through the various 'stalwarts' of the British bureaucracy. The important points made by some of them are summarised below:

H.G. Stokes in his note dated 1.7.1910, suggested that while policy issues could be taken up at this stage, administrative issues may be taken up separately. According to him, the first question was whether, as a matter of policy, it was desirable to further compulsory primary education and should the Government of India undertake legislation or press local governments to do so. There was a genuine desire for extending primary education but this may not remain so if there was a proposal to impose additional local taxation. It would be a dangerous step. The initiative should be left to the local bodies as far as possible. We cannot afford to estrange large sections of population.

He suggested that the first step in the direction of compulsion should be taken with extreme caution and that utmost latitude should be given to local governments.

Mr. Gokhale's proposal to introduce compulsion for boys where 33 per cent enrolment was available was also *premature and dangerous* (emphasis added). The local governments should be enabled to force the pace on local bodies; a general power be conferred on them to compel local bodies to prepare bye laws. We should not go further than this, if indeed we should go thus far.

Mr. J.L. Jenkins, Member (Home) in his note dated 20.7.1910, opposed any step whatever being taken in the direction of compulsory education. According to him, at present, compulsory education was clearly impossible and would remain impossible for a very long time. Even Bombay city was not ripe for it. Compulsory education in Baroda was a mere pretence. The number of schools was wholly inadequate and, in villages where there were schools, the children of lower castes were not required to attend. If they did attend, the schools would be vacated by children of higher castes. If there was to be compulsory education, then we will have to have two schools in each village.

Mr Jenkin continued:

"We have to have more schools; better teachers. That was our present task and it was quite enough. The future may safely be left to take care of itself and I do not think we should be justified forestalling those who come after us in laying down the lines upon which compulsion should be introduced."[1]

He also rejected the suggestion made by Mr. Orange about holding a conference to discuss the issue. According to him, there was no use in holding a conference to discuss a policy which we know to be impracticable or in passing legislation, which we know must be ineffective. This disposes of Mr. Gokhale's proposal so far as I am concerned.[2]

The Bill was officially opposed and thrown out by 38 to 13 votes. Thus ended the pioneering effort made by Mr. Gokhale to introduce free and compulsory primary education. In fact, the vehemence with which the officials found faults with his resolution forced the redoubtable Mr. Gokhale to withdraw the resolution.

At the time of the impending defeat of his historic mission, Mr. Gokhale made a prophetic statement in which he expressed the hope that in spite of the Bill being rejected by the majority of the British Legislatures, at that time, it will come again and again till it becomes a reality. He said:

"My Lord, I know that my Bill will be thrown out before the day closes. I make no complaint. I shall not even feel depressed... I have always felt that we, of the present generation in India, can only hope to serve our country by our failures. The men and women, who will be privileged to serve her by their success will come later. We must be content to accept cheerfully the place that has been allotted to us in our onward march. The bill thrown out today will come back again and again till on the stepping stones of its dead selves, a measure ultimately rises, which will spread the light of knowledge throughout the land... But my Lord, whatever fate awaits our labours, one thing is clear, we shall be entitled to feel that we have done our duty and where the call of duty is clear, *it is better even to labour and fail than not to labour at all* (emphasis added)."

It may be stated that the hope expressed by the crusader of free and compulsory elementary education did come true. During the next 15 years, four Resolutions were tabled in the Council, but all were rejected. Even in independent India, it has taken the Government about 63 years to legislate Right to Education Act, which makes it incumbent on the Government to provide free and compulsory education to children between the ages of six and fourteen.

The Aftermath

It took another one year for the Government to reassess the demand for free and compulsory primary education.

In a note dated Thirteenth May, 1911, S.H. Butler, Member, Legislative Council admitted that the demand for free primary education throughout India had grown in intensity. "Hindus and Muhammadans alike have made it part of their platforms. It is advocated in legislative councils, at public meetings and in the press, by land owners no less than by lawyers; and philanthropists and politicians are starting free institutions, night schools and the like."[4] The note also stated that Mr. Gokhale's Bill contemplates the payment of fees by parents, whose income exceeded Rs.10 per mensem; but the public prefers the abolition of fee to the contingent introduction of the compulsive principle and that was Mr. Gokhale's own attitude in the Imperial Legislative Council a year ago.[5]

The Government of India in their letter dated 22nd November, 1906 had expressed a definite opinion in favour of free vernacular education for boys and girls as soon as the finances of the country would bear the strain and this opinion was kept alive in spite of the criticism of the local bodies.

Mr. Butler underlined the urgency of providing free primary education which he considered was of vital consequence "not only because I foresee that we shall be forced to concede it within a year or two, nor because I think that more than any measure it will remove the deep rooted belief in India and outside it, that we are afraid of education and put difficulties in its path, but mainly because I am convinced that the economic and political conditions of the country require it."[6] He warned that unless we move in harmony with popular opinion in this matter, *we shall find control slipping through our fingers.*

The viceroy (Lord Hardinge) in his order dated 27.5.1911, warmly supported the proposal of Mr. Butler. He was of the view that free primary education is a measure that is bound to come, even if we were opposed to the idea and in that case it would be far better that we introduced it on our own initiative rather than be forced into doing it so or by a reiterated expression of Indian public opinion........ Having said this, he agreed with the opinion of the honourable Member that education should not be at present made compulsory. .... "It would be a great mistake for Government to press forward too fast or to allow ourselves to be hustled by Mr. Gokhale into making education compulsory at present. Free elementary education would be only the first step in our campaign against illiteracy. It is an important one and will cost a good deal of money. To make it compulsory at once would cost a good deal more. *Therefore, on financial grounds also, it is best to take one step at a time*" (emphasis added).[7]

Government's Policy Outlined

The thinking of the Government in regard to free and compulsory education was crystallised in a letter dated 18th April, 1912 from Secretary of State for India on – Improvement and Expansion of Education in India – Draft Resolution on Educational Policy addressed to Governor General. Extracts:

1. The first place has been wisely given to primary education, the predominant claims of which depend upon the means (at your disposal) are fully recognised by His Majesty's Government.
2. Time has not arrived at which it would be practicable to dispense, wholly with fees, without injustice to many villages, which are waiting for the provision of schools.
3. Mr. Gokhale raised the question of free and compulsory primary education. He withdrew the proposal on the government promising to examine them. The result of examination are:
   (a) Legislation conferring powers on local bodies to make elementary education compulsory was accepted;
   (b) Primary education should be made compulsory for boys and not girls;
   (c) Compulsion should be between the ages of six and ten. This provision would in no sense prejudice education upto a later age.
4. Education would be compulsory for boys in areas where 33 per cent of boys are actually at school. It would be safer for local governments to compel local bodies to make byelaws, when the local government thought fit.
5. Education, wherever compulsory to be gratuitous at least for children of parents whose income is below Rs. 25 per month.
6. Extra cost divided between Government and local bodies in proportion of 2:1.
7. A post of secretary and finally a member in separate charge of education should be created.
8. Administration and control of education to be divided instead of being a provincial head.
9. Statement describing progress of education to be published with *the General Financial Statement.*

The Government's position was further elaborated by Mr. Montague's Budget speech of 30th July 1912. Excerpts[8]:

"...The house will have heard of the proposals associated with the name of that eminent Indian educationist, Mr. Gokhale, who has introduced a bill for what I may describe shortly as free compulsory primary education on a permissive basis. What I mean by that is that education is to be free and compulsory where, under certain conditions, the local authority chooses to apply it. He estimates that the cost of his proposal would ultimately be about £3,500,000. We are induced to believe this is a sanguine estimate.

I hope that Mr. Gokhale and those, who sympathise with him, will not misunderstand me when I urge a quality always irksome to self-sacrificing reformers like himself – the quality of patience. He thinks that primary education as it exists at present in India is sufficiently valuable to force it on the whole school going population of India as early as possible; *we do not*, Universal and free education in India must come as it has come in all other countries, but the time is not yet ripe and I am confident that the Government of India has a policy dictated for the present by the same hopes and aims of Mr. Gokhale, whose bill which will have a better result. We and he together are working for the same end – the breaking down of illiteracy in India. No one who also knows anything about the matter knows that his energy and speeches have helped us to create public opinion, without which our activity would be useless, but we believe that the greatest expansion of education can be secured not by making it free or compulsory but, at the present moment, by the improvement and multiplication of schools...compulsion can really be worked where education is popular and where, therefore, the need of putting compulsioxn into force would not show itself to the very large bulk of the population. There is not much use in applying it to resentful districts."[9]

To bolster his claim, Montague quoted the Maharaja of Rajpipla, 'a progressive chief' in the Bombay Presidency:

"Make primary education as free as you choose; add as many further inducements as you can, but do not make it compulsory. In the case of the most advanced classes, it is absolutely unnecessary and would serve only to create irritation. In the case of the poor 'backward classes', it would inflict harm, where good was meant, would subject them to great harassment, would be positively cruel and unjust and would be deeply, though silently, resented as such."[9]

Thus ended, though temporarily, the pioneering effort to introduce free and compulsory primary education for Indians.

It may be recalled that after Mr. Gokhale withdrew his resolution at the instance of the officials of the British Government, four more resolutions relating to primary education were tabled in the Legislative Council. Although none of them survived the onslaught of colonial representatives, it would be interesting to recall the proceedings of the Council and to see how British officials viewed the problem of mass education.

The following are in brief, the statements made by the movers of the resolutions and the reactions of the officials and non-official members in the debates on the subject:

(ii) Mazhar-ul-Haque

The Resolution moved by the Honourable Mr. Mazhar-ul-Haque on 7th of March, 1911 in the Legislative Council stated:

> 'That this Council recommends that the grants to local governments be increased by such an amount as will enable them to remit the fees payable in primary schools for the coming year'.

Explaining the purpose of the Resolution, Mr. Haque said that his proposal was a very small beginning in the advancement of the grand scheme of free and compulsory education moved by Mr. Gokhale to which he gave his whole hearted support. The idea was that education should become universal in India. He referred to the letter by Sir Herbert Risley addressed to the local governments in November 1906, in which he had declared that universal primary education was the aim in view. To insist permanent retention of fees was manifestly incompatible with universal school attendance. They would, therefore, desire to abolish fees as soon as the finances of the country permit...

Mr. Haque further stated that a perusal of the reactions of the local governments revealed that out of the administrations consulted, only 3 out of 12 had supported it. This was mainly because of the feeling that money would be better spent on the extension of schools in backward areas and the bettering of teaching staff. These views were the personal views of the administration. The people were unanimous that education should be made free. A large number of officials were in favour of the proposal. There was also a view that the first priority was to make education compulsory and then free. According to Mr. Haque, education cannot be made compulsory until it is made free.

In the discussion that followed, the following points were made:

Malik Umar Hayat Khan was of the opinion that, "education on an extensive scale was a question which will decide the destinies of India one way or the other, and to deal with it in an off-hand way, by moving a resolution, would be merely rushing things. Again to draw all people from their forefathers' occupations and to be unable to provide them with any other suitable openings was a gross mistake. He also referred to the cost and the sources from which it would be met. If free primary education was forced upon the people, it will mean trading and non-agricultural classes will benefit at the cost of agriculturists; surely from the Government revenues, which were mainly contributed by the agricultural classes. Further, if an agriculturist had to send his son to school, he would have to employ another person to help him. That will mean financial loss for him. Mr. Umar Hayat Khan also argued that if a Zamindar boy goes on working like his father, he would get hardy and be able to work efficiently while on the other hand, if he is sitting down in school and carrying on his studies, he would not have that bodily development and his limbs would become so weak that he would be unable to follow his father's occupations and also develop a false honour which will prevent him from doing such works.

Through these bizarre arguments, he opposed the Resolution.

Mr. Gokhale stated that it was a matter of Rs. 32 lakhs a year to begin with and if the government so chooses, they could do it. The government had given a non-recurring grant for buildings for training institutions. In order to make it really effective, it should be supplemented with a recurring grant and that should be done in the current year.

Babu Bhupendranath Basu stated that the government had always assured that if expenses did not stand in the way, it would not stand in the way of introducing compulsory primary education. Allaying the fears of Malik Umar Hayat Khan, Mr. Basu stated that a person with a little knowledge of reading and writing, would be more useful to the Zamindar and the Mahajan. We should not be overpowered by the fear of large sums involved in introducing free and compulsory primary education. For the present, a few selected areas could be taken up. We do not expect that the resolution would be approved. But we must put question to the country and the Government.

Mr. Sachidananda Sinha referred to Lord Antony Macdonnell's: address to Allahabad University where he stated that what the Government of India afraid of was not education but the ignorance of the masses. The agricultural classes were as much at a disadvantage against money lenders and it was in their own interest to support a measure of this kind.

Mr. Shams-ul-Huda said that Mohammeden opinion was at one with the Hindu opinion that primary education should be made free in India. About the question, whether it should be compulsory, the opinion was divided.

Mr. Quin, a government representative, reminded the members that the resolution on which they were asked to vote ran like this:

"That this Council recommends that the grants to local governments be increased by such an amount as will enable them to remit the fees payable in primary schools for the ensuing year.

Mr. Quin opposed the resolution. According to him, the proposal was not desirable and should not be accepted by the Council. To make grants to the local governments for this purpose would necessitate a large financial scheme to cover the additional expenditure. We may not be able to continue the scheme for years to come. Facilities for education were not available in all villages. Qualified teachers were also not available. It would be unjust to provide for remission of fees to existing students, while a large bulk of them were denied education by the government. Fee remissions did not always increase the number of students. In support of his contention, he quoted figures for the Bombay Presidency. He concluded by saying, "The proposal made by the Honourable member is both inadequate, unjust and unnecessary. He hoped that it will not be accepted by the Council".

Mr. Madge, while opposing the motion, said that employment of young people in agricultural farms was a necessary part of the then domestic economy and compulsory education applied to that class would become absolutely tyrannical. "Great injustice and hardship would be done to many poor families if you dragged their children to school and compelled them to undergo a course of primary instruction" he emphasised.

Mr. Mudholkar quoted Baroda experiment of compulsory and free education. According to him, we have yet miles to go to introduce free and compulsory education all over India. I have heard no new reason for introducing free and compulsory education. The question remains at the stage of last year when mr. Gokhale's proposal was discussed.

The mover of the resolution, Mr. Mazhar-ul-Haque regretted that the non-officials are so much in minority. He, therefore, never expected that his resolution would be immediately accepted. "We have to bring this proposal year after year, because we have set our hearts upon providing free and compulsory education for the people of the country and one shall not be satisfied unless they get it."

The Resolution was put to vote and rejected.

(iii) B.N.S. Sarma

The story did not end there. Eight years later, on 13th March 1918, Honourable Rai Bahadur BNS Sarma moved another Resolution regarding introduction of free and compulsory education after the War and financing of primary education out of Imperial revenues.

The Resolution read:

'The Council recommends to the Governor General in Council that one of the post-war reforms should be the introduction throughout British India of free and compulsory primary education immediately after the war'.[11]

Mr. Sarma said: The Home Government has promised that self-government is to be the goal of Indian administration. Whatever progress has been made in the past, we have not been able to overtake the growth of population.

The world has advanced considerably since Mr. Gokhale advanced his proposal and besides that Mr. Gokhale knew the difficulties he had to contend against and was, therefore, desirous of introducing the thin end of the wedge then by inducing the Government to accept the principle. What was an improbability then the Government have been forced by the public opinion to accept as a possibility now.

The voluntary principle has been preached ad-nauseam by the Government and their advocates. Two propositions have been put in support of this policy:

(a) We have not enough funds to found schools
(b) The quality has to be improved. Unless free and compulsory education is introduced, you cannot have quality."[12]

In the debate, the following points were made:

C. Sankaran Nair

We oppose this Resolution as we did last year.

(i) There is increasing government expenditure on education – Rs. 468 lakhs last year, Rs. 502 lakhs this year and it is expected to be Rs. 616 lakhs next year.

(ii) Compulsion every year is a colossal task. We cannot raise the money necessary for maintaining it.

(iii) Mr. Gokhale estimated that the cost would be Rs. 4½ crores. It would be about Rs.12 crores, now.

Dr. Tej Bahadur Sapru

Can we take pride in the fact that UP is a little higher than Baluchistan in the matter of primary education?

Pandit Madan Mohan Malaviya

Further time should not be lost.

Sir William Meyer

The expansion of primary education should rest with the local bodies and local government.

H. Sharp

We must apply the principle of assistance to those who cannot help themselves.

K.K. Chanda

When we ask for self government, the answer we get is, that the people are illiterate and therefore it cannot be granted. When we ask for universal education we are met with the objection that it will cost a mint of money and therefore it cannot be granted. That is our position. How are we to get out of that circle?

The motion was considered by the Council on 13th March 1918 and put to vote: 12 members voted for and 43 against.

The motion was negated[13].

(iv) Other Resolutions

Two separate Resolutions were moved by Haji Wajihuddin (21st July 1923) and Mr. N.M. Joshi (9th June 1925). One of them read:

"This Assembly recommends to the Governor General in Council to take immediate steps to introduce compulsory primary education in those territories in British India, which are under the direct control of the Government of India."[14]

As usual, the Resolutions were rejected.

It may be recalled that at the time of rejection of Mr. Gokhale's proposal in 1911, a statement was made by the Education Member, Sir Harcourt Butler, to the effect that it would be open to the Provincial Legislatures to initiate legislation for the purpose of rendering education compulsory within the limits of such local bodies as might desire compulsion and be ready to defray the additional expenses entailed by it. In pursuance of this, a private bill to allow the adoption of compulsory education by district municipalities in Bombay was introduced into the Bombay Legislative Council by Hon'ble Mr. Patel and was passed into Law. A similar bill was proposed by a non-official member of the Bengal Council and another for Bihar and Orissa, while the Punjab Government published for criticism a government bill on similar and even more comprehensive lines....

The government of India, however, felt that adoption here and there of measure of compulsion in certain areas in a sporadic manner was not desirable for two reasons:

1. In an important matter of this kind, it was incumbent on the government to indicate the principles on which it considers that the country should proceed and as we have satisfied ourselves as to the principles we believe to be suitable for adoption, we see no reason for postponing their publication or for subjecting ourselves to the approach that private agencies are forced owing to our inactivity to enter the field, which the government should occupy.
2. We are convinced that the subsidiary schemes of compulsory education now before the public are in every way inferior to that which we ourselves support.[15]

In pursuance of this letter, B.D. Macalagon, Secretary to the Government of India communicated to the provincial governments the following suggestions in his letter dated nil, 1918:

1. The Government of India have for sometime past, been satisfied that keen demand exists over large areas for a more rapid realization of their desired policy that has been possible during a period of financial stringency and that the country, as a whole, is prepared for a solid advance towards mass education. They have, therefore, during the last two years, been constantly occupied with the consideration of this important question and during the autumn of 1917, they found themselves in a position to formulate proposals which are as follows:
   - (i) that effort should be made to double the present number of pupils in boy's primary schools in ten years;
   - (ii) that of the additional expenditure involved, one third should be met by Imperial government, one third by provincial governments and one third by local bodies, and
   - (iii) that local bodies should be under obligation to establish and maintain the facilities requisite for carrying out the above scheme and should, where necessary, be empowered to raise further taxation for the purpose.

In order to render the scheme effective, it was recognised that it would require an additional number of trained teachers and an additional inspecting staff. The additional expenditure on this account would be met by the Imperial and Provincial governments and not by the local bodies. The responsibility for carrying out the proposed expansion of primary education would rest with the reformed provincial administration and local bodies and the introduction of a system of educational development will constitute one of the first of the serious and responsible duties, which will fall to the lot of these bodies...

Conclusions

It has been a long way since the British Government in India adopted the so called 'Downward Filtration Theory' which, in effect, meant that the Government should take care of the education of the classes rather than of the masses. The idea was that this would make it possible for education to filter down in course of time from the elitist classes to the lower sections of society – the hewers of wood and the drawers of water. This policy was firmly reversed by the 'Woods Despatch' of 1854, which recommended the involvement of government in the education of the masses. This period also witnessed the great controversy about the type of education – Oriental or European – which the government should promote. The government, on the advice of Lord Macaulay, Law Member of the Governor General's Council, decided that encouraging English language and scientific education should be the sheet-anchor of the government policy.

The period also witnessed the pioneering efforts made by the Indian members of the Legislative Council to coax and cajole the government to move towards providing for free and compulsory education. The first resolution was tabled by Hon'ble Gopal Krishan Gokhale, a member of the Legislative Council, in which the officials outnumbered the non-officials. The official opinion was solidly against the resolution forcing him to withdraw it. Thereafter, four more attempts were made to make the government aware of their responsibilities towards education of the masses. All these resolutions were outright rejected.

It is difficult to surmise how far the country would have progressed towards achieving the target of universalising elementary education if the resolutions sponsored by the Indian members of the Legislative Council had not met the rock of official apathy and cynicism. The position at the time of India's independence was, however, not very encouraging as would be evident from the following facts:

1. Over all educational facilities were available for only 40 per cent of the children of the age group 6-11, 10 per cent in the age group 11-17 and 0.9 per cent for the age group 17-23.
2. The literacy percentage was roughly 17.2 per cent.
3. Whereas 82.8 per cent of the population lived in rural areas, the percentage of the total number of pupils in recognized primary, middle and high schools that were studying in them in 1949-50 was 60, 67 and 26 respectively. The respective percentages in 1937-38 were 82, 72 and 28. At the university level, facilities were practically non-existent. Expenditure on recognised educational institutions in rural areas fell from 36 per cent of the total expenditure in 1937-38 to 30 per cent in 1949-50 although the total expenditure on education in rural areas had considerably increased.

4. At the primary stage, there was incidence of large wastage. Of the total number of students entering schools in class I, only 40 per cent reached class V in 1948-49. The position of girls was much worse.

(*Source:* First Five Year Plan)

Post Script

After the rejection by the Government of the last Resolution about providing free and compulsory education to children in 1925, India had to wait for more than three quarters of a century to achieve the long cherished goal which was envisioned by Gopal Krishan Gokhale in 1910. It was only in 2010 that the Government of India notified Right to Education Act[16], which provides for free and compulsory education to children in the age group of six to fourteen. This comes nine years after the Constitutional amendment, which declared education as a fundamental right for every child in the above-mentioned age group.

It may be recalled that the Indian Constitution had recognized the need for providing free and compulsory education to children till they attain the age of 14, under Article 45 of the Directive Principles of State Policy. This was, however, a policy guideline and was non-ad-judicable. Except for periodically repeating it in the five-year plans and other official documents, not much was done by way of enforcing compulsory education of the provision of Article 45.

The Right to Education Act makes it obligatory for the Government, central, states and local bodies, to provide and enforce the provision. It also entitles parents to sue the Government for not making available requisite facilities for education of children of the age group. Action can also be taken against schools for not providing the requisite facilities. The problem is, however, of stupendous dimensions and its implementation is fraught with numerous difficulties – financial, socio-economic, academic and administrative. It is earnestly hoped that in course of time, the problems will be sorted out and it will be possible to attain the objective for which pioneering efforts were initiated in the early days of the twentieth century (18th March 1910), by reformists like Gopal Krishan Gokhale and other members of the Legislative Council who sponsored resolutions in the Council on the subject only to be rejected by the Government.

References

1. *Source:* National Archives of India (files).
2. It is interesting to note that in his note dated 5-9-1910, Mr. G.F. Wilson, while agreeing with Mr. Jenkins, remarked that while in Bombay, he was told by Indians, who should know that this whole thing would be a farce; in Baroda was it not that every unfortunate native has to bribe an education officer to avoid sending his child to school. This statement was made in Mr. Gokhale's presence and he remained silent.
3. The sentiments expressed by Gokhale are reminiscent of the statement made by Brutus – a close confidant of Julius Caesar - who, having lost the battle against Antony said: "I have glory by this losing day! More than Octavious and Mark Antony" – (The killers of Julius Caesar) (Shakespeare: Julius Caesar) – W.G. Craig (ed.) p. 199.

4. National Archives of India files.
5. *Ibid.*
6. *Ibid.*
7. *Ibid.*
8. Department of Education proceedings, March, 1913 IA No. 103-108, National Archives files.
9. *Ibid.,* Proceedings.
10. Department of Education, Proceedings, March, 1913 (A).
11. Proceeding No.53, Education Dept. (National Archives of India files), August 1918.
12. *Ibid.*, August, 1918.
13. Proceedings, 53, National Archives of India files.
14. Proceedings 68-78 (B), January 1926.
15. Extracts from a letter dated 15th April, 1918 from the Viceroy Lord Chelmsford and all members of the Legislative Council addressed to Secretary of State for India (Edwin Montague) London.
16. The 'Right to Education Act' has been fully discussed in a separate Chapter.

8

Protagonists of Indian Education

(i) Swami Dayanand Saraswati (1824-83)*

Maharishi Dayanand Saraswati, the founder of Arya Samaj and a born rebel against religious dogmas and practices based on myths and legends; a crusader for Vedic renaissance and an eminent social reformer, was born as Mool Shankar in 1824 at Tankara in princely state of Morvi in the Saurashtra region of Gujarat. His father Karshanji was a landlord and a staunch worshipper of Shiva (one of the trinity of gods). At the age of 14, Mool Shankar was taken to a Shiva temple by his father to keep a 24 hour fast and a night long vigil on the occasion of Mahashivaratri. This proved to be a turning point in the life of the young boy. He saw to his horror that, when everybody was dozing, rats started nibbling the offerings and defiling the idol. He asked his father as to why Shiva, the omnipotent, could not protect himself from these inroads. He was not convinced with his father's explanation, went home and broke his fast. At the age of 21, he decided to renounce the world. Parental efforts to bind him in wedlock failed to restrain him. At the age of 22, he left his home for good in search of a guru.

He wandered from place to place and ultimately came across his Guru–Swami Virajanand, a frail yogi, an erudite scholar of the Vedic lore and a strict disciplinarian. He stayed with his Guru till 1863. He was admitted to the clan of Sanyasis and rechristened Dayanand. At the end of his education, which was a rigorous exercise under a very strict Guru, he was asked not to give the customary Dakshina (offering) but a pledge that he would work throughout his life for the supremacy of *Aarsha* works over the *Aanarsha*[1] ones. Dayanand pledged to devote his entire life to the propagation of Vedic scriptures and to fight against the social evils and religious malpractices that had plagued the Hindu society.

---

* The main sources for write up are:

(a) Dr. Charanjiva Bharadwoja; Light of Truth; An English translation of Satyarth Prakash, 1975; Sarvedeshak Pratinidhi Sabha; New Delhi, 1975.

(b) J.M. Sharma, Swami Dayananda; A Biography, UBS Publishers, New Delhi.

(c) S.R. Sharma, Life and Work's of Swami Dayanand Saraswati, 2004; Book Enclave, Jaipur.

Thus was born the apostle of Vedic learning, who devoted his entire life to the rejuvenation of the Vedic Dharma. that was contained in the four Vedas but had become corrupted over the centuries. It was his aim to propagate "the truth of that religion, to reinstate it in its purity, thereby to reinstate the Indian people in their forgotten glory.....".[2] It is significant to note that this task was accomplished not through his mother tongue – Gujarati – but through Hindi, which was spoken and understood widely in most parts of India.

While fulfilling his life's mission, Swamiji was confronted with untold trials and tribulations, intrigues, indignities and physical assaults; even attempts to murder him. He, however, continued with his life's mission. He left his mortal frame as a result of poisoning by his cook, who performed the nefarious act at the behest of a dancing girl, whom Swamiji had antagonized by advising her patron to leave the immoral ways. On his death bed, Swamiji sat in a Samadhi (meditation) and breathed his last with these words: 'God, Your Wish is Supreme'!

Dayanand's Educational Philosophy

Dayanand was a profound thinker who believed that it was through education that the moral and spiritual upliftment of the individual could be brought about. He, therefore, worked out a comprehensive system of education starting from the pre-natal stage to the very advanced years of an adult's life. He was in fact a votary of life-long education. Unlike Raja Ram Mohan Roy, who had vehemently pleaded for the introduction of the western system of education with English as the medium, Dayanand advocated education based on the Vedas and other religious scriptures through Sanskrit and Hindi medium. Further, he stressed training in martial arts, aesthetics and vocations, in addition to the Vedic version of the subjects like– geography, astronomy, mathematics and languages. He had also given instructions about teacher education and the manner in which teachers should perform their duties.

Dayanand believed that a person would become a good scholar only if he had the advantage of three good teachers: mother, father and the preceptor. According to him, the mother's healthy influence on her children surpassed that of everyone. "Blessed is the mother, who never ceases to impart religious tone to the mind of her child from the time of conception, till his knowledge is perfected."[3]

Swamiji had given instructions about the manner in which, parents should take care of a child's education from early stages to his growth as an adult: "The mother has been advised to instruct her children so as to make them refined in character and manners and they should never be allowed to misconduct themselves in any way. When the child begins to speak, his mother should help him pronouncing the words accurately. He should also be taught how to behave with and respect his elders. Parents should endeavour to inculcate in the minds of their children intense desire for the love for knowledge, elevating company and control of senses."[4] Swamiji warned that "parents who neglect the education of their child are his veritable enemies. To give their children the highest education possible, to instruct them in the ways of truth, to make them refined in character and manners; in short to devote all their resources, body and mind to accomplish this object, is the paramount duty, the highest virtue and the glory of parents."[5]

Dayanand was a votary of compulsory education for children of both sexes. He quoted Manu, who had ordained in the *Manusmriti*: "Both state and society should make it compulsory upon all to send their children (both male and female) to schools after 5th or 8th year. It should be made a penal offence to keep the child at home after that age"[6] (a precursor to Right to Education Act [RTE] passed recently by Indian Parliament).

Dayanand laid down a strict code of conduct for teachers. They were supposed to ensure that children are kept aloof from sexual excitement and thus perfect them, cultivate amiable dispositions and manners, gain in strength both of body and mind and thereby grow in happiness.

As for personal qualifications, a teacher was supposed to be not only a learned person, well versed in the Vedas and other scriptures, but also a person of high moral character. He should not only ensure that the children get good theoretical knowledge, but also perform daily prayers, tend the cows and perform other household chores at the residence of the teacher. The teachers were required to train the student not only in various science and humanities courses but also watch his growth as an adolescent and provide him with the necessary guidance in reforming his behavioural pattern. According to Dayanand, the teachers should instruct their pupils in the following way:

"My children, always speak the truth, lead a virtuous life; abstain from sexual indulgence, never be negligent in learning and teaching, devote yourself to sciences (physical and spiritual) till your knowledge is perfect... Never be indifferent to truth and religion. Never neglect your health and the cultivation of any skill. Never neglect your studies, never neglect to serve your father, mother, teacher and all preachers of the true religion..."[7]

As regards the syllabus of studies, Dayanand abhorred superficial knowledge of a few subjects, but wanted the students to go through a wide variety of subjects, beginning with grammar, literature, the Vedas, Upanishads, *Ramayana*, *Mahabharata*, *Ayurveda* (the science of health), *Dhanurvidya* (the science of war), Gandarveda (aesthetic arts), *Arthveda* (economics), vocational training, Astronomy, Algebra, Arithmetic, Geology, Space Science, etc. All these would, however, depend upon the interest and intellectual capabilities of the aspiring students. Swami Dayanand has given detailed instructions about the manner in which the various subjects are to be studied.

Dayanand was totally against any distinctions based on the gender and socio-economic position of the students. He underlined the need for providing education to all, regardless of the caste and class to which they belonged. The educational system was to be non-discriminatory, all embracing and universal. According to him if Brahmans only acquired knowledge "there could be no advance in knowledge, religion and government, nor increase in wealth.... When all classes are well educated and cultured, no one can set up any false, fraudulent and irreligious practices."[8]

Dayanand was a staunch believer in the need for educating women and '*Shudras*', the down-trodden segment of the Hindus. According to him, "all the classes: Brahmans, Kshatriayas, Vaishyas, Shudras, women, servants, aye even the lowest of the low, so should you all do, i.e., teach and preach the Vedas. He quoted Manu to support his point: "...Does not God desire the welfare of the Shudras? Is God prejudiced that he should allow the study of the Vedas to *Dwijas* (high castes) and disallow it to *Shudras*? Had God meant that the Shudras should not study the Vedas or hear it read; why should He have created the organs of speech and hearing in their bodies? As He has created the sun, the moon, the earth, the water, the fire, the air, various food and drinks, etc., for all, so He has revealed the Vedas for all..."[9]

As for the medium of instruction, he preferred the lingua franca of India Hindi to be the language of communication in educational institutions as also in day to day conversation. This was in spite of the fact that his own mother tongue was Gujarati and he himself was a Sanskrit scholar.

The D.A.V. Mission

Swami Dayanand's advocacy of the supremacy of education being an instrument for socio-cultural development flowered into the setting up of a chain of educational institutions in India. On June 1, 1886, the foundation stone of a Dayanand Anglo Vedic institution was laid at Lahore. This school was later on converted into a college. This was followed by a gigantic movement to set up educational institutions of all types all over India. According to the latest report, there are more than 700 educational institutions managed by the Dayanand Anglo-Vedic Managing Committee. These include D.A.V. Schools, Arts and Science Colleges, Colleges of Education, Law, Engineering and Technology, Agriculture; Vedic institutions and a recently set up university. These institutions have been set up to fulfil the 'D.A.V. Mission', which aims at:

1. Providing holistic education by homogenizing the western knowledge while remaining anchored to the Indian culture moorings;
2. To act as catalyst of change by spreading education by dismantling the cobwebs of ignorance and illiteracy;
3. To develop individuals, who are morally upright, intellectually well informed, socially concerned, emotionally balanced, physically well developed and culturally conscious;
4. To stimulate a scientific culture by crusading against superstitions and outmoded customs;
5. To sensitise the individuals towards social welfare; and

6. To nurture creative minds, who think big, think fast and think ahead, who care for the nation and the weaker sections of the society and are imbued with humanistic passions and values."[10]

Swami Sharadhanand, a devoted follower of Swami Dayanand, established a Gurukul on the banks of river Ganga in Haridwar, to impart, among others, knowledge of Sanskrit and study of and research on the Vedic scriptures. The Gurukul has now become a deemed university under the UGC Act. Till now, a large number of Gurukuls both for boys and girls, have been established all over the Indian landscape.

In order to propagate Vedic knowledge, a society named Arya Samaj was set up. This society, which has branches in the nook and corner of India, conducts *Havans* and *Sandhyas* as enjoined in Vedic scriptures. It also conducts seminars and workshops to spread the message of the Vedas and Upanishads and other Hindu scriptures. The Samaj is guided by ten Principles[11], which were evolved by Swami Dayanand. The first Principle says "God is the primary source of all true knowledge and all that is known through Him." About the attributes of God, it is believed that "God is Existent, Intelligent and Blissful. He is formless, Almighty, Just, Merciful, Unborn, Infinite, Unchangeable, Eternal, Incomparable, the support and Lord of all, Omniscient, Imperishable, Immortal, Fearless, Holy and the Maker of the Universe. To him alone, worship is due."[12]

About education, the 4th Principle beckons that "the Vedas are the scriptures of all true knowledge. It is the paramount duty of all Aryas to read them, to teach them to others, to listen to them and recite them to others."[13] The specific Principle (8th) which extols education says, "We should aim at dispelling ignorance and promoting knowledge." Though very brief, this is the Magna Carta of spreading knowledge to everybody, so that he should be taken out of the abyss of ignorance.

To sum up: The educational system advocated by Swami Dayanand is based on the principles of education for all without discrimination based on gender, class or caste. He emphasised the building of character, the purity of mind and abstinence from worldly pleasures while receiving education. In this task, the role of parents is of paramount importance. He emphasised that the parents should set as examples to the child with their own behaviour. Example, and not the precept, was to be the guiding force in the educational system evolved by Maharishi Dayanand. In this, the teacher has to play a vital role. He is expected to be a learned person, who has mastered the craft of teaching students by his own flawless, honest, truthful behaviour. Likewise, a student is expected to practice celibacy (*brahmacharya*) all through the span of his education. In fact, Swami Dayanand has laid down a code of conduct for teachers, parents and students of which character, i.e., purity of behaviour, honesty, truthfulness and performance of one's duty are the guiding forces. All this is to be achieved by following the rules and regulations laid down in ancient scriptures, the Vedas, the Upanishads, the Manusmriti, which have been elaborated in Swami Dayanand's magnum opus, the *Satyarth Prakash* and other ancient Sanskrit literature, some of which has been translated by him.

(ii) Sir Syed Ahmed Khan (October 17, 1817 - March 27, 1898)

Sir Syed was a prolific writer both in Persian and Urdu; "a historian, who tried to bring the Muslims out of their centuries old cultural stagnation through re-interpretation of Islamic teachings; a fearless fighter for social justice and above all a scholar of comparative religion."[14] Sir Syed wrote a commentary on the Bible in Urdu and impressed upon the Muslims that religio-cultural interaction between them and European Christians would be beneficial for them. Sir Syed had respect for all religions of the world and had all praise for non-Muslim religious leaders who endeavoured to restore their religious tradition to its pristine purity.

The Scientific Society founded by him was joined by Hindus and Muslims. The aim of the society was to provide Urdu translation of European works. His scheme resulted in the Aligarh Movement and the establishment of the Anglo-Oriental College at Aligarh. The doors of the college were kept open for all Muslims and non-Muslims. The college was later converted into a full-fledged university.

Sir Syed had his critics also. Aziz Ahmed in his essay: 'Islamic Reform Movements' has stated: "Sayyid Ahmed Khan's political activity began with the propagation of the view that was futile to challenge the British Role in India, that it was to be accepted as a reality, and as such the Muslim Community should adjust itself to a *modus vivendi* with it. This should take the form of a staunch loyalism and support for *Pax Britannica*....."[15]

Dr. Zakir Hussain, who had resigned his lecturership of the Mohammadan Anglo Oriental College, expressed his anguish at the indiscretion of the trustees of the university to call the police and evict the agitating students in the wake of Non-Cooperation Movement launched by Mahatma Gandhi. According to Zakir Sahib, "This can hardly be denied that Sir Syed lacked insight as a leader. We may give him some allowance as there was strong opposition to his efforts to introduce western education among his own people. There were few immediate needs to be fulfilled after the unsuccessful revolt of 1857, when Indian Muslims were particularly made victims of vengeance let loose by the Government on Indian people. In this condition, what could Sir Syed do? But to be carried away so much by the condition of the day is nothing but short-sightedness.[16]

Be that as it may, there is no denying the fact that Sir Syed was a social reformer, alongside a theological, political and educational thinker. He stressed a scientific attitude of mind, adopting a secular approach in all matters of human relationship. He believed in the supremacy of reason in all matters; spiritual or temporal. In spite of being an oriental scholar, he advocated modern education among the Muslims, who were rather backward in education. He insisted upon the Muslims to imbibe the liberal ideas and give up traditional mode of thinking and to adopt the modern system of education.

Sir Syed's Scheme of Education[17]

Sir Syed held the view that education was essential for the all round development of human personality. Defining the meaning of education, he said: "Human spirit is just like a mountain of marbles having several black spots on it, and unless the sculptor touches it, removes its dimness and roughness, turns it into a model, polishes and shines it, its beautiful nerves, charming colour and nice designs remain hidden. Similar is the condition of human spirit. A human being may be pious from the very core of his heart, but unless he is subjected to education, his piety and other noble qualities lie hidden in him. They can be brought into prominence only by means of education."[18]

He emphasised the need for self reliance in education. He strongly held the view that the nation wishing betterment could not do so unless it provided for education of the young. He made it clear that Indians would progress only when they themselves, without the interference of the Government, arranged for the education of their young boys out of their voluntary contribution and themselves administered and controlled their schools and colleges.

Sir Syed was painfully aware of the fact that the education of Muslims had remained confined to the traditional and religious learning through the medium of Arabic and Persian and that modern education in English was a *bête noire* for them and considered to be a cause for weakening their religion. Sir Syed considered this attitude as suicidal. He was convinced that modern education was the panacea of all social and political ills of India.

Aims of Education

Sir Syed believed that education was a means of fostering and cultivating the inherent potentialities of the child. It was the only instrument of bringing out the best in the child to equip him to face the challenges of life with confidence and to make his contribution to the socio-economic development and cultural regeneration of the country. He believed that the greatest aim of education and training was to engender piety, morality and humaneness in human beings. Education should aim at the harmonious development of the child's personality – physical, moral, intellectual and aesthetic sides of human nature. His thinking was akin to that of Mahatma Gandhi who advocated that education should aim at the all round development of the child – body, mind and spirit.

Sir Syed summed up his views on the role of education in the following words:

"The purpose of education has always been to create an awareness in man by which he may distinguish between good and bad, may give thought to the natural phenomena spread out before him. By acquiring knowledge, he may become more refined in his manners, may earn his livelihood in a better way and may give his thought to life hereafter. The plea of government that they are not concerned with the discipline and training of mind to this extent, but want that much education which may enable a man to earn his bread and which may remain confined merely to the teaching of geography, arithmetic and digits, is unwarranted."[19]

Courses of Study

The courses of study proposed by Sir Syed were to aim at bringing about the socio-economic, educational and cultural transformation of the students and through them of the nation. Sir Syed was of the view that the traditional curriculum taught in Muslim managed institutions was inadequate. There was, therefore, need for introducing modern curriculum which emphasised secular and general courses in sciences. After consulting community leaders, Sir Syed evolved a curriculum which had two parts: general education curriculum; and special education curriculum.

The general curriculum was expected to meet the general needs of the Muslims – secular as well as spiritual. It consisted of a study of religion, moral sciences, mathematics and natural sciences. The special curriculum included subjects like engineering, physiology, zoology, botany, geology, mineralogy and chemistry.

Transacting Education

Sir Syed was not satisfied with the traditional methods of teaching like lecture method in which the teacher reels out information on the subject and the students are, very often, passive listeners. Sir Syed advocated methods of teaching which assured active involvement of students in the teaching learning process. According to him, learning by doing and observation, rather than rote learning were the most effective modes of teaching. He also stressed freedom of expression on the part of students. Sir Syed also recommended experimental methods of teaching. According to him - "In old times, theories could be propounded and rebutted in the sequestrated places; now it is the experimental age. To prove or disprove anything, you have to be in the laboratories."[20]

To sum up, Sir Syeds' concept of education was an amalgam of the traditional and the modern system of education. In emphasising modern scientific education, he must have incurred the ire of Muslim orthodoxy. He was, however, able to implement his scheme of education because he firmly believed that the community cannot progress unless the system of education is modernised and education in subjects like science, engineering and technology is introduced. He also stressed teaching through English because that language had become a world language and was the repository of modern knowledge in Arts, Sciences and technology. He firmly believed that the community can ignore this fact only at its peril. The magnificent edifice of the Aligarh Muslim University built by Sir Syed speaks volumes about his vision and foresight about the future of the Muslim community and the emerging educational needs of a democratic, resurgent India.

(iii) Jamsetji Nusserwanji Tata (1839–1904)

The legendary Jamsetji Nusserwanji Tata, the patriarch of the illustrious Tata family[21] and the founder of the Tata Group of Industries, was born in a non-descript town Navsari in Gujarat State. He was the only son of Nusserwanji Tata - the scion of the family of Parsi priests. He completed his graduation at Elphinstone College, Bombay in 1858. Before that he had joined his father's business at the age of 14. Less than twenty years later, he set up the Empress Mills at Nagpur to coincide with the proclamation of Queen Victoria as the Empress of India. From that day onward, there was no looking back.

Jamsetji was a great visionary, who believed that India's poverty could be reduced by large scale industrialization. Alongside, he also believed that in order to reach that goal, it would be necessary to identify and nurture talented persons, who would contribute their best for accelerating the process of socio-economic development and cultural rejuvenation of the Country. According to him:

> "Freedom without strength to support it and, if need be defend it, would be a cruel delusion. And the strength to defend freedom can itself only come from wide-spread industrialisation and the infusion of modern science and technology, into the country's economic life".

To achieve the objective, Jamsetji established J.N.T. Endowment in 1892 to enable Indian students, regardless of their caste or creed, to pursue higher studies in England. He also offered the then Indian government a large sum of money as also buildings to establish a post graduate institute for scientific research. Thus was laid the foundation of the Indian Institute of Science at Bangalore. Unfortunately, this did not happen during the life time of Jamset ji.

Jamsetji was a realist, a staunch believer in action, a nationalist to the core, a philanthropist and pioneer, who not only brought India on the industrial map of the world but also laid the foundation stone of two of most prestigious research institutions; the Indian Institute of Science at Bangalore (now Bengaluru) and the Tata Institute of Fundamental Research at Bombay (now Mumbai).

Indian Institute of Science (IISc), Bangalore

The Institute was established in 1909 - 5 years after the death of the person, who visualized it: Jamsetji N. Tata. The conceptual framework of this Institute was worked out in 1893, when Jamsetji met Swami Vivekananda on a ship while travelling from Japan to Chicago. Besides discussing Tata's plan of establishing steel industry in India, they discussed Tata's scheme of establishing a Research Institute of Science in India. With the blessings of Swami Vivekananda, a committee was formed which worked out the proposal which was submitted to Lord Curzon in 1898. The land and other facilities were provided by the then Maharaja of

Mysore - H.H. Sir Krishnaraja Wodeyar and Tata himself. The proposal was formally approved by Lord Minto, the then viceroy of India in 1909. The foundation stone of the Institute was laid by the Maharaja of Mysore in 1911. On 24th July, the Departments of General and Applied Chemistry were set up to be followed by establishing Department of Organic Chemistry. The first Director of the Institute was Morris Travers, Sir William Ramsay's co-worker in the discovery of the noble gases. The first Indian Director was the Nobel Laureate, Sir C.V. Raman.

The Institute was the first to introduce Master's degree course in engineering. It has also started an integrated Ph.D. programme in Biological, Chemical, Physical and Mathematical Sciences for science graduates. The Institute has been given the status of a Deemed University by the University Grants Commission.

Tata Institute of Fundamental Research (TIFR), Mumbai

The Institute was established in 1945 in response to Homi J. Bhabha of the Atomic Energy Commission's request to Sir Dorabji Tata Trust to set up a Scientific Research Institute in India. With support from J.R.D. Tata, the then Chairman of the Tata Group, the Institute was set up with Homi J. Bhabha as its first Director. In the beginning the Institute started its activities at the Indian Institute of Science, Bangalore to be later shifted to Bombay.

In 1949, the Indian Council for Scientific and Industrial Research (CSIR) designated TIFR to be the centre for all large-scale projects in nuclear research. The first theoretical physics group was organized in December, 1950.

In 1957, India's first digital computer, TIFRAC, was built at TIFR. At the instance of Bhabha, Obaid Siddiqi set up a research group in Molecular Biology. This resulted in the establishment of the National Centre for Biological Sciences in 1970. Research at the TIFR is distributed in three schools working over the mathematical sciences, natural sciences, technology and computer science.

TIFR attained Deemed University status in 2002 - 40 years after the inauguration of its new campus at Colaba (Mumbai) by India's first Prime Minister, Jawahar Lal Nehru on 15th January, 1962.

(iv) Rabindra Nath Tagore (7th May, 1861 – 7th August, 1941)

The Poet Laureate, Nobel Prize Winner and a great thinker, Rabindra Nath was the youngest son of Debendranath Tagore, a leader of Brahmo Samaj, which attempted to revive the monistic basis of Hinduism as laid down in the Upanishads. He was raised mostly by servants; his mother had died in his early childhood and his father was always busy with his travels. Tagore generally avoided classroom schooling and preferred to roam about in the manor or the nearby idylls, which the family visited. He learnt drawing, anatomy, geography and history, literature, mathematics, Sanskrit and English – his least favourite subject. Because his father wanted his son to become a barrister, Tagore joined a public school in Brighton (England) in 1878. He studied law at University College, London, but again left the school. Instead, he opted for an independent study of Shakespeare's: *Antony and Cleopatra*. In 1880, he returned to Bengal without a degree.

In 1901, Tagore moved to Santiniketan to set up an *ashram*, with a marble floored prayer hall – the *Mandir*; an experimental school, groves of trees, garden and a library. There his wife and four of his five children died. He published *Naivedya* (1901) and *Kheya* (1906). In 1913, Tagore was awarded the Nobel Prize in Literature for his monumental work: '*Gitanjali*'. In 1915, the British Government 'honoured' him with Knighthood, which he renounced after the massacre at Jalianwala Bagh (1919).

In 1921, Tagore and agricultural economist Leonard Elmhirst set up the 'Institute for Rural Reconstruction' later renamed as *Sriniketan*. In 1930, he targeted abnormal caste consciousness and untouchability. In order to give vent to his ideas, he campaigned successfully to open Guruvayoor Temple to Dalits.

Tagore despised classroom based schooling. In 'The Parrot's Training' a bird is caged and force-fed text book pages – to death. Visiting Santa Barbara in 1917, he conceived of a new type of University; he sought to make Santiniketan, the connecting thread between India and the world – a world centre for the study of humanity somewhere beyond the limits of nations and Geography. The foundation stone of the school *Visva Bharati* was laid on 24th December, 1918 and was inaugurated three years later. It was based on the Gurukul system – Gurus gave personal attention to pupils – emotional, intellectual and spiritual – under the trees.

Tagore was a visionary. He has described the various attributes of India of his dreams in a poem in his magnum opus – *Gitanjali*:

"Where the mind is without fear and the head is held high;
Where knowledge is free;
Where the world has not been broken up into fragments by narrow domestic walls;
Where words come out from the depth of truth;
Where tireless striving stretches its arms towards perfection;
Where the clear stream of reason has not lost its way into the dreary desert sand of dead habit;
Where the mind is led forward by thee into ever-widening thought and action—
Into that heaven of freedom, my Father, let my country awake"

One of the important factors that would create this 'utopia' was education, which he strived to innovate as a life-long mission.

Tagore had a many splendoured personality. Amaratya Sen considered Tagore a 'towering figure', a deeply relevant and many sided contemporary thinker'. Tagore's contribution to art and literature, poetry, fiction, music, theatre and education is colossal. He transcended time and space barriers. Two of his poems: *Amar Shonar Bangla* and *Jana Gana Mana* have become national anthems of Bangladesh and India respectively.

The Chairman of the Nobel Committee of the Swedish Academy in the presentation speech on December 10, 1913 said:

"Tagore's *Gitanjali*: Song offerings (1912) a collection of religious poems was one of his works that especially arrested the attention of the selecting critics. Since last year the book, in a real and full sense, has belonged to English literature, for the author himself who, by education and practice, is a poet in his native Indian tongue, has bestowed upon the poems a new dress, alike perfect in form and personally original in inspiration. Quite independently of any knowledge of his Bengali poetry, irrespective, too, of differences of religious faiths, literary schools, or party aims, Tagore has been hailed from various quarters as a new and admirable master of that poetic art which has been a never-failing concomitant of the expansion of British civilization ever since the days of Queen Elizabeth. The features of this poetry that won immediate and enthusiastic admiration are the perfection with which the poet's own ideas and those he has borrowed have been harmonized into a complete whole; his rhythmically balanced style, that, to quote an English critic's opinion, combines at once the feminine grace of poetry with the virile power of prose; his austere, by some termed classic, taste in the choice of words and his use of the other elements of expression in a borrowed tongue – those features, in short, that stamp an original work as such, but which at the same time render more difficult its reproduction in another language."

On Education

Tagore identified the lack of educational facilities as the basic cause of India's social and economic backwardness. According to him: 'In my view the imposing tower of misery, which today rests on the heart of India has its sole foundation in the absence of education, caste division, religious conflicts, aversion to work, precarious economic condition, all are on this single factor'.

Tagore not only pleaded for the expansion of educational facilities all over India, particularly in rural areas, but also wanted the educational system to be more lively and joyful. He emphasised self motivation on the part of students rather than on discipline; on fostering intellectual curiosity rather than on competitive excellence.

Tagore preferred education of the general mass of people rather than university education. He was quite concerned about the prevalence of illiteracy particularly among the women. This had occurred because of neglect of the British rulers reinforced by India's traditional bias for elitist education.

Visva Bharati

Visva Bharati evolved out of a school for children at Santiniketan. The school Brahma Vidyalaya, which started functioning in 1901 with no more than five students, was in part, a fulfilment of the wishes of Tagore's father. From 1925, this school came to be known as Patha Bhavan. The school sought to realise the intrinsic value of ancient Indian education. Its curriculum departed from the usual curriculum introduced in schools in the society. Simplicity was the cardinal principle; classes were held in open under the shade of the trees, where man and nature entered into a cordial relationship. Teachers and students shared the single integral socio-cultural life. The curriculum included music, painting, dramatic performances and other similar activities. Besides academic and intellectual pursuits, opportunities were made available for invigorating and sustaining the manifold faculties of the human personality.

The aims and objectives of Santiniketan are:

1. To study the mind of man in its realisation of different aspects of truth from diverse points of view;
2. To promote more intimate relation with one another, through patient study and research, the different cultures of the East on the basis of their underlying unity;
3. To approach the west from the standpoint of such a unity of life and thought of Asia; to seek to realise in a common fellowship of study the meeting of the East and the West; to strengthen world peace through free communication of ideas between the two hemispheres.
4. To make Santiniketan a centre of culture, where research into and study of religion, literature, history, science and art of various religions may be pursued along with the culture of west for true spiritual realisation, in amity, good fellowship and cooperation between the thinkers and scholars of both Eastern and Western countries.

The centre at Santiniketan conceived by Tagore aimed at undertaking a coordinated study of the different cultures. In the centre, music and art were to be given a prominent place. The centre was not only a centre of the intellectual life of India, but of the economic life as well.

Vidya Bhavan or the Institute of Higher Studies and Research was expected to be a centre of comprehensive study of the cultures of East and West. It was viewed as a community of scholars, Indian as well as foreign, who would be engaged in creation and dissemination of systematised and philanthropic reasoning. The concern was epistemological. The centre attracted luminaries from different countries who worked with Indian scholars and creative artists.

In 1937, Cheena Bhavan, the department of Sino-Indian studies, was established. In 1939, Hindi Bhavan was founded. Kala Bhavan, which was originally an institution for both Fine Arts and Music was split into two distinct institutions, Kala Bhavan and Sangeet Bhavan, each with its own distinct disciplines.

In 1951, Visva Bharati was declared to be a Central University and an Institute of National Importance by an Act of Parliament. It was given the status of a unitary, teaching and residential university. The status and function of the major institutions were redefined.

Sriniketan

The Institute for Rural Reconstruction was founded in 1922, with the following objectives:

1. To win the friendship of villagers and cultivators by taking real interest in all that concerns their life and welfare, and by making an effort to assist them in solving their most pressing problems;
2. To initiate a dialogue between academic study and research of rural economy, culture and field experiences.

In order to help in the reconstruction of village life, a school primarily meant for the children of neighbouring villages, who would eventually use their acquired knowledge in reforming the village community life, was started at Santiniketan in 1924. The school was shifted to Sriniketan in 1927. In 1936, an organisation '*Lok Shiksha Sansad*' was started for the propagation of non-formal education among those, who had no concern to formal school education. *Shiksha Charcha* for training of school teachers was also set up in 1937.

The aim of all these organisations was to reform the village life through education and training.

Tagore was a pioneer in the field of education. His emphasis was on the all round development of the child which could be achieved by a holistic education, encompassing education at home, in the street and in the play field besides the school. His motto was learning by doing in the natural surroundings rather than rote learning.

Long before the world had heard of Globalisation, which has now become the sheet-anchor of international cooperation in the socio-economic field, Tagore had visualised Visva-Bharati as a meeting ground for the East and the West, apart from being a centre for the dissemination of India's cultural heritage, in addition to being a seminary for Eastern studies. The poet selected for its motto an ancient Sanskrit Verse: '*Yatra Visvambhavaticka nidam*' – "where the whole world meets in a single nest." Visva Bharati, according to Tagore, represents India, where she has her wealth of mind, which is for all. Visva-Bharati acknowledges India's obligation to offer to others the hospitably of the best culture and India's right to accept from others their best.

(v) Pandit Madan Mohan Malaviya (1861-1946)

Pandit Madan Mohan Malaviya was born on 25th December 1861 at Prayag, Allahabad. He received his early education in Sanskrit *Pathshalas.* Thereafter, he passed entrance examination from Allahabad Zila School. He graduated in 1884 from Muir Central College. Subsequently, he joined Law and started taking interest in Public affairs. He joined the Indian National Congress in 1886. He became a member of the Allahabad Municipal Council and subsequently, the Legislative Council. He was elected president of the All India Congress Committee at its Lahore session. He was also a member of the Viceroy's Council.

Pandit Malaviya had unparalleled capacity for collecting funds for the university. An instance in his life, which indicates his passion for providing adequate finances for the University, is very revealing. He approached His Exalted Highness, the Nizam of Hyderabad for some donation for the university which the latter flatly refused. This did not dishearten Malaviya ji. He came to know that the Nizam was in the habit of giving alms to beggars on every friday after finishing his prayers at the mosque. Malaviya ji joined the line of beggars outside the mosque waiting for munificence of the ruler of Hyderabad. Nizam was taken aback when he found Malviya ji among other aspirants for his generosity. He invited him to his palace and is said to have given him a substantial amount for the University. No wonder that Mahatma Gandhi called him the 'prince among the beggars'.

Pandit Malaviya was a champion of secular democracy. He frequently declared that India is a common motherhood of all Hindus, Muslims, etc. He stood for an efficient impartial administration. He was a great educational reformer and favoured the spread of education in every nook and corner of India. He, however, chose Varanasi and founded the Banaras Hindu University. He was Vice Chancellor of the University for more than two decades.

The Banaras Hindu University

Education claimed Pandit Malaviya's attention from the very beginning of his life. His passion for education fructified in the establishment of the Banaras Hindu University when Annie Besant handed over to him the Central Hindu College founded by her. He made it a national (university level) institution in 1916 with Sir Sunder Lal as the Vice Chancellor. He was succeeded by Sir P.S. Sivaswami Iyer. Alfred King, an Englishman, was appointed as Principal of the Engineering College. The faculty of the University was drawn from all over India. He himself became the founding Vice-Chancellor. Subsequently, the mantle of vice-chancellorship was passed on to Dr. S. Radhakrishnan, who was destined to become the President of India.

The Banaras Hindu University is an epitome of selfless service, devotion and love for education of Malaviyaji. It is an institution, which is non-discriminatory, open to all communities and religions. It is a unitary institution in the sense that its jurisdiction is limited to the city of Varanasi. The existing Central Hindu College was declared by an Act to be a college maintained by the University. Quality-wise the university is among the best institutions that country can boast of. It is an embodiment of the secular character of the country. It has places of worship of the three major communities – Hindus, Muslims and the Sikhs. It has received donations from the followers of all religions. The Muslims like the Nawab of Rampur, Nawab Chhatari and the Aga Khan were the prominent donors to this seat of learning.

The University also encourages education of the depressed classes. They are given special facilities and financial assistance during their education at the University.

During the freedom struggle, the Government of India stopped its financial assistance to the University. In order to keep it going, the faculty, on their own volition, took a cut on their salaries and made the University get over the financial crises that was staring in the face of the university.

To sum up, Pandit Madan Mohan Malaviya, was one of the brightest stars on India's social, political and educational firmament. He devoted his entire life to the social well being of the people. In spite of being deeply religious, he was secular and non-partisan. His contribution to the field of education is phenomenal. The Banaras University is an eloquent testimony to his capacity to provide higher education of super-quality to generations of students aspiring to become the torch bearers of India's socio-economic development and cultural regeneration.

(vi) Mohan Das Karam Chand Gandhi (2nd October 1869 – 30th January, 1948)

Mohan Das Karam Chand Gandhi was born in Porbandar, a small town on the Western Ghats of India in a small Kathiawar state. At the age of seven, the family moved to Rajkot. He got married at a very young age. Gandhi sailed to England in spite of the opposition of the orthodox members of his community. In England, he studied Law and was called to the Bar on June 10, 1881. He went to Durban in South Africa in 1893. There he came across racial discrimination at its worst. In spite of his holding a valid ticket in the train in the capital of Natal, he was thrown out of the compartment at about 9 p.m. without his luggage. Gandhi shivered and sat all through the cold night. He decided to fight it out.

In 1901, at the end of the Boer War, Gandhi decided to return to India. He participated in the Calcutta session of the Indian National Congress which passed a resolution against South Africa Apartheid. Soon after, he received a cablegram from the Indian Community in Natal. He sailed back to South Africa. When Transvaal received independence, it passed a 'Black Act' which required all Indians, men and women to register themselves and give their finger prints. Gandhi advised Indians to refuse to do so. He was arrested and sentenced to four months imprisonment. After his release, the Indians resisted the registration system and made a bonfire of the registration certificates. Gandhi was re-arrested. The strike spread, Gandhi was released and a provisional agreement was signed between him and General Smuts. The main demands of the Indians were accepted. Gandhi sailed to England, where Gokhale had called him. In January 1913, he returned to India and after a year's wanderings, settled down at the river Sabarmati in Ahmedabad, where he founded an Ashram.

His first Satyagraha was in Champaran in Bihar undertaken at the request of poor peasants, who were exploited by the British masters. Mahatma Gandhi arrived at the place and was arrested to be released forthwith because of the large following that had gathered there. This was followed by a few more civil disobedience movements at Kheda district in Gujarat. Gandhi had a many splendoured personality. He was in fact the guiding force in all the socio-political movements that occurred in India during the twilight years of the British rule.

Here we are concerned with two of these movements:

1. The Non-cooperation Movement so far as it affected the education system in the earlier twenties and

2. Gandhi's efforts to make the education system productivity oriented – the emergence of the Wardha Scheme of Basic Education.

The non-cooperation movement has been discussed separately under 'the Significant Events that Impacted Education.' Here we take up his scheme of Basic Education, the ideology behind it and the problems that it had to face.

Before discussing the Wardha Scheme of Education, it would be pertinent to give a brief life sketch of Dr. Zakir Hussain, who was the prime mover of the Scheme of Basic Education. In fact, the Wardha Scheme owes its origin to Dr. Zakir Hussain.

Zakir Hussain was born in 1897 at Hyderabad in a respectable Pathan family of Quanganj in Uttar Pradesh. His early education began with the Quran. He was taught Persian and Urdu. He studied at Islamic high school at Etawah, a famous residential institution.

After passing the matriculation examination, he got admission in Mohammdan Anglo Oriental College (which later developed into the Aligarh Muslim University in 1913) and passed Intermediate in science. He was admitted to the Aligarh Muslim University and did his Masters in Economics. He was appointed as a lecturer at the University.

Zakir Hussain joined the Non-cooperation Movement launched by Mahatma Gandhi in association with the redoubtable Ali Brothers. He resigned his lecturership after the refusal of the trustees of the Aligarh Muslim University to join the national movement. A new national university – Jamia Millia Islamia – was set up at Aligarh and later on shifted to Delhi. After his stay at Jamia for two years, he went to Germany for higher studies and got his doctorate in Economics from the Berlin University.

Zakir Hussain had great respect for Gandhiji. He gave practical shape to Gandhiji's concept of learning by giving a central place to craft in education and making it an instrument of educational transaction.

The Basic Education Scheme was worked out by a Committee under the chairmanship of Dr. Zakir Hussain. He was closely associated with introduction of the scheme on an all India basis. Zakir Husain became the President of the Republic of India.

Wardha Education (Basic) Scheme

(The Demise of an Ideology)

The significance of the educational proposals of Mahatma Gandhi – basic education and its elaborated version of Wardha Scheme – lay in forging a system of education which would act as an instrument for social and economic transformation of the country. It is, therefore, important to consider the context –social, economic and political – in which the proposal to provide compulsory education of seven years through mother tongue and with content of education built predominantly around a productive activity was made. Some of the important features of this context were:

- the predominantly rural character of Indian society; farming as the main activity of the majority of people (80 per cent or more);
- a sizeable work force self-employed as artisans and craftsmen, practising generally home and community based economic activities;
- a fragmented society consisting of castes, minorities, religious and socially stratified groups etc.
- existence of two systems of education, one patronized by the affluent and powerful; providing education through the medium of English and the other available for the poor with few opportunities for economic and social mobility; and
- political turmoil that preceded the attainment of freedom from foreign yoke – the period during which the scheme was launched.

A system of education suited to the conditions prevailing in the country – with little prospect of any radical change – had to take cognizance of this context.

The other consideration for basic education was the structure of Indian society and socio-economic development that Mahatma Gandhi envisaged. In his scheme of things, the regeneration and reconstruction of rural economy was of paramount importance. He emphasised the need of creating a community where peace prevailed among different groups, where economic and social tasks were cooperatively organised without undue competition; where individuals, families and communities were more or less self-reliant and where decisions affecting them were taken by communities rather than by a distant authority. Considering that India in 1930s consisted largely of villages and its economy was based on farming and handicrafts, Mahatma Gandhi felt that the basis for economic development in India had to be the village and its economy. Basic education, by promoting competencies in rural crafts and other related activities, was expected to be the prime mover of achieving this task.

Further, economic development, according to Mahatma Gandhi, was not the sole purpose of education. Education had to be all inclusive leading to the highest physical, mental and emotional development of the child. By education, I mean "an all round drawing of the best in child and man – body, mind and spirit"; This could be achieved by revolutionising the existing stereotyped system of education, which depended primarily on theoretical learning and shunned practical activities. Basic education, by emphasising working with hands, was the expected answer to the problem.

The Zakir Hussain Committee

In the backdrop of these ideas, a Committee under the Chairmanship of Dr. Zakir Hussain was constituted to draw up a detailed scheme. The Committee was critical of the western system of education, which had been imposed on the Indian society and had failed to meet the most urgent needs of national life. According to the Committee: "It (the western system of education) is neither responsive to the realistic elements of the present situation, nor inspired by any life giving or creative ideal... It has no conception of the new cooperative social order which education must help to bring into existence to replace the present competitive and inhuman regime based on exploitation and violent force."[22]

The main components of the scheme were:

(a) The duration of primary education should be extended to at least seven years and should include the general knowledge gained upto matriculation standard, less English, plus a substantial vocation;

(b) For the all round development of boys and girls all training should, as far as possible, be given through a profit yielding vocation;

(c) The primary education, besides training the mind, should equip boys and girls to earn their bread by State guaranteeing employment in the vocations learnt and by buying from the schools their manufactures at prices fixed by the state;

(d) Such education taken as a whole can and must be self supporting; and

(e) Higher education should be left to private enterprise and the state universities should be purely examining bodies.

The B.G. Kher Committee

The scheme was considered by a Committee under the Chairmanship of B.G. Kher, the then Chief Minister of Bombay (now Maharashtra). Dr. Zakir Hussain, the Chairman of the Wardha Education Scheme attempted to allay the misgivings of some members about the scheme. The Committee arrived at the following conclusions:

1. The scheme of 'Basic' education should be first introduced in rural areas.
2. The age range for compulsion should be 6 to 14 years, but children can be admitted to "Basic" schools at the age of 5.
3. Diversion of students from 'Basic' schools to other kind of schools should be allowed after the 5th Class or about the age of 11 plus.
4. The medium of instruction should be vernacular of the pupils.
5. A common language for India is desirable. This should be Hindustani with both Urdu and Hindi scripts. Option should be given to children to choose the script and provision should be made for teaching them in that script. Every teacher should know both these scripts viz. Urdu and Hindi. Some members of the Committee suggested that the adoption of the Roman script might prove a solution to the language difficulty and greatly minimise the work of both scholar and teacher.
6. The Wardha scheme of Basic education was in full agreement with the recommendations made in the Wood-Abbot Report as far as principle of learning by doing was concerned. This activity should be of many kinds in the lower classes and, later, should lead to a basic craft; the products of which should be saleable and proceeds applied to the upkeep of the school.

7. Certain elements of cultural subjects, which cannot be correlated with the basic craft, must be taught independently.
8. The training of teachers should be reorganised and their status raised.
9. No teacher should receive less than Rs. 20 per mensem.

There were other recommendations like need for revision of curriulum, non introduction of English even as an optional subject in Basic schools, provision of facilities by the government to every community to give religious teaching; no external examination at the end of basic education etc.

The CABE Adopts the Scheme

The Central Advisory Board of Education in their meeting held on 6th and 7th May, 1940 at Simla considered the report submitted by the B.G. Kher Committee. The Board accepted most of the recommendations of the Committee and felt that the Report, read in conjunction with the report of the previous Committee appointed by the Board to consider the Wardha Scheme, might well prove a valuable contribution towards the exploration of most important problem.

The Board, however, expressed its reservations about the possibility of meeting the costs of education by the sale of the articles produced by the students. It also did not agree with the hope expressed in the scheme that the educational system would produce craftsmen, whose products would compete with those prepared by skilled craftsmen.

The Path Breaking Scheme

There was tremendous enthusiasm in official and non-official circles about the path-breaking scheme propounded by the government. The First Five Year Plan (1951-56) termed the introduction of basic education as an important development in the field of education and as the pattern for education of children of the age group 6-14. The Plan, however, lamented that work done in this direction has varied to such an extent in the matter of approach and quality in different places that it is impossible to get an idea of the work done from statistics alone. This was in spite of the clear lead given by the Central Advisory Board of Education in March 1952 when they emphasised: "A system of education cannot be considered as basic education unless: (a) it provides an integrated course, including both the junior and the senior stages and (b) places adequate emphasis on craft work in both its educational and productive aspects."

The Plan recognised that although broad framework of basic education has been worked out and given inspiring expression at some places, it has to be recognised that "many of its details remained to be worked out and we are far from having fully developed the potentialities of basic education."[23]

The Plan also pointed out that the progress of basic education was retarded because of the following problems:

(a) Non-provision of adequate land, initial equipment and insufficient capital expenditure;

(b) The problems faced by agriculture centred school;
(c) Little attention to the disposal of the products of basic schools;
(d) Inadequate facilities for the training of basic school teachers. It was also stressed that the selection of teachers for training should include assessment of their personality traits, which should be given due weightage;
(e) Buildings for basic schools should be simple in design – not very costly but adequate for children's educational requirements;
(f) Non-officials should be associated with the administrative machinery consistent with efficiency and broad uniformity of policy.

Progress of Basic Education

In view of the difficulties like lack of trained teachers, buildings, equipment, etc., the progress of the scheme of basic education was very slow. In 1949-50, out of a total number of 2,64,826 primary schools, the number of basic schools was 32,182, i.e., 12 per cent of the total. Curiously enough, out of the 32,182 schools claiming to be basic, 31,036 (96 per cent), were in one single state viz. UP. The total number of pupils in these schools was 25,35,710, which works out to 14.5 per cent of the total enrolment in primary schools (including basic), i.e., 1,74,18,544.

Twelve years later i.e. in 1961-62, the position had somewhat improved. The enrolment in junior basic schools rose to 78,62,438, which was about 26 per cent of the total enrolment of 2,98,42,269 at that stage. Similarly, the number of junior basic schools rose to 73,982, which was 20.9 per cent of the total number of 3,53,670 primary schools. In the case of higher stages, the position was far from encouraging. The enrolment at the post-basic stage (higher secondary) was a mere 4,712, which was 0.0001 per cent of the total enrolment of 30,61,992 at that stage. The high school stage was better. The enrolment in senior basic schools was 35,89,550 out of a total enrolment of 89,57,279, which worked out to about 40 per cent of the total enrolment.

As far as institutions for basic education were concerned, there were only 31 post basic schools out of 13,729 higher secondary schools. In the case of senior basic schools, the number stood at 15,405 against a total of 40,430 denoting a percentage of 38. At the junior Basic (Primary) stage, the number of schools imparting basic education was 73,982 out of a total number 3,53,670 schools (including primary schools). This worked out to 29.7 per cent of the total schools at the primary stage.

The position highlighted above indicates that, except for the post-basic stage, there was some improvement in enrolment as well as the number of basic education institutions. This is, however, subject to the assumption that the schools claiming to be basic education institutions were really following the guidelines laid down in the Wardha Scheme of Education Committee. This may not be entirely correct. As already stated in the First Five Year Plan, "work in the direction of implementing the scheme of basic education has varied to such an extent in the matter of approach and quality in different places that it is impossible to get an idea of the work done from statistics alone."[24]

The Failure of the Scheme

The half-hearted manner in which the scheme was implemented, the non-availability of adequate academic and administrative support needed for nurturing an innovative idea, partly because of lack of conviction among those who were charged with its implementation and mostly for lack of effort to develop suitable institutional arrangements led to its eventual failure, notwithstanding the patronage it received at the hands of the high and mighty of the academic world and the blessings of Mahatma Gandhi. The causes of the failure of the scheme and the ultimate demise of the ideology on which it was built were not merely the traditional conservatism of the educational system to adapt itself to any radical transformation and its inability to adopt innovating and efficient practices, but lie much deeper in the emerging socio-economic fabric that India sought to weave for itself in the post-independence period. Apart from the factors that are endemic to the education system – lack of resources, inadequate working out of operational details, lack of adequate support system, lack of adequately trained teachers, etc.– the failure of basic education to take roots can be attributed to the socio-economic situation that prevailed in the thirties and in the decades that followed the initiation of economic planning in the fifties. The rejection of the development model that Mahatma Gandhi had in view and that he proposed was a strong characteristic of the latter period. In the different model, the instrumental relevance and appropriateness of basic education was neither accepted nor worked out.

The acceptance of the education system, its effectiveness and the support it was able to get depended significantly on the perceptions of those who availed of it. In late thirties, when adoption of basic education was advocated, and also in the decades that followed the attainment of independence, the clientele of basic education consisted mostly of the upward mobile segments of the society. With free, compulsory and universal primary education yet not an important component of the state policy, education was largely a preserve of the English knowing classes, steeped in, and appreciative of, the Western culture, institutions and modes of thinking; the general mass of the people, much less those who lived in rural areas, had little access to education. For the affluent, the main motivation for seeking education was remunerative employment in civil services and professions. Basic education, with its emphasis on craft (work-centred education) and designed largely for meeting the needs of the 80 per cent inhabiting the countryside, was perceived by this class to be a hindrance and stumbling block for educational advancement. This class not only patronised the system, the legacy of Macaulay, but also was in a position to decide what education for India should consist of and how it should be delivered. In spite of the considerable spread of education – a consequence as much of government effort as of the aspirations of the people – "elite" institutions providing education through the medium of English continued to flourish and thrive since they were patronised by those who can pay for the education of their wards; for this section, education was a never ending enterprise until the wards landed in cushy jobs. The institutions that they supported introduced what is called the "socially useful productive work", with the ostensible intention of promoting dignity of labour among students who, and whose families, were never destined to work with hands.

It must also be recognised that societal rewards – in terms of status and remunerative employment – then (and now), were largely available for those who studied "English" education. With private sector establishments largely absent, except in the form of low return farming and household/community practised crafts, government was the sole provider of jobs of high and low remuneration for the educated. With employment seekers and their families cued to the requirements of the job market, it was no surprise that basic schools did not attract the clientele whose perceptions and patronage would establish their credibility and lead to its acceptance. Basic schools remained confined to the hinterland of the country, patronized by those who, in spite of appreciating the value of education, could not even afford it.

The tendency to seek English medium education was and continues to be strengthened by entry requirements of third level institutions. In spite of the increasing use of regional languages as media of instruction in higher education, particularly at the under-graduate stage, there is a preference for institutions providing education through the medium of English; all professional education institutions have English medium. Although somewhat dormant during the freedom struggle, English as the medium of education continues to hold sway. With proficiency in English as a major requirement for remunerative employment, most school systems in the country prefer teaching through English; these days the introduction of English takes place in a large number of schools as early as grade I and even earlier. Coaching institutions, promising proficiency in the use of English, have proliferated and are found in lanes and by-lanes of even small towns. It is, therefore, not surprising that institutions providing quality education use English as the medium. This is as true of schools as of colleges. In a way, therefore, the education system prevailing in the pre-independence period had much greater credibility and acceptance. Poorly endowed basic schools did not have the capacity and support to compete with this system much less to dislodge it.

As stated earlier, basic education was conceived of in the context of development strategy that took note of the prevailing social and economic conditions. The development model chosen with the initiation of economic planning in the fifties was a significant departure from this model. The latter emphasised self-reliance through large scale industrialisation, with emphasis being on developing heavy machinery that will make machines. Not that this model was in any way faulty and not needed; the model, however, did not deal squarely with the concerns of the large majority of people living in impoverished villages and pursuing farming and village crafts. The neglect of agriculture and of economic activities of the rural households has all along been voiced. While the effort at Green Revolution did usher in a new era of agricultural development, rural handicrafts did not receive the knowledge and skill inputs that they required. Even now the education and training system does not deal squarely with the needs of this sector, although it, along with farming, provides employment to the large majority of the work force.

In this context it is interesting to note that even now self-employed and casual labour constitute 85 per cent of the employed (83 per cent in rural areas and 59 per cent in urban areas) while wage employment consists of 15 per cent of the employed.

Among the reasons that led to the failure of basic education, the following need mention:

- The academic content of basic education, encompassing all the stages of education was not adequately elaborated to demonstrate how the proposed system would fully meet all the needs of all learners. The proposition that only that knowledge was worth, which could be acquired through productive activity did not cut much ice, particularly in the context of considerable explosion of knowledge that had and was taking place. It was obligatory to recognise that with country changing fast – economically, socially and politically – the competencies of people would have to be many more and of different varieties and levels than work centred education could provide.
- The unquestioned acceptance of correlation as the strategy to develop content and to promote learning prevented the recognition of important learning gaps that needed to be filled through other transactional strategies of teaching and learning. Institutions made unsuccessful attempts to build content through what came to be known as "forced correlation".
- Craft-centred education needed teachers who had a knowledge base of craft as also the skills to impart training. Such teachers were hardly available despite the establishment of basic teacher training institutions. Even the teachers, who trained basic education teachers, were not fully equipped to impart knowledge and techniques of transacting education through the basic mode.
- Basic schools were never able to obtain resources – raw materials, equipment, working capital, kitchen gardens, workshops, etc. – that would allow them to introduce productive activities that went beyond spinning and weaving and kitchen gardening. The teaching of craft remained confined to *Takli* (spinning needle) and in a few cases to spinning wheel and flower pots. That was, obviously, inadequate.

The Axe Falls

Basic education, as conceived by Mahatma Gandhi and worked out by the Committees of the CABE could not pass muster with the Education Commission (1964-66). The Commission felt that if in practice basic education has become *largely frozen around certain crafts* (emphasis added), there is no denying the fact that it always stressed the vital principle of relating education to productivity".[25] The Commission, therefore, stressed that there is need for reorientation of the basic education programme to the needs of society that "has to be transformed with the help of science and technology; in other words work experience must be forward looking in keeping with the character of the new social order".[26] By implication, the Commission did not very much approve of the crafts –weaving and spinning, etc. – suggested in the original scheme as modes of education.

In effect, the Commission suggested different types of work experiences for the rural and urban areas. According to the Commission, while the work experience in rural areas may be built around agriculture, programme oriented to industry and simple technology should be introduced in fair proportion in rural schools. In such schools, where school workshop cannot be provided, suitable kits of tools and materials may be manufactured at low cost and made available to the pupils. For urban areas, gardening may be introduced. Training in farm work may be provided to at least a small population of urban pupils. In order to introduce work experience in rural and urban schools, the Commission visualised three problem areas:

1. Training of teachers would need special attention. For this purpose, working craftsmen or graduates of vocational schools may be appointed.
2. Facilities and equipment: In rural areas, farms should be attached to schools wherever possible. Alternatively, the students may be permitted to work on private farms. The help of industrial houses might be enlisted to design and manufacture cheap kits for schools, which may be used by groups of students. ITIs, vocational schools may also be encouraged to manufacture the required equipment and material.
3. A good deal of spade work will need to be done before the scheme is launched. It will include preparation of necessary literature about the scheme and its introduction to teachers and schools; short orientation courses would need to be held for officers of the department, principals and headmasters.

The Commission concluded its discussion about the concept of basic education, somewhat apologetically though, that in their view the essential principles of basic education were so important that they should guide and shape the educational systems of all levels. This is the essence of our proposal and in view of this we are not in favour of designating any one stage of education as basic education.[27]

Lest we forget, the basic principles as enunciated by Mahatama Gandhi and subsequently by the Zakir Hussain Committee were:

1. The course of primary education should be extended to at least seven years;
2. Education should be given, as far as possible, through a profit yielding craft;
3. Such education should be self-supporting;
4. Higher education should be left to private enterprise.

The scheme worked out by the Commission circumvents the major recommendations of the Wardha (basic) education scheme. None of the above principles have been owned by the Commission in their entirety. One would have wished that the Commission was candid enough to admit that they did not agree with the basic principles of the Wardha Education Scheme and would like to make fundamental changes in the scheme in order to make it in tune with the economic, social and educational needs of newly emerging resurgent India, in which modern industry has to play a very significant role along with agriculture.

References

1. Arsha works are the authenticated scriptures like the Vedas, upanishads, Manusmriti, Patanjali's Yog Shastra, etc. The Anarsha literature are those based on myths and legends, which have no religious sanctity.
2. J.T. F. Jordens: Hindu Religious and Social Reforms in British India', A Cultural History of India; A.L. Basham; (ed.) Delhi, Oxford University Press (1975), p. 372.
3. Satyarth Prakash, p. 20.
4. *Ibid.*, p. 22.
5. *Ibid.*, p. 30.
6. *Ibid.*, p. 33.
7. *Ibid.*, p. 49.
8. *Ibid.*, p. 51.
9. *Ibid.*, p. 78.
10. The Dayanand Anglo Vedic Movement; 125 years; Annual Report; 2010-2011; DAV College Managing Committee, New Delhi; p. 3.
11. The Dayanand Anglo Vedic Movement; op. cit; Back Page.
12. *Ibid.*
13. *Ibid.*
14. Shahabuddin Iraqi (ed.); Sir Syed Ahmed Khan; Vision and Mission, 2008, Department of History, Aligarh University, Aligarh; p. 11.
15. Aziz Ahmed; Islamic Reform Movements in A.L. Basham (ed.), A. Cultural History of India; op. cit. p. 387.
16. Dr. Zakir Hussain in an article 'Eternity or Toy' dated 7.4.1920 as quoted in Zakir Hussain on Eduction by Salamatullah et. al., National Council for Teacher Education, Nagri Printers, Delhi, p. 5.
17. Based on a Paper: Sir Syed's Scheme of Education submitted by Professor Ali Ahmed to a seminar organised by the Department of History, Aligarh Muslim University, 2008; p. 162.
    The contribution is gratefully acknowledged.
18. Shah Mohammad, Sir Syed Ahmed Khan, A Political Biography, Meerut, Meenakshi Prakashan, 1969, p. 210.
19. Quoted from seminar papers, op. cit. p. 166.
20. Quoted from Ali Ahmed, 'Sir Syed's Scheme of Education op. cit., p. 170.
21. Notable among the Tata family are Dorabji Tata; JRD Tata and Ratan N. Tata.
22. Zakir Hussain Committee on Basic Education.
23. First Five Year Plan, 1951-56, Planning Commission, p. 8.
24. *Ibid.*, p. 8.
25. Education Commission (1964-66) p. 202.
26. *Ibid.*, p. 202.
27. Education Commission, *Ibid.*, p. 209.

PART-2—EDUCATION IN INDEPENDENT INDIA

In this part, an analysis has been made of the progress, problems and perspectives of Indian Education during the post-independent period, i.e., 1947 to 2013. The subjects discussed are almost the same as those of the Colonial period. The discussion has, however, been undertaken in the context of the social, political and constitutional developments that have impacted Indian education during the period under review. These include the emergence of planning as a strategy for socio-economic development, the ushering in of the New Economic Policy with liberalisation, privatisation and globalisation (LPG) as its sheet anchors; and the constitutional reforms culminating into the enforcement of the Right to Education Act and its implications. The role of the teacher in the emerging socio-political and educational situation has also been discussed.

As has already been clarified, the discussion should not be considered as a comparative study of the two periods. The circumstances impacting the course of education during the two periods are fundamentally different. In the pre-independence period the decision makers were foreigners for whom the interests of the 'mother country' were of paramount importance. As a consequence, education of the 'natives' did not occupy a place of importance in their mental frame work. In the post-independence period, however, the socio-economic, educational and cultural development even of the lowliest of the low has been of supreme importance, and therefore, an all out effort has been made to provide educational facilities – both quantitatively and qualitatively to the *'aam admi'* – the common man inhabiting this divided country.

The discussion starts with the evolution of the National Policy on Education in independent India and wades through educational development – overall and sectoral; educational finance and the imperatives of the New Economic Policy. At the end, the discussion has been summed up in the form of Epilogue.

9

National Policy on Education

There have been two main policy documents in the post-independence India. The first policy for educational development was framed in 1968, 21 years after India attained freedom. The second policy was evolved 18 years later in 1986. In between, an aborted policy was worked out in 1979, which could not be placed before the Parliament because of the change in the Government. It should, however, not be inferred that the country was without a policy framework for education for the first two decades of independence. There were quite a few Commissions and Committees appointed by the Government of India and state governments from time to time, which delineated the broad contours of the directions towards which the educational system of the country should move. Further, India adopted planning as a means of achieving socio-economic development. Each plan indicated the broad educational goals that the country should strive to achieve during the five year period. For example, the first five year plan (1951-56), emphasised the role of education as of basic importance for achieving the specific tasks, which the nation sets for itself through the plan so as to make available, in the various fields, personnel of suitable quality at the required rate. The plan also set out the priority areas as also the targets to be achieved during the coming five years in a longer term perspective of about 15 years. The practice was repeated in the subsequent plans.

We shall discuss the main policy guidelines about educational development laid down by the Commissions and the policy documents evolved by the Government of India. Before that, however, it would be prudent to go over the main Constitutional provisions relating to education, adopted by the country in 1950.

Constitutional Provisions

Education, according to Indian Constitution, is included in the list of Concurrent Subjects. This empowers the Central Government to legislate on education. The Centre has however, refrained from bringing about any major legislation, (except the recently enacted 'Right to Education Act') which would impinge on the rights of the states, which continue to be the main players in the field of education.

In the initial stages, it was provided, under the Directive Principles of State Policy (Article 45) that the State shall endeavour to provide for free and compulsory education to children till they attain the age of 14. The Supreme Court in 1993 (Unnikrishnan case) gave a verdict declaring right to education as a fundamental right to children until the age of 14 years. The Parliament amended the Constitution by introducing Article 21A which laid down that the State shall provide free and compulsory education to all children of age six to fourteen in such a manner as the State may, by law, determine. The amendment also introduced a new Article 51-A, which imposed a duty on the parents and guardians to provide free and compulsory elementary education. The Right of children to Free and Compulsory Education was enacted and came into force with effect from 1st April, 2010. The Act makes it incumbent on Government to provide free and compulsory education to all children of 6-14 years of age; ensure compulsory admission, attendance and completion of elementary education by every child of 6 to 14 years of age. It also makes it mandatory for the State to ensure availability of neighbourhood school within three years of commencement of the Act. The state has to provide infrastructure, including school buildings, trained teaching staff and learning equipment as well as to ensure good quality elementary education according to specified norms and standards. The Act also mandates private schools to reserve 25 per cent of the seats to students from weaker sections of the society. It also prohibits donations or capitation fee in admissions and interviewing the child or parent as part of the schooling process.[1]

It is undoubtedly an epoch making legislation coming about a century after Gopal Krishan Gokhale's heroic but futile effort to persuade the British Government to enact on similar lines.

Policy Guidelines Enunciated by the Commissions Appointed by the Government of India

(a) University Education Commission (1948-49)

Soon after the attainment of independence, the Government of India thought of seeking the advice of experts about the various stages of education. Curiously enough, instead of starting with the school stage, the first Commission that was appointed related to university education (1948). The Commission was set up under the chairmanship of Dr. Sarvapalli Radhakrishnan – an erudite scholar, philosopher and a great thinker.

The Commission's major recommendations included the extension of the first degree course to three years after 12 years of school education, introduction of variety of courses in the field of science, technology, commerce and humanities; setting up of rural universities; increasing the number of working days of university institutions to 180. Another important recommendation was the setting up of an organisation to oversee the work of the universities and to provide financial assistance to universities.

Although the recommendations of the Commission were approved by the Central Advisory Board of Education and the Government, the implementation seems to have been half hearted. As per Commission's recommendations, the University Grants Commission was set up by an Act of Parliament in 1956, with the task of determination and maintenance of standards of teaching, examination and research. In the initial stages, the states did not show any enthusiasm to introduce three year degree course. The recommendation about the setting up of Rural Universities was not accepted but on the advice of the Rural Higher Education Committee, Rural Institutes were set up, which were initially expected to provide facilities for higher education to students who complete their post basic or higher secondary courses in subjects such as rural hygiene, agriculture, rural engineering, extension etc. The Government also appointed a Council for Rural Higher Education to oversee the progress and problems of 14 Rural Institutes which were set up. Unfortunately, the scheme of Rural Institutes could not be sustained due to a variety of reasons including the apathy of the sponsoring authorities and lack of interest by students. The Institutes were either closed down or merged with the existing universities.

(b) Secondary Education Commission (1952)

Keeping up its penchant for going upside down – resembling the much maligned 'Downward Filtration Theory' adopted by the British Government in the initial stages of their rule – the Government of India appointed Secondary Education Commission in 1952. The Commission made the following major recommendations;

(a) Secondary education which was regarded as the weakest link in the system of education in India should be made more broad-based, by introducing greater diversity in the syllabus and preventing wastage.

(b) A period of 4 or 5 years of primary or junior basic education would be followed by three years of middle or senior basic and a further period of 4 years in the higher secondary stage. The total period at the secondary stage may be extended to 11 years followed by a graduation course of 3 years duration.

(c) Multi-purpose schools with technical schools separately or as part of multi-purpose schools should be established. It also recommended agricultural education in rural schools.

(d) Adequate provision should be made for vocational guidance to students.

It has been reported that the programmes suggested by the Commission came into actual operation by the end of the first Plan (1951-56). During the Plan period, 470 multi-purpose schools were approved by the Ministry of Education and 334 schools were actually established. Proposals for improving teaching of science were taken up in 214 schools; for improving existing teaching facilities in general in 1072 schools; for improving libraries in 1479 schools and introducing crafts in 1190 schools. An important project taken up in the last year of the Plan was the establishment of extension departments in 24 post-graduate training colleges.[2]

A number of institutions to provide academic and technical support to school education were set up. Among others, they included Central Institute of Education, Central Bureaus of Textbook Research and of Guidance, National Institute of Basic Education and of Audio-Visual and Adult Education, Directorate of Extension Programmes for Secondary Education etc. By merging them into an all comprehensive institution, the National Council of Educational Research and Training was established in 1961.

(c) Education Commission (1964-66)

After getting the two upper stages of education examined by two Commissions, the Government thought of having a comprehensive view of the state of educational developments, its progress and problems, its priorities and programme of action. To achieve this, the Education Commission was appointed in 1964, under the chairmanship of Dr. D.S. Kothari, the then Chairman of the University Grants Commission. The Commission submitted its Report on 26th June, 1966.

The Commission made detailed recommendations about the reconstruction of the educational system. The main points stressed by the Commission were:

1. Introducing uniform structure of education:
   10 years of high school followed by three years of higher secondary and three years of first degree course;
2. Introduction of work experience (which includes manual work, production experience etc.) and social service as integral parts of general education at all levels of education;
3. Stress on moral education and inclusion of a sense of social responsibility. Schools should recognise their responsibility in facilitating the transition of youth from the world of school to the world of work and life;
4. Vocationalisation of secondary education, with diversion of students at different stages to vocational courses leading to employment;
5. Strengthening of the Centres of Advanced Study and the setting up of a small number of major universities which would achieve. international standards;
6. Special emphasis on training and quality of teachers of school;
7. Research in agriculture and allied sciences to be given a high priority in the scheme of educational reconstruction. Energetic and imaginative steps required to draw a reasonable population of talent looking for advanced study and research in agricultural sciences;
8. Development of quality or pace setting institutions at all stages and in all sections.[3]

Educational Policy, 1968

The first National Policy on Education was evolved in 1968 mainly on the basis of the recommendations of the Education Commission (1964-66). The guiding principles were that a national reconstruction of education on the broad lines recommended by the Education Commission was essential for the economic and cultural development of the country for national reconstruction and for realizing the ideal of a socialistic pattern of society. This would involve a transformation of system to relate it more closely to the life of the people; a continuous effort to expand educational opportunity; a sustained and intensive effort to review the quality of education at all stages; an emphasis on the development of science and technology and the cultivation of moral and social values. The educational system must produce young men and women of character and ability committed to national service and development....

The specific recommendations to achieve the above objectives are:

1. Strenuous efforts should be made for the early fulfilment of the Directive Principles under Article 45 of the Constitution seeking to provide free and compulsory education for children up to the age of 14. Suitable programmes should be devised to reduce the prevailing wastage and stagnation in schools and to ensure that every child, who is enrolled in school, successfully completes the prescribed course.
2. Teachers are the key factor in the determination of quality of education. They, therefore be accorded an honoured place in society. Their remuneration should be adequate and satisfactory having regard to their qualifications and responsibilities. They should be given academic freedom to pursue and publish independent studies and researches. Teacher education, particularly in-service education, should receive due emphasis.
3. The energetic development of Indian languages and literature is the sine-qua-non for educational and cultural development. Urgent steps may be taken to adopt regional languages as media of education at the university stage also.
4. Equal educational opportunities should be provided to all. To achieve this objective, common school system should be promoted. The quality of education in these schools should be improved.
5. Systematic hunt for talent at an early age will help in cultivation of excellence. It should be given priority.
6. Schools and community should be brought together under suitable programmes. Work experience and national service should be brought closer through viable schemes.
7. Science, Mathematics education and research should be accorded high priority. Special emphasis should be given to agricultural education right from the school stage.

8. There is need to extend technical and vocational education facilities at the secondary stage of education keeping in view the manpower needs.
9. University education needs to be reorganised, extended and its academic quality should be improved. More post-graduate courses should be added and research must be extended.

The above are the main features of the educational policy delineated in 1968, which was broadly based on the recommendations of the Education Commission (1964-66). The recommendations were accepted by the Government of India vide a Resolution issued by the Ministry of Education. The Resolution, inter-alia, expressed the Government's conviction that a radical reconstruction of education, based on the recommendations of the Education Commission, is essential for accelerating the process of socio-economic and cultural development as also for national integration and realising the ideal of a socialistic pattern of society. This would involve a transformation of the system of education to relate it more closely to the life of the people; a continuous effort to expand educational opportunity; a sustained and intensive effort to raise the quality of education at all stages; an emphasis on the development of science and technology and the cultivation of moral and social values. The educational system must produce young men and women of character and ability committed to national service and development. Only then will education be able to play its vital role in promoting economic progress, creating a sense of common citizenship and culture and strengthening national integration.

The Resolution also laid down principles according to which the development of education would take place. In effect, the Resolution reiterated the main recommendations of the policy and modus operandi to achieve them. The Resolution also indicated that the government will review the progress achieved in regard to the major recommendations made in the policy and suggest guidelines for future development.

Policy on Education (1979) – Draft

There was a change of Government in 1979. The incoming government decided to revise the Policy drawn up by the previous government. The revised policy spoke about an 'ideal' system of education to enable individuals to know and develop, to the fullest, their intellectual potentialities and promote their awareness of social and human values so that they can develop a strong character and live better lives as responsible members of the society. The aim of education should be the growth of the individual through truthful life without detriment to the welfare and progress of the society and our cherished ideals of freedom, equality and social justice. To this end, education should strengthen values of democracy, secularism and socialism. It should also promote national unity, pride in our cultural heritage and faith in the country's future. The effort must be made to include scientific and moral values and facilitate pursuit of knowledge.

Within these idealistic paradigms, the policy suggested reforms that should be brought about in the educational system. It reiterated, more or less, the objectives set out in the 1968 Policy on Education. It laid down the specific targets to be achieved in relation to various sectors of education. Unfortunately, the Government sponsoring the Policy was voted out of power and the educational policy so meticulously worked out became dysfunctional.

Challenge of Education (1985)

Before discussing the main recommendations of the Policy evolved in 1986, it would be pertinent to mention the policy perspectives worked out in the Ministry of Education's document: **Challenge of Education** – The document was prepared in a year before the 1986 Policy of Education. It was in pursuance of the suggestions made in the 1968 Policy that the working and progress of the new policies and programmes should be reviewed after every five years.

The 'Challenge of Education' discussed in details the role of education in socio-economic development; the progress and problems encountered by the educational system in achieving the goals of personal, economic, social, political and cultural development. It also attempted to analyse the salient features of the achievements in education during the post-independence period.

Recapitulating the goal of orientation for educational planning, the Document stated that the "educational system is expected to generate new knowledge in all fields within the reach of the human mind. In addition, it has to evolve principles, methodologies and guidelines for the application of knowledge for benefiting society. It is also expected to provide knowledge and skills for solving the problems of development. It must also enable the students to develop understanding and a perspective of the physical and social environment. Research and Development and extension, therefore, have to be accepted as essential ingredients of the education process.[4]

Further, emphasis has to be laid on the socio-economic well being, competence and creativity of the individual... In addition, education has to assume the responsibility for imparting knowledge about concepts and facts relating to different subjects and for developing skills in the area of languages and communication as also interest in hobbies, games and sports.[5] Education has also to play an important role in integrating the individuals into the social system, besides equipping them with competence, in terms of knowledge and skills in various combinations at different levels of understanding, relating to the opportunities of employment in the context of a particular pattern and rate of development.[6]

The Document concluded by saying that, "in broad terms', the task of evolving the new Education Policy would consist of laying down a long term strategy for education in which the requirements of universalisation of elementary education, production of sophisticated manpower in adequate numbers to deal creatively with new technologies, diversified vocationalisation; and the creation of overall environment for change and development through adult and continuing education would be integrated with measures to improve the quality and outputs of all other educational sections. In this integrated strategy, specific roles will be assigned to different agencies for drawing up and implementing detailed programmes. To ensure functional and sequential complementaries, it will be necessary to set forth the framework for interaction and integration."[7]

National Policy on Education – 1986

The 'Challenge of Education' was widely discussed at various levels and forums. It became the basis for evolving the National Policy on Education (NPE) in 1986. Six years later, the Programme of Action was worked out though it would have been appropriate if it had immediately followed the Policy paradigms accepted by the Government.

The main recommendations of the 1986 Policy were:

1. The concept of the national system of education implies that, up to a given level, all students, irrespective of caste, creed, location or sex, have access to education of a comparable quality. For this, emphasis will be laid on the common school system recommended in the 1968 Policy. The need for common educational structure – 10+2+3 system which has been adopted all over the country – was stressed. It will also have a National Curriculum Framework, containing a common core along with other flexible components.
2. Education has to strengthen the concept of treating the world as one family and motivate the younger generation for international cooperation and peaceful co-existence.
3. To provide equality, special emphasis will be laid on the removal of disparities and ensuring the provision of equal educational opportunities by attending to the specific needs of those who have been denied equality so far.
4. Minimum levels of learning will be laid down for each stage of education. Steps will also be taken to foster among students an understanding of the diverse cultural and social system of the people living in different parts of the country. Besides the promotion of basic language, programmes will also be launched to increase substantially the translation of books from one language to the other and to publish multi-lingual dictionaries and glossaries.
5. In higher education in general and technical education in particular, steps will be taken to facilitate inter-regional mobility by providing equal access to every Indian of requisite merit, regardless of his origins.
6. In the area of research and development and education in science and technology, special measures will be taken to establish net-work arrangements between different institutions in the country to pool their resources and participate in projects of national importance.
7. Lifelong education is a cherished goal of the educational process. This presupposes universal literacy. Opportunities will be provided to the youth, housewives, agricultural and industrial workers and professionals to continue education of their choice, at the pace suited to them. The future thrust will be on open and distance learning.

8. The Institutions like the University Grants Commission, All India Council for Technical Education, Indian Council of Agricultural Research, the Indian Medical Council will be strengthened to play their role in giving shape to National System of Education.
9. The nation as a whole will assume the responsibility for providing resource support for implementing programmes of educational transformation, reducing disparities, universalisation of elementary education, adult literacy, scientific and technological research etc.

All this will be achieved by bringing about a meaningful partnership between the Union Government and the states. The Union Government will, however, have to assume a larger responsibility to reinforce the national and integrative character of education; to maintain quality and standards; to study and monitor the educational requirements of the country as a whole in regard to manpower for development; to cater to the needs of research and advanced study; to look after the international aspects of education; cultural and human resource development and, in general, to promote excellence at all levels of the educational pyramid throughout the country. Concurrency signifies a partnership, which is at once meaningful and challenging; the National Policy will be oriented towards giving effect to it in letter and spirit.

Programme of Action, 1992

In July 1991, a CABE Committee was constituted to review the various parameters of the 1986 Policy and other relevant developments. The Committee, in its Report submitted in 1992 said that while very little of the NPE (1986) required reformulation, a programme of action (POA) needed to be prepared. Accordingly, 23 Task Forces wee constituted to suggest strategies and programmes to be implemented along with time frame. The reports of these Task Forces were compiled in a document: Programme of Action (POA). The draft POA was discussed in a conference of State Secretaries and Directors of Education in August, 1992. On the basis of their suggestions, the POA was revised. The revised document was endorsed by CABE on 8th August, 1992.

The POA worked out the priority areas in education and strategies to implement the recommendations made by the NPE (1986). The priority areas included universalisation of elementary education and adult education, qualitative development of all sectors of education and developing effective human resources of various categories to accelerate the process of socio-economic development of the country. Emphasis was also laid on providing educational facilities to backward sections – scheduled castes, scheduled tribes, other backward sections, minorities and handicapped persons. Secondary education was to be expanded ensuring high participation of girls, scheduled castes and scheduled tribes. Need based and non-formal programme of vocational education was stressed. In higher education, dynamic efforts were to be made for consolidation and expansion of institutions; development of autonomous colleges, redesigning of courses and strengthening of research. Further, open-university system was to be encouraged and expanded and stress was to be laid on delinking of degrees from jobs. Manpower planning was to be emphasised.

In 1991, the National Front Government appointed a committee under Acharya Ramamurthy to review the NPE (1986). The Committee produced a perspective paper 'Towards Enlightened and Humane Society', which made some suggestions about reforming the educational system and strengthening the process of implementation of the programmes suggested by the NPE (1986). An important recommendation of the Committee was that right to education should become a fundamental right so that people are able to learn the competencies needed for work.

To Conclude

It would be noted that apart from the aborted National Policy of 1979 and the Ramamurthy Committee which was constituted to review the 1986 National Policy, there have been only two National Policies, which reported in 1968 and 1986. The first National Policy (1968) was in effect, an extension of the Education Commission (1964-66). It laid down the priorities in the field of education and strategies for implementing the policy guidelines laid down by it. The second Policy (1986) was based on a review of educational development undertaken by the Ministry of Education in its analytical document – Challenge of Education. The Programme of Action (1992), in effect, reviewed the progress of education on an all India basis and identified the problems that were impeding the expansion of facilities and effecting qualitative improvement of various sectors. The POA in fact brought out the recommendations of the National Policy from conceptual to ground level.

It may be pointed out that the first policy document (1968) came out 21 years after India attained freedom from foreign rule. The second document saw the light of the day 18 years thereafter. It would, however, not be correct to conclude that there was no policy framework about educational development during first 2 decades after freedom. Soon after India became free, the Government appointed two Commissions – University Education Commission in 1948 and Secondary Education Commission in 1952. Although these Commissions were not in a sequential order, they provided much useful information about the progress in their sectors, the problems that thwarted progress and the manner in which they should be resolved. The Commission also worked out the future policy of development of that sector in the overall context of education as a whole. Further, four years after political emancipation, the country adopted planning as an instrument of socio-economic development. The Commission, in its annual and five yearly reports, is mandated to assess progress and identify problem areas in development sectors including education. It also makes recommendations about the strategies to be adopted for implementing the programmes of development.

It would have been useful to evolve a mechanism of assessing the progress of various programmes initiated on the recommendations of the Policy documents. Although this assessment is attempted by the Ministry of Human Resource Development and the Planning Commission, a standing expert body, possibly under the Central Advisory Board of Education; should have been constituted to be on constant look out for the manner of and extent to which the implementation of various programmes is being done. This body should have representation from the various stake holders: the Ministry of HRD and its specialised organisations, the state governments and experts from various fields.

References

1. For details, see Chapter 10.
2. Review of the First Five Year Plan, 1957, Planning Commission; 255.
3. Excerpts from Dr. Kothari's (Chairman of the Education Commission) letter dated 29th June, 1966 to M.C. Chagla, Union Minister for Education, Government of India.
4. Challenge of Education – a policy perspective, Ministry of Education, New Delhi – 1985, pp. 66-67.
5. *Ibid.*, p. 67.
6. *Ibid.*, p. 68.
7. *Ibid*, p. 117.

10

Educational Development: Progress, Problems and Perspectives

With the dawn of independence, the role that education plays in accelerating the process of socio-economic development and cultural regeneration has been recognised. Education is considered to be of vital importance in planned development of the country. According to the Planning Commission, 'The success of planning in a democracy depends also in the growth of the spirit of cooperation and the sense of disciplined citizenship among the people and on the degree to which it becomes possible to evoke public enthusiasm and build leadership. It is essential for the successful implementation of the plan that educational programmes help to train people to place responsibilities before rights and to keep the self regarding outlook and the force of the acquisitive instinct within legitimate bounds. The educational system should also satisfy cultural needs, which is essential for the healthy growth of a nation..."[1]

The recognition of the important role of education as an instrument of socio-economic development impelled the government and the people to accelerate the process of quantitative expansion and qualitative development of education. We shall critically analyse the progress of education in the post-independence period beginning from 1951, when the process of socio-economic planning was set in motion. Before doing so, however, it appears appropriate to have a birds' eye view of the state of Indian education just at the time when India threw away its yoke of slavery.

State of Education in 1947

There were 2,03,873 recognised and 14,292 unrecognised institutions, consisting of 1,72,661 primary, 12,843 middle and 5297 high schools. Further, there were 17 universities, 297 degree colleges and 199 intermediate colleges. There were also 140 professional colleges, including 16 engineering colleges. The total enrolment in 1946-47 was 1,77,56,375 out of which, 170,01,541, i.e.,

95.75 per cent, were at the school stage. The rest were in universities and colleges of humanities and sciences as also in professional institutions. The total population of India was estimated to be 34,03,74,335 in 1947. In other words only 5 out of a thousand persons were in educational institutions.

Education in 1951

The position of educational development soon after the attainment of independence, as indicated by the Planning Commission, is summarised below:

1. Considering the size of the population, the overall provision of educational facilities was very inadequate. Only 40 per cent of the children in the age groups 6-11, 10 per cent of children in the age group 11-17 and 0.9 per cent of those in the age group of 17-23 were provided a semblance of educational facilities. The literacy, percentage was only 17.2 per cent. The literacy level among the female was abysmally low.
2. The overall structure was top heavy. Although the provision at the secondary stage was properly proportional to the primary stage, that at the university stage was larger than the base structure could profitably support. Further, expenditure on primary education was disproportionally lower than other stages of education, particularly the university stage. There were large disparities in the educational expenditure among different states.
3. Educational facilities were not properly distributed between rural and urban areas. Whereas 82.8 per cent of the population lived in rural areas, the percentage of the total number of pupils studying in recognised primary, middle and high schools in rural areas in 1949-50 was 60, 67 and 26 respectively. This was much lower than the percentages in 1937-38, which were 82, 72 and 28 respectively. At the university stage, facilities were practically non-existent in rural areas.
4. Whereas women constituted almost 50 per cent of the total population, the percentage of girl students at the primary, middle and high school stages in 1949-50 were only 28, 18 and 13 respectively of the total number of pupils at these stages. At the university stage, girls constituted only 10.4 per cent of the total number of students.
5. Wastage and stagnation that occurs at various stages was another disturbing feature. Only 40 per cent of the pupils entering in class I in 1945-46 reached class IV in 1948-49. The expenditure on the remaining 60 per cent was apparently wasteful.
6. The absence of adequate facilities for technical and vocational education resulted in a much larger number of students opting for general education courses. The undue emphasis on academic and theoretical education retarded the development of practical sense, initiative and resourcefulness among large number of students. Education, therefore, needed to have a more practical bias at the very beginning and at the post-secondary stage, there had to be greater adjustment between the needs of the country and the output of educational institutions.

7. A large number of teachers were untrained. In 1948-49, the percentage of untrained teachers was 41.4 at the primary and 46.4 at the secondary stages. There was acute shortage of women teachers.
8. There was undue emphasis on examinations and rote learning.
9. There was general neglect of the study of our culture. Literature on the cultural and political identity and creating awareness about building up civic loyalties and creating understanding of democratic citizenship, although necessary, was absent.

Keeping in view the deficiencies of the educational system observed during the period immediately following political independence of the country, the following steps for remodelling it were identified:

1. Reorientation of the educational system and integration of different stages and branches;
2. Expansion in various fields, especially in those of basic and social education, remodelling secondary education, technical and vocational education;
3. Consolidation of existing secondary and university education and the design of a system of higher education suited to the needs of the rural areas;
4. Expansion of facilities for women's education, especially in rural areas;
5. Training of teachers, especially women teachers and teachers for basic schools and improvement in their pay scales and conditions of service; and
6. Helping backward states by giving preferential treatment to them in the matter of financial assistance; and promotion of adult literacy.

Review of Progress of Education

Keeping in view, the position of education soon after India attained political freedom, we shall review the progress of education during the post-independence period in order to identify remedial measures and their impact on the state of education in that period. The progress is reviewed in two sections:

(A) Overall Progress Covering all Sectors
(B) Analytical Study of the Progress under different Sectors

(A) Overall Progress of Education

There has been tremendous expansion in educational facilities in the post independence period. We shall discuss the progress of education during this period in two phases:

(a) **Phase One** – Between 1951 and 1985: In 1951, the country launched its first five year plan. It was during this period that two commissions: Secondary Education Commission (1952) and Education Commission (1964-66) reviewed state of Indian education and made recommendations about its future course. 1985 was an important watershed in Indian education because it formed the basis of the 1986

Policy formulation, which guided the course of educational development during the next quarter of the century.

(b) **Phase Two** – The Progress of education during the period following the National Policy of Education formulated in 1986 up to the present time. It is also intended that the problems that emerged in the system of education during these phases may be critically examined.

(A) Phase One: 1951-1985

Growth of Education

There was a threefold increase in the number of institutions in India during the period under review: from 2.3 lakh, the number of institutions increased to 6.9 lakh. About 73 per cent of the institutions (5.04 lakh) were primary schools. The growth of primary schools has, however, not been uniform in all states. The number of middle schools increased from 13.4 thousand in 1950-51 to 123.3 thousand in 1982-83, thus registering an annual increase of 7.2 per cent. In 1950-51, there were 7,300 secondary schools. The number increased to 52,279 in 1982-83 registering an annual growth of 6.3 per cent.[2]

The growth of vocational schools, which began with the adoption of the 10+2 pattern of secondary education, was not very satisfactory. By 1976-77, the programme had taken shape only in three states. However, by 1983-84, it had been adopted by 11 states. More than half of the vocational institutions existing in 1983-84 were in Tamil Nadu. Maharashtra with 250 institutions ranked number two.

The number of Polytechnics increased from 323 in 1975-76 to 515 in 1982-83. The largest number of Polytechnics was in Tamil Nadu followed by Karnataka, Uttar Pradesh and Maharashtra. The number of Engineering Colleges increased from 108 in 1975-76 to 200 in 1982-83 registering an increase of 9.2 per cent per annum.

There were 5246 colleges and 140 universities in 1982-83 indicating a rate of growth of these institutions of 6 per cent per annum.

Enrolment

There was significant expansion in the enrolment during the period. Total student population had a fourfold increase from 2.8 crore in 1951 to 11.4 crore in 1982-83. The compounded growth rate of girls' enrolment was 5.5 per cent, while that of boys was 3.9 per cent. On a decadal basis, the growth rate of primary education declined. In the fifties, the growth rate was 6.2 per cent. In the sixties, it was reduced to 5 per cent and in seventies, it came down to a still lower level of 2.5 per cent. Further, the proportion of overage and underage children at the primary stage was as high as 25 per cent.

Gender-wise, highest enrolment ratio for boys among major states was in 1960-61 in Tamil Nadu; the lowest being in Jammu and Kashmir, Madhya Pradesh and Bihar. By 1982-83, the picture had changed substantially. Except for 4 states – Assam, Karnataka, Madhya Pradesh and Orissa, all other states reported 100 per cent coverage for boys.

In the case of girls, the least enrolment ratio (16) was in the states of Rajasthan, Jammu & Kashmir, Bihar and Madhya Pradesh. By 1982-83, tremendous improvement had been registered across all states. Uttar Pradesh had, however, the dubious distinction of being the lowest (49 per cent).

At the middle education stage, the number of pupils increased from a paltry 26 lakh in 1951 to 1.47 crore in 1982-83. The girls' enrolment in relation to the relevant age group was 30.6 per cent against 56.3 per cent for boys.

At the secondary stage, the total enrolment increased from 12.2 lakh in 1951 to 94.9 lakh in 1980-81, indicating a growth rate of 7.8 per cent per annum. The girls enrolment at this stage was, however, much lower than that of boys – 0.16 girls for one boy in 1950-51 increasing to 0.42 for one boy in 1980-81.

Higher education enrolment increased at the overall rate of 9.7 per cent per annum during the period under review. The rate of growth, however, slowed down in the seventies – from about 13 per cent in the fifties and sixties to 3.8 per cent in seventies. There was substantial increase in the enrolment in all faculties and specializations. As compared to the enrolment for general education (4.5 per cent), enrolment for professional courses increased by 2.5 per cent per annum.

Retention and Dropouts

There was some improvement in the retention rates for boys and girls at the primary stage; for classes I-V improving from 35.5 per cent in the case of 1968 batch and by 38.6 per cent for 1974 batch.

Non-formal Education and Literacy

Non-formal education for pupils of the age group 9-14, who could not avail of the regular formal education was emphasised during the Sixth Plan. In educationally backward states, more than 68000 centres were opened – 90 per cent of these centres were for primary education. Most of these centres were located in Madhya Pradesh and Uttar Pradesh – the educationally backward states. In these centres, about 15 lakh students were enrolled across nine backward states.

The literacy rate during the post-independence period increased from 16.67 per cent in 1951 to 36.23 per cent in 1981. The number of literates thus increased from 6 crore in 1951 to 24.8 crore in 1981. There were, however, glaring disparities between the males (46.9 per cent) and female (24.8 per cent). In rural areas the position was worse – 40.8 and 18 per cent respectively against 65.8 and 47.8 per cent in urban areas. Kerala topped the list with a literacy percentage of 70.4 against 24.38 per cent - the lowest - in Rajasthan. Only 5.46 per cent females were literate in Rajasthan.

It would thus be seen that although there was expansion of facilities in terms of enrolments and institutions, there were quite a few deficiencies, particularly in the educationally backward states, which lacked in providing educational facilities for females, had deficient arrangement for vocational education and lagged behind in adult literacy.

The Position in 2007-08

The progress of education recorded during the period 1951-86 continued unabated. The number of schools in 2007-08 was the following:

1.	Primary/Junior Basic	7,83,827
2.	Middle/Senior Basic	3,25,174
3.	High/Post Basic	1,13,824
4.	Higher Secondary/Intermediate Colleges	59,165
	Total	**12,81,990**

Enrolment

The total enrolment at the school stage (classes I-XII) was 23,71,50,741 in 2007-08. If the enrolment at the pre-primary stage is also included, the total would rise to 27,76,38,099. Thus while the enrolment during the period 1951-83 increased four times, the increase during 1983-2008 was about 2½ times. It may also be stated that gender disparities still remained in spite of attempts at accelerating the girls' enrolment; boys were about 54 per cent, while the girls were about 46 per cent. At the primary stage, the percentages were 52 for boys and about 48 for girls. At the secondary stage, the girls constituted about 44 per cent of the total enrolment.

Out of the total enrolment at the school stage, the enrolment at the primary stage accounted for 57 per cent, Middle stage 24 per cent, while secondary stage registered about 19 per cent of the total enrolment.

Table 1 explains the position as follows:

Table 1: Enrolment at the School Stage – 2007-08

1. *Pre Primary*	*Boys*	*Girls*	*Total*
(a) Age Group 3-6	1,73,27,695	1,65,83,178	3,39,10,873
(b) Pre-Primary	35,18,498	30,57,985	65,76483
Total	2,08,46,193	1,96,41,163	4,04,87,356
	(51.49)	(48.51)	(100.00)
2. *Primary Schools*			
Classes I-V	7,10,89,547	6,43,81,014	13,54,70,561
	(52.48)	(47.52)	(100.00)

3. *Middle Schools*			
VI-VIII	3,10,50,441	2,61,54,263	5,72,04,704
	(54.28)	(45.72)	(100.00)
4. *Secondary Schools*			
(a) IX-X	58,98,127	1,23,16,570	2,82,17,697
	(56.34)	(43.66)	(100.00)
(b) XI-XII	92,58,131	69,99,648	1,62,57,779
	(55.85)	(44.15)	(100.00)
Total School Education I-XII	**12,72,96,246**	**10,98,54,495**	**23,71,50,741**
Percentages	**(53.68)**	**(46.32)**	**(100.00)**

Source: Tables of School Education: 2007-08, Mimeo; Ministry of HRD.

It would be seen that at all stages of education, girls lagged behind the boys in terms of percentages of the total enrolment.

Enrolment of Backward Classes

Table 2 indicates the enrolment of the scheduled castes and scheduled tribes students at the school stage.

Table 2: Enrolment of Scheduled Castes/Tribes (2007-2008) (I-XII)

Total	*Enrolment*	*Scheduled Castes*	*Percentage*	*Scheduled Tribes*	*Percentage*	*Total Backward Classes*	*Percentage*
Boys	12,72,96,246	2,26,90,535	17.82	1,17,73,015	9.25	3,46,63,550	27.07
Girls	10,98,54,495	1,99,00,896	18.12	1,01,49,992	9.24	3,00,50,888	27.36
Total	23,71,50,741	4,25,91,431	17.96	2,19,23,007	9.24	6,45,14,438	27.20

(*Source:* Statistics of School Enrolment 2007-08).

It would appear that out of the total enrolment of about 24 crore, (which is in classes I-XII in schools), the Scheduled Castes account for about 18 per cent and the Scheduled Tribes about 9 per cent. This compares favourably with their percentage in the total projected population of India for 2007-08, which is about 16 and 8 per cent respectively. It has also been noted that girls and boys of these communities are almost equally represented in schools. This is a very important development in the post-independent India.

Enrolment in Rural Areas

Table 3 explains the percentages of enrolment in terms of population in rural areas:

Table 3: Population/Enrolment in Rural Areas at School Level

	Percentage Enrolment to Total Enrolment	*Percentage Population to Total Population*
Boys	62.84	71.71
Girls	70.39	72.69
Total	69.02	72.36

(*Source:* Statistics of School Enrolment 2007-08)

It is worth noting that while 72.36 per cent of the total population in India lives in rural areas, only 69.02 per cent of the total enrolment at the school level is in rural areas. It is also interesting to note that the percentage of girls' enrolment to the total enrolment is higher than that of the boys'. This is a step in the right direction.

(B) University Stage

There was substantial increase in the number of university level institutions. From 140 in 1982-83, the total number of degree awarding institutions rose to 636 in 2012. This included 43 (7 per cent) Central Universities, 227 (47 per cent) State Universities, 100 (16 per cent) Private Universities, 129 (20 per cent) 'Deemed' Universities, and 65 (10 per cent) Institutions of National Importance. Besides there were 33,023 colleges and 1914 polytechnics. The bulk of colleges are Arts, Fine Arts, Science and Commerce Colleges. The largest number of universities (59) is in Tamil Nadu followed by 58 in Uttar Pradesh, 48 in Rajasthan, 44 in Maharashtra; 42 in Karnataka, 25 in Delhi and three each in Arunachal Pradesh, Mizoram, Sikkim, Tripura and Chandigarh. Goa with 2 universities is at the bottom line.

Enrolment

The total enrolment at the university stage was 1,72,95,086 in 2009-10, consisting of 1,03,25,236 boys (59.70 per cent) and 69,69,850 girls (40.30 per cent). Besides there were 34,45,654 students in open universities. The number of Scheduled Castes students in all categories of universities was 24,39,585 (19.60 per cent) and that of Scheduled Tribes was 10,80,896 (8.69 per cent).

The Gross Enrolment Ratios of the age group 18-23 were 15 per cent as a whole – 17.1 per cent for males; 12.7 per cent for females. The corresponding ratios for Scheduled Castes, was 11.1 per cent for the entire student body consisting of 13 per cent for males and 9 per cent for females. The corresponding percentages for Scheduled Tribes were 10.3, 13.1 and 7.5 respectively.

The preceding review of progress of education during the post-independence period indicates a phenomenal increase in number of institutions of all types as also enrolment of various age groups. It, however, appears to be a phenomenon of lights and shades. Within the overall growth there were regional, social and gender disparities. Steps will need to be taken to reduce and, if possible, eliminate these disparities, which are against the principles of equity, access and excellence, which should form the basic structure of the educational system.

(B) Sectoral Programmes (Analytical Study of Progress)

We shall now discuss the policies, progress and problems of development of education on sectoral basis during the post-independence period. We shall start with Adult Literacy Programmes.

(a) Adult Education

The National Policy of Education (1986), emphasising the need for strengthening programmes of Adult Education stated: "Our ancient scriptures define education as that which liberates i.e. provides the instruments for liberation from ignorance and oppression. In the modern world, it would naturally include the ability to read and write, since that is the main instrument of learning. Hence the crucial importance of adult education, including adult literacy."[3]

India was a seat of learning in ancient times. It attracted seekers of knowledge from countries far across the Indian borders. During ten centuries of foreign rule, it lost its place in the world of knowledge and relapsed into the darkness of illiteracy. The first census during the British rule in 1901, showed that only 5.3 per cent – 9.8 per cent males and 0.6 per cent females were found to be literate. After fifty years i.e. in 1951, the literacy percentages crawled to 16.7 overall, 24.9 males and 7.9 females. By 1981, the overall literacy was 36.2 per cent – 46.9 per cent for males and 24.8 per cent for females.

According to the 2011 census, overall literacy has increased from 64.8 per cent in 2001 to 74.0 per cent in 2011. Improvement in female literacy has been more rapid than male literacy and the gender gap has declined (6.7 by percentage points) from 21.6 percentage points in 2011. The mean years of schooling of the working age population (over 15 years) has increased from 4.2 years in 2000 to 5.12 years in 2010. However, this remains well below the level in other countries such as China (8.17 years) and Brazil (75.4 years).

According to 2011 census, apart from gender disparities in literacy rates, there were wide disparities among the socio-economic groups. The literacy rate among the Scheduled Castes was 54.69 per cent overall – 66.44 among the males and 41.90 among the females. The corresponding percentages among the schedule tribes were 47.10 overall; 59.17 males and 34.76 among the females.[4]

Considered state-wise data, while the overall literacy rate in rural areas was 58.74, seven states – Andhra Pradesh (54.50); Arunachal Pradesh (47.83); Bihar (43.92); Jammu & Kashmir (49.78); Jharkhand (45.74); Meghalaya (56.29) and

Rajasthan (52.53) were below the all India level. In the urban areas, 8 states – Andhra Pradesh (76.09); Arunachal Pradesh (78.36); Bihar (71.93); Haryana (79.16); Jammu & Kashmir (71.92); Jharkhand (79.14); Punjab (79.10) and Rajasthan (76.20) were below the all India average of 79.92 per cent. Similar differences were noticed in the coverage of the socially disadvantaged groups – Scheduled Castes and Scheduled Tribes, in various states.

The preceding analysis of the literacy levels among the states and socio-economic groups indicates that in spite of a substantial progress in the post-independence period, much more remains to be achieved in this field. Keeping this in view, the Government in May 2009 announced that literacy would be the key programme instrument for emancipation and empowerment of women. With this end in view, the **National Literacy Mission (NLM)** was started in 1998; as a programme instrument it has been recast as *Sakshar Bharat* with an enhanced focus on female literacy. The programme will cover all adults in the age group of 15 and beyond, though its primary focus will be on women. Basic literacy, post literacy and continuing education programmes form a continuum, rather than sequential segments. The objectives of the National Literacy Mission are:

(i) Impart functional literacy and numeracy to non-numerate adults;
(ii) Enable the neo-literate adults to continue their learning beyond basic literacy and acquire equivalency to formal educational system;
(iii) Impart non and neo-literates relevant skills to improve their earning capacity and living conditions and;
(iv) Promote a learning society by providing opportunities to neo-literate adults for continuing education.

The Mission is expected to impart literacy to 70 million adults of age group of 15 years and beyond. Further, 1.5 million adults will be covered under basic education and an equal number under vocational (skill development) programme. Emphasis will be on women of socially and economically backward groups.

Under the **Adult and Continuing Education Programme**, *Sakshar Bharat* is aimed at providing impetus to achieving the goal of fully literate society engaged in lifelong learning through:

- Development of quality human resource to meet the demands of Bharat in transition;
- Empowerment, transformation and application of literacy skills, beyond 3 R's;
- Use of ICT, media and innovatively designed cultural and library based activities in specially designed Continuing Education Programmes;
- A uniform pattern of Equivalency framework across the country to open avenues for further education through Open and Distance Learning Systems. The government will meet the entire cost of teaching-learning including materials and assessment.

- To prepare a specially designed programme for neo-literates of about 200 hours, the completion of which will merit a learner literacy levels equivalent to Standard V.
- Given the diversity of contexts, needs and target groups, diverse strategies like arrangement for resident camps, resident instructor mode and theme based literacy interventions, etc. as per the needs and requirements of the learners are to be made available.
- A specially designed Basic Education Programme to facilitate neo literates and school dropouts to continue their learning beyond basic literacy and acquire equivalency to formal education system up to class XII.
- Special importance to skill development programme to equip the neo-literates and non-literates with skills to improve their livelihood opportunities.
- Jan Shikshan Sansthans to be institutionally networked with the Adult Education Centres in the villages for imparting vocational training programmes.

Besides, there are programmes of providing assistance to Voluntary Agencies for Adult Education and Skill Development, establishing State Resource Centres to provide academic and technical resource support to adult and continuing education through development and production of material and training modules; establishing Jan Shikshan Sansthans to provide training to non literates, etc.

The success of adult literacy programme is vital to the personality development of the individual as also for socio-economic progress of the country. The programme was, however, always starved of funds. In the post-independence exuberance, about 3.5 per cent of the total plan allocations for education were earmarked for 'social education' – the then nomenclature of adult education. The percentage was reduced substantially in the subsequent plans; Second Plan (1.6 per cent), Third Plan (0.3 per cent), Fourth Plan (0.1 per cent) and in the Fifth Plan it was allocated 0.3 per cent of the total allocation. That the funding has not improved till now would be evident from the fact that in 2007-08, the allocation (plan and non-plan) accounted for 0.30 of the total expenditure on education. The percentage for 2008-09 was 0.29 and for 2009, 0.38. Needless to say that although the success of a programme depends on a multiplicity of factors, financial inputs are not an unimportant causative factor. Any deficiency on that account would certainly thwart the progress of the programme, and so has it happened in the case of adult education.

Sectoral Programmes

(b) Elementary Education

There has been sizeable increase in the number of pupils at the elementary stage of education.

In 1960-61, the overall gross enrolment ratio (GER) was 62.4 per cent for the 6-11 age group. The coverage for the boys was 82.6 per cent and for girls, it was almost half of that of the boys i.e. 41.4 per cent. The corresponding percentages for the age group 11-14 were 33.2 for boys, 11.3 for girls within an overall percentage of 22.5. The position improved considerably in 1984-85, raising the overall percentage to 94.1 for 6-11 age group and 49.8 for 11-14 age group. The girls' percentage was, however, still very low; in the case of 11-14 age group being 35.7. State-wise, Kerala with 119.1 per cent coverage for the age group 6-11 and 63.5 for 11-14 age group topped the list among the major states. Rajasthan had the dubious distinction of having the lowest percentage among the major states averaging 35.8 per cent coverage of the age group 6-11. In the case of 11-14 age group, West Bengal registered the lowest coverage of 34.4 per cent.

The position improved considerably by 2007-08. The overall GER was 113.97 – 115.26 for boys and 112.58 for girls in the age group 6-11. The coverage of the age group 11-14 was however, lower – 78.6 per cent; 81.48 for boys and 74.36 for girls. Considered state-wise. Madhya Pradesh recorded the highest overall coverage at 153.44 per cent; the lowest being that of West Bengal (70.24) for the age group 6-11.

For elementary education (classes I-VIII), the Gross enrolment Ratio was overall 100.28 per cent; boys 102.38 per cent and girls 98.2 per cent. At this stage, there were wide variations among the states – Bihar with 82.57 per cent coverage was the lowest and Madhya Pradesh with 133.47 per cent was the highest. It may also be mentioned that in the case of 6-11 age group, the overall coverage was 111.81, for the age group 11-14 only 69.99 per cent was covered by school education. Further, 96.26 per cent of the population in classes I-VIII was in schools.

A Word of Caution

The coverage of the various age groups at the elementary education stage should be viewed with caution. The Gross Enrolment Ratio (GER) includes underage and overage students. For example, at the primary level 13.79 per cent of children belong to underage and overage category. The corresponding figure for upper primary stage is 19.98. The figures for urban areas are still higher: 15.37 at the primary stage and 20.61 per cent at the upper primary stage.[4] It would mean that when 111.81 per cent of student population is stated to be covered at the primary stage, the actual coverage of the relevant age group is 97.51, much lower than the stated figure.

Gender Parity Index

According to the analysis made by the National University of Educational Planning and Administration, there is marked improvement in the participation of girls in education. Table 4 explains:

Table 4: Gender Parity Index (GPI) in Enrolment: 2005-06 to 2008-09

Grades	All Areas	Rural Areas	Urban Areas Managements	All Government Managements	All Private Managements
2005-06					
I-V	0.92	0.91	0.92	0.95	0.80
VI-VII/VIII	0.84	0.82	0.91	0.87	0.81
I-VII/VIII	0.90	0.89	0.92	0.93	0.80
2006-07					
I-V	0.93	0.93	0.92	0.96	0.81
VI-VII/VIII	0.87	0.85	0.92	0.90	0.82
I-VII/VIII	0.91	0.91	0.92	0.95	0.82
2007-08					
I-V	0.93	0.94	0.91	0.97	0.81
VI-VII/VIII	0.89	0.88	0.91	0.93	0.81
I-VII/VIII	9.92	0.92	0.91	0.96	0.81
2008-09					
I-V	0.94	0.94	0.91	0.99	0.81
VI-VII/VIII	0.91	0.90	0.92	0.97	0.81
I-VII/VIII	0.93	0.93	0.91	0.98	0.81

(*Source:* Elementary Education in India, NUEPA, 2011; p. 104).

It would be seen that Gender Parity Index in respect of 35 states/UTs in 2008-09 was 0.94 in classes I-V; 0.93 in 2007-08 as also in 2006-07 and 0.92 in 2006-07. The corresponding figures for classes I-VII/VIII were 0.93, 0.92, 0.91 and 0.90 respectively. Further, there was no marked difference in GPI in rural and urban areas. There was, however, sizeable difference in the GPI between Government managed and privately managed schools – the latter being much lower than the former.

Drop Outs

Even after being admitted to schools, a large number of students leave without completing the course. In 2007-08, the dropout rate in classes I-V was – over all 25.09 – 25.70 for boys and 24.41 for girls. The dropout rate became larger in classes I-VIII. It was 42.68 per cent overall – 43.72 for boys and 41.34 for girls. Further, about 57 per cent drop out before completing their matriculation course. The dropout rate is larger for girls – 57.33 per cent than that for boys – 56.55 per cent. The dropout rate is also larger in the case of students from Scheduled Castes – 30.09 per cent in classes I-V, 52.47 in classes I-VIII and a huge 68.42 per cent in classes I-X. The dropouts among Scheduled Tribes are still larger – 30.42 per cent in classes I-V; 62.48 per cent in classes I-VIII and 76.85 per cent in classes I-X.

Physical Facilities

In spite of the tremendous expansion of facilities at the elementary education stage, it has not been possible to reach one hundred per cent coverage, particularly at the upper primary school level. Further, there are glaring disparities on account of gender, location and social groups. Besides the general poverty of the population and lack of appreciation on the part of the general public of the utility of education, the lack of physical facilities at the elementary education stage, are also important reasons. Only 88 per cent schools had drinking water facility, 67 per cent had common toilet facility. Only 54 per cent schools had separate toilets for girls. Further, only 36 per cent of schools managed by Government have kitchen sheds to operate the mid-day meal programme. All these deficiencies have the potentiality of retarding the progress of education at the elementary education stage.

Strategy for Universalising Elementary Education

We have described the attempt made by the Government of free India to give a legal status to the provision of free and compulsory education to children of the age group 6-14 leading to the passage of Right to Education Act (Annexure). The Act makes it incumbent upon the central and state governments to provide facilities for education to children of the said age group. The Act came into force on 1st April, 2010 – a century after Gopal Krishan Gokhale introduced his famous bill in the Imperial Legislation. The country has to watch, with bated breath, the impact that the Act is going to make on the expansion of elementary education.

The mechanisms for implementing R.T.E. Act are:

1. Sarva Shiksha Abhiyan (SSA)

SSA is intended to achieve universal elementary education. Its various schemes like the National Programme of Education for Girls at the Elementary Level (NPEGEL) and Kasturba Gandhi Balika Vidyalaya scheme, which provides for setting up of residential upper primary schools for girls of SC, ST or OBC and Muslims have been continued so as to address the educational needs of girls in educationally backward areas.

The specific goals of SSA as indicated in the 10th Plan are:

- All children to be in regular schools by 2005.
- Bridging all gender and social category gaps at primary stage by 2007 and at elementary level by 2010.
- Universal retention by 2010.
- Focus on elementary education of satisfactory quality, with emphasis on education for life.

2. Mid Day Meal Programme

The programme was launched on 15th August, 1995 in 2408 development blocks as a dry ration scheme with a view to enhance attendance and simultaneously improve nutritional level of primary school going children. A hot cooked mid-day meal is served to the students of classes I to VIII in Government aided and local body schools and to Education Guarantee Scheme/Alternative and Innovative Education Centres, including Madrassas, Maktabs supported under Sarva Shiksha Abhiyan across the country.

The scheme was revised in 2009-10. The food norms for upper primary children were revised. The cooking cost was increased. Transport assistance to 11 special category states, (8 North Eastern and 3 other hilly areas), was also revised upwards.

3. Quality, Access and Equity

Government will focus on providing education facilities in districts with substantial population of SC, ST and minority (Muslim) communities, as well as more than 50,000 out of school children. Further, special efforts will be made to identify districts lacking infrastructure and to provide the requisite financial assistance. It has also been realised that retaining disadvantaged children enrolled in schools is a far more challenging task than enrolling them. This is especially true in the case of girls. In order to attract and retain girl students, female teachers are to be appointed.

4. Educational Development Index (EDI) at the Elementary Education Stage

The University of Educational Planning and Administration and the Ministry of Human Resource Development have attempted to work out an EDI separately for Primary and upper primary classes as also for the entire elementary education based on the data provided by the state governments under Sarv Shiksha Abhiyan (DISE). For this purpose, 24 indicators were used, which were regrouped under four sub-groups-Access, Infrastructures, Teachers and outcome indicators. Based on this analysis the States/UTs were ranked. The following table indicates the composite Educational Development Index (EDI) relating to all schools, all managements at the elementary education stage in repeat of major states.

Table 5: Statewise EDI at the Elementary Education Stage

State	*Primary level*		*Upper Primary Stage*		*Composite Primary and Upper Primary Stage*	
	Index	*Rank*	*Index*	*Rank*	*Index*	*Rank*
1. Andhra Pradesh	0.558	14	0.635	17	0.597	15
2. Assam	0.460	33	0.442	24	0.451	35
3. Bihar	0.477	32	0.453	32	0.465	33
4. Gujarat	0.568	12	0.682	8	0.625	9
5. Haryana	0.517	29	0.666	12	0.591	17

6. Himachal Pradesh	0.593	8	0.645	15	0.619	11
7. Jammu & Kashmir	0.550	17	0.606	19	0.578	18
8. Karnataka	0.636	3	0.751	2	0.693	2
9. Kerala	0.616	6	0.658	13	0.637	7
10. Madhya Pradesh	0.524	22	0.519	28	0.521	26
11. Maharashtra	0.587	10	0.667	11	0.627	8
12. Odisha	0.554	16	0.532	25	0.543	22
13. Punjab	0.557	15	0.654	14	0.606	13
14. Rajasthan	0.497	29	0.575	21	0.536	23
15. Tamil Nadu	0.680	1	0.699	5	0.689	3
16. Uttar Pradesh	0.527	20	0.412	35	0.470	32
17. West Bengal	0.536	19	0.453	33	0.495	29

Source: NUEPA, Elementory Education in India, Progress Towards UFE. 2013, p. 43.

As would appear there are wide inter-states and intra-state disparities in respect of the various indicators set out for the study. For example, Tamil Nadu, which ranks number 1 in respect of primary stage indicators, goes upto 5 in respect of Upper Primary, coming down to 3 in respect of composite elementary education stage. Bihar has the dubious distinction of being the most backward state in respect of elementary education as a whole as also separately at the Primary and Upper Primary Levels.

Keeping in view the above analysis, it would need to be emphasised that the concerned authorities of the central and state levels will have to sharpen their tools of implementation in order to the achieve the objectives of universalising elementary education.

(c) Secondary Education

There has been substantial expansion of secondary education. From 4,000 schools in 1947, the number increased to 52,279 in 1982-83 and further to 1,72,990 (including 59,166 higher secondary schools and junior colleges) in 2007-08. During this period, the enrolment in secondary schools increased from 7 lakh in 1947 to 140 lakh in 1982-83 and to 4,44,75,476 in 2007-08. The girls enrolment, however, was 1,93,19,218, which works out to about 43 per cent of the total enrolment in 2007-08. Further, the number of teachers increased from 93,000 in 1947 to 9,93,000 in 1982 and 21,26,875 in 2007-08. The teacher pupil ratios (TPR) in 2007-08, were 1:37 at the higher secondary stage and 1:33 at the high school stage. State-wise the teacher-pupil ratio at the higher secondary stage was as high as 1:65 in Uttar Pradesh followed by West Bengal (1:51), Karnataka, (1:50) and Gujarat (1:38) among the major states. Among the lower TPR states, mention may be made of Jammu & Kashmir 1:17; Odisha 1:17, Madhya Pradesh 1:24 and Himachal Pradesh (1:25). At the high school stage, West Bengal had the dubious distinction of having the highest TPR of 1:60 followed by Bihar 1:52. Jammu & Kashmir, and in the case of higher secondary schools, had the lowest TPR 1:11. The widely varying TPRs in different states would have certainly affected the quality of education in different states.

The Grey Areas

In spite of the large scalc expansion in enrolment at the secondary stage, only 58 per cent of the population in the age group is enrolled in classes IX-X and 33 per cent in classes XI-XII. The corresponding figures for girls are 53 and 30 per cent respectively. Further, the Gross Enrolment Ratio (GER) for Scheduled Castes students is as low as 28 per cent overall and 25 per cent for girl students in classes XI-XII. For scheduled tribes, the corresponding percentages are 20.3 overall and a merely 16 per cent for girls in classes XI-XII.

The outreach of secondary education in rural areas presents a dismal picture. Only 35 per cent of the age group 14-17 are enrolled in classes IX-XII; the girls being only 32 per cent. Taking classes XI-XII separately, the position is appalling; only 19 per cent of the overall age group entered the school – the girls being as low as 17 per cent.

The dropout rates in classes I-X in 2008 for all categories of students were 56.71 per cent – 56.55 per cent for boys and 57.33 per cent for girls. The corresponding figures for SC students are 68.42 per cent overall – 68.05 for boys and 68.90 for girls. The position of ST students is much worse – 76.85 per cent students in the overall category: 76.02 per cent boys and 77.97 girls dropout between classes I-X.

It has also been noted that only 68.22 per cent of all categories of students (66.02 boys and 71.34 per cent girls) pass the matriculation examination. The pass percentage for SC students is only 58.61 – 55.95 per cent for boys and 62.27 per cent for girls. The results of the ST students are slightly better: 59.60 overall, 59.60 per cent boys and 59.59 per cent girls pass the matriculation examination. The success rate in the high school examination in open schooling is very low: 38.58 per cent students of all categories – 35.59 per cent SC and 38.61 per cent ST students succeed in the matriculation examination. The position of girls is precarious: only 14.88 per cent of the girls are able to make the grade.

The position of higher secondary examination is somewhat better. The overall pass percentage in class XII Board examination was 74.36 in 2008 – for girls it was 80.65, faring much better than boys, whose pass percentage was 69.72. The overall pass percentage of Scheduled Castes students was 69.08 and of the Scheduled Tribes students was 65.14. In both these categories the girls outshone the boys in the higher secondary examinations.

Vocationalisation

The National Policies on Education (1968 and 1986) had emphasised the introduction of 'systematic, well planned and vigorously implemented vocational education, which is crucial in the proposed educational reorganisation.'[5]

The programme of vacationalisation at the secondary stage has, however, remained marginal and confined to a few states. "The courses started with little imagination and with poor wherewithal that have also lacked in prestige and attracting power."[6]

It may be recalled that the Education Commission (1964-66) had visualised that 25 per cent of the students at the lower secondary stage and 50 per cent of the total enrolment at the higher secondary stage would go for vocational stream by 1986. In spite of 50 years having elapsed after the Commission made this recommendation, only 5 per cent of the population of 19-24 age group, has acquired some sort of skills through vocational education. This is in spite of a centrally sponsored scheme launched for boosting vocationalisation of secondary education which is being implemented since 1988. The scheme provides financial assistance to states for setting up administrative structures, carrying out vocational surveys, preparing curriculum guides/training manuals, organising teacher training programmes etc.

Universalising Secondary Education

In the backdrop of these deficiencies, the government intends to launch programmes of quantitative expansion and qualitative improvement of secondary education. It has launched a comprehensive centrally sponsored scheme: *Rashtriya Madhyamik Shiksha Abhiyan* with the objective of making good quality secondary education available, accessible and affordable to young persons, irrespective of gender, socio-economic condition, disability, geographical and other barriers. Under this a secondary school of acceptable norms would be available within 5 kilometres of every habitation in the country. The objective is that universal secondary education will be accessible by 2017 and universal retention by 2020.

The aim of the Government for universalising secondary education is laudable. But the task is formidable. One can only hope that problems like disparities in availability of academic and physical facilities among the states; teacher pupil ratios; gender and regional disparities; dropouts and high rates of failures in the examinations will be sorted out in course of time.

Diversification of courses at the secondary stage has to be addressed on a priority basis. As already stated, in spite of the various Commissions and National Policies emphasising vocationalisation at the secondary stage of education, even the modest target of 25 per cent of students to be covered under the scheme has not been realised. It is incumbent on the educational authorities to provide need based practical education so that the students leaving the schools can look for a purposeful, productive life after they leave the school.

(d) Higher Education

The system of higher education in India, as also in other countries of the world, is subject to an inexplicable ambivalence on the part of the government as well as the society. It is extolled as a crucial factor for survival – for it provides people with "an opportunity to reflect on the critical, social, economic, cultural, moral and spiritual issues facing humanity" (National Policy on Education, 1986). It is also regarded as a potent instrument for producing scientific and technical manpower of the highest calibre. The Punnayya Committee (1994) has rightly said that for India, to attain the cutting edge of technology, it is institutions of higher learning that offer hope. Further, they provide an excellent opportunity of vertical mobility to the deprived sections of society.

Higher education has also been facing sharp criticism for its apparent in ability to provide education relevant to the needs and aspirations of the ever-escalating numbers of seekers of knowledge. It has also been castigated as the exclusive preserve of the elitist groups who are, generally, alienated from the socio-cultural mores of the country of their origin. It is quite often contended that the system of higher education has developed an in-built process of metabolic degeneration in that quite a large number of students entering the portals of university institutions are thrown by the way side resulting in a huge loss of human and financial resources. The phenomenon of ever escalating unemployment and under-employment of educated youth in the developing countries has further aggravated the situation, giving rise to its outright, but undeserved, condemnation in these words: "The whole process of higher education has become warped, dysfunctional, producing a number of unemployable young men and women."[6]

In the welter of denunciations, it is conveniently forgotten that institutions of higher education have been inundated by never-ending streams of young men and women aspiring to get university degrees; quite a few of them being ill-prepared, on account of poor schooling facilities, to benefit from higher education. It is also not appreciated that a number of universities/colleges have been established without adequate physical and academic infrastructure depending upon inadequate financial support from the Government as also private bodies sponsoring them. This undermines their autonomous character and saps their capacity for free and unfettered intellectual inquiry. Even the old and established institutions have been subjected to an unprecedented financial squeeze, which has afflicted the system since the early seventies and does not yet seem to be loosening its stranglehold.

Higher education in the erstwhile British Colonies, particularly India, is facing a 'crisis of identity' in that it has become heterogeneous in complexion, size and quality. The quality could not be maintained because of the absence of proper planning and adequate academic and physical facilities. In spite of concerted efforts at structural reorganisation, it has not developed a personality of its own. The institutional pattern is marked by a sort of academic stratification; a few financially viable institutions co-existing with the vast multitude of what may be called academic "ghettos" perennially afflicted by paucity of resources. The bulk of affiliated colleges (which are responsible for a sizeable proportion of student enrolment on the Indian sub-continent) do not appear to be of much concern to the governments and hence do not seem to be a significant part of the academic configuration. Even the University Grants Commission (UGC) has abandoned about half of these colleges by describing them as academically non-viable institutions and ineligible for its assistance. This underlines the pathetic academic condition of these colleges mainly affiliated to some state universities. It is worthwhile to mention that India still needs more expansion in higher education because; out of over one billion people in the country, only 6 per cent of the relevant age group study in colleges and universities. Further expansion, however, would have to proceed in a systematic and planned manner, keeping in view the availability of physical and academic facilities.

The causes of educational morass are complex and varied. The unregulated institutional expansion, the lack of a firm policy about student admissions, particularly in general education courses, the somewhat irrelevance of university curriculum to socio-economic milieu of the country, the antiquated methods of teaching, the stifling stranglehold of examination system and continuing paucity of physical and financial resources could be mentioned as the main causative factors of the malady afflicting the university education system. Any improvement of higher education would, therefore, call for a multi-dimensional approach.

In the context of these general remarks, we shall discuss the state of higher education and the problem areas in the sector.

Expansion of Facilities

There has been large scale expansion of facilities for higher education during the post independence period. Table 5 explains:

Table 6 : Number of Institutions of Higher Education, Enrolment and Faculty

Year	*No. of Colleges*	*No. of Universities*	*Enrolment*	*Teachers*
1950-51	750	30	2,63,000	24,000
1990-91	7346	177	49,25,000	2,72,000
2003-04	16885	302	99,53,506	4,56,742
2010-11	33023	634	1,69,75,000	8,16,966

(*Source:* UGC's Higher Education in India at a Glance, 2012 and MHRD; Statistics of Higher and Technical Education (2009-10).

Equity, Excellence Syndrome

Does the large expansion of facilities, ipso facto, lead to the conclusion that there is equitable distribution among the various stakeholders of higher education? The following facts would throw some light on this:

1. There are wide disparities in coverage of higher education in respect of various social groups. For example, in 2009-10, the Gross Enrolment Ratio (GER) for all categories was 15 per cent; it was 17.1 per cent for boys and 12.7 per cent for girls. The corresponding ratio for Scheduled Castes were11.3 and 10.3 for STs.

2. The enrolment of girls was about 40 per cent of the total enrolment; corresponding figures for SC were 17.78 per cent. The tribal students constituted 4.69 per cent of the total enrolment, indicating that their share in enrolment was significantly less than their proportion in the total population.
3. The Gender Parity Index for higher education (age group 18-23) was 0.74 for all categories of students; 0.69 for SC and 0.57 for ST students.
4. The total number of students in open universities was 21,19,364, which works out to 15.35 per cent of total enrolment. Scheduled Castes students constituted only 9.44 per cent and Scheduled Tribes 7.8 per cent of the total enrolment.

It would be seen that behind the facade of quite a large expansion, the iniquitous distribution of facilities among the various social groups is large. Further, there is sizeable difference among the students on the basis of gender.

It is admitted that equity does not mean equality, particularly, at the higher education stage, in which admissions should be based on the intellectual capabilities of students to profit from higher education. It may, however, be stated that in quite a few cases, it is not the lack of academic brilliance but that of opportunities which restrict the student's entry into academic institutions. Such students need to be provided with financial and other support to pursue their academic activities without any hindrance. The socio-economic groups which are lagging behind need to be provided with physical and financial support from the state.

Keeping in view the need to provide facilities for the disadvantaged socio-economic groups, the UGC has taken several remedial measures, including remedial coaching at UG and PG level, coaching classes for preparation for National Eligibility Test (NET), Post graduate studentships, establishment of centres in universities for study of social exclusion and inclusive policy, special seats reserved for SC, ST and Other Backward Classes in central institutions.

The UGC has also launched a number of schemes to achieve gender parity. These include scholarships for single girl student for pursuing higher and technical education, support for construction of hostels for girls, post-doctoral fellowships offered for women students. Further, schemes for encouraging higher education among the minorities have been launched.

For improving access, special programmes for targeted expansion in central universities, facilitating the setting up of new universities and colleges and additional assistance to underfunded institutions have been launched, Open and Distance Learning has been recognised as an important mode for achieving enhanced access, developing skills, capacity building, training, employability, life-long education and continuing education. These programmes are to be continued and expanded to meet the burgeoning requirements for access to higher education.

Globalisation–Its Impact on Higher Education

India embarked upon deregulation and liberalisation of its economy since 1980s. The process received a major thrust from early nineties, when significant changes were introduced by abolishing licensing for most of the domestic industries and allowing private sector to enter areas formally the exclusive domain of the public sector. Globalisation became the password for India's socio-economic system. Education, particularly higher education, was impacted by the process set in motion by the new economic policy. As stated by Azad: "In a market oriented competitive world, education has to assume a somewhat different role. It cannot afford to be conventional, rigid and imperious to change. It has to keep abreast of the latest developments in various fields and has to become capable of creating, absorbing and transacting neo-technology and information systems that are sweeping across countries of the world. There has also to be a paradigm shift in the content of education and the transactional technologies with substantial emphasis on the productivity aspects of the curriculum."[7]

The impact of globalisation on higher education has been explained in details in a subsequent chapter. At this stage, the following may be briefly stated:

1. It will lead to internationalisation of education with its good and bad effects.
2. It will lay emphasise on market oriented courses to the neglect of courses in humanities and basic sciences.
3. It may emphasise privatisation of education; will boost self financing courses in areas, which have a readily available market.

Research in the Doldrums

There is need for emphasising Research and Development in the universities. Our attempts in this direction are, however, not very encouraging. It has been reckoned that leaving aside the specialised Research Organisations like Council of Scientific and Industrial Research and its regional set ups; agricultural and medical research, the expenditure on research in universities and colleges is 0.1 per cent of the GDP. Further, the UGC, which is expected to provide financial support for research and development in universities, spends meagre amounts on research. For example, during the 8th Plan, the Commission's grants to universities for excellence and research were 15 per cent of the total grants given by it. The share of excellence and quality improvement was reduced to 13.15 per cent of the total grants during the Ninth Plan. It went further down to 11 per cent in 2005-06. So far, the non-plan grants are almost inconsequential. Table 6 explains:

Table 7: Scheme-wise Distribution of Non-Plan Grants (in Percentages)

Scheme	*1992-93*	*1997-98*	*2005-06*
Research Fellowship	1.07	2.68	2.08
Research Fellowship in Humanities	0.00	0.32	0.22
Total	**1.07**	**3.00**	**2.30**

Source: Ministry of HRD's Statistical reports for various years.

It may be conceded that UGC's funds being limited and its commitment to finance the qualitative development of universities, besides providing total funding for the maintenance and development of the central universities, the Commission finds it difficult to provide adequate funds for research and development to university level institutions. Since the industrial and commercial houses are the main beneficiaries of research in universities, it would be appropriate for them to share the financing of research in universities and similar institutions. The Government may consider levying a cess for research on the industrial houses so as to ensure a stable financial input for research in universities. The philanthropic organisations may also be approached for financing research programmes in universities.

To conclude, it may be worthwhile mentioning that the Planning Commission in its approach to the Twelfth Five Year Plan has laid emphasis on bringing back the 'lost' Research Culture of the Indian Universities so as to create new knowledge and improve teaching standards. According to the Commission:

"...Collaborative research, setting up industry incubation parks in universities and institutions providing more research fellowships, promoting innovation through inter-disciplinary research in new and emerging fields, strengthening Inter-University Centres, etc., need to be emphasised.... This would require more funding for university based research and funding policies that create right incentives for quality research and promote collaboration among institutions."[8]

Managing Higher Education

There are quite a few organisations at the central level concerned with management and financing of higher education. Among the specialised bodies, mention may be made of the University Grants Commission, the All India Council for Technical Education, the Indian Council for Agricultural Research, the Medical Council of India; the Indian Council of Medical Research etc. All these bodies are concerned with their specialised subject areas and work almost independently without much interaction with one another.

The University Grants Commission, which was set up under Entry 66 of the Union List of the Constitution for coordination and determination of standards in institutions of higher education or research and scientific and technical institutions of university education has, in actual fact, an extremely truncated role to play. Its writ does not run beyond higher education of a general type. According to Azad "the nomenclature of the Commission smacks of a sort of terminological inexactitude. It can also exercise a restraining influence on its role. The Commission's jurisdiction transcends the universities and its functions are much more than giving grants to institutions of higher education. A rechristening of the Commission might be in the best interests of higher education."[9]

As stated above, all these bodies/organisations are concerned with higher education work autonomously without any kind of constructive interaction among them. The Education Commission (1964-66) had expressed the view that the UGC should represent the entire spectrum of higher education... This is necessary for various reasons but principally because, in the contemporary world, no discipline can develop fully in isolation from the main stream of academic life.[10]

In pursuance of this recommendation, the Planning Commission, in mid seventies, held discussions with various stake holders: the Ministries of Education, Health and Agriculture along with their specialised bodies. It was, however, difficult to persuade the various ministries/specialised organisations to set up an overall organisation to have a coordinated view of the programmes and policies of various disciplines of higher education.

The Ministry of HRD has drawn up a bill for the setting up of a National Commission on Higher Education and Research (NCHER) for prescribing standards of academic quality and defining policies for advancement of knowledge in higher education institutions based on the principle of enhancing autonomy of universities and institutions of higher learning and research.

The bill, at present in a formative stage, will have to be drawn up in details giving the objectives, constitution of the Commission, its modus operandi, etc. Based on past experience, it appears difficult to persuade the concerned Ministries/organisations to part with their sphere of work and influence.[11] It is however, worth making an effort to bring about an organisation of the type envisaged by the Education Commission and later by the Planning Commission.

To Sum-up

The preceding analysis of the progress of education during the post-independence period can be summed up briefly as follows:

The state of Indian education represents a phenomenon of 'lights and shades'. All the sectors of education have shown phenomenal progress. But the dazzling brilliance of the advancement is interspersed with a plethora of dark spots, which eclipse its glitter.

We shall describe the position sector by sector during the period under review.

1. India, soon after independence, recognised the importance of education as a means of socio-economic development and cultural regeneration. The process of educational development, both quantitatively and qualitatively, was accelerated as part of planning, which was ushered in as a means of socio-economic development.
2. At the time of the initiation of the First Five Year Plan, i.e. 1951, the position of education was not very encouraging. Only 40 per cent of children in the age group 6-11, 10 per cent in the age group 11-17 and 0.9 per cent of those in the age group 17-23 were provided with some sort of educational

facilities. The literacy rate of the India's teeming millions was abysmally low – only 17.2 per cent. The female literacy percentage was still lower.

3. Educational facilities were unevenly distributed between rural and urban areas. In spite of the rural areas having about four fifths of India's population, the percentage of students studying in primary, middle and high schools in rural areas was 60, 67 and 26 respectively. At the university stage, facilities in rural areas were practically non-existent.
4. The enrolment of girls was abysmally low – only 28, 18 and 13 per cent of the total enrolment in primary, middle and high schools respectively.
5. About 41 per cent of the teachers at the primary stage were untrained. The percentage of female trained teachers was very low.

In the backdrop of these unsavoury conditions, the country set out to improve its educational system through process of planning. It launched schemes of reorientation of the educational system, expansion of facilities at the primary education, remodelling secondary education and technical and vocational education; consolidation of university education, expansion of facilities for women's education; training of teachers, helping the backward states to improve their educational systems. A review has been made of the state of education in two periods:

1. 1951 to 1985
2. 1986 to the present position.

There has been tremendous expansion of educational facilities at all stages of education. This expansion has been region-wise and gender-wise at all stages of education. There has also been some improvement in retention and drop outs of students as also in the literacy levels of both males and females – the latter of course lagging behind their male counterparts.

The Position in 2007-08

The position of the educational development is reviewed below:

1. The number of schools of all types increased to 12,75,990 in 2007-08. The total enrolment at the school stage was 23,71,50,710 in 2007-08. If the pre-primary stage is also included, the number would rise to 27,71,38,099.
2. In spite of the tremendous increase in the overall enrolment at the school stage, girls were 46 per cent of the total enrolment while boys constituted 54 per cent of the total enrolment.
3. The Scheduled Caste students were about 18 per cent of the total enrolment.
4. The Scheduled Tribes were much lower in that they constituted about 9 per cent of the total enrolment – the boys and girls were almost equal in percentage terms i.e. about 9 per cent.

5. While population in rural areas constituted about 72 per cent of the total population, enrolment in rural areas was about 69 per cent – the girls at about 70 per cent faring better than that of boys, i.e., about 63 per cent.
6. At the university stage, boys were much ahead of girls in terms of percentage of the total enrolment – about 60 per cent of the total, while the girls were only 40 per cent.
7. The Scheduled Castes coverage at the university stage was much lower (about 20 per cent of the total enrolment); the Scheduled Tribes registering an abysmally low percentage at about 9.

The conclusion that could be drawn is that in spite of stupendous increase, there are wide disparities on the basis of gender, social groups and regions.

Sectoral Progress

(a) Adult Education

1. There has been quite a bit improvement in the level of adult literacy, which according to the 2011 census stood at 74 per cent – a 9 per cent increase compared to 10 years earlier, i.e., 2001. Further, the gender gap has declined by about 7 percentage points.
2. The literacy rate among Scheduled Castes was much lower than the overall rate, i.e., about 55 per cent against 74 per cent. The Scheduled Tribes were at a still lower level of 47 per cent.
3. There are quite a few schemes launched by the Government to accelerate the literacy level among the population especially the backward sections of the society. The most prominent among the schemes is the National Literacy Mission, which provides basic literacy, post literacy and continuing education programmes for all adults, specially the women. It is expected to impart literacy to 70 million adults in the age group 15 and above.

(b) Elementary Education

The Gross Enrolment Ratio (GER) for 6-11 age group, which was 62.4 per cent in 1960-61 improved to about 114 per cent in 2007-08. The girls, however, lag much behind the boys.

For elementary education as a whole, the GER was overall about 100 per cent – boys 102 per cent and girls 98 per cent. There are, however, wide disparities among the states – Bihar with about 83 per cent coverage being the lowest. The Gender Parity Index in respect of 35 states and union territories in 2008-09 was 0.94 in classes I-V and 0.93 in classes VI to VIII. There were marked differences among the stages.

The dropout rate in classes I-V was 25 per cent; 43 per cent in classes VI-VIII. It was much larger in the case of backward classes.

Strategies for Universalising Elementary Education

The most important step taken by the Government is the passage of the Right to Education Act, which makes it incumbent upon the Government to provide free and compulsory education to children of the age group 6-14; ensure compulsory admission, attendance and completion of elementary education by every child in that age group. The Act has come into force with effect from 1st April, 2010. The Act has given rise to various 'teething' problems. It is, however, hoped that these problems will be sorted out in course of time.

The main instrument of achieving the objective of introducing free and compulsory education at the elementary stage is the Sarva Siksha Abhiyan, which is aimed at providing good quality education at the elementary education stage for the targeted age group. Further, the schemes of Mid-Day Meals and Quality Improvement Programmes are intended to help in achieving the target aimed at by the Act. The loopholes discovers in the states' inplementation of programmes of universaling elementary education as identified in the analysis of Educational Development index will need to be plugged, if the programme is not to remain a distant dream.

(c) Secondary Education

There has been substantial increase in the number of schools and enrolment at the secondary stage. The institutions increased from 4,000 in1947 to 1,72,990 i.e. a staggering 43 times in sixty years. The enrolment increased from 7 lakh to 445 lakh in that period. The girls' enrolment is, however, 43 per cent of the total enrolment. There is substantial increase in the number of teachers although there are large variations in the teacher-pupil ratios among the states – the lowest being in Jammu & Kashmir (1:14) to the highest 1:65 in U.P. at the higher secondary stage. At the high school stage, the lowest (1:11) was again in Jammu & Kashmir and the highest in West Bengal (1:60). The malevolent effect of higher TPR on the quality of education can be easily surmised.

The coverage of the age group 14-17 is 58 per cent at the high school stage and 33 per cent at the higher secondary stages. The G.E.R. among the scheduled castes is as low as 28 per cent; for S Ts it is even lower; 20 per cent. The G.E.R. in rural areas is 35 per cent overall and 32 per cent for girls. Only 19 per cent of the overall age group is enrolled in classes XI-XII; the girls being as low as 17 per cent.

There is huge dropout in classes I-X – about 57 per cent of those, who enter dropout of the schools – 57 per cent of the girls and about 51 per cent boys. The dropout among the backward classes is much higher – 68 per cent for SC and 77 per cent for ST.

The courses offered to bulk of students at the secondary stage are largely theoretical. The programme of voationalisation has remained marginal – only 5 per cent of the 19-24 age-group has acquired some sort of skills during the 50 year period since the Education Commission made this recommendation.

These deficiencies notwithstanding, the government has set its eyes on universalisation of secondary education. It has launched a centrally sponsored scheme: '*Rashtriya Madhyamik Shiksha Abhiyan*' to provide good quality secondary education at affordable cost to the eligible students. While the aim of the government is laudable, the task undertaken by it is formidable keeping in view the deficiencies in the system analysed in this report.

(d) Higher Education

Higher Education has earned applause for being a crucial factor for survival; a potent instrument for providing scientific and professional, manpower of the highest calibre. It has also been condemned for its inability to provide education relevant to the needs and aspirations of the ever escalating number of seekers of knowledge. The reality lies somewhere in between.

There is sizeable increase in the enrolment, institutions and teachers at higher education stage. There are, however, wide disparities in the coverage of higher education on the basis of gender, socio-economic groups and regions. Keeping in view these deficiencies, a number of schemes have been launched to encourage the backward groups to join institutions of higher education.

There is very meagre allocation for encouraging research in humanities and basic sciences. The amount allocated for research by U G C was 1.7 per cent of its total budget, which increased to 2.30 per cent during the period 1992-93 to 2005-06. It is necessary, to persuade the industrial and commercial houses, through legislation if necessary, to provide funding for research programmes of which they are the prominent beneficiaries.

A major development in the world's socio-economic system has been the on-set of globalisation since early nineties in India. It has affected India's educational system, particularly, higher education, which is now exposed to the international system of education. It is also expected to lay emphasis on market oriented courses rather than traditional curriculum. Further, privatization is fast becoming an important instrument of managing and financing of education, particularly of higher education. The educational system in India, while making the required changes, has to guard itself against being swayed by the whirlpool of globalisation and losing its socio-cultural identity.

Managing Higher Education

There are quite a few organisations, at the central level concerned with financing and management of institutions of various types at the higher education level. Among them, the University Grants Commission is concerned with the coordination and determination of standards in institutions of higher education. Ironically, its writ does not go beyond higher education of a general type. There is no mechanism of continued interaction among the various bodies concerned with higher education.

The Education Commission (1964-66) had suggested that the UGC should represent the entire spectrum of higher education. In pursuance of this suggestion, the Planning Commission organised inter-ministerial and inter-organisation meetings to bring about some sort of coordination among the various stakeholders. No tangible action emerged out of these discussions.

After a lapse of almost 40 years, the Ministry of HRD is considering a proposal for setting up of a 'National Commission on Higher Education and Research' for prescribing standards of academic quality and defining policies for advancement of knowledge...

The idea of establishing a central organisation for coordination of policies in respect of higher education is laudable. It is, however, doubtful whether the MHRD will be able to wade through the cobwebs of vested interests and exclusiveness that the various organisations have woven around themselves.

Annexure

RIGHT TO EDUCATION ACT

A little more than a century ago, when the British Raj was at its zenith, an Indian visionary, Gopal Krishan Gokhale, introduced a bill in the Imperial Legislature, to provide free and compulsory education to children at the elementary education stage. The bill was thoroughly debated and thrown out on flimsy grounds, by the overwhelming majority of the British legislators. It was followed by attempts by other Indian legislators; the last being made by N.M. Joshi in 1925, but the result was no different. The matter was put in the cold storage for the remaining period of the British rule. Some provinces, soon after the introduction of reforms of 1919 and 1935, introduced compulsory education at the elementary education stage.

Attempts after Independence

Soon after the dawn of political independence, the government committed itself to introduce free and compulsory education for children in the age group 6-14. The Constitution of India recognised the significance of providing facilities to children up to 14 years. Article 45 in the Directive Principles of State Policy laid down that the State shall endeavour to provide within a period ten years from the commencement of the Constitution for free and compulsory education for all children until they complete the age of fourteen years. This Article, however, being non-justiciable, depended on the discretion of the governments at the centre and in states. The ice was broken when in 1993, i.e., 42 years after the commencement of the Constitution, the Supreme Court legalised the right to education in a historic verdict by declaring right to education as a fundamental right of children until the age of 14. This led to the amendment of the Constitution with the introduction of Article 21-A, which called upon the State to provide free and compulsory education to all children of ages six to fourteen years in such manner as the State may, by law, determine. The amendment also introduced a new Article 51-A, which imposed a duty on the parents and guardians to educate their children. In order to legitimise the right of children, of the age group 6-14, for free and compulsory education, the Parliament on 27th August, 2009, passed a Bill providing for free and compulsory education to all children aged 6-14. The 'Notification' to enforce Article 21-A in the Constitution and the corresponding legislation as 'Right of Children to Free and Compulsory Education' came into effect from 1st April 2010.[12]

The Salient Features of the Act are:

1. It is incumbent on the government to provide free and compulsory education to all children of 6-14 years of age; ensure compulsory admission, attendance and completion of elementary education by every child of six to fourteen.
2. It makes it mandatory for the state to ensure availability of a neighbourhood school within three years of the commencement of the Act.
3. The state needs to provide infrastructure including school buildings, trained teachers, and learning equipment as well as to ensure good quality elementary education according to the specified standards and norms.
4. The Act mandates unaided private schools to reserve upto 25 per cent of their seats for students from weaker sections.
5. The Act prohibits donations and charging of capitation fee for admission and interviewing the child or his/her parents as part of a screening process.
6. The Act lays down that teachers ensure that children complete elementary education with requisite learning competencies. Physical punishment, expulsion and detention of the child and deployment of teachers for non-educational purposes other than census and election duty, disaster relief, is strictly prohibited.
7. The Act leaves out of its ambit the age group of 3-6 which educationist regard as crucial for human development. This transitional stage for learning and scholar readiness is of particular significance for children belonging to disadvantaged segments in which case the household environment is not conducive, stimulating and supportive of a child's learning and advancement.

The Act Comes into Force

The RTE Act came into force with effect from 1st April, 2010 after the Supreme Court judgement upholding the validity of the Right of Children to free and compulsory education. It has completed the three year compliance period. It is however, too early to assess its impact. Undoubtedly, there are, quite a few misgivings/ problems about certain provisions of the Act which, it is felt, may affect its potentiality to bring about universal free and compulsory education for the age group 6-14 – the avowed objective of the Act.

Problems Galore

The main problems relate to private schools, which are charged with the responsibility of providing 25 per cent seats for the children of the deprived and backward sections of the society. According to them, the RTE will increase the cost of education, which at present is of the order of Rs. 1200 to Rs. 3000 per student per month. The reimbursement fixed by the government, varying between Rs. 6000 to Rs. 19,000 per year, is seemingly inadequate, particularly in high fee charging private schools. As a consequence, they will be forced to raise tuition fees for the general category students. Otherwise, they will have to put on hold schemes of qualitative improvement of infrastructural and academic facilities. The problem will be more acute in the case of so called 'international' schools, which charge a fee of a whopping amount of Rs. 4-5 lakh a year. It is also feared that integrating students from under-privileged sections would face a serious challenge. RTE may also be used as an instrument for infringement of the academic autonomy of the institutions.

It has also been argued that the provisions in the Act about teacher-pupil ratio and physical infrastructure which include all weather buildings with play grounds, well equipped library, separate toilets for boys and girls, proper sports equipment etc. to be provided within three years of the commencement of the Act are 'draconian' in that non-implementation of the norms would lead to derecognition of the school under section 19 of the Act. Further, any school violating this stipulation can face a fine of Rs. one lakh. The Ministry of Human Resource Development is already considering a grace period of three years for enforcement of this provision.

There is the problem of providing adequate number of qualified and trained teachers on the basis of the recommended pupil-teacher ratios. This does not concern the private schools only. There is an overall shortage of teachers, which may hinder the implementation of the R.T.E. within the stipulated period of one year that is upto 1st April, 2013. According to the analysis made by the Ministry of Human Resource Development "there are 23 lakh vacancies of school teachers at the elementary level and there would be an additional requirement of around 5.1 lakh teachers to fulfil the provision of teacher pupil ratio (laid down in the R.T.E. Act). Even more worrying is the fact that 7.74 lakh teachers are untrained or ill qualified for the job."[13] The problem is likely to be compounded by the provision in the Act against hiring contract teachers.

All this is likely to add up to a very serious problem of teacher shortage which is unlikely to be solved in the near future.

It has also been feared that the R.T.E. Act's provision of doing away with the rigour of examination based assessment will not give the right incentive to students to learn and teachers to teach, leading to deterioration in standards.

Quality of education, as mandated under the R.T.E. Act, is also a matter of serious concern. Several studies about the learning outcomes have painted a gloomy picture in this regard. It has been revealed that nearly half of the children in grade 5 are unable to read a grade 2 text. This would necessitate concerted efforts to ensure that minimum levels of cognitive skills are acquired by all children during the eight years of schooling. Thus "quality issues and determinants such as ensuring availability of trained teachers, good curriculum and innovative pedagogy that impact on learning outcomes of children must be addressed on priority basis."[14]

Doubts have also been raised about the possibility of meeting the cost of implementing the Act, which has been estimated to be Rs. 182 lakh crores.

It is difficult to question the genuineness of some of the above problems. It should, however, not be beyond the ingenuity of the Government and the people to come out with solutions to these problems. As stated by the Planning Commission: "Effective enforcement of this Right requires that vision, strategies and norms of the S.S.A. are aligned with the mandate under the R.T.E. To achieve U.E.E. in a planned and time bound manner, a much higher level of funding and also better targeting of uncovered and under-covered population will be necessary. Isolated habitations, educationally backward blocks and districts shall require special attention. Flexible approach and concerted efforts are needed to reach out to the out of school children (OoSC) including children with special needs and street children. Bridging the social and gender gaps in enrolments with regard to SC, ST and minorities would receive special attention. Given the fact that several states face serious limitations of funds in implementation of R.T.E. Act, innovative ways would have to be found to address resource constraints."[15]

To Sum-up

Undoubtedly, there are bound to be a plethora of problems to be addressed. But, hopefully, those committed to see the historic measure through will not allow these impediments to stand in the way of its implementation. We fully agree with the hope expressed by the author of the Act – Kapil Sibal, when he says:

> "The RTE Act is an opportunity to break gender, caste, class and community barriers that threaten to damage the social fabric of our democracy and create fissures that could be ruinous to the country. I believe that the RTE Act is visionary in its objective and scope, and if understood and implemented in the right spirit by the government authorities, school managements and all the other stakeholders, could well become a model for the world to emulate."[16]

References

1. First Five Year Plan, Planning Commission, p. 1.
2. Statistical information has been culled out from the Ministry of Education publication Challenge of Education, 1985.
   Information about 2012 has been taken from UGC's publication: Higher Education at a glance; February, 2012.
3. National Policy on Education, Ministry of HRD, p. 9.
4. Elementary Education in India, NUEPA 2011; p.148. The percentages relate to 2008-09.
5. National Policy on Education, 1968, p. 13.
6. The Challenges of Education, 1985, Ministry of Education, p. 44.
7. Azad J.L.; Financing and Management of Higher Education in India (2008), Gyan Publishing House, Delhi, p. 256.
8. Faster, sustainable and More Inclusive Growth; An approach to the Twelfth Five Year Plan, Planning Commission, 2001, p. 102.
9. Azad J.L. Financing of Higher Education in India; 1975, Sterling Publishers, pp.125-26.

10. Education Commission (1964-66) Ministry of Education, p. 343.
11. The Bar Council is already up in arms because the proposed Commission will strip the B.C.I. of all its educational regulatory functions. The Ministry of H.R.D., however, has maintained that B.C.I's autonomy, so far as specifying standards of higher education concerning practice in courts will not be affected as a result of the Bill.
12. The Act crossed its final hurdle when the Supreme Court upheld the Constitutional validity of the Act, in particular relating to the clause, which requires all unaided private schools to reserve 25 per cent of their seats for children from economically weaker sections.
13. As reported in the *Times of India,* dated 7th May, 2012.
14. Planning Commission's Faster, Sustainable and more inclusive Growth; An Approach to the Twelfth Five Year Plan; (Mimeo) p. 96.
15. *Ibid.,* p. 96.
16. As reported in the *Times of India,* dated April 20, 2012.

11
Financing Indian Education

India has been a seat of learning from the hoary past. Her centres of learning have attracted seekers of knowledge from far off countries. Her teachers have commanded respect from the high and mighty of the land. Education has been extolled not only for its deep philosophical and ideological outpourings but for the practical training that it imparts.

The reverence for education has remained unabated over time. After the attainment of independence from the foreign rule, education has continued to be given the place of honour that it richly deserves. The University Education Commission (1948-49), speaking about the task of universities said, "If India is to face the confusion of the time, she must turn for guidance, not to those who are lost in the mere exigencies of the passing hour, but to her men of letters, and men of science, to her poets and artists, to her discoverers and inventors. These intellectual pioneers of civilization are to be found and trained in the universities, which are the sanctuaries of the inner life of the nation".[1]

In a similar vein, the Education Commission (1964-66), describing education as an 'investment of change' pointed out, "If this change on a grand scale is to be achieved without violent revolution (and even then it would still be necessary), there is one instrument only that can be used: EDUCATION.

Similarly, the National Policy on Education (1986), describing education as a unique investment in the present and future and fundamental to all round development (material and spiritual) said, "Education has an acculturating role. It refines sensibilities and perceptions that contribute to national cohesion; a scientific temper and independence of mind and spirit – thus furthering the goal of socialism, secularism and democracy enshrined in our Constitution."[2]

Providing adequate and sustained financial support to the educational system is an essential pre-requisite so as to enable it to perform its role of being a catalyst for nurturing human capital of the requisite quality, who will not only be a decent human being with a sharpened intellect but also a viable instrument for accelerating the process of socio-economic development and cultural regeneration. In this chapter, attempt has been made to analyse different contours of educational finance as they have emerged in the post-independence period. The analysis will centre around the following:

1. The behaviour of educational finance—All India and State-wise;
2. Inter-sectoral priorities—Plan and Non-Plan; and
3. Measures for raising resources for educational programmes.

Part I – The Behaviour of Educational Finance

1. All India

There has been a rapid growth in educational expenditure in India since independence. In 1950-51, an amount of Rs.114 crore was spent on education. According to the latest estimates, the total government expenditure on education was Rs.1,98,430 crore in 2009-10. If the expenditure incurred on education by departments other than the department of education is also included, the total budgeted expenditure on education and training would amount to Rs. 2,39,783 crore. This works out to about 3.85 per cent of the Gross Domestic Product (GDP).

Expenditure on Education by Centre and States.

Table 1 indicates the break-up of expenditure incurred by central and state governments:

Table 1: Expenditure on Education by Education and other Departments Years – 1971-2010

(Rs. in Crore)

	Centre		*States*		*Total*	
	Education Depts.	*Total expenditure by all Depts.*	*Education Depts.*	*Total expenditure by all Depts.*	*Education Depts.*	*Total expenditure by all Depts.*
1970-71	659.40	659.40	8,284.10	9,048.90	8,943.50	9,708.30
1975-76	1,261.00	1,730.70	16,830.00	19,121.40	18,091.00	20,852.10
1980-81	2,239.00	3,128.50	31,503.00	36,924.10	33,742.00	40,052.60
1985-86	5,285.00	9,151.80	69,284.70	81,591.60	74,569.70	90,743.40
1990-91	1,644.21	2,420.45	15,819.62	18,340.88	17,463.83	20,761.33
1995-96	3,317.53	5,551.02	28,789.66	33,217.67	32,107.19	38,768.69
2000-01	8385.96	12817.30	56898.68	65419.24	65284.64	78236.54
2005-06	18337.04	26998.77	79210.62	91418.06	97547.66	120346.83
2009-10	44532.21	61180.55	153897.57	178602.53	198429.53	239783.08

Source: Trends of Expenditure on Education and Analysis of Budgeted Expenditure on Education, MHRD for various years.

It would be seen that while there has been about 22 times increase in overall expenditure on education by education departments, the expenditure of the central government increased about 67 times as against about 18 times by state governments.

It may also be stated that while the percentage expenditure incurred by the central and state governments was in the ratio of about 7:93 in 1970-71, the central share of expenditure rose to about 22 per cent of the total expenditure in 2005-06 and to 26 per cent in 2010. This shows increasing investment on the part of the central government in education over the years. Much of the central government expenditure is on account of the Sarva Shiksha Abhiyan (SSA).

2. Central and States' Contribution by Stages of Education

Table 2 explains the relative financial inputs in education by central and state governments for different stages of education.

Table 2: Role of centre-states in financing different levels of education (total expenditures)

	Centre			*States*			*Total*		
	Centre	*States*	*Total*	*Centre*	*States*	*Total*	*Centre*	*States*	*Total*
	(in %)		*(Rs. in crs)*	*(in %)*		*(Rs. in crs.)*	*(in %)*		*(Rs. in crs.)*
1980-81	1	99	1537	2	98	1036	20	80	484
1985-88	1	99	3448	4	96	2293	20	80	1047
1990-91	3	97	7956	7	93	5531	21	79	2312
1995-96	8	92	15218	7	93	10344	18	82	3871
1996-97	9	91	17850	6	94	11735	17	83	4288
1998-99	11	89	25115	6	94	16721	26	74	6117
1999-00	10	90	27905	5	95	20845	27	73	8248
2000-01 (R)	10	90	31756	6	94	20489	25	75	10342
2009-10 (BE)	22.6	77.4	98660	11.8	88.2	60309	37.8	62.2	55541

It would appear that upto early Nineties, the central contribution for school education was very modest. From 3 per cent of the total expenditure in 1980-81, it rose to 10 per cent by 1990-91. The bulk of the central contribution during this period was on higher education for which the central government contributed about one fifth of the total expenditure in 1990-91. From 1995-96 onwards, the Central Government's contribution to school education got a boost rising from about 15 per cent of the expenditure in 1995-96 to an all time high of about 34 per cent of the total expenditure in 2009-10. The main beneficiary of the central munificence was elementary education for which the central contribution in 1990-91 rose from a meagre 3 per cent to about 23 per cent of the total expenditure in 2009-10. The expenditure on education has, however, increased more than threefold between 1981 and 2010. This happened primarily because of the commitment by the Central Government to introduce free and compulsory education at elementary education stage for which various schemes like Sarva Siksha Abhiyan, Mid-day Meals Scheme etc. were launched. The Central Government's recognition of its responsibility towards free and compulsory education was affirmed by the enactment of the Right to Education (RTE) Act, which came into force from 2010.

3. Expenditure on Revenue and Capital Account

Table 3 indicates the break-up of expenditure under Revenue and Capital account incurred by the central and state governments

Table 3: Expenditure on Education by Centre and States

(Rs. Crore)

	1984-85 (Actuals)	*Percentage of Edn. Exp. to Total Budget*	*1995-96 (Actuals)*	*Percentage of Edn. Exp. to Total Budget*	*2005-2006 (Actuals)*	*Percentage of Edn. Exp. to Total Budget*	*2009-2010 (Budgeted)*	*Percentage of Edn. Exp. to Total Budget*
Centre								
Revenue	445.32	1.60	5550.52	3.97	28928.75	6.48	61180.55	6.81
Capital	0.07	0.00	0.02	0.00	0.00	0.0	0.00	0.00
Loans and Advances	0.35	0.00	0.50	0.00	0.00	0.0	0.00	0.00
Total	445.74	1.60	5551.07	3.05	28928.75	5.62	61180.55	5.99
States/ Union Territories								
Revenue	5908.46	20.20	32627.57	22.30	90101.12	19.58	178415.66	20.31
Capital	60.21	1.40	379.06	2.01	1300.49	0.19	3758.07	2.25
Loans and Advances	8.74	0.30	211.04	2.56	16.47	0.12	28.80	0.16
Total	5977.41	16.40	33217.67	19.15	103118.08	8.48	178602.53	17.07
Total: Centre and States/UTs								
Revenue	6353.78	11.00	38178.09	13.40	119029.88	13.13	235996.71	13.42
Capital	60.28	0.50	379.06	1.04	1300.49	0.17	3758.77	1.30
Loans and Advances	9.09	0.10	211.54	0.64	16.47	0.10	0.00	0.16
Total	**6423.15**	**7.80**	**38768.69**	**10.90**	**120346.84**	**7.19**	**239783.88**	**11.61**

Source: Analysis of Budgeted Expenditure on Education for 1984-85, 1995-96, 2005-2006 and 2009-10.

As is obvious from Table 3, bulk of expenditure on education both of Central and state governments is on revenue account. There was slight increase in the percentage of expenditure on capital account; from 0.5 per cent to a little over one per cent during the period 1984-85 and 1995-96. In 2009-2010, the percentage rose to 1.30 indicating that some priority was given to building the infrastructure facilities like buildings, furniture and roads. The fact, however, remains that educational expenditure primarily consists of recurring expenditure like teachers' salaries, maintenance of buildings, procurement of consumables items, etc. The very low percentage of expenditure on capital account does not augur well for an integrated development of the educational system.

4. Public Expenditure on Education as Percentage of GDP

It has been contended that one of the important factors responsible for the inadequacy of resources for education is the inability or unwillingness of the government – both central and of states – to provide an adequate share of GDP for educational development. The percentage of GDP has not even reached four not six as recommended by the Education Commission about half a century ago.

Table 13 (Annexure-I) indicates the percentage of GDP spent on education during the period 1961-62 to 2009-10. It would be seen that it remained less than 2 during the first decade, i.e., 1961-62 to 1969-70, signifying that the Education Commission's recommendation did not make any tangible impact on the allocation of resources. Even in the next decade, during 1970-71 and 1980-81, it remained in the realm of 3 per cent. Thereafter, it has remained less than four per cent except for the year 1999-2000 and 2000-2001 when it touched a figure of four per cent. This is, however, inadequate to meet the burgeoning requirements of an ever-rising enrolment at different levels and the urgent need to enhance quality and relevance of education. This is cited as one of the important causes of the sluggish rate of educational development and also lack of quality in education. Ironically, the Education Commission's recommendation had been accepted by the Government of India and reiterated in the National Policies on Education and in successive five years plans. The issue for consideration is of national significance and deserves to be examined in depth.

It is an indisputable fact that, in spite of spending large amounts on education, year after year, the quality of education has been deteriorating. The large drop-outs at the elementary education stage, the continuing wastage at the secondary and higher education stages – of about 50 per cent of students failing to make the grade – are indicative of the deep malaise that afflicts the educational system. Further, the successive educational surveys conducted by the National Council of Educational Research and Training (NCERT) as also the National University of Educational Planning & Administration (NUEPA) have highlighted the deteriorating physical and academic infrastructural facilities of educational institutions.

While we would welcome a larger percentage of GDP being spent on education, we would like to examine the question in a wider context, that is, the appropriateness of earmarking a specified proportion of GDP for a particular sector. While not going into the merits of the case, it does not appear to be prudent to insist on providing a pre-determined percentage of GDP even for an important sector like education without assessing the needs of other sectors, which may be equally starved of resources. It also does not appear to be an economically viable proposition to provide a large quantum of resources without an objective assessment of needs and the spending capacity of the education sector. In case, earmarking of specific proportion of GDP for various sectors becomes an accepted method of resource allocation, we may end up in an economically unenviable position of piercing through the ceiling of 100 per cent!

It would be logical not to insist upon an ad hoc percentage of GDP being earmarked for education. The allocations of resources should be based on realistically assessed needs of education in the context of requirements of other sectors, the capacity of the system to effectively and meaningfully utilise the amounts provided and the ability of the economy to provide resources of that order. Further, it would also be necessary to mobilise community support for education. This aspect has been examined in a subsequent part of this chapter.

International Experience

The experience of the international community is an indicator of the validity of the above argument. Table 4 indicates the quantum of educational expenditure as percentage of GNP in some selected countries.

Table 4: Educational Expenditures in Selected Countries

Country	*Year*	*Educational Expenditure as Percentage of GNP*	*As Percentage of Total Government Expenditure*
South Africa	1986	6.0	15.8
	1996	8.6	14.9
	2005	5.3	NA
Canada	1970	8.6	17.8 (1975)
	1994	6.9	12.9
USA	1985	4.9	15.3
	1994	5.4	14.4
	2005	5.6	15.5
China	1970	1.3	4.3
	1996	2.3	12.2 (1993)
	2005	NA	NA
India	1970	2.6	10.7
	1998-99	3.7	11.6
	2005	3.8	NA
Israel	1970	5.7	8.1
	1994	4.9	12.3 (1993)
	2005	NA	NA
France	1970	4.8	24.9
	1996	6.0	10.9
	2005	5.4	NA
Russia	1970	3.9	NA
	1996	3.0	NA
	2005	3.8	11.5
Australia	1970	4.1	13.3
	1995	5.5	13.5
	2005	4.9	NA

(Figures in parentheses indicate the years)

Source: UNESCO, Statistical Year Book, Various Year.

It would appear that, barring South Africa, no country was spending more than 6 per cent of their GNP on education. Even the USA, one of the most advanced countries of the world, was spending 5.6 per cent of its GNP on education.

The following points need emphasis:

1. Educational expenditure should be determined by assessed needs and not on the basis of a pre-determined percentage of GDP.
2. Utilisation of resources is also important in this regard, because it determines the capacity of the system to gainfully utilise the investment.
3. Community should be encouraged to provide resources for education. It would, among other things, ensure community's involvement in education.
4. Costs of education should be partly shared by the beneficiaries/utilisers of educated manpower.

5. Educational Expenditure as Percentage of overall Expenditure

Table 13 (Appendix) I indicates the percentage of expenditure on education as a whole in terms of the overall expenditure. It would appear that, in spite of yearly fluctuations, there has been increase in the percentage of educational expenditure in terms of the overall expenditure. From a percentage of 10 in the first decade 1961-71 – with minor fluctuations for some years – the percentage oscillated between 12 and 13 in the decade ending 2005-06. In the intervening years, 1998-99 to 2000-01, it reached a figure of a little over 14 per cent.

It could be concluded that no set pattern is discernible in the percentages over the four decades under study, signifying that the allocation of resources for education depends more on the availability of resources for each year than on fixed percentage of allocation of resources.

2. States

Although education has been included in the Concurrent List of the Seventh Schedule of the Indian Constitution, state governments remain the main agencies for administration and financing of educational programmes, particularly at the school stage. While the overall proportion of revenue budget being spent on education was 13.42 per cent, most states except for Andhra Pradesh were spending more than the average percentage indicated above of their revenue budget on education. There were, however, sizeable variations among the states. Table 5 indicates state-wise position:

Table 5: Percentage of Expenditure on Education to Total Revenue Budget State-wise – 2009-10

Below 10	*10-15*	*15-20*	*20-25*	*25 and above*
NIL	Arunachal Pradesh (10.33)	Madhya Pradesh (15.67)	Himachal Pradesh (20.00)	Delhi (25.60)
	Puducherry (11.29)	Gujarat (17.30)	Haryana (20.38)	Uttrakhand (25.46)
	Andhra Pradesh (11.40)	Tamil Nadu (17.41)	Rajasthan (22.25)	
	Goa (13.16)	Chandigarh (17.79)	Bihar (22.31)	
	Sikkim (13.17)	Karnataka (17.97)		
	A & N Islands (13.49)	West Bengal (18.18)		
	Manipur (13.93)	Uttar Pradesh (18.33)		

J & K (13.97)	Tripura (18.38)
Meghalaya (13.98	Punjab (18.70)
Mizoram (14.73)	Orissa (18.76)
Assam (14.94)	Jharkhand (19.39
	Maharashtra (19.77)
	Kerala (19.63)

(Figures in parentheses indicate percentages).

Source: Analysis of Budgeted Expenditure on Education, 2009-10; Ministry of Human Resource Development (MHRD), 2009.

Andhra Pradesh having spent 11.40 per cent of its revenue budget on education had the dubious distinction of being the lowest among the major states in terms of educational expenditure. In contrast, Delhi and Uttarakhand were spending over 25 per cent of their revenue. Curiously enough, Madhya Pradesh was spending a lowly 15.61 per cent of its budget on education.

States' Investment in Education

In order to find out the position of states' investment in education in relation to their economic capacity to spend on it as reflected in the State Domestic Product, the State Governments were classified in terms of these two variables. Table 6 sums up the position:

Table 6: Percentage Total Budget on Education and Training (Rev.) to States Net Domestic Product (2009-10)

Below 2	*2-5*	*5-10*	*10 and above*
Gujarat (1.53)	Punjab (2.07)	Himachal Pradesh (5.25)	Sikkim (11.02)
Delhi (1.87)	Tamil Nadu (2.10)	Bihar (5.47)	
	Maharashtra (2.45)	Assam (5.51)	
	Andhra Pradesh (2.67)	Jammu & Kashmir (5.71)	
	West Bengal (2.75)	Manipur (5.84)	
	Haryana (2.86)	A & N Islands (6.78)	
	Kerala (3.10)	Mizoram (8.49)	
	Madhya Pradesh (3.41)		
	Rajasthan (3.68)		
	Uttar Pradesh (3.79)		
	Orissa (3.84)		
	Pudducherry (3.93)		
	Chandigarh (4.09)		
	Meghalaya (4.90)		

Source: Analysis of Budgeted Expenditure on Education, 2005-2006; Ministry of Human Resource Development (MHRD), 2009-10.

It may be stated that 16 states were spending 2-5 per cent of State Domestic Product, while 7 states were spending 5-10 per cent of their Domestic Product on education. Curiously enough, Gujarat and Delhi were spending less than 2 per cent of their SDP on education.

Relationship between States' Investment in Education and State Domestic Product (SDP).

The relationship between the per capita expenditure on education, overall and sectoral, and per capita state domestic product (SDP), is sought to be examined statistically by working out Rank Coefficients of Correlation between the two variables. The underlying assumption is that there would be a positive relationship between the two variables. Table 7 explains.

It would be seen that:

(i) There is a significant correlation between per capita expenditure on education as a whole and per capita State Domestic Product, although the relationship has fluctuated over the years. Further, downward trend has been observed since 1990-91;

(ii) The relationship between the two variables in regard to elementary education does not appear to be significant. The coefficient has declined substantially over the years, upto 1996-97. The situation, however, improved substantially in the decade ending 2006-07. This indicates, Government's realisation, though somewhat belated, to enhance its investment in elementary education contradicting the current assumption that states have been giving high priority to elementary education;

Table 7: Rank Coefficients of Correlation (R) between per capita SDP of States and the per capita Expenditures on Education - Total Education, Elementary, Secondary and Higher Education

Rank Coefficients of Correlation Between:

Year	*SDP and Total Education*	*SDP and Elementary Education*	*SDP and Secondary Education*	*SDP and Higher Education*
1960-61	0.78	0.50	0.63	0.74
1965-66	0.63	0.39	0.71	0.58
1970-71	0.65	0.42	0.73	0.43
1975-76	0.71	0.42	0.82	0.37
1980-81	0.56	0.30	0.54	0.19
1990-91	0.81	0.41	0.83	0.84
1996-97	0.62	0.26	0.72	0.64
2006-07	0.69	0.57	0.68	0.72

Source: For 1960-61 to 1980-81, see J. L. Azad: Government Support for Higher Education and Research, (1984). For Subsequent Years, Calculations were made on the basis of data taken from Selected Educational Statistics for the relevant years. For SDP, data were collected from Government's Economic Surveys for various years.

(iii) There is significant relationship between the two variables so far as secondary education is concerned; and

(iv) Although the coefficient in respect of higher education has been quite significant, there has been a steep decline in the relationship between the two variables between 1961 and 1981. The position improved significantly after 1990-91. It sustained itself thereafter.

To sum up, it could be stated that there is an overall positive relationship between states' economic capacity and expenditure on education, in spite of some states not providing financial inputs consistent with their economic development. It is heartening to note that dwindling relationship between the two variables upto 1996-97 improved perceptibly during the decade 1997-2007 in respect of elementary education.

Part-2 – Inter Institutional Priorities

(a) Distribution of Expenditure by Levels of Education

Table 8 indicates the distribution of educational expenditure by levels of education for the period extending from 1990-91 to 2009-10.

Table 8: Distribution of Expenditure on Various Levels of Education: States and Union Territories (Percentages)

(Rs. in lakhs)

	Elementary			*Secondary*			*University*		
	1990-91	*1999-00*	*2009-10*	*1990-91*	*1999-00*	*2009-10*	*1990-91*	*1999-00*	*2009-10*
Direction Inspection and Administration	2.4	2.4	3.13	2.30	1.38	7.87	0.8	1.1	1.19
Assistance to Government Schools and Colleges	37.5	49.5	34.41	32.9	32.46	33.46	22.2	25.1	22.65
Assistance to Private Schools and Colleges	25.9	21.4	18.79	51.7	53.45	47.13	45.0	47.3	44.58
Assistance to Local Bodies	22.7	22.2	26.37	7.5	7.37	9.23	—	—	—
Assistance to Universities	—	—	00	—	—	—	29.2	25.5	30.14
Teacher Education	6.5	0.3	0.71	0.8	0.43	2.18	—	—	—
Non-Formal Education	0.5	0.1	6.77	0.7	0.17	0.07	—	—	—
Scholarships	—	0.2	0.75	0.2	0.12	0.33	0.6	0.15	0.27
Text Books -	0.3	0.35	0.8	0.34	0.50	—	—	—	
Others	4.5	3.6	9.72	3.6	4.28	9.23	2.1	0.89	1.17
Total Expenditure	**7,729**	**27,905**	**97,255**	**5,154**	**20,844**	**5,97,048**	**1,836**	**8,248**	**2,39,793**

Source: Analysis of Budgeted Expenditure on Education for Various Years.

It would be noted that bulk of government expenditure on various sectors of education is on the establishment and maintenance of educational institutions. There is very little expenditure on qualitative development, i.e., for Teacher Education, Scholarships, Text Books etc. This is a cause of concern and needs to be looked into.

Table 9 indicates the expenditure on education during the five year plans:

Table 9 : Educational Expenditure in Five Year Plans

(Rs. in crore)

Five Year Plans	*Elementary Education*	*Percentage*	*Secondary Education*	*Percentage*	*Higher Education*	*Percentage*	*Total*	*Others**	*Percentage*	*Grand Total*
I	85	56	20	13	14	9	119	34	22	153
II	95	35	51	19	48	18	154	79	28	273
III	201	34	103	18	87	15	391	198	33	589
IV	239	30	140	18	195	25	574	212	27	786
V	317	35	156	17	205	22	678	234	26	912
VI	803	30	736	25	530	18	1069	461	27	2530
VII	2849	34	1829	22	1201	14	5879	2621	30	8500
VIII	4007	47	1538	18	1056	12	7101	1921	23	8522
IX	16365	66	2323	10.5	2271	10	20959	3950	13.5	24909
X	**Information incomplete**									
2009-10	34330	59.6	9506	16.5	7227	12.54	51063	6556	12	57619

*Includes Technical Education, Languages, Adult Education, etc.

Source: Figures upto Ninth Plan are taken from Planning Commission's Chapter 2.3 (pp. 42) and (65) of the Tenth Plan. Information about the outlays/expenditures in the X Plan given in the same Report was incomplete and hence not included in the table. Information about 2009-10 has been taken from Ministry of HRD's Analysis of Budget Expenditure on Education, 2007-08 to 2009-10, p. 3).

The following may be noted from Table 9:

1. Elementary education started with a formidable percentage of 56 in the First Plan. Thereafter, there was a sharp downward trend with the Fourth Plan registering an all time low of 30 per cent. Thereafter, there has been a gradual rise culminating into 66 per cent of the Plan allocations being earmarked for this sector in the Ninth Plan and about 60 per cent in 2009-10, which pertains to the Eleventh Plan.
2. Secondary education, starting with a modest percentage of 13 in the First Plan, reached an all time high of 25 per cent in the Sixth Plan. Thereafter, however, there has been a steep decline with Ninth Plan reaching a modest figure of about 11 per cent, rising again to about 17 per cent in 2009-10.
3. Higher education also started with an insignificant 9 per cent in the First Plan. The Fourth Plan recorded an all time high of 25 per cent, where after,

there has been a continuous downward trend, culminating into a lowly percentage of 10 in the Ninth Plan – recovering again to about 12 per cent in 2009-10.

4. The case of other sectors, which include technical education, is no different. From 22 per cent of the outlay provided for this sector in the First Plan, the percentage went up to 33 in the Third Plan, (which corresponded to the post Chinese incursions period). Thereafter, however, there has been a steep downward trend with Ninth Plan registering 13.5 per cent for this sector. In 2009-10, the percentage stood at 12 – the lowest in the Plans.

(b) Over all Sectoral Expenditure

The same picture emerges, when sectoral expenditures are considered for selected years. Table 10 indicates the plan and non-plan expenditure during the period 1986-87 to 2009-10.

Table 11: Plan and Non-Plan Outlays/ Expenditure: Centre and States

(Figure in percentages)

	1986-87 (Actual)			*1991-92 (Actual)*			*2007-08 (Actual)*			*2009-10*		
	Plan	*Non-Plan*	*Total*	*Plan*	*Non-Plan*	*Total*	*Plan*	*Non-Plan*	*Total*	*Plan*	*Non-Plan*	*Total*
Elementary Education	35.3	44.5	43.3	37.1	44.9	43.8	73.48	47.43	54.89	59.58	45.92	49.97
Secondary Education	20.2	33.3	31.5	25.1	32.2	31.2	10.34	35.50	28.28	16.88	37.11	31.11
Adult Education	3.4	0.2	0.6	8.7	0.3	1.5	0.76	0.12	0.32	0.94	0.14	0.38
University Education	15.2	14.2	14.3	10.3	13.7	13.2	8.62	12.52	11.41	12.54	12.85	12.76
Physical Edn, Sports and Youth Welfare	2.3	1.2	1.3	0.3	0.1	0.1	0.12	0.07	0.82	0.10	0.07	0.07
Other Programmes	11.9	3.1	4.4	4.9	5.4	5.4	1.41	1.24	1.31	1.05	0.75	0.84
Total (General Education)	88.3	96.5	95.4	86.4	96.6	95.2	94.73	96.88	97.03	91.09	96.84	95.13
Technical Education	11.7	3.5	4.6	13.6	3.4	4.8	5.27	3.12	2.97	8.91	3.16	4.87
Total Education	100	100	100	100	100	100	100	100	100	100	100	100

There has been substantial increase in plan expenditure for elementary education in the years under study. From 35.3 per cent of the overall plan outlay for all sectors, the percentage for elementary education increased to more than double of the expenditure in 2007-08. Two years later i.e. in 2009-10, it plummeted to 59.58 per cent. The increase in expenditure on elementary education seems to have happened at the cost of secondary and higher education; the former going down from about 20 per cent in 1986-87 to a meagre 10 per cent in 2007-08; recovering slightly to about 17 per cent in 2009-10. In the case of higher education, the percentage got reduced from 15.2 in 1986-87 to about 9 in 2007-08; recovering to about 13 in 2009-10.

The non-plan budget has remained almost stable in the case of elementary and university education. In the case of secondary education, however, there was some increase – the percentage rising from about 33 in 1986-87 to about 37 in 2009-10. The worst sufferer was Adult education; the percentages going down from 3.4 per cent of the plan expenditure to a meagre 0.94 per cent in 2009-10 during the period under review.

Considered in terms of the overall expenditure on general education there was substantial increase in the percentage of plan expenditure allocated to education – it rose from about 88 per cent in 1986-87 to about 91 per cent in 2009-10. Correspondingly, the plan expenditure on Technical Education was reduced to less than half – from about 12 per cent, it got reduced to about 5 in 2007-08 but rose to respectable 9 per cent two years later.

It may also be noted that programmes like physical education, sports and games and languages were the worst sufferers both in terms of plan and non-plan expenditure. For both of these programmes, about 6 per cent of the expenditure was incurred in 1986-87. By 2009-10, the percentage got reduced to less than one. This does not appear to be conducive to the overall development of education.

These sectors are very vital for the all round development of the students personality and any attempt to starve them of financial inputs would not be in the best interests of educational development.

(a) Share of Various Sectors of Education in the G.D.P.

Table 11 explains the share of various sectors of Education in the G.D.P.

Table 11: Public Expenditure on Education as Percentage of GDP

Year	*Elementary Education*	*Secondary Education*	*University*	*Adult Education and Higher*	*Technical*	*Total Education*
2001-02	1.09	0.98	0.43	NA	NA	3.81
2007-08 (Actual)	1.52	0.78	0.83	0.01	0.25	3.40
2008-09 (RE)	1.64	0.89	0.90	0.01	0.33	3.77
2009-10 (BE)	1.61	0.98	0.91	0.01	0.34	3.85

(*Source:* Analysis of Budgeted Expenditure on Education, op. cit).

It would appear that except for Secondary Education, which has down slided, but stabilised in the last year and Adult Education, which has remained constantly low, the share of expenditure in terms of GDP of all sectors has gone up. The overall expenditure in terms of percentage of GDP after going down during the intermediate years has also improved. This, however, does not ensure the adequacy of outlays for these sectors. It also does not ensure the adequacy of expenditure of these sectors to meet the burgeoning requirements of these sectors.

The Deleterious Impact of Inflationary Pressures

The one single factor that has played havoc with investment in education, as also in other sectors, is the ever-increasing inflationary pressures during the post-independence period. This has substantially eroded the real value of financial inputs. Table 12 sums up the public expenditure on education at current and constant prices.

Table 12: Public Expenditure on Education (At Current and Constant Prices)

Year	*At Current Prices*			*At Constant Prices – 1993-94*		
	Total	*Per Capita)*	*Per Student*	*Total*	*Per Capita)*	*Per Student*
1950-51	114.4	3.2	35.6	1683.8	46.6	524.0
1960-61	344.4	7.8	53.7	4376.4	99.9	663.8
1970-71	1118.9	20.4	141.7	7837.9	143.0	993.1
1980-81	3640.6	53.3	319.7	11211.9	164.1	984.6
1990-91	20491.2	243.0	1071.6	27828.7	330.0	1453.3
2000-01	78236.5	761.8	3957.1	49208.7	479.2	2488.9

(Adapted from J.B.G. Tilak's *Financing Education in India: Current Issues and Changing Perspectives*, 2003).

Dwindling Private Resources

The problem of inadequacy of government funding of education has been accentuated by the fast dwindling private contribution to investment in education in the post independence period. In 1950-51, government, including local bodies, contributed about 68 per cent of total resources for education. By 1992-93 (for which authentic information is available) the government contribution had increased to over 94 per cent of the total expenditure. Perceptible decline has occurred in the case of income from tuition fees (from about 20 per cent to above 3 per cent) and endowments and other sources (from 11.6 per cent to about 3 per cent). It is quite apparent that unless some special measures are taken, these two sources can virtually be written off even as modest contributors to funding of education.

(b) Measures for Raising Resources for Educational Programmes

We shall discuss some of the measures that can be adopted for augmenting resources for education. These measures include enhancing student fees and encouraging private philanthropy to contribute for education.

Student Fee

According to the Indian Constitution, the government is committed to provide free and compulsory elementary education (Age group 6-14). Therefore, fee as a resource for education can only be considered at the secondary and university stages. Even at these stages, the extent to which fees can be raised depends on the paying capacity of the parents. It has to be ensured that high fees do not become a deterrent factor for the education of students from backward sections of the society.

The question of fees as a measure for mobilizing resources, particularly for higher education, has been examined by various commissions and committees. The Education Commission (1964-66) termed student fees as the most regressive form of taxation, which falls heavily on the poorer classes of society and acts as an anti-egalitarian force. The Commission, therefore, suggested that they should be made progressive by relating them on a graduated scale to the income of the parents and size of the family. This, according to the Commission, would not be an administratively feasible proposition. The Commission, therefore, suggested that while education at the elementary and lower secondary stages should be free, the policy of levying fees at the higher secondary and higher education stages, with a liberal freeships, for deserving and needy students, should be continued.

The UGC set up a number of committees on financing of higher education with particular reference to the generation of resources through revision of fees at that stage. We shall describe briefly the views expressed by these committees relating to the fee structure at the higher education stage:

The Arguments for Raising Fees

- When the nation needs to achieve universal elementary education and total literacy and lacks funds for education, it becomes imperative to provide adequate resources for that sector even by diverting resources from higher to primary levels of education. Higher education should be financed largely by student funding through fees. Thus, increase in fees may augment the required funds for the cash-starved institutions of higher education, as government does not have adequate resources to finance higher education.
- Expenditure on higher education will have to be borne by the society. The affluent sections should meet reasonable cost of higher education in the form, among other things, of fees which reflect both ability of and willingness to pay for education.
- Since private rates of return to higher education are said to be high, an individual needs to finance his or her own education either from his present or future income. Further, it is argued that subsidies to higher education are regressive in nature, redistributing the income from the poor to the rich. This arrangement requires that, subsidies to higher education should be reduced and eliminated in the long run.
- Higher fees would improve internal efficiency of the system as fees are adequately and regularly realised and therefore students inevitably pursue their academic goals more seriously. An increase in fees would be viewed as a mark of respectability to the system in so far as higher fees give prominence

to an institution and are also helpful in making institutions and their personnel and clientele accountable.

- It is generally perceived that fees are extremely low and have not been revised for decades and need to be revised and adjusted to inflation and also revised periodically in accordance with the rise in costs of higher education.
- Differential fees have the merit of enhancing recovery of expenditure, removing subsidy from those who are in a position to pay and enabling the financially weaker students to undertake professional and higher studies.

The Arguments Against Hike in Fees Include:

- While 'Education For All' provides the foundations of a nation, higher education determines the nature and level of its economic and technological development, particularly in the context of developing a knowledge society. Further, it needs to be realised that all levels of education are inter-dependent and, that an organic relationship exists among them. Indeed, the quality of primary and secondary education itself depends on the quality of higher education.
- Hike in fees would lead to elitism in higher education since high fees will force the poor not to opt for higher education or seek higher education of an indifferent quality such as that offered in poor quality colleges.
- High fees would accentuate iniquities in the system as children from high income groups would spend more and be able to make more advantageous choices while children from low-income families would spend less and therefore would have to be content with the leftovers.
- Hike in fees is advocated on the basis of full cost recovery or no-profit-no-loss principles, which treat education just like any other commodity. This is contrary to the nature and basic philosophy of education. It also ignores the aspects of human capital investment.
- Except in case of tuition fee, other forms and kinds of fees are already high and are increasing substantially.

Specific Recommendations

In the backdrop of the arguments for and against raising tuition fees, the committees have made specific recommendations about enhancing student fees. These are:

(i) Tuition fee should be revised upwards and be periodically adjusted keeping in view inflation and rise in costs of providing higher education, including increases in faculty remuneration. The revision of fees must be related in a meaningful manner to the recurring cost of the courses of study and employment opportunities offered by them (Justice D.K. Punnayya Committee, UGC, 1993, p. 77).

(ii) Full cost recovery is suggested in government and aided institutions so that the government funded/aided colleges may be allowed to start new specialised programmes for specific target groups on self-financing/net revenue earning basis (AICTE, 1994).

(iii) Tuition fees should seek to recover the actual cost of imparting education. Tuition and all other fees, which are not to be charged on a one time basis, should be leviable for 12 months. Modified unit cost method i.e. 3 per cent of the unit cost worked out by Punnayya Committee should be the basis of fee structure. Annual upward revisions may be made at 2 per cent of the suggested rate and after every five years the University Grants Commission may consider the entire issue again for upward revision in the fee structure. It is recommended that certain mandatory provisions be made to ensure that the revised fee structure being suggested by the Committee is implemented (UGC Annual Report, 2000, pp. 41-44 and p. 16).

(iv) Institutions should raise fees in such a way that at least 15 to 25 per cent of the annual recurring cost per student is recovered from students in the form of fees and from other sources by the end of ten years. The government should, in course of time, shift funding of universities to a system of student funding (UGC 1993, 1999 and 2000). Tuition fee for the government funded and government aided institutions should be revised by at least 20 per cent of the recurring expenditure per student per year. Fees so fixed may be reviewed and refixed once every three years (AICTE 1994, p. 19).

Differential Fee System

The differential fee structure proposed by Azad (1975) and Tilak and Varghese (1985) seems to be a viable alternative with high income groups meeting 75 per cent, 'middle income group paying 50 per cent' and the low-income group paying 25 per cent of the per student cost. As they have argued, this proposal attempts to ensure the twin principles of equity (access to low income groups) and efficiency (raise revenue of higher education institutions). Differential fees have been recommended by the UGC (1993; 2000) and AICTE (1994). Committees constituted by them have recommended that as the size and variety of higher education is complex, it is not pragmatic to suggest a detailed fee structure; differential fees may be charged from students coming from different economic background and for subjects/courses and their employment prospects, etc. Some committees have recommended uniform hike in fees, which will have serious repercussion on equity.[3]

It is recognised that it is somewhat difficult to operationalise differential fee system because of lack of precise information about the economic capacity of all the beneficiaries. As noted by Azad (1975, 1984), "there are a number of difficulties involved in implementing this type of reform. The main arguments against this proposal are that it is not practicable to introduce such a scheme on a large scale and it is discriminatory.... However, the long term advantages of this proposal outweigh the disadvantages and the suggested reform in fee structure warrants serious consideration and implementation ...."[4]

Other Sources of Income

Income from other sources comprises income from endowments, university press, rent from university land, buildings, space, infrastructure, income from consultancy services and research projects, etc. Income from sale of publications, self-financing courses, and income from interest are some other sources of internal income of universities. The search for additional resources and the introduction of income-generating activities have been undertaken in many institutions. While such efforts need to continue, they should not be at the cost of primary goals of equity, academic excellence and relevance of higher education.

It is evident that the Government of India now encourages augmentation of resources by each institution for recovering a larger proportion of the cost of education. The recent policy direction in India suggests full cost recovery ('user pays' principle) from students even in public higher education institutions through hike in fees and introduction of self-financing courses and seats in tune with liberalisation policies.[5] Under the impact of globalisation and competitive market oriented economy, economic rationale for government funding for higher education is often down-played. With economic reforms and other pressures, higher education is proposed to be shifted to the list of non-merit goods[6] from the list of merit goods. This tends to ignore expenditure on education as a social investment and the complementary nature of public and household expenditure on education. Funding of higher education requires both public and private resources even in a situation of economic austerity. However, the role of the state and public support to higher education remains essential to ensure its educational, social and institutional objectives.

Private investment in higher education alone would be socially *sub-optimal,* because households do not, or are not able to, invest on non-market oriented courses in higher education and research and development activities. This is also true of private enterprises. Increased role of market in determining nature and character of education is likely to jeopardise participation of meritorious students from economically disadvantaged groups, women and minorities. Very steep increase in fees might compel a large number of students from low and middle income families and women not to seek higher education, and some rich students to opt for studies abroad. Further, it is important to notice that self-financing courses are often of short duration; heavy reliance on them will have repercussions on equity and quality of higher education system in the long run. This will also adversely affect the availability of qualified and competent teachers and researchers in pure and basic disciplines in the near future.

Student Loans

Student loans are currently in operation in a large number of countries around the globe. Of late, educational loans have become popular among students because of their simple and appealing logic, despite their inherent weaknesses. It is argued that in order to safeguard poor students against rising costs of higher education (both tuition and maintenance), a number of countries in the developing and developed world have initiated student loan programmes. However, cost recovery cannot be implemented equitably without scholarship programmes that would guarantee necessary financial support to academically meritorious and economically backward students. Further, imperfections in capital markets related to lack of collateral security for education investments restricts the ability of poor students to take advantage of loans available for higher education.

Keeping in view the vast changes occurring around the world, the present Educational Loan Scheme was introduced in India following an announcement in the budget 2000-01. The scheme administered by commercial banks covers a wide range of courses in higher studies from post-matric education to research studies, both in India and abroad. Eligibility criterion is that any student who secures admission in domestic/foreign educational institution is eligible for a loan, which covers both instructional cost and living expenses. The loan can be repaid in a specified period and repayment would commence one year after completion of the course or six months after getting employment, whichever is earlier. Simple rate of interest is charged during the period of study and up to the commencement of repayment.

It has however to be noted that there is no income ceiling on students/parents for being eligible for loan. Academic achievement is also not considered as an essential eligibility criterion, that is, there are no minimum qualifying marks required. There are no special provisions of any kind for weaker sections in terms of security, government guarantee, lower rate of interest or repayment period, repayment in accordance with earnings, waivers, etc. The scheme does not adhere either to the efficiency or equity principles unlike in many other countries, where merit-cum-means determine the eligibility for student loan.

Given the world experience on student loan schemes, the scheme in India is insensitive to the needs of the poor and does not consider equity aspects; there are no special provisions of any kind for the weaker sections. The scheme is a sheer commercial venture in tune with private commercial higher education and, in its present form, has the potentiality of doing more harm than good for the quantitative growth and qualitative development of higher education. Hence, an alternative scheme, which avoids the pitfalls of the present scheme and genuinely caters to the needs of the weaker sections of the society, should be worked out. It should be ensured that loans are for helping talented, but economically weaker students to pursue their education without being thwarted by lack of financial resources. From this point of view, loans are an investment in human capital and not a commercial enterprise.

In order to increase affordability for higher education, the Government launched a scheme in the year 2009-10 to provide full interest subsidy during the period of moratorium of educational loans for students for the economically weaker sections of society, whose parental income was less than Rs. 4.5 lakhs per annum. Loans availed of from Scheduled Banks under the Educational Loan Scheme of the Indian Banks' Association to pursue technical and professional courses of study are covered under the scheme of Interest subsidy. The Government, in fact, intends to move to a position where banks will lend freely to students, who have obtained admission to certified institutions against a loan guarantee given by a National Student Loan Guarantee Corporation.[7] These are the steps in the right direction. They will certainly enable the economically weaker but meritorious students to enter the haloed precincts of institutions of higher education and continue to be there till they achieve their objective.

Educational Development Bank

It would be desirable to set up an Educational Development Bank with equity participation from the Central and state governments, financial institution, private industrial and commercial houses and non-resident Indians. This Bank may provide soft loans to educational institutions mainly for capital works and purchase of sophisticated instruments. This Bank, which will have branches in states, may also administer the scheme of loan scholarships.

(c) Community Contributions

It has been mentioned earlier that private donations, as a source of educational finance, are fast drying up. There are historical reasons for this phenomenon. The abolition of the Zamindaris, the dwindling of the patronage of Rajas and Maharajas and lack of incentives by way of relief in taxation could be cited as the main factors responsible for this problem. It is necessary that a concerted effort is made to mobilise community resources for meeting some part of educational expenditure. These should include, besides relief in taxation, the following measures.

1. Regulatory barriers limiting the entry of private sector in education should be minimised.
2. Users of technical manpower should pay part of the educational costs.
3. Collaboration between industrial establishments and universities which could take the form of sponsored research, creation of special chairs, consultancy, endowments for specialised discipline etc. should be encouraged.
4. Educational institutions should approach the community for financial assistance. This can happen only if educational institutions shed their aura of academic exclusiveness, become a part of the society around them and provide education and extension which is relevant to community needs. An educational institution should function as the centre for social life around it and not a place, which is alien to its social and physical environment.

Capitation Fee Colleges

While we recommend mobilisation of resources for education through raising fees and persuading the community to contribute to education, we do not support the charging of capitation fees as is being done in some of the states. In fact, we would suggest curbing the growing menace of capitation fee colleges, which have mushroomed in some of the states, without any viable academic justification. The prime motive of these institutions is to sell seats to the highest bidder regardless of the student's merit or capacity to profit by education. In the process they make a fast buck, but at a cost, which in terms of educational standards is non-affordable. The recipients of such education, having paid hefty amounts as capitation charges, tend to look upon education as a means of making easy money to compensate themselves in the shortest possible time. The practice is ethically immoral, academically indefensible and socially undesirable. Under the garb of liberalisation and decontrol let us not allow the educational system to be vitiated by the Frankenstein of capitation fee charging institutions, which are threatening to tear our social fabric to shreds and lower the academic standards, which are already on a declining trend.

(d) Avoiding Wastage

While making a case for mobilizing additional resources, mind boggling wastage of resources that occurs in the form of irrelevant courses and failures and drop-outs at the various stages of education, has to be prevented. The dropout rate at the primary and upper primary stage is 40 per cent and 57 per cent respectively. At secondary and higher education stages (in humanities and social science) about 50 per cent students fail to pass in public examinations. According to a study conducted by the present author, only one out of eight students, who enter universities, comes out with a reasonably good grade.

Another important aspect of this colossal wastage is the migration of trained manpower to economically advanced countries. Thus financing of education of these people is supported without any tangible returns to the country although remittances from them have shown some increase. Further, an economically backward country like India seems to supply the cream of its professionally trained manpower to developed countries without any quid-pro-quo, giving rise to a form of foreign assistance in reverse direction. While it is not intended to suggest that this outflow of the creamy layer of the professional manpower is stopped, it would be desirable to tax these emigrants to the extent that they reimburse the full cost of their education in case they permanently settle down in foreign countries.

(e) Optimal Utilisation of Resources

In a resource deficient country like India, no amount of resource generation will be of any significance unless the existing educational infrastructure is put to the maximum use. It is a strange phenomenon to witness the educational institutions being rendered dysfunctional on the flimsy grounds like strikes, lockouts, etc.

According to the UGC norms, the universities and colleges should function for at least 180 days in a year. It is, however, observed that the actual functioning of a number of institutions is far less than the stipulated period. It has also been observed that the physical and academic facilities available with the institutions are less than optimally utilised. It should, therefore, be the constant endeavour of all institutions to put the available resource to maximum use.

(f) Institutional Proliferation

An important facet of this problem is the unhindered proliferation of low quality institutions of higher education. It has been noted that, with or without the approval of the UGC, colleges and universities are being opened regardless of their academic viability and without due consideration to the needs of the area, which they are expected to serve. In this game of indiscriminate expansion of institutions, the motivating factors are generally extra-academic and are usually born out of political and commercial considerations. It is not surprising that the UGC has declared more than one third of the colleges as non-viable institutions.

In order to enable institutions to have adequate resources for quantitative expansion and qualitative development, the propensity to set up new institutions, without much academic justification, should be curbed resolutely.

(g) Academic Accountability 12

The extent of wastage that occurs in the educational institutions has already been pointed out. Further, the under utilisation of academic and physical facilities, particularly in the universities and colleges, due to strikes, *bandhs* and other politically inspired events does not need any statistical evidence. In the process, substantial amounts invested in education are rendered infructuous.

It is, therefore, necessary that educational institutions are made accountable to the public. In case they do not show good performance and all efforts to improve their working fail, they should be closed down. There should be a system of continuously monitoring their efficiency and they should be subjected to rigorous standards of excellence. It should be possible for educational institutions to pass the test of accountability without compromising their autonomy, which is essential for the nurturing of talent and for the blossoming of the intellect, which is the prime responsibility of the institution of higher education.

To Sum-Up

1. There has been a rapid growth of the quantum of expenditure on education during the post-independence period. From about Rs.58 crore in 1946-47, the total expenditure on education, by all departments has risen to a formidable Rs. 239783 crore in 2009-10. The bulk of the expenditure is, however, on revenue account. This means that it is mainly for maintenance of the system rather than for providing better infrastructural facilities – so vital for the integrated development of education.

2. Public expenditure on education as percentage of the overall Gross Domestic Product started from less than two per cent in 1961-62 and remained so till 1969-70. Thereafter, it has remained a little more than three per cent, except for 1999-2000 and 2000-2001, wherein it touched the percentage of a little over four. Thereafter, it has remained less than 4 till 2009-10. In this context, without endorsing the recommendation of the Education Commission that it should rise to 6 per cent of the National income, it may be said that it is much below that magic figure even though about half a century has elapsed when the Commission made its recommendations. Ironically, the Government has been endorsing this recommendation all through the plans, including the Eleventh Plan!
3. A bulk of states were spending between 10 to 20 per cent of their revenue budget on education. Further, 15 states were spending two to five per cent of their Domestic Product (SDP) on education. Only eight states were spending five to 10 per cent of their SDP on education. It has also been reckoned that there is significant correlation between the per capita expenditure on education and the per capita SDP. The relationship between these two factors was, however, insignificant in the case of elementary education upto 1996-97. By 2006-07, the position improved considerably – the coefficient of correlation reaching a respectable figure of 0.57. This contradicts the general perception that the states are giving higher priority to elementary education in terms of providing financial resources.
4. An analysis of the object-wise allocation of resources for various sectors of education reveals that bulk of expenditure is on the maintenance of institutions rather than on quality improvement programmes.
5. There have been significant changes in the allocation of resources for different sectors in the five year plans. Elementary education, which started with a formidable percentage of 56 in the First Plan plummeted to an all time low of 30 per cent in Fourth Plan to go up to 66 per cent in the Ninth Plan and 60 per cent in 2009-10. Correspondingly, the percentage expenditure on higher education went down from an all time high of 25 per cent in the Fourth Plan to a lowly 10 per cent in the Ninth Plan. Similar but drastic reductions took place in the case of secondary education. All these changes occurred because of the Government's Commitment to provide free and compulsory education at the elementary education stage.
6. Considered in terms of plan and non-plan expenditure as a whole, elementary education rose from about 43 per cent in 1986-87 to about 50 per cent in 2009-10; the university sector declined from about 15 per cent to about 13 during the same period.
7. Programmes like games, sports were the worst sufferers in terms of plan and non-plan expenditure. From about 13 per cent of the total expenditure in 1986-87, these programmes plummeted to 0.07 per cent in 2009-10.

8. Contribution from private sources including fees has dwindled considerably over the years. There is, therefore, need for raising resources. The question of raising tuition fees has been discussed in details based on the recommendations made by various Committees/Commissions appointed from time to time. It has been recommended that there is scope for raising fees, particularly at the university and secondary education stages. It is, however, necessary that it should not be a dampening factor for students, who are intellectually endowed but economically not in a position to pay for education. In this context, a differential fee system has been suggested. Suggestions have also been made for raising resources by attracting endowments and contribution from corporate houses. In all these efforts, it would be necessary to take steps to guard the primary goals of equity, academic excellence and relevance of education.
9. In order to operationalise the student loan scheme, there is need for setting up of an Educational Development Bank, as a joint venture of Central and state governments and NRIs corporate houses.
10. The tendency to set up capitation fee charging colleges should be resolutely curbed.
11. There is need for avoiding wastage in terms of student failures and dropouts at all stages of education.
12. Optimal utilisation of existing resources – physical and academic – is the sine-qua-non of any reform. There should be restriction on unplanned institutional proliferation that is taking place in some of the states. In fact, even the existing institutions should be subjected to continuous academic and financial scrutiny. This should, however, not compromise their academic autonomy, which is vital for nurturing excellence and integrated development of educational institutions.

We may conclude by emphasising that in the context of globalisation, economic rationale for government funding, especially for secondary and higher education tends to be given inadequate priority. This is a retrogressive development. Public support for these sectors is essential to ensure a balanced achievement of educational and social objectives, apart from ensuring national survival in the knowledge-based society. Sequencing of priorities, i.e., universal primary education first, secondary and higher education later (as and when resources are available or/leaving these sectors to private initiatives) will prove to be a very costly strategy in the era of globalisation.

It is equally important to bring about a fundamental transformation at both the systems level and institutional structure of higher education. Effective financial management at institutional level should be an essential pre-requisite. It is also necessary that funding sources be diversified; but cost-sharing with students has social and political limits, and excessive commercialisation of higher education should be discouraged.

The challenge to public policy on secondary and higher education in India requires that private providers are encouraged to contribute to the financing of these sectors as also for providing management and academic support. The government should, however, continue to discharge its responsibility of funding, regulating, guiding and monitoring the progress of institutions of secondary education as also of higher education so that there is a balance between equity (assurance of access to low-income students) and efficiency (quality and academic coverage). It may also be ensured that increased access of private bodies to the financing and management of education and higher education in particular does not end up in commercialisation of the system.

Table 13 : Public Expenditure on Education in India

(Rs. in crore)

Year	*Government expenditure on education (Trg. and Rev) by education and other Deptt. (centre + states)*	*Total Government Expenditure on all sectors (Rev)*	*GDP at current prices (at factor cost) base year 1993-94*	*Percentages of Expenditure on Education to Expenditure on all sectors*	*Percentege of Education Expenditure to GDP*
1	2	3	4	5	6
1961-62	260.3	2225.4	17116	11.70	1.52
1962-63	278.76	2942.67	18302	9.47	1.52
1963-64	313.93	3488.97	20916	9.00	1.50
1964-65	369.29	3844.91	24436	9.60	1.51
1965-66	432.61	4404.82	25586	9.82	1.69
1966-67	487.83	5100.24	29123	9.56	1.63
1967-68	593.14	5619.77	34225	10.55	1.68
1968-69	649.13	6922.07	26092	9.38	1.80
1969-70	760.23	7908.09	39691	9.61	1.92
1970-71	892.36	8787.12	41111	10.16	2.11
1971-72	1011.07	10610.89	44923	9.53	2.25
1972-73	1150.43	11863.56	49415	9.70	2.33
1973-74	1300.72	12884.48	60560	10.10	2.15
1974-75	1570.67	14626.03	71283	10.74	2.20
1975-76	1849.47	17958.9	75709	10.30	2.44
1976-77	2039.09	20482.83	84381	9.96	2.51
1977-78	2630.6	22666.31	92881	11.61	2.83
1978-79	2994.69	26134.84	99823	11.46	3.00
1979-80	3347.57	30915.39	108927	10.83	3.07
1980-81	3884.2	36398.39	130178	10.67	2.98

1981-82	4298.29	41715.71	152056	10.30	2.83
1982-83	5509.17	43996.18	169525	12.52	3.25
1983-84	6229.53	61889.25	198630	10.52	3.25
1984-85	7455.88	63025.45	222705	10.80	3.35
1985-86	8713.05	67091.41	249547	12.99	3.49
1986-87	9479.13	80454.66	278258	11.78	3.41
1987-88	11798.35	92518.38	915993	12.75	3.73
1988-89	14069.82	107549.75	378491	13.08	3.72
1989-90	17192.5	126045.97	438020	13.64	3.93
1990-91	19615.85	146711.53	510954	13.37	3.84
1991-92	22393.69	170370.38	589086	13.14	3.80
1992-93	25030.3	190327.45	673221	13.15	3.72
1993-94	28279.69	218535.15	673221	13.15	3.72
1994-95	32606.22	251691.92	917058	12.95	3.56
1995-96]	38178.09	286194.55	1073271	13.34	3.56
1996-97	43896.48	329389.92	917058	12.95	3.56
1997-98	48552.14	380728.45	1390148	12.75	3.49
1998-99	61578.91	439768.11	1598127	14.00	3.85
1999-2000	74816.09	512519.33	1786525	14.60	4.19
2000-2001	82486.88	572160.14	1925017	14.42	4.28
2001-2002*	79866.00	619713.15	2097726	12.89	3.81
2002-2003*	85079.00	678547.31	2761415	12.60	3.28
2003-2004*	89079.25	743668.96	2261415	11.98	3.51
2004-2005*	96694.00(RE)	819231.90 (RE)	2971464 (Q)	12.76	3.26
2005-06	113229	—	3389621	—	3.34
2006-07	137384	—	3952241	—	3.48
2007-08	155798	—	458122	—	3.40
2008-09	198986	—	5282086	—	3.77
2009-10	235996	—	6133230	—	3.85

P-Provisional estimates. Q-Quick estimates, RE – Revised estimates.

Source:

1. National Accounts statistics published by C.S.O.
2. Expenditure on Education Figures are taken from Ministry of Educations' Analysis of Budgeted Expenditure on Education published by Department of Higher Education, Planning, Monitoring and Statistical Bureau for various years.
3. Selected Educational Statistics, MHRD, New Delhi, for various years.

References

1. University Education Commission, Ministry of Education (1949).
2. National Policy on Education, 1986, Ministry of Education, 1986, p. 3.
3. Differential fee structure seems to be incompatible with the Supreme Court Judgement on the Writ Petition (Civil) 317 of 1993 in TMA Pai Foundation and Others and State of Karnataka and Others on October 31, 2002.
4. Azad J.L., Financing of Higher Education in India, 1975.
5. Some students in each department pay full cost fee, while the rest of the students pay normal (subsidised) fees. It is to be noted that the normal fee itself has been increasing.
6. According to a discussion paper; Government subsidies level falls outside the ambit of 'merit' category because the benefits of subsidy accrue to the recipient... thus secondary and higher education are non-merit goods and not worthy of Government subsidisation. (For a detailed discussion, see J.L. Azad; Higher Education – A Non-Merit Good (?) published in University News; June 15, 1998 pp. 32-47.
7. 11th Five Year Plan, p. 32 and Report to the People on Education; 2009-10, Ministry of Education; Human Resource Development; p. 35.

SIGNIFICANT EVENTS/ PROCEDURES THAT IMPACTED INDIAN EDUCATION

In the post independence period, three important events/procedures have the potentiality of influencing the course of Indian education. They are:

1. Initiation of planning as a technique of socio-economic, including educational, development;
2. Globalisation as a part of the economic reforms introduced in the early nineties; and
3. Public Private Partnership (PPP) in education.

We have discussed the main features of these events in the Chapters that follow.

12

Initiation of Planning for Socio-Economic Development

In view of the worsening socio-economic situation soon after India attained political freedom, it was realised that some drastic action plan was required to bring about some order in the chaotic state of affairs that had bedevilled the country's socio-economic system. The system of planning in vogue in the USSR provided an example and was considered to be a suitable model and mechanism that could help rejuvenate the development process. Centralized initiation in this was considered of utmost significance because of the uneven economic conditions of the former princely states which were integrated into the Union of India.

This chapter, critically analyses the process of planning, its organisational arrangements and its impact on the prevailing state of education. For obvious reasons, discussion is focussed on educational planning, of course in the contextual framework of overall planning.

The Origin

India embarked upon planning as a strategy for accelerating the process of socio-economic development in 1951. The plan had to be all pervasive, incorporating all sectors of economy, including social services of which education was an important component. The specific objectives of the First Five Year Plan which was mainly, attuned to provide a healing touch to the country, grievously wounded by the twin catastrophes of a prolonged war and an unsolicited partition, were:

1. It aimed at correcting the disequilibrium in the economy caused by the war and partition of the country.
2. It proposed to initiate simultaneously a process of all round balanced development, which would ensure augmentation of the national income and a steady improvement in the living standards over a period.

3. It emphasised that the aim was not merely to plan within the existing framework but to change the framework progressively and by democratic methods in keeping with the larger ends of policy enunciated in the Constitution.
4. About education, the objective of planning was the reorientation of the educational system and integration of its different stages and branches; expansion in various fields, particularly basic and social education, increasing access to education, particularly of women; remodelling and expanding facilities for technical and vocational education; consolidation of secondary and university education; the designing of a system of higher education suited to the needs of rural areas.

The Process of Planning

We shall briefly discuss the process of educational planning as it has evolved in the Indian context including the machinery of planning in order to give an idea of the manner in which planning of education takes place. Before doing so, an attempt has been made to give a peep into the history of planning.

A Historical Review

The first systematic attempt at planning for socio-economic development was made in 1923 when the U.S.S.R. launched its First Five Year Plan. The idea of planning got an impetus after the Second World War due to the complete breakdown of the economic system of most of the warring nations of Europe and the demographic explosion that followed it. Apart from the socialist countries, which adopted planning as their model, the United Kingdom, through its Education Act of 1944, made it mandatory for each of the local Boards of Education (now Local Educational Authorities) to draw up a development plan. France, which had not included education among the fields covered by its first plan in 1946, set up a Commission in 1954 and education became an integral part of the national plan. One after the other, most European countries adopted some sort of planning for repairing their war-shattered economies.

In India, various attempts were made at economic planning. They preceded the onset of planning as an instrument of socio-economic development in 1951. As early as 1934, M. Visveraya brought out a ten year plan with the objective of doubling the national income.[1] Ten year later, three private plans were published, out of which the best known was the "Bombay Plan" sponsored by some of the top industrialists of India. This plan emphasised industrialisation and proposed quintuplicating of industrial production in 15 years. Priority was to be given to the production of power and capital goods. But to avoid hardship, prevent inflation, provide employment and economise capital resources, fullest possible use was to be made of small scale and village industries in the production of consumer goods.[2] The 'People's Plan' drawn up by M.N. Roy and the Indian Federation of Labour emphasised the desirability of socialism and was concerned with the expansion of the public sector at the expense of the private sector.

The first concerted effort at comprehensive planning was made towards the end of 1938, when the National Planning Committee was appointed by the President of Indian National Congress, Subash Chandra Bose, in pursuance of the resolution of the Ministers of Industries which, inter alia, stated that "the problems of poverty and unemployment in general cannot be solved without industrialisation. As a step towards industrialisation, a comprehensive scheme of national planning should provide for the development of heavy key industries, medium scale industries and cottage industries, keeping in view our national requirements, the resource of the country, as also the peculiar circumstances prevailing in the country.[3]

During the war years of 1939-45, the Government of India realised the need for initiating a coordinated programme of development needed to make the war efforts a success. They set up a Planning and Development Department of their own. This included the setting up of an elaborate machinery, which consisted of a Consultative Committee panel, Policy Committee etc. Provincial Governments also prepared their own plans to absorb demobilised veterans in the normal life of the country and to develop the latent resources of each unit. Taking their cue from the Government, the industrialists, public persons and businessmen also prepared plans which were of varying degrees of comprehensiveness. In the field of education, the Central Advisory Board of Education worked out a plan of educational development (known as Sargent Plan). "There was abundant seed, many sowers and a rich harvest; but all the crop that could be realised was absorbed by the war demand".[4]

Planning in Independent India

Soon after attainment of political freedom, the need for planning as "the intellectual matrix of the entire modernisation ideology"[5] was realised. The edifice of planning, however, had to be built keeping in view the political-administrative set up visualised by the Indian Constitution, particularly, the federal character of the Indian states, under which the constituent units were as much responsible for plan formulation and implementation as the Union Government. Further, adherence to democratic socialism necessitated the involvement of people in the process of planning. The Government of India's Resolution of 1950, which set up the Planning Commission, attempts to embody these basic concepts in the administrative configuration of Indian planning.

Basic Structure of Indian Planning

India, being a Federation of the Union and the States, needs to have a system of planning which is based on the co-operation between the central and the constituent units. This spirit of cooperation, which has been described as 'Cooperative Federalism', by the Planning Commission has to permeate the relations between center and states; among the states as also between the states and the

Panchayati Raj Institutions (PRIs) and the Urban Local Bodies (ULBs). According to the Planning Commission: "The essence of Cooperative Federalism is that the centre and the states should be guided by the broader national concerns of using the available resources for the benefit of the people. Cooperative Federalism encourages the government at different levels to take advantage of a large national market, diverse and rich national resources and potential of human capabilities in all parts of the country and from all sections of society for building a prosperous nation. This requires a harmonious relationships and cooperative spirit between center and states and among the states themselves… Cooperative Federalism is intended to ensure a minimum bundle of basic services and a nationally acceptable level of living for all the people of the country".[6]

The implications of Cooperative Federalism for educational planning would be in the nature of a joint enterprise in which the participation of all the units becomes an essential pre-requisite. It would also mean that educational planning cannot be carried out in isolation. It will have to work in tandem with other sectors of development, like industry, agriculture, health and social welfare etc.

The Process of Educational Planning

The process of educational planning has been succinctly explained by the UNESCO, which regards educational planning as the application to education itself of what real educators seek to instil in students; and a rational scientific approach to problems. In this context, the process of planning involves identifying objectives and available resources, examining the implication of alternative courses of action and choosing wisely among them, deciding on the specific targets to be met within specific time limits, and finally developing the best means of systematically implementing the choices made.

It may be stressed that educational planning is an instrument to channel all knowledge about education and related disciplines into the preparation and implementation of long-term and short-term educational development; it can be applied to the most widely varying socio-political environments and adapted to the goals of each country. It involves willingness to size up the situation and to measure action to be taken. Educational planning necessarily implies a global approach. By placing these in proper perspective, it ensures a balanced distribution of energies and resources both for short term and long-term action.

In addition, educational planning has the difficult task of ensuring that education fits harmoniously into the pattern of change; that it is sufficiently progressive to produce the kind of social and technical leadership and qualified manpower required for development while at the same time preserving the continuity and development of society's cultural identity. There can be differences of opinion on what should come first but there can be no disagreement on the need for a harmonious blending and development of both.

The process of educational planning may be summed up as follows:

"Educational planning is a process of drawing up the most realistic blueprint of educational development for a specified period, based on a critical study of the existing situation within a broad perspective of educational development over a long term time span keeping in view the priorities emerging from the socio-economic goals that the country has set for itself and taking due note of the various constraints-physical, financial and academic that have a bearing on the realisation of targets of educational development."[7] Planning should lay down specific goals to be achieved, resources required and how they need to be utilised and an administrative framework for implementation, monitoring and evaluation.

Organisational Arrangements

(a) All India Level

At the all India level, there are two organisations, which are responsible for drawing up plans for the country as also over-seeing its performance. We shall explain the composition of these bodies as also their responsibilities relating to the drawing up of plans for development.

The National Development Council

We have already explained the basic structure of Indian planning, which rests on what has been called Cooperative Federalism. A large country like India is always subject to political, administrative and social stresses and strains. There is, therefore, need for an all India body to provide a safety valve to deal with different viewpoints and also to accommodate different needs of states. This is sought to be achieved through the National Development Council (NDC), the apex body in Planning set up in August, 1952. The Council consists of the Prime Minister as the chairman; all the State Chief Ministers and some central ministers as members. The NDC is expected to strengthen and mobilise the efforts and resources of the nation in support of the Plan, to promote common economic policies in all vital spheres and to ensure a balanced development of all parts of the country. Its functions are:

(i) To prescribe guidelines for the formulation of the National Plan, including the assessment of resources for the Plan;

(ii) To consider and approve the goals to be achieved and strategies to be adopted as worked out by the Planning Commission and in consultation with states and central ministries.

(iii) To consider the draft of the National Plan as formulated by the Planning Commission;

(iv) To consider important questions of social and economic policy effecting national development; and

(v) To review the working of the Plan from time to time and to recommend such measures as are necessary for achieving the aims and targets set out in the National Plan, including measures to secure the active

> participation and cooperation of the people, improve the efficiency of the administrative services, ensure the fullest development of the less advanced regions and sections of the community and, through sacrifice, borne equally by all citizens, build up resources for national development.

The Planning Commission

The concept of joint responsibility for development was in a way concretized in the setting up of the Planning Commission, which was established in March, 1950, by a Resolution of the Government of India and which is charged, theoretically at least, with overall responsibility for planning in the country. The Resolution, setting up the Planning Commission refers to the fundamental rights of the people in regard to the promotion of a social order "in which justice; social, economic and political, shall inform all the institutions of national life" and makes the Planning Commission responsible for formulating a plan for the most effective and balanced utilisation of the country's resources in the light of assessment of the material, capital and human resources of the country. The Commission has also to determine priorities, define the stages in which the Plan should be carried out and investigate the possibilities of augmenting such resources as are found deficient.

Apparently, the Resolution setting up the Planning Commission seems to invest the Commission with almost absolute powers of planning; assessment of human and material resources of the country, formulation of the plan and even defining the stages in which the plan should be carried out. This, however, does not represent the *spirit* of the Resolution. The Planning Commission is expected to be an organisation composed of professional experts drawn from various fields, which will formulate the plan in close cooperation with the Central and the State Governments and non-official experts. The very fact that the magnificent edifice of the Planning Commission rests only on a Resolution of the Government rather than on any Constitutional or Statutory basis should militate against the possibility of any role other than purely advisory being assumed by the Planning Commission. To achieve this, however, the Commission has to have a strong data base particularly relating to the availability of resources – physical, financial and academic – and a competent and knowledgeable professional and technical manpower to advise the states and Central ministries. The Commission has also to work in tandem with the Finance Commissions, which are concerned with providing resources for non-plan expenditure. It has also been ensured that the Planning Commission should have no executive responsibility and should act through discussion and persuasion. It has also been insisted that the states should set up planning bodies consisting of experts and officials to replicate the functions of the central Planning Commission in their respective areas. In the field of education, besides state and regional plans, institutional plans are also insisted upon. That not much progress has been achieved in the formulation of institutional plans is due more to the traditional conservativeness and imperviousness to change on the part of those concerned with educational planning than lack of will or guidance on the part of the Planning Commission.

(B) State Level

State Planning Boards

Most of the state governments have set up State Planning Boards to work out plans of socio-economic development. These bodies are patterned on the model of Central Planning Commission and consist of members of the state bureaucracy as also professionals drawn from outside. Planning Commission has also encouraged decentralisation of the planning powers by the setting up of District and Taluk level Planning Committees. With the enactment of 73rd and 74th Amendments to the Constitution in 1993, constitutional status has been conferred on the Panchayati Raj Institutions (PRIs) and the Urban Level Bodies (ULBs) as also the District Planning Committees (DPCs). The objective is that the central government, the state governments, the Panchayati Raj Institutions as also the non-government organisation (NGOs) and the people at grass root level should be involved in the process of formulation and implementation of the plans. They should also be involved in monitoring and evaluation of plan outcomes.

To Sum-up

The basic structure of Indian planning rests on the edifice of what has been aptly called 'Cooperative Federalism'. This involves the working together of the center, states and other administrative units in the process of planning for the larger benefits of the country. In order to achieve this objective, the National Development Council has been set up to lay down policy guidelines for over all planning; to oversee its progress and discuss policy issues arising from time to time. The Planning Commission is the operational wing of planning charged with the task of working out a national plan of socio-economic development and having responsibility for its effective implementation through a process of continuous monitoring and evaluation. At the state level also, Planning Boards have been set up. The Planning Commission works in consultation with the state governments keeping in view the policy guidelines determined from time to time. The review of progress of plans is undertaken through the annual plans and ad-hoc studies and surveys, which assess the progress achieved as also the problems that arise during the year. Based on this exercise, corrective action is taken.

Impact of Planning on Educational Development

While discussing the shattering blow that partition of the country inflicted on socio-economic development as also on education, it had been stated that Planning was conceived as an instrument of bringing about some sort of order in the chaotic socio-economic system. The process of Planning introduced in 1950 has been in vogue for more than six decades. During this period, the Indian economy has achieved tremendous progress, barring a few hiccups that have recently retarded its growth. Similarly, educational development has also undergone a multi-dimensional process of quantitative expansion and qualitative improvement.[8]

India is also having quite a few institutions of quality, which are among the best in the world. It has produced technical and professional manpower of outstanding quality, which has withstood fierce international competition and occupied positions of eminence in the world.

It is difficult to attribute all this to the introduction of planning in education as an instrument of accelerating the process of educational development. It must be emphasised that planning is a multifaceted process in which a number of elements interact with one another. It involves a scientific study of the educational situation in the base year, visualising a long term perspective of educational development, working out rational pattern of priorities keeping in view the availability of infrastructure, financial and academic resources. Most importantly, it involves working out a contingency plan so that if there is any change in the economic, social and political situation, the plan model could be adjusted accordingly. Further, as already stated, the success of planning, depends on the cooperation of and inputs by all the stakeholders.

We would conclude by saying that though the process of planning has the capability of accelerating the pace of educational and socio-economic development through providing the requisite inputs of adequate quantity and quality, phasing of the programme in a scientific manner, introducing corrective factors through an inbuilt process of monitoring and evaluation, it has its limitation in ensuring the achievement of the pre-determined targets. As emphasised by UNESCO, "educational planning is not a wonder-drug to cure all educational ills. It is not a standardised formula applicable to all situations regardless of their vast differences".[9] The success of educational planning depends on a number of variables and postulates, which may undergo a sea-change soon after the plan has been conceived. It is humanly impossible to visualise the behaviour of these variables. Hence there is need for an inbuilt process of continuous monitoring and evaluation of the progress of the plan and readjusting the priorities.

And that is what the Indian system of educational planning has been attempting to do during the last 62 years of planning.

References

1. M. Visveswaraya, *Planned Economy for India*. (Second Edition), Mangalore, 1938.
2. A.H. Manson – The Process of Planning – A Study of India's Five Year Plans, 1950-64, (Oxford University Press, London).

3. Report: National Planning Committee, (Vora and Co. Publishers, Bombay) 1949, p. 5.
4. *Ibid.*, p. 14.
5. Gunnar Myrdal: *Asian Drama; An Inquiry into the Poverty of Nations*; Penguin Books Ltd., England), 1969; p. 711.
6. Planning Commission; Ninth Plan; Vol. I, p. 241.
7. Azad, J.L.; The Process of Educational Planning; published for the M.Ed. Programmes of the Indira Gandhi National Open University and Kurukshetra University.
8. For details, see Chapter 10 Educational Development in the Post-Independence period.
9. For a fuller description, see Educational Planning; A world survey of problems and prospeets; UNESCO; 1970.

13

Globalisation and its Impact on Education

(A Challenge and an Opportunity)

India embarked upon the process of deregulation and liberalisation of its economy from 1980s. The process received a big boost from early nineties, when significant changes were introduced by abolishing licensing for domestic manufacturing for all but a few industries and private sector was allowed to enter areas hitherto reserved for the public sector. Further, import tariffs were drastically reduced. Considered in international context, Globalisation as the on-going process of economic, technological, social and political integration of the World is reported to have started after the Second World War. It is impacting the institutional framework in both developing and industrialising countries; changing the way in which governments perceive their role in the society. It has also far reaching implications for socio-economic development and educational systems of countries all over the World.

The Main Themes

The Impact of Globalisation on education will be discussed under the following themes:

1. The Concept and Ramifications of Globalisations
2. Globalisation and Education
3. Impact on Education:
    (a) Reforms within the Educational System
    (b) The Fall out of Globalisation

1. The Concept and Ramifications of Globalisation

Globalisation is a newly emerging phenomenon. It has been defined as: "a set of processes by which the world is rapidly being integrated into one economic space via increased international trade, the internationalisation of production and financial markets; the internationalisation of a commodity culture promoted by an increasingly networked global telecommunication system" (Graham, 1996)[1].

Globalisation transcends socio-economic and political barriers that the countries of the world are prone to build around themselves. It is not only a process "integrating just economy, but culture, technology and governance. It is giving rise to new markets, foreign exchange and capital markets linked globally, new tools, internet links, cellular phones, media network, new actors; the World Trade Organisation with authority over national governments, the multi-national cooperation with more economic power than many states, new rules, multi-national agreements and intellectual property, multi-lateral agreements on trade".[2]

Globalisation is expected to have a positive influence on the volume, quality and spread of knowledge through increased interaction among the various nations. "In a globalised world, as technology becomes its main motor, knowledge assumes a powerful role in production, making its possession essential for nations, if they are successfully to pursue economic growth and competitiveness" (Stromquist, 2000). Education, being the most potent instrument of creating, assimilating and transmitting knowledge, assumes a central role in the process.

In a market oriented competitive world, unleashed by the forces of globalisation, education has to assume a somewhat different role. It cannot afford to be conventional, rigid and impervious to change. It has to keep abreast of the latest developments in various fields and be capable of creating, absorbing and transacting new-technology and information systems that are sweeping across the countries of the world. There has also to be a paradigm shift in the content of education with substantial emphasis on the productivity and efficiency aspects of the curriculum. It also calls for adequate emphasis on research and development (R & D).

It is, however, necessary to guard against being swept off our feet by the new 'cult of technology', and consequently, 'the diminution of respect for spiritual and cultural values' (Maugey, cited in Namer, 1999). An unfettered and ruthless pursuit of economic goals in an aggressively competitive world, without regard to considerations of moral and social values, is bound to be disastrous for the people, particularly in developing countries.

Not an Unmixed Blessing

In spite of the cataclysmic changes taking place in most countries, it would be wrong to consider globalisation as a panacea for all economic and social ills. As stated by the Planning Commission, "the accelerated process of liberalisation and globalization in the world has increased the opportunities for growth and development, but it has also added new complexities and risks in the management of global interdependence".[3] Some of the complexities identified at the international level are:

(i) Although globalisation is forging greater interdependence, yet the world seems more fragmented–between the rich and the poor; between the powerful and the powerless.

(ii) Economically, politically and technologically, the world has never seemed more free and at the same time more unjust.
(iii) If the present global progress continues at such a snails' pace, it will take more than 130 years to rid the World of hunger.[4]
(iv) Globalisation is a "tricky term for some; it connotes free flow of ideas, capital, people and goods around the world. For others, it implies the hegemony of the capitalist system, the domination of rich nations and corporations and the loss of national identity" (Madeline Green et. al. 2002).
(v) A globalised world will ultimately require the outsourcing of human skills in regions, which will witness a demographic deficit, skilled human capital will have to be imported to certain regions to sustain economic growth (Ministry of HRD, Report to People; 2009-10 (p. 4).

The Humane Face of Globalisation

It would thus appear that globalisation is not an unmixed blessing. It may promote "growth through increased technology and knowledge transfers in developing countries but it could also be sometime a source of instability....".[5] It should, therefore, not be construed purely as a faceless economic mechanism but be based on:

(a) *Ethics:* ensuring less violation of human rights;
(b) *Equity:* resulting in reducing disparities within and between nations;
(c) *Inclusion:* less marginalization of people and countries;
(d) *Human security:* less instability of societies and less vulnerability of people;
(e) *Sustainability:* less destruction of environment;
(f) *Development:* less poverty and deprivation; and
(g) *Productivity Orientation:* to education in regions with deficit in skilled manpower of the requisite capability.

2. Globalisation and Education

Education, as a service industry, is part of the globalisation process under the umbrella of General Agreement on Trade in Services (GATS). There is, however, distinct possibility that this might "force countries with quite different academic needs and resources to conform to structures inevitably designed to service the interest of the most powerful academic systems and corporate educational providers... breeding inequality and dependence"[6] (Altbach, 2002). Further, "Globalisation... can lead to unregulated and poor quality higher education, with the worldwide marketing of fraudulent degrees or other so-called higher education credentials[7]..." India, is likely to turn into "an increasingly attractive market for foreign universities and hence other nations are going to use GATS' provisions to their advantage."[8] While these are obvious problems, globalisation can also have advantages, particularly for India, which has a large educational system and infrastructure and diverse human capabilities.

Given the array of theoretical and epistemological perspective presented in the general social science literature on 'globalisation', it is difficult to assess not only the nature and dimensions of globalisation, but also what it might mean to the field of education. "Globalisation imposes new ways of thinking by researchers, teachers and administrators in the process of creation, dissemination and the management of knowledge."[9]

It appears as though the phenomenon of globalisation will mean many different things for education. Most certainly, in the near future, "it will mean a more competitive and deregulated educational systems modelled after free market but with more pressure on it to assure that the next generation of workers are prepared for some amorphous 'job market of 21st century'.

In fact, "a globalised world will ultimately require the outsourcing of human skills in regions which will witness a demographic deficit." This can offer tremendous opportunities for employment and growth provided the youth are equipped with requisite knowledge and skills.

Globalisation as a Reality

We have discussed the main features of globalisation and its likely impact on socio-economic development. At this stage, it must be emphasized that globalisation, though a recent phenomenon, is a reality, which cannot be wished away. It is, however, difficult to measure its long-term effect on the course of socio-economic development in various countries. Because of the large disparities in the economic position of the countries inhabiting the globe, it would be imprudent to arrive at any standardised formula of assessing the effects. Each country is an entity in itself with specific socio-economic and cultural configuration and requires to be studied differently. It is, however, necessary to stress that a thoughtless and unimaginative entry into the globalised market would not be in the best interests of the countries, particularly those, which are striving to grapple with the problems of slow economic and social development.

3. Impact of Globalisation on Education

Globalisation has a wide ranging potential to influence all sectors of development. Besides its impact on the pace and pattern of economic development, it also casts its shadow on the system of education. It would, therefore, be pertinent to analyse its impact on the process and progress of education. The impact of globalisation on education and the manner in which the system should respond to the needs of globalisation would require to be studied basically under two broad heads:

1. The needed reforms within the educational system like content, equity and excellence aspects, and
2. The fall out of globalisation, which will entail determining strategies relating to the impending internationalisation of education; finance related issues and privatisation of secondary and higher education.

(a) Needed Reforms within the Educational System

(i) Content of Education

(a) Curriculum Upgradation

The modern advances in information technology have revolutionised, among others, the content of knowledge and the processes of educational transaction. The ever-growing use of electronic media, as a constituent of the ever-expanding open learning system, has brought education to the doorsteps of the common man. Information processing technologies provide an efficient framework for the storage, management, analysis and application of information. In the process, the behavioural pattern, education and the way of living have adopted what may be called 'computational paradigm', the use of computer language, to understand how human beings cognize themselves and the world.

The operative part of the introduction of the information technology is the need for a continuous upgradation of the curriculum in order to introduce the latest developments relating to various disciplines in the curriculum. Alongside, pruning of the existing curriculum would be a necessary condition in order to remove the obsolete and irrelevant details. It also needs to be stressed that education should help to engender a new "humanism that contains an essential ethical component and sets considerable store by knowledge of, and respect for, the culture and spiritual values of different civilisations, as a much needed counter weight to a globalisation that would otherwise be seen only in economical or technological terms. The sense of shared values as a common destiny is in fact the basis on which any scheme of international cooperation must be founded."[10]

The fast developing stock of knowledge and the need for its continuous upgrading has also initiated an era of lifelong learning. No longer is education confined to a particular period of life. It is a continuum with no artificial time and space barriers restricting the process.

(b) Productivity Orientation

The basic objective of globalisation is to enhance productivity and to make educational system an instrument of preparing students, who can compete in world markets as productive members of the society. This would necessitate making skill training as an integral part of the curriculum besides making attitudinal changes so that the students do not consider it infra-dig to work with hands.

Unfortunately our experience of introducing an element of skill training has not been adequately successful. The schemes of vocationalisation, both at the school and college stages, have been languishing for want of enthusiasm on the part of students (and teachers). They have also not received the required social recognition. It may be recalled that the scheme of vocational education at the secondary stage was launched in 1988 as a centrally sponsored programme. Against a target of diverting 10 per cent of students to vocational stream by 1995 and 25 per cent by 2000, only 11 per cent of students have been covered at the plus-two stage. At the college stage also, scheme of vocationalisation has been in operation since 1994. It has, however, languished for want of an adequate number of students opting for vocational courses. Further, according to the recent National Sample Survey Organisation (NSSO) data, only 5 per cent of the population of 19-24 age group in India have acquired some sort of skill through vocational education. The corresponding figure for Korea is 96 per cent (Eleventh Five Year Plan; p. 20).

The reasons for the slow progress of these programmes are many, but the most significant is lack of acceptance–by the parents, teachers and students–of introducing an element of skill training as a part of the general education curriculum. Education is still considered as an academic discipline in which the intrusion of vocational training is considered unacceptable. Further, the craze for degrees is also an important retarding factor. There is also lack of parity of status between students and teachers of vocational and general streams leading to the former hesitating to join vocational courses. Another limiting factor is lack of mobility between vocational, general and technical education and absence of multiple entry and exit options.

(c) Value Education

In order to ward off the evils of untrammeled competitiveness and use of unethical practices to move up in the socio-economic ladder, it is necessary that education should lay stress on value education, which emphasizes cooperation rather than competition; sharing of experience rather than personal aggrandizement and learning to live together rather than living in mutually hostile camps.

(d) Research

Indian professionals, particularly in information technology, have successfully competed in the world markets especially in software development and data analysis. This, however, cannot continue for a long time, especially because competition from other developing countries is likely to be very intense in times to come. It has been reckoned that there have been low level of R & D efforts mainly due to inadequate number of highly trained and knowledgeable R & D personnel – particularly, at the level of Ph.D. (about 450 per annum in

Engineering and Technology); relatively low level of investment in R & D by the corporate sector and lack of synergy among R & D institutions and universities. This underscores the need for emphasizing Research and Development (R & D) particularly in the newly emerging areas in our university institutions. As suggested by Iyengar (2000): "Our human resource development in the future should be planned such that there are identified areas in which India could compete effectively, and be innovators rather than just followers. These could include areas such as biotechnology, new power sources, education etc. The Government should focus on these areas, and offer incentives to researchers for innovative research in these fields".

(ii) Equity, Excellence Syndrome

An important component of globalisation in relation to education is the need for producing higher quality manpower that can successfully face competition in the world markets. This would imply selecting the best possible human material and giving them education of the highest quality. This would naturally be relevant to secondary and higher education, because education at the primary level has been considered as the fundamental right of every child in the relevant age group. It would also be necessary to grant financial and other incentives to the meritorious students so that want of resources is not an impediment in their ascent towards the highest form of education.

It can be argued that nurturing of excellence will be inequitable in that it may deny opportunities to a very large segment of student population, who are not so intellectually endowed, to get into institutions of higher education. It is also feared that the present day techniques of students' assessment are not very reliable tools for measuring the potentiality of students, particularly from rural areas and those belonging to the deprived sections of the society.

It is difficult to deny the force of these arguments. The remedy, however, lies not in denigrating the need for nurturing excellence but in creating opportunities by expanding the *field* of excellence, so as to enable more and more promising students to join institutions of higher learning. The emphasis needs to be placed on providing financial and other support to institutions catering to the students from backward sections of society, physically challenged and girl students, who should be given special scholarships, fellowships, hostel facilities, etc. This would necessitate qualitative upgradation of the academic and physical infrastructure, reforming teacher education and improving the system of student assessment so that no student with potentiality for benefiting from education is denied that opportunity. It may also require special coaching facilities for the students belonging to the traditionally deprived sections of the society.

(b) The Fallout of Globalisation

(a) *Internationalisation of Education*

Implicit in the system of Globalisation is the inevitability of internationalisation of the educational system, particularly at the higher education stage. This is not peculiar to India but has become a worldwide phenomenon. The entry of the World Trade Organisation (WTO) and the inclusion of educational services under the general Agreement on Trade in Services (GATS) has given a boost to the internationalisation of higher education. It has been rightly felt that higher education is an increasingly global enterprise, hence Indian institutions should embrace internationalisation that could provide them with new opportunities. According to the Planning Commission, "Country's rationale for internationalisation would be to enhance its soft power, improve standards of domestic provision and produce graduates with international competencies and skills. This can be best achieved by having more and more innovative partnership."[11]

The other merits of internationalisation of higher education are:

(i) It will provide global opportunities and promote international good will;

(ii) It will encourage exchange of scholars. This can be done by involvement of reputed scholars in the respective countries in curriculum designing and transaction of knowledge; and

(iii) Internationalisation of higher education is an 'emerging trend'. India, because of its very advanced state of educational development, particularly among the South and East Asian countries, should assume the role of a provider/exporter of education, particularly at the higher education stage.

A Word of Caution

Notwithstanding the merits of internationalisation, it will be necessary to tread cautiously and not to allow an unregulated entry of foreign institutions in India. According to latest information, foreign education institutions have increased more than fourfold during the last decade; from 144 in 2000 the number shot up to 631 in 2010. Curiously enough, of the 60 foreign education institutions, who have collaboration programme with local institutions, only 25 local institutions were affiliated to Indian universities or approved by regulatory bodies. Further, only 32 of the 49 foreign institutions operating under twinning arrangements have approval or affiliation.[12] A legislative proposal to regulate entry and operation of foreign educational institutions has recently been introduced in Parliament.

In a Study ***"Partnership of Private Sector in Financing and Management of Higher Education" (2008),***[13] undertaken by the present author, the following guidelines were suggested about the entry of foreign institutions in India in consultation with academics, educational planners and representatives of the industry:

- While the foreign institutions may be allowed to set up their campuses in India, they should function under the control of the government or specialised bodies like the National Assessment and Accreditation Council (NAAC) set up by the Government for the purpose;
- The universities which want to function in India should have been accredited in their own countries;
- The foreign institutions should be subjected to pre-entry academic audit and accreditation norms devised by the designated government agencies;
- They should sign Memoranda of Understanding (MOU) with the government or a body designated by it. The Memorandum should give details of the courses of study, infrastructural facilities, both academic and non-academic and the amount of expected cost recov ies from Indian students;
- They should provide a stipulated level of investment in academic infrastructure and physical facilities;
- The entry of foreign institutions should be allowed on the basis of reciprocity. The countries exporting education to India should also permit the opening of Indian university campuses in their countries. There should be provision for exchange of faculty among the various countries participating in the programme; and
- In the entire process of the entry of foreign institutions, the paramountcy of national interests should be the crucial guiding factor.

Regulatory Mechanism

The Ministry of the Human Resource Development, in pursuance of the recommendations made by the University Grants Commission, has notified the rules governing the setting up of campuses in India by foreign education providers (F.E.P.). The important rules are:

1. The FEPs would have to run as a non-profit legal entity. They are required to first form a company under section 25 of the Companies Act-1956. Companies under this Act are non-profit entities.
2. The degrees awarded by FEPs would be treated as foreign degrees only and they would be subject to the equivalence accorded by the Association of Indian Universities as per their rules.
3. FEPs, before being notified would have to maintain a corpus of not less than Rs. 25 crores for each campus, the maximum being four campuses. FEPs would not be allowed to utilise more than 75 per cent income for the purpose of development. The rest of the income would have to be deposited in the corpus foud.
4. FEPs, who are placed in the top 400 institutions, as per university rankings by Times Higher Education or world university Rankings by Quaequarelli

Symonds (QS) or Academic Rankings of world universities by Shanghai Jia Tong University will be allowed to operate.

5. FEPs that have been for more than 20 years in the parent country and are accredited there would be allowed to set up campuses in India.[14]

It is hoped that these regulations will bring in some order in the chaotic state of affairs that prevails at the apex stage of Indian education.

(b) *Down Sizing Secondary and Higher Education*

Indian higher education has attracted special attention by the 'Reformists', particularly by the international organisations. Based on the 'Rate of Return' studies, the World Bank came to the conclusion that its lending strategy should emphasise primary education relegating higher education to a relatively minor place in its development agenda. The plea has been repeated by Carnoy (1999). According to him: "Higher education is a high cost level of schooling and basic education is relatively low cost. In addition, in many countries, public university education costs are heavily weighted toward non-teaching and non-research expenditures such as student subsidies and administrative costs... The shift of emphasis, it is argued, would enhance opportunities for larger number of primary students at the expense of subsidizing a relatively elite group of families that could bear the cost of university education".[15]

That the Government of India succumbed to these specious arguments would be evident from the fact that in 1997, the Ministry of Finance circulated a note on 'Subsidies', in which, among other things, higher education was described as a 'non-merit' good, unworthy of government subventions.

A deeper consideration of this suggestion will bring out its utter shortsightedness. In the first place, it is wrong to presume that at the higher education stage, costs are heavily weighted towards non-teaching and non-research expenditure. Moreover it is academically preposterous to segmentalise education, whose different stages are complementary rather than competitive. For example, if university education is starved of funds, will it be possible to provide good and competent teachers for the school stage? As emphasised by Panchamukhi (2002); "At any point of time, weakening of higher education sector would weaken the forces of competitiveness and efficiency in the functioning of different sectors of economy..."

The implementation of this too simplistic suggestion will also impede the progress of basic research, which is an important responsibility of the universities. Further, any scaling down of the financial inputs for higher education would result in the qualitative deterioration of the highly trained scientific and technical manpower, which is the mainstay of our economic and social development.

It may be noted that a Task Force of the World Bank (2000), while fully supporting the continuation of larger investment in primary and secondary education rebutted the traditional economic argument, which is based on "limited understanding of what higher education institutions contribute". The Task Force challenged the notion that public investment in higher education is socially inequitable. It emphasised that: 'Rate-of-Return' Studies treat educated people as valuable only through their higher earnings and the greater tax revenues extracted by society. But educated people clearly have many other effects on society. Educated people are well positioned to be economic and social entrepreneurs, having far reaching impact on the economic and social well being of their communities. "Rates of return analysis entirely misses the impact of university based research on the economy – *a far reaching social benefit that is at the heart of the argument for developing strong higher education system*".

It may be stressed that education is a continuum in which the various stages are complementary rather than competitive. Any attempt at compartmentalising education in order to deny the requisite funding to a particular sector would be retrogressive and retard the progress of education.

(c) Privatisation of Secondary and Higher Education

As a corollary to the suggestions about reducing public investment in secondary and higher education, a plea has been made to hand over these sectors to private bodies. It has also been suggested that institutions beyond primary basic education should increasingly depend upon tuition fees, the philanthropy of the general public and the support of industrial and commercial organisations, which should be allowed to set up, manage and finance institutions of post elementary education.

The question of the role of private sector in education has been discussed in a subsequent chapter[16]. At this stage, suffice it to say that while the participation of private bodies in investment and management of education should be encouraged, complete privatisation of these sectors of education should be ruled out. Further, market needs should be kept in view while developing the curriculum. In fact, productivity orientation should guide the formulation of curriculum framework. Further, while deciding about the fee structure and other student levies, the tendency towards commercialisation of education should be guarded against.

To Conclude

We have attempted to traverse the entire spectrum of globalisation with a focus on studying its impact on and implications for the educational system. Even at the cost of repetition, it may be stated that globalisation is a recent phenomenon in the world's socio-economic system. Although it is too early to assess the impact of globalization on India's economy, it has so far not yielded any spectacular outcomes. It has accelerated the pace of development in some areas but has led to certain incongruities in others. It is, therefore, necessary that steps should be taken to reduce, if not remove, its baneful fall out.

Globalisation, as an effective instrument of international exchange of goods and services, has to have a humane face, based on ethical considerations rather than on cut-throat competition. It should play a positive role in reducing economic and social disparities within, and among, the nations. It should also be an effective tool for promoting sustainable development.

Globalisation has a multi-dimensional impact on the system of education. It has underlined the need for reforms in the educational system with particular reference to the wider utilisation of information technology; giving productivity dimension to the educational system and emphasis on research and development. It has also given rise to controversies relating to introducing changes in the inter-sectoral priorities in the allocation of resources leading to the misconceived policy of downsising of social services sector in general and secondary and higher education in particular. It has also advocated privatisation of higher education without realising the dangerous possibility of making the system a commercial enterprise. Further, internationalisation of education particularly higher education has been advocated without due regard to the needs and susceptibilities of the developing countries.

It is, therefore, necessary that each country should decide the nature and extent of globalisation that can be constructively introduced in their socio-economic and educational systems. While it is difficult to resist the temptation of falling in line with the international community, it is necessary that while doing so, the paramountcy of national interests should be kept in view. This is more so in the field of education which is intimately concerned with the development of human capital. Any thoughtless entry into the global education market may end up in harming the vital interests of students for generations to come.

The discussion may be concluded by quoting the prophetic statement of Mahatma Gandhi made long before globalisation was ever thought of: "I do not want my house to be walled on all sides and my windows to be stuffed. I want the culture of all the lands to be blown about my house as freely as possible. But I refuse to be blown off my feet by any." This should be the guiding principle of our entry into the comity of nations that Globalisation has opened up for India and also other developing countries.

References

1. Parikh, Kirti S., (ed.), 2002, *India, Development Report*, Indira Gandhi Institute of Development Research, Oxford.
2. Human Development Report; (UNDP Oxford).
3. Tenth Five Year Plan, Vol. I, Planning Commission; p. 97.
4. The Human Development Report, 2002, UNDP.
5. The Human Development Report in South Asia; (ed.) UNDP, 1999.
6. Altbach Philip, G. *Private Promoters*; Centre for Institutional Higher Education, Massachusetts, USA.
7. World Bank; 2002, Higher Education in Developing Countries; Peril and promise; The Report of the Task Force on Education and Society.
8. Arun Nigvekar; GATS and Higher Education; UGC, (Mimeo).

9. Ministry of Human Resource Development: Report to the People on Education; 2009-10, Mimeo: p. 4.
10. UNESCO; Learning, The Treasure Within; International Commission on Education for the Twenty First Century, 1996.
11. Faster, Sustainable and More Inclusive Growth: Planning Commission, 2011, p. 103.
12. Reported in the *Times of India* dated September 13, 2013.
13. The Study was conducted at the instance of the Planning Commission at the National University of Educational Planning and Administration (NUEPA) under the direction of the present author.
14. Reference: *Times of India* dated 3rd June, 2012.
15. Carnoy Martin; Globalisation and Educational Reforms in Globalisation and Education; (2000), (ed.) Stranguist, Nally P., Rouman and Little Field Publications.
16. See Chapter 14.

14

Public Private Partnership in Education

India has been a seat of learning since times immemorial. The ancient Indian scriptures have extolled the value of education in no uncertain terms. *Vidya Dan* was considered as the noblest benevolence and the *Guru* (the preceptor) was held in the highest esteem. The nobility and the laity voluntarily participated in setting up and maintenance of educational institutions.

With the passage of time, education ceased to be the prerogative of the elitist groups and was recognised as the basic human right. The state emerged as the largest single agency for the establishment and maintenance of educational institutions. The private sector, however, continued to participate in the process of providing education to the teeming millions of the country.

We shall discuss the role of private sector in education under the following heads:

(i) The Role of Private Sector in:
  (a) the Pre-independence Period, and
  (b) the Post-independence Period;
(ii) Evolving a Policy Framework Towards Private Participation; and
(iii) Augmenting Private Resources.

I

(a) Role of Private Sector in Pre-Independence Period

(i) The Ancient Times

The ancient Indian education started as a family concern, both for literary and professional education. As education became more complex and exacting, the specialist came into the field in the form of private teacher. *'Guru Griha'*, i.e., the abode of the preceptor became the centre of education where the high and mighty of the land flocked to get education and training in literary and vocational skills. During the Buddhist period, corporate educational institutions were established. They were the counterparts of the *Gurukuls*, which were also essentially residential institutions. Some of the universities like *Taksashila, Vallalbhi, Nalanda* grew as famous institutes of higher learning and attracted seekers of knowledge from foreign countries like China, Sri Lanka, Vietnam, Cambodia, etc. The main sources of finance were donations by the royalty and the nobility as also by the community. Most of these institutions were residential. Tuition fee, as considered in the modern sense, was conspicuous by its absence. The practice of the royalty and the nobility of providing finances for educational institutions continued during the medieval period.

(ii) Colonial Period

The system of financing of education under the Colonial rule was subjected to strange vicissitudes of time. It took the East India Company more than a century to officially recognise their responsibility for the education of the vast masses of people, over whose destinies they had the privilege to preside. Well up to the end of the 19th century, the British rulers of India fought shy of direct administration of education and insisted upon a policy of gradual withdrawal from education leaving the field to the munificence of private bodies.

In the early twentieth century, the central and the provincial governments evinced greater interest in education. But two consecutive economic depressions, which occurred between 1919-24 and 1929-32, forced the provincial governments to economise on educational expenditure. As a consequence of the financial squeeze caused by the First World War, educational budgets were drastically cut and a number of organisations set up by the government were abolished. The transfer of education to popular ministers under the 'Dyarchy' and later on under the Government of India Act, 1935, was expected to improve the financial position of educational institutions but the Second World War (1939-45) added to the financial difficulties of the government and thwarted attempts at providing a sound financial base to educational institutions.

In spite of the financial squeeze that had been the hallmark of the Indian economy almost all through the colonial rule, private bodies–religions and otherwise–entered into the educational field in a big way to set up institutions, some of which are outstanding models even in the present times. In 1885, the Decan Education Society set up the Fergussan College at Pune. Under the aegis of the newly established Arya Samaj, the first Dayanand Anglo Vedic (DAV) College was established at Lahore in 1886. Dr. Annie Besant of the Theosophical Society set up the Central Hindu College at Varanasi, which was handed over to Pandit Madan Mohan Malaviya to be converted into a full-fledged university – Banaras Hindu University–in 1917. Similarly, Gurudev Tagore established the Visva Bharati University, which developed out of a school for children at Santiniketan established in 1901.

The rulers of some of the princely states also took keen interest in developing educational facilities in their states. Among them, the classic cases of the rulers of

Baroda, Travancore and Cochin and Hyderabad stand out as refreshing examples of the rulers giving boost to education in their respective states. M.S. University, Baroda (now Vadodra), Osmania University (1918) and Annamali University (1921), were set up by the enlightened rulers of the princely states. During the Non-cooperation Movement (1920), a number of institutions – Gujarat Vidyapeeth, Kashi Vidyapeeth, Tilak Maharashtra Vidyapeeth and Jamia Millia Islamia were established.

(*Source:* K.B. Pawar, Veena Bhalla; "Private Higher Education in India" in Asha Gupta (ed.). *Private Higher Education,* Shipra: 2008).

Internationally Acclaimed Institutions set up by Private Trusts

Apart from setting up institutions of the usual type, some of the individuals/ trusts were able to set up institutions catering to specific disciplines at the post secondary level. These institutions, under the inspiring leadership of their mentors, who were imbued with the desire to set up world class institutions, have attained international acclaim. To mention a few:

1. Indian Institute of Science, Bangalore and Tata Institute of Fundamental Research at Mumbai were established by J.N. Tata with the vision and aim of advancing scientific capabilities of the country.
2. Santiniketan, presently Viswabharati, was set up by Nobel Laureate, Rabindranath Tagore. The aim of the university has been to reform the village life through education and training.
3. Xavier Labour Relations Institute set up by Fr. Quinn Enright in Jamshedpur with a vision of 'renewing the face of the earth'.
4. The Birla Institute of Technology and Science founded by G.D. Birla, which was started as a small school at Pilani. It has now grown as a premier engineering institution with campuses at Ranchi and in Goa, Hyderabad and Dubai.
5. The Tata Institute of Social Sciences, established in 1936 as Sir Dorabji Tata Graduate School of Social Work, was recognised as a deemed university by the UGC in 1964.
6. The International Institute of Information Technology, Hyderabad – an autonomous self-supporting institution with major international I.T. Companies being actively involved in its academic programmes through their corporate schools on the campuses.
7. Vidyanagari Baramati offers courses from primary education to Master's degree. The Trust runs a Law College, Engineering College, Biotechnology College and an Institution of Information Technology.

(*Source:* Planning Commission, Eleventh Five Year Plan).

(b) Role of Private Sector in the Post Independence Period

(1) Institutions under Private Management

The post-independence period witnessed a spurt in government administered institutions. In 1949-50, private institutions formed 36.4 per cent of total educational institutions. In 1995-96, they formed an abysmal 16.66 per cent. There has however, been considerable improvement in the position of privately managed institutions during the first decade of the twenty first century. At the pre-degree higher secondary level, out of 59,166 institutions, the privately managed institutions accounted for about 65 per cent of the total in 2007-08. According to the Planning Commission: "A welcome development during the Tenth Plan is that share of private unaided higher education institutions increased from 42.6 per cent in 2001 to 63.21 per cent in 2006. The share of enrolments also increased from 32.89 per cent to 51.53 per cent during the same period. This trend is likely to continue during the Eleventh Plan and, therefore, it is reasonable to expect that about half of the incremental enrolment targeted for higher education will come from private providers".[1]

(2) Private Investment in Education

(i) Over all Education

Over the years there has been a sharp decline in the private contribution to education. At the dawn of the twentieth century (1901-02), the contribution of private bodies including donations, endowments and 'other sources' was 24.3 per cent of the total expenditure on education. In 1946-47, when India attained freedom from the British stranglehold, the percentage contribution had come down to 14. Even in the post-independence period, while there has been increase in the number of private institutions, there has been a sizeable decline in private investment in education. In 1950-51, private investment in education was Rs. 13.29 crores out of a total expenditure of Rs. 114.38 crores, which worked out to about 12 per cent of the expenditure. In case income from tuition fees is also added, the contribution from private sources would go up to Rs. 36.5 crores i.e. 32 per cent. In 1993-94, private investment increased to Rs. 543.4 crores. In percentage terms, however, it was 3.15 per cent of the total expenditure; indicating a steep decline. Even if income from fees is added, the percentage would be 7.20, which is far short of the percentage in 1950-51.

(ii) Higher Education

An analysis of the relative contribution from different sources for higher education reveals substantial decline in the share of private bodies. Contribution from government registered considerable increase that is from 49.4 per cent in 1950-51 to 75.9 per cent in 1986-87. On the other hand, fee income drastically declined from 36.8 per cent to 12.6 per cent during the same period. Other sources, which include private philanthropy, contributed around 11 per cent throughout the period. As would appear from Table 1, higher education has been largely a state funded activity with about three-quarters of the total expenditure being borne by government. The relative share of non-government sources, such as fees and voluntary contributions, has been declining. It is to be noted that the latest year for which such information is available is 1986-87.

Table 1: Sources of income for Higher Education in India

	Government	*Fees*	*Others*	*Rs. Crores*
1950-51	49.4	36.8	13.8	114.38
1960-61	53.5	34.8	11.7	344.38
1970-71	61.0	25.5	13.5	1118.28
1980-81	72.8	17.4	10.8	3766.71
1986-87	75.9	12.6	11.5	9011.98

Source: Education in India Vol. II (S).

(iii) University-wise Sources of Finance

A recent study of sources of finances of about 30 universities of all types (Manju, 2004) revealed that government continues to be the main source of funding for the universities although there has been a steady decline in the government funding, i.e., from about 65 per cent in 1996-97 to about 57 per cent in 2001-02. In the case of state universities, the decline was from about 60 to 51 per cent during the corresponding period. In the case of deemed to be universities, the reduction was from about 39 per cent to 26 per cent. The contribution from fees of all kinds, however, increased from about 20 per cent to 26 per cent in the case of all universities. The income from 'other sources', which include donations from trusts, general public, industries and corporate houses, sale of publications, etc., registered a substantial decline from about 25 per cent in 1996-97 to about 17 per cent in 2001-02.

It would thus be seen that in spite of some decline in proportionate terms, the government continues to be the main source for funding higher education. The private contributions, including cost recoveries from the students, have registered a substantial decline both in over all university finances as also in the case of individual universities.

International Experience[2]

In most countries, private and public sectors co-exist. In some countries like Japan, Republic of Korea, Philippines and Latin American countries mass private and restricted public sectors have developed. However, in South Asian countries, including India and Africa, and Western Europe, mixed system prevails. In some countries like the Netherlands and Belgium, both co-exist under public funding. Countries where the role of private sector is limited are Sweden, United Kingdom, France, Spain, Thailand etc. "Asia presents the most varied picture, from non-existence to majority shares. The Philippines (85 per cent), South Korea (77 per cent), Bangladesh (67 per cent) and Indonesia (67 per cent) all show private majorities, with India close, and Turkey and Nepal roughly one fourth private trailed by Malaysia and Papua New Guinea". (*The Encyclopedia of Higher Education*, 1992-1184).

Types of Private Universities

Primarily, there are two types of private universities:

(i) Corporate Universities

According to Middlehurst, (2001)[3] there are corporate universities in Europe and parts of the Commonwealth, but most are in the USA. They take a variety of forms and are generally linked with some multi-national companies or other large organisations. The driving force behind the corporate universities is the business requirements.

In the first type of corporate university – exemplified by the McDonald's Hamburger University – learning is driven by the need to enhance employee performance and productivity and to ensure consistency of service and the spread of a common culture. Its focus tends to be upon employees, but may extend to suppliers and customers (including small and medium-sized enterprises). In the second type, learning is conceptualised more broadly, to include both individual and organisational development. Features include education and training, but also, perhaps, research, consultancy, best-practice benchmarking and knowledge management (as in the case of the British Aerospace Virtual University).

The UK Report indicates the features of corporate universities that appear to be widely shared. These include:

"Professional development activities that are aimed at company and individual needs, specialist in-company departments/colleges which are staffed by a combination of professional educators/ trainers and practitioners from the businesses and an increasing emphasis on the use of technology for the delivery of education and training. Further notable elements include an emphasis on competency-based training, linked to assessment of outcomes and credit accumulation, with a particular focus on professional/vocational subjects and training that forms a necessary part of assuring the quality of products and services, for example, through programmes offered to suppliers and customers. Where degrees are offered, there is generally a partnership with existing universities and in all the education and training offered there, a strong emphasis on quality through close attention to curriculum design, staff selection, mandatory teacher training, control of class size and course cohorts, and rigorous evaluation of every process from student admissions to teacher performance and adherence to curricula."[4]

(ii) 'For-profit' Institutions

Flexibility, convenience and relevance are the key features of 'for-profit' education businesses, which include:

(a) *Location:* Phoenix has set up nearly 80 learning centres in 32 US states on the edge of freeways or in shopping malls in order to minimise student time lost in travelling between work and home;

(b) *Access for students:* Provision and support is often available online (Unexus University, launched recently in New Brunswick, offers twenty-four hours access, seven days a week); enrolment times are also convenient – Jones International University enables students to enroll every four weeks; Keller Graduate School of Management runs a five semester year (ten weeks each) and holds all classes in the evenings or on Saturdays;

(c) *Length and intensity of study:* Courses and programmes tend to be shorter (Phoenix has courses of five or six weeks contributing to a two-year programme) with credit accumulated for awards at different levels. Teaching is focused and intensive and classes are small (14-15 students for face-to-face tuition at Phoenix; 8-11 students for online classes);

(d) *Credit accumulation and transfer:* Sylvan Learning Systems, in an arrangement with Regent's College of New York State, gives credit, and transfers credits from different institutions and gives Regent's examinations in Sylvan's Technology Centres across the US; and

(e) *Curriculum:* 'Learn tonight, apply tomorrow' is a motto for curriculum relevance, Keller Graduate School of Management offers 'practitioner-led management education' where all faculty are practicing professionals; Phoenix designs and delivers customised programmes for corporations along similar lines.

Our Reaction

It may be mentioned that, so far none of the above types of universities has found a place in the Indian educational system. It may, however, he stated that while we can introduce elements of flexibility, efficiency and convenience in our university system, it would not be in consonance with our academic ethos to introduce commercialisation and profit making as the objective of universities notwithstanding the not-so-comfortable financial position of these institutions. The basic tenets of our educational philosophy are much more inclined towards benevolence rather than money spinning.

II

Evolving a Policy Framework Towards Public Private Participation

Given the governments' pre-occupation with the universalization of elementary education and the on-set of economic reforms, which emphasize liberalisation and privatisation, the government seems to be slowly, but steadily, veering round to the view that private sector should be encouraged to play a far greater role in the financing and management of education, particularly of higher education. The first indication of this paradigm shift in government policy became evident from the recommendations made in the Eighth Plan (1992-97), which stated that the opening of new conventional universities and colleges should not be encouraged. Further, a significant recommendations was the involvement of voluntary agencies and private sector participation in the opening and conduct of higher education institutions with proper checks to ensure maintenance of standards and facilities to make *higher education, as far as possible, self-financing.* (emphasis added) To assuage the feelings of the academic community, a rider was also added: 'the quality of education is not to be compromised at any cost'.

As already stated, another milestone towards privatization of higher education was the Ministry of Finance's paper on Government Subsidies (1997), which was much more damaging for Indian higher education. It dubbed higher education as a 'non-merit' good.[5] This controversial statement was based on the reasoning that higher education benefited individuals more than the society. In view of this, it was suggested that government should not subsidise higher education. Instead, it should be left to private bodies to provide the requisite finances.

The move towards privatisation of higher education got a boost from the Birla Ambani Report (2001) submitted to the Prime Minister in which, among other things, it was suggested that government subsidies to higher education should be minimal and the funds thus saved should be invested in expanding facilities for primary and secondary stages of education.

The fallacy of the above arguments can be gauged by the fact that education is a continuum and all stages of education are complementary to one another. It is difficult to visualise the expansion and qualitative development of primary and secondary education without the availability of qualified teachers, who have to be produced in universities and colleges. Further, universities are concerned with the production of highly trained scientific and technical manpower, which is an essential pre-requisite for the socio-economic development of the country. Any slackening of effort towards the expansion and qualitative development of higher education, by reducing financial investment for this sector, is bound to be counter-productive.

It may be pointed out that the government has not, so far, *explicitly* shown its preference for complete privatisation of higher education. It has, however, stressed greater involvement of private bodies, including industrial and commercial houses in financing and management of institutions of higher education.

We think that the best course would be: to work out a well-considered policy framework of not only to 'manage' but to encourage private bodies' participation in higher education. It would also be necessary to devise ways and means of mobilising financial resources from other than government sources. The basic components of this policy framework would be mobilising private resources and adopting other measures to ensure that the available sources go the longest way.

III

Augmenting Private Resources

The following measures for augmenting non-government resources for higher education are suggested:

(a) Encouraging Private Participation in Higher Education

(i) Private participation in the financing and management of higher education should be promoted. It will bring about efficiency in the system and make it more effective and relevant. It is expected to promote excellence. It will also enable the universities to come out of the stifling confines of academic exclusiveness and become a part of the wider social milieu.

(ii) Private bodies should be encouraged to contribute substantial amounts for the maintenance and development of institutions at least to the extent of about 20 per cent of the recurring expenditure. Barring elementary education, student fee contribution should be pegged between 20 to 30 per cent. The balance should come from government and industrial/commercial houses.

(b) Introducing Self-financing Courses

Introduction of self-financing courses is expected to be another step towards mobilising private contribution. These courses are expected to be market driven, which may help the students to enter into gainful employment. Some of the courses could be in professional subjects like Medicine, Engineering, Business Administration, Bio-Technology etc.

While recommending self-financing courses, it is necessary to sound a note of caution. Undue stress on self-financing courses could lead to the possible neglect of courses like Social Sciences and Humanities, Languages, particularly classical languages, Fine Arts, Creative and Performing Arts, History, Philosophy, Anthropology, Archaeology etc. It is also likely that "pedagogies less linked to market will lose importance e.g. classroom discussions, based on critical theory as opposed to problem solving tasks" (Stromquist et.al 2000).

It is, therefore, suggested that effective steps should be taken to prevent the neglect of courses, which may not be completely job-oriented, but nevertheless are essential for the social, cultural and moral development of the society. In order to promote these courses, a scheme should be introduced under which special assistance can be provided for courses, which are likely to be relegated to the background. It is also necessary that self-financing institutions/courses should not end up in commercialisation of university education. They should be periodically subjected to public scrutiny by the regulatory bodies like UGC, AICTE, NCTE, MCI and NAAC.

(c) Bringing About Closer Industry-University Relationship

Industry has a vital stake in higher education. It is not only because of the fact that institutions of higher education provide trained manpower for jobs in the industry, but also because they, through research and development, open up new vistas of scientific and technological development. It is, therefore, essential that there should be a closer relationship between industry and universities. Unfortunately this is precisely what is not happening as evidenced by a study of 300 industries having an annual turn-over of Rs. 200 crores and above (Ansari 1999). The main findings of the study are:

- Over 50 per cent of companies have no interaction with higher education institutions.
- Very few companies provide research fellowships.
- Very few major companies have endowed chairs.
- The forms of collaboration, wherever they exist, include sponsored research, sharing of facilities, awarding of fellowships, strengthening infrastructure through donation of equipment, funds, collaborative research programme etc.

(d) Promoting Industry University Linkages

In order to involve industry in the financing and management of higher education, the following measures are suggested:

- Industry should be involved in curriculum development and designing of courses, which have integral relationship with industrial processes. The universities should identify specific needs of the industry and draw up their curriculum and research programmes taking them into account.
- Industry should also be represented on the decision making bodies of the universities.
- Industry should provide faculty support in subject areas, where industry has expertise.
- While student admissions should be the sole prerogative of the universities, industry may be consulted about the type of students that would be admitted specially to professional courses. Industry could, however, sponsor its employees for advanced refresher courses.
- Industry may provide fellowships and scholarships to meritorious but economically weaker sections of students. They should also finance the establishment of chairs in various disciplines.
- Industry should provide financial and material support to universities for Research and Development Programmes. They should also provide facilities for supervised 'Hands on Training' to the university students particularly those pursuing professional courses.

The Policy and Legal Framework

It would be interesting to know how the existing legal framework may be modified to promote private sector's active participation in higher education. In a study conducted by the author (2008)[6], a selected group of academics, Vice-Chancellors, Planners and Industrialists were asked to give their views about this problem. A majority of respondents suggested framing new acts/ laws and also changing the existing laws so that private participation may be encouraged. The views of respondents given on this aspect are summarised below:

(i) There was an urgent need to bring necessary changes in the Acts and Statutes of universities so that representation of trade, commerce and industry may become possible on the decision making bodies of the universities like Court,

Senate, Executive Council, Syndicate, Academic Council, Faculty Committee, Board of Studies etc. It may also be provided that industrial houses may establish/ adopt university institutions.

(ii) The territorial jurisdiction of universities should be extended so that they can expand their working freely in the country and abroad.

(iii) The accountability procedures for academic and administrative staff should be developed and followed strictly. Term appointments of faculty and staff may be considered. Extension may be given purely on merit/ performance bases.

(iv) The monopoly of the state in establishing and managing universities should be done away with so that industrial and corporate houses may consider starting private universities. However, it should be ensured that it does not lead to commercialising of higher education. An act may be passed which would provide for incorporation, monitoring and regulation of universities and colleges under private management.

(v) Private investment in higher education should be made tax-free.

Nature and Level of Participation

(a) Management

The universities should be given complete operational freedom in management. The role of funding agencies and government is to provide guidelines for maintaining the standards and ensuring that the norms laid down by them are adhered to properly. Representation of trade, commerce and industry and the parents' associations should be increased in decision making bodies of universities. They can lend their expertise in strategic planning, organisational management, finance, human resource development and monitoring the progress of various programmes. From this stand point, they need to be represented on Management/ Executive Councils.

(b) Curriculum Development

The regulating authority should lay down broad guidelines for curriculum development. The representation from academic community and public institutions should be invited. The market needs must be kept in view while developing the curriculum.

(c) Admission of Students

University may invite sponsored students from employers. However, merit may not be neglected altogether. Special courses may be developed to suit the needs of sponsors. The university should be allowed to have some sponsored seats against which candidates fulfilling the requirements for admission may be admitted.

(d) Determining Fee Structure

The fee structure should be revised. It should, however, not take the form of commercialisation or profiteering. The regulating authority should decide differential fee structure but the fee structure should accommodate students from weaker sections and also meritorious students.

(e) Recruitment of Staff

Although procedure for appointments has been laid down for many years, they have not led to improvement in the quality and performance of teachers. Funding agency should provide guidelines and also suggest procedures.

(g) Other Measures

(i) Tuition Fees

Tuition fees levied on students have not kept pace with the ever escalating costs of education. In the process, at the post-elementary level, large subsidy is built into the present fee structure. This subsidy is given indiscriminately to each and every student regardless of his or her capacity to pay for education. There is a very strong case for raising tuition fees at secondary and higher education stages. The best method of levying fees is to relate them uniformly to costs of education. But this step could be construed as a regressive form of taxation. In the circumstances, a sort of differential fee structure should be considered (Azad, 1976). Under the system, the economically well off should be made to pay enhanced fees (meeting at least 20 per cent of the recurring costs) while weaker sections will pay subsidised fees. Further, foreign students may be charged at the international rates.

(ii) Loan Scholarships

A scheme of loan scholarships, rather than outright grants to students, who are in need of financial assistance has been recently introduced in India. Under this scheme, students are entitled to get loans for various university courses in India and abroad. The students are charged at the prevailing rates of interest.

The scheme, as worked out at present, does not seem to be in a position to meet the requirements of the needy students. It is based on the same principles, which govern other loan schemes like car loans or housing loans. Education being an investment in human capital should not be treated like any other consumer good.

It is recognised that in India, a host of administrative problems are likely to arise in implementing loan assistance programmes. This is particularly so in case of students enrolled in general education courses who are likely to be subjected to prolonged periods of unemployment and under-unemployment, which would seriously undermine their capacity to repay their loan. In spite of these problems, the scheme is worth trying if only for the fact that it will, eventually, develop self-confidence among students; will reduce wasteful expenditure and will generate a revolving, self-sustaining fund.

(iii) Community Contributions

It has been mentioned that private donations, as a source of educational finance, are fast drying up. It is necessary that a concerted effort is made to mobilise community resources for meeting some part of educational expenditure. This would happen only if educational institutions shed their academic exclusiveness, become a part of the society around them and provide education, which is relevant to community needs. An educational institution should function as the centre for social life around it and not a place, which has nothing to do with its social and physical environment.

To Conclude

It needs hardly to be emphasised that in spite of the private bodies' dwindling contribution to the financing of educational institutions, they have played an important role in the establishment and maintenance of educational institutions of all types. They have to be encouraged to contribute more substantially to education. While it is difficult to endorse the apparent shift in government policy of withdrawing from financing of higher education and leaving the field primarily to private sector, it is necessary that constructive and viable steps should be taken to augment private resources for all types of educational institutions, particularly higher education. Higher education is at the apex of the educational pyramid and any indifference towards its maintenance and development will lead to the weakening of the entire educational super-structure. It will thwart the harmonious development of education and retard the process of socio-economic development and cultural regeneration of the country. We can neglect higher education only at our peril.

References

1. Planning Commission; Eleventh Five Year Plan; p. 23.
2. For details, see J.L. Azad, *Financing and Management of Higher Education in India,* Gyan Publishing House, 2008.
3. Robin Middlehurst, University Challenges, Minerva, 2001.
4. Robin Middlehurst, op. cit.
5. See page 354-55 for detailed discussion.
6. Financing and Management of Higher Education in India; op. cit.

15

Teacher of the New Millennium

> The world around us is undergoing cataclysmic transformation not only in academia but also in socio-economic and political systems. A sort of revolution is occurring relentlessly in information and communication technology as also in transactional techniques. In spite of all the changes in technology, the teacher, representing the community at large, remains an important constituent of the educational process. It is he/she who has to be nurtured and equipped adequately to meet the emerging challenges.

We have discussed briefly the changes that are occurring in the field of Indian education consequent upon the onset of economic reforms launched in the nineties of the last century. The policy of Liberalisation, Privatisation and Globalisation (LPG) and breath-taking advances in information and communication technology have transformed the world into a global village. Under the provisions of the General Agreement on Trade in Services (GATS), Indian education is going to face formidable global competition. It will also become an attractive market for foreign institutions giving rise to a host of problems for our educational institutions, particularly at the higher education level.

As a major component of Reforms, Privatisation of Indian Education is also on the cards with all its beneficial and baneful implications. Further, in spite of very large expansion at all stages of education, there are quite a few deficient areas in the educational system. The content of education needs to be continuously upgraded and enriched in order to keep pace with breath-taking advances taking place in various disciplines all over the world. Education has also to become productivity oriented in order to produce persons who are capable of developing the socio-economic system rather than being a drag on the society.

Role of Teacher

The challenges thrown up by the exposure of Indian Education to the somewhat diverse systems of the outside world as also the inadequacies in our educational system would necessitate introducing requisite structural reconstruction and academic transformation in our educational system so as to enable it to synchronise with the developments taking place around the globe. In this task, the role of the teacher – an important component of the educational process - would need to be redefined.

Before attempting to delineate the role of the Indian teacher in the fast changing socio-economic and academic scenario around us, it would be useful to have a bird's eye-view of the quantitative and qualitative aspects of the teaching personnel in Indian institutions. The position, according to the Planning Commission, does not appear to be very encouraging. According to the Commission: "The effort to expand access is severely constrained by lack of suitably qualified, appropriately trained human resources in adequate numbers. There are half a million vacancies of teachers in the country and another half a million are required to meet the Right to Education Act norms on pupil-teacher ratio. Besides 0.6 million teachers in the public school system are untrained. Pre-service and in-service training of teachers has to be mounted on a mission mode during the twelfth Plan for which information and communication technologies could be effectively leveraged.... There is acute shortage of high quality teachers. Efforts in this direction should also focus on research in curricular and pedagogic practices and address the paucity of teacher educators..."[1]

In the context of this grim scenario of the teaching personnel, the role of teachers assumes added significance. While remaining at the centre stage of the teaching learning process, the teacher has to participate in redesigning the educational system to meet, among others, the diverse and complex challenges thrown up by forces unleashed by globalisation of the socio-economic systems of the countries across the globe.

Paradigm Shift

Thus, a paradigm shift has to occur in the role and responsibilities of the modern day teacher. The world has traversed a long way since Arnold Goldsmiths' description of the 'Village School Master', who would subject his students to an endless tyranny of words. The teacher of today has to be quite different from his predecessor. Sri Aurobindo, with his divine foresight, has summed up the fundamental change that has occurred in the role of the teacher thus:

"The first principle of true teaching is that nothing can be taught. The teacher is not an instructor or taskmaster; he is a helper and a guide. His business is to suggest and not to impose. He does not actually train the pupil's mind; he only shows him how to perfect his instruments of knowledge and helps and encourages him in this process. He does not impart knowledge to him; he shows him how to acquire it. He does not call forth the knowledge that is within; he only shows him where it lies and how it can be habituated to rise to the surface..."[2]

The Profile of the Teacher

Before elaborating Sri Aurobindo's perception of the role of the teacher and the method of knowledge transaction propounded by him, it would be appropriate to make an attempt to delineate the physical and intellectual capabilities of the person, who would make a good teacher. For this purpose, we would reproduce the constituents of the personality make up of such a person outlined by the seers of the days of yore in the Rig Veda.[3] It underlined the following traits of teachers:

1. He should be a scholar of eminence. Alongside, he should; have humility;
2. He should be an experienced person;
3. He should be able to provide education to the pupils and help remove their ignorance;
4. He should be a specialist in certain arts and crafts and have the capacity to go to the root of the problem;
5. He should be healthy and capable of undergoing rigours of life.

Coming back to Sri Aurobindo's concept of the teacher's responsibilities, the role of the teacher would be:

(i) He should arouse the analytical capabilities of the students by encouraging them to think for themselves. As stated by Clay P. Bedford: "You can teach a student a lesson for a day, but if you can teach him to learn by creating curiosity, he will continue the learning process so long as he lives".

(ii) He should make teaching-learning process a joyful experience, and not a sordid, soulless activity. He/she should be perennially involved in the creation of new knowledge and concepts; should have a vision of the future; the kind of society that we are trying to build; and in that process, to what extent, and in what way, education system, and he/she, can become an effective catalyst.

(iii) He should involve himself in curriculum development. He is expected to sift knowledge; to separate the grain from the chaff and help the students to distinguish between lasting and ephemeral knowledge. He should help students in developing a sense of discrimination so that they do not carry the burden of unwanted knowledge.

(iv) His own personality affects students' personality development. He/she is, in fact, the role model for them. If he/she has self-confidence, honesty, truthfulness, tolerance etc. the students will develop these qualities. It may be stressed that value oriented education is possible only if the teacher has a system of values and puts them into practice in actual life situations. Further, integrated development of students' personality is possible only if the teacher himself has an integrated personality.

(v) He has to strengthen bonds between the community and school. School is a microcosm within a broad social macrocosm; a place where future citizens are nurtured. It is a matter of concern that urban oriented education is driving children away from their hearths and homes, fields and workshops. The system has, therefore, to be community oriented so that the children become useful members of the society and not aliens on their own soil. In this social transformation, the teacher has to play a vital role.

In sum, the teacher has to perform the important task of nation building by providing right kind of education to the students, at the most formative stages of their lives. According to the National Policy on Education (1986), "The country has placed boundless trust in the educational system. The people have a right to expect concrete results. The first task is to make it work. All teachers should teach and all students study."[4] To achieve this, the National Policy has suggested: "The Government and community shall endeavour to create conditions which will help motivate and inspire teachers on constructive and creative lines. Teachers should have the freedom to innovate, to devise appropriate methods of communication and activities relevant to needs and capabilities of and the concerns of the society."[5]

A Committed Teacher

The one single factor that enables a teacher to fulfil his responsibilities to nation is his commitment to the cause of education. The commitment is multi-dimensional. Some of the components of teachers' commitment are:

(a) *Commitment to Students*: The teacher has to have abiding love for the children under his care. The children have vastly different capabilities. Their intelligences and emotional quotients and capacity to respond to emerging academic situations are materially different. A good teacher has to be aware of the individual differences and has to attune his teaching to meet the varied requirements of subjects. Any attempt to impose uniformity would be counterproductive.

(b) *Commitment to the Profession*: Teaching profession is expected to be an oasis of idealism, devotion to duty and love for humanity amidst a vast desert of materialism, competitiveness and unconcern for the good of others. In spite of the vast expansion of education and the quantum jump in the number of teachers, there is no dearth of selfless, devoted teachers, who do not always look for material gains; who have a commitment to their profession, and a strong desire to inspire the budding, blooming children who happen to be placed under their care. This kind of teacher will keep in touch with the latest developments in the field of education, be conversant with the modern means of expanding the vistas of knowledge, and experiment with new ideas and new methods of curriculum transaction.

(c) *Commitment to Society:* The teachers' commitment to society manifests itself in many ways – the most important being that the children should come to school regularly and punctually. This is more so at the present time, when education has been declared as a Fundamental Right and Right to Education has become a statutory responsibility of the Government. To achieve this, the persuasive acumen of the teacher, rather than his coercive or punitive capabilities should be brought into play. In this task, the help of the parent teacher associations (PTAs) could be of immense help.

With increasing access to education, intended or driven by people's perception of education's economic and social significance, institutions are now drawing children from the disadvantaged segments of society. The teacher needs to be conscious of their disadvantages and disabilities and design measures to facilitate their education and learning. This will require a great deal of sensitivity on the part of the teacher.

(d) *Commitment to Ethical Value System*: The world is in a state of turbulence because of conflicts arising out of growing economic and social disparities, ethnic conflicts, religious fanaticism, aggressive competitiveness and the tension between the spiritual and the material. These conflicts can be reduced by inculcating value system among the students. The teachers can play an admirable role in this grim situation. It is, however, essential for the teachers themselves to have an undiluted commitment to the basic value system governing the society.

Facilitating Teachers' Job

It is firmly believed that the teacher cannot do justice to his job unless his social and financial status is improved and the society and the government repose their trust in him. For this purpose, the following steps are suggested:

(i) Involving teachers in planning and management of education including curriculum development. The teachers cannot be expected to show excellence in performance unless they are a part of the process of academic and non-academic management systems. The policy of thrusting on them decisions taken from above will not encourage them to show good performance.

(ii) Promoting innovative practices among teachers. It needs hardly be emphasised that intellect blossoms in an atmosphere of unfettered academic freedom. The teachers should be given complete freedom to experiment and innovate in academic matters. Any interference from non-academic segments of school administration should be resolutely curbed.

(iii) Reforming the procedures of teachers' selection so that merit is the sole criterion of teachers' recruitment.

(iv) Preparing a code of professional ethics for guiding teachers in their professional activities. In this connection, it may be stated that the All India Federation of Primary and Secondary Teachers and a group of educationists, in collaboration with the National Council of Educational Research and Training, have evolved a Code of Professional Ethics, which addresses itself to the various aspects of teachers' relationship with students, parents/guardians, society and nation and peer groups on the one hand and professional organisations and management and administrative systems on the other. This could be a good starting point in preparing a code of professional ethics for all types of teaching personnel.

Upgrading Teachers' Competencies

The kind of teacher that has been envisaged in the preceding section will be a mere chimera of imagination unless steps are taken to upgrade his academic and professional competencies. According to the Planning Commission: with vast expansion of education and training, sizeable number of teachers has little understanding of the material they teach, have poor teaching skills and poor motivation levels.

To remedy the situation, it is necessary to introduce an integrated plan of pre-service and in-service teacher education programme. The general objectives of the programme should be to enable teachers to act as agents of modernisation and social change, to sensitise teachers towards the promotion of social cohesion, international understanding and protection of human rights; to transform student teachers into competent and committed professionals willing to perform the identified tasks; to develop competencies and skills needed for becoming effective teachers, and to enable teachers and teacher educators to be abreast of the newly emerging issues such as environment, ecology, population, gender equality, legal literacy etc.

To achieve these formidable tasks, it is necessary that the curriculum of teacher education should be continuously reviewed. Attention should also be given to making practice teaching a really useful experience for the teachers aspiring to enter this profession. It would also be necessary that the teacher education institutions should be strengthened to perform their tasks with a fair degree of competence.

Duration of Teacher Education Courses

It would be extremely desirable to extend the duration of teacher education courses to at least two years. This is particularly relevant to B.Ed. and M.Ed. programmes, whose duration is extremely inadequate. Extending these courses to two years is essential because of the need for enlarging the teacher education curriculum so as to include many new areas of teacher education like environmental education, population education, economics of education, etc. Further the modern day teacher has to perform diverse roles in the society. All this would necessitate expanding their period of professional education. In this context, the existing NCERT's scheme of Regional Colleges of Education, providing an integrated course of teacher education, should be suitably expanded.

In-Service Training

There is also need for a continuous, well-organised and comprehensive in-service training programme for teachers. According to the Delors Commission (1996): "The World in general is evolving so rapidly today that teachers, like most other professional groups, now must face the fact that their initial training will not see them through the rest of their lives: they need to update and improve their own knowledge and techniques throughout their life time...."[6]

It is recognised that in such a vast country like India, with teachers' strength at about 70 lakh, it is difficult to organise institutional training for all teachers. It would, therefore, be useful to utilise the non-formal/distance education mode for this purpose. It will provide training material to teacher at their work places and keep the cost of training within affordable limits.

To Conclude

We may conclude by saying that the challenges of the new millennium are vast and varied. Our educational system has to be remodelled and made an effective instrument of accelerating the process of socio-economic development and cultural regeneration of the country. The government alone can never be in a position to bring about the requisite changes in the educational system of the country. For this purpose, the role of teachers' organisations, which can give free, frank and unbiased views about the various issues concerning education and teacher education, is of crucial importance. Any complacency on our part will leave us behind in the race for socio-economic and cultural advancement, and make us hostage to the research agenda of the developing countries which are out to exploit the situation to their utmost advantage.

References

1. An approach to Twelfth Five Year Plan (2012-17), Planning Commission; p. 97.
2. Manoj Das; Sri Aurobindo on Education, NCERT, 1999; p. 74.
3. "*Om Sam Dvibarha Mahi Tigma*
   Bhrishti Tu-Vishman
   Padam Na Gorop
   Guol Han Vivid Van Agnirmayam
   Prado Vachan Manisham"
4. The National Policy on Education 1986, Ministry of Human Resource Development, May 1986; p. 20.
5. *Ibid.*, p. 25.
6. UNESCO; Learning, The Treasure Within; International Commission on Education for the Twenty First Century; 1996, p. 149.

16
Epilogue

We have traversed through the saga of education in India – its progress, problems and perspectives – during the period spanning over two centuries. Although the British got suzerainty over this vast country after winning the Battle of Plassey in 1757, education of the natives did not attract their attention for about half a century, till 1813, when the Charter Act, followed by the Despatch of 1814, enjoined on the Governor General in Council to provide a sum of not less than Rs. one lakh each year for the revival and improvement of literature and the encouragement of the learned natives of India and for the introduction and promotion of the knowledge of sciences among the inhabitants of the British territories of India. We have described, in details, the controversy that ensued about the manner in which the paltry amount earmarked for education should be spent and the way in which the solution was hammered out.

The period under review was a mute witness to frequent, and sometime large scale, turbulence and turmoil, which impacted adversely the progress of education. The earliest was India's war of independence in 1857, which was termed as 'Sepoy Mutiny' and crushed with all the brutality that the British Government could command. In the last decade of the nineteenth century, the country was afflicted with natural calamities – plague, cyclone and earthquakes – which devastated large areas in the eastern region of the country. The two World Wars – fought during 1914-18 and 1939-45, in which India was forcibly involved by its British masters, brought about unbearable economic distress, besides an almost administrative collapse, resulting into slowing down of the process of educational development and abandoning of a large number of educational programmes.

In spite of a number of impediments like two wars, economic depression and natural catastrophes, there was some development of education during the first half of the twentieth century. There were, however, quite a few deficient areas. For example, the coverage of the relevant age group at the primary stage was hardly 40 per cent. Further, there were disparities in the coverage of students on account of gender and regions. Adult literacy was abysmally low, particularly among women. Further, education remained predominantly literary in character; vocationalisation and work experience were not given much importance. There was large scale wastage and stagnation at various stages of education. The period, however, saw the establishment of quite a few prestigious institutions like the Indian Institute of Science; Tata Institute of Fundamental Research, Pusa Institute of Agricultural Research, besides a few universities and colleges.

During the period under review, India was fortunate to have quite a few eminent persons, who impacted Indian education. They included Raja Ram Mohan Roy, Gopal Krishan Gokhale, Swami Dayanand Saraswati, Jamshetji Tata, Pandit Madan Mohan Malaviya, Sir Syed Ahmed Khan, Rabindra Nath Tagore, Swami Vivekananda and Jagadish Chandra Bose. Each one of these Indian luminaries contributed substantially to the process of educational development based on Indian traditions and cultural moorings.

Among the crusaders of mass education, the foremost place was occupied by Gopal Krishan Gokhale, whose prophetic statement about the enactment of the bill for free and compulsory education to children of 6-14 age group, introduced in the Imperial Legislature in 1910, has been given a concrete shape; a century afterwards; in 2010. Similarly, Swami Dayanand's emphasis on education, being an instrument of moral and spiritual upliftment of the individual, has blossomed into the creation of more than 700 institutions, which provide modern education by homogenising the western knowledge with education, anchored to Indian culture and traditions. Similarly, the Nobel Laureate Rabindra Nath Tagore's Visvabharati has become an international centre, which aims at, besides teaching in the natural atmosphere, becoming a meeting ground for the East and the West. It is a place for the dissemination of India's cultural heritage, in addition to being a seminary for Eastern studies. The institutions set up by Pandit Madan Mohan Malaviya and Sir Syed Ahmed Khan, are the torch bearers of amalgamating Eastern culture with modern scientific and technological studies.

In sum, the colonial period, which started with indifference, apathy and somewhat hostility towards Indian education, ended up with considerable progress in its development. In fact, it was the edifice built up during that period on which the massive structure of education in the post-independence period rests.

Post Independence Period

The initial years of the post-independence India witnessed gruesome events arising out of the partition of the country on religious grounds. A sizeable number of people, inhabiting the two newly carved countries, seemed to have lost their reason and were out to kill, maim and do all kinds of fiendish acts on their compatriots with whom they had lived in peace for centuries. There was massive unplanned exchange of population, which wrought havoc on the socio-economic systems of both the countries. Education seemed to be nowhere in the reckoning in the early years of independent India. Even when it seemed that the situation had somewhat stabilized, India had to face the unprovoked Chinese incursions in 1962, followed by wars with Pakistan; in 1965 and then in 1971. Kashmir, being the bone of contention between the two countries, has been in perpetual turmoil. Organised war has now been replaced by acts of terrorism, subterfuge, subversion and unprovoked killings. The situation is far from being stable.

In spite of the gloomy picture painted above, there has been an all round development, not only of the economy, but also in the field of education.[1] Indian education is, however, confronted with a plethora of problems that need to be addressed so as to enable the system to perform its crucial role of accelerating the process of socio-economic development and cultural regeneration. Some of the problems are discussed briefly:

1. Access, Equity, Excellence Syndrome

There are widespread gender, community and regional disparities in access to the school and higher education. Besides, there is large scale wastage and stagnation at all stages of education. The quality of education leaves much to be desired. The system needs a multi-pronged remedial action in order to make it an effective instrument of bringing about the desired changes in the socio-economic set up.

In order to attract to, and retain all sections of society in, the educational institutions, there is need for providing education at affordable cost, with large number of incentives like free-ships, scholarships and other facilities like mid-day meals, games and sports etc. The system should be attractive and relevant not only in terms of competencies required for economic development but also in enabling a person to become a creative, socially conscious and productive member of the society. Further, there should be provision to empower people to select institutions, courses of study and professional careers for their future life. These choices should be available to all, regardless of their socio-economic status.

There is large scale drop out and reversal to illiteracy among disadvantaged groups, particularly scheduled castes, scheduled tribes and physically and mentally challenged sections. A very small proportion of such students reach a level of competence and quality, which would enable them to benefit from and contribute to the process of socio-economic development. Special schemes of attracting them, to and retaining them in, the educational institutions would need to be drawn up.

While emphasising an equitable distribution of educational facilities, it has to be clarified that equity does not mean equality, particularly at the higher education stage in which merit and ability of students to profit by education should be a deciding factor. In quite a few cases, however, even the intellectually endowed students are not able to avail of educational facilities because of, among other things, lack of financial wherewithal. Such students need to be provided with adequate financial support so that they can pursue their academic activities without any hindrance. The students from the disadvantaged sections also deserve all kinds of physical, financial and academic support because, who knows, how many 'mute, inglorious Miltons' may form a part of those sections and may wither away for want of proper encouragement and support.

2. Research and Development

It is an important area, which needs special attention. Besides providing adequate financial inputs, which are abysmally low at present; being less than 1 per cent of the GNP; it is necessary to provide adequate academic and physical facilities for the intending researchers. Another factor that has, in an indirect way, retarded the growth of research programmes in the universities is the emergence of specialised research bodies, like the Council of Scientific and Industrial Research, the Atomic Energy Commission etc. with a reasonable quantum of physical and financial back up. They have, though unintendedly, denuded the universities of talented and intellectually endowed persons; adversely affecting their capacity to promote next generation scientific manpower. This has also prevented university – industry collaboration. While it is not intended to minimise the importance of specialised research bodies, it would be necessary to promote specially designed research and development programmes in the university institutions – the universally acclaimed citadels of scholarly and academic activities and producers of professionally trained scientific and technical manpower.

3. The New Economic Policy and its Impact on Education

India launched its policy of economic reforms in early nineties. It has thrown up a very serious challenge to the educational system, particularly higher education which is now confronted with the entry of foreign institutions, not all of which are of the requisite academic standard; some of them even not accredited in their own countries. A well thought out policy of regulating the entry of foreign universities has to be worked out and implemented. In any case, while falling in line with the imperatives of Globalisation, the paramountcy of national interests should be kept in view. Further, while private participation in educational development, particularly, at the secondary and higher education stages, may be a welcome step, complete privatisation of these stages is not in the best interests of the country. It may lead to commercialisation as also neglect of certain subjects, which have no immediate market value.

4. Adult Education

Education for adults is another area, which needs attention. In spite of large number of schemes, the overall literacy is still very low for a country of India's size, diversity and growth, it was 74 per cent only (2011 census). This figure, however, conceals large disparities among males/females and socio-economic groups. There are wide disparities among the States as also between urban and rural areas. It would hardly be denied that education is a liberating force – it saves one from ignorance and oppression. We can ignore it only at our own peril.

5. The Stranglehold of Examinations

The system of education lays too much stress on examinations with the result that motivation for hard or sustained work and willingness to excel is adversely affected. There is need for devising new methods of assessing scholastic and professional achievement so that the entire personality of student and not his power of memorisation alone becomes the deciding factor.

6. Education and Society

The educational institutions are an integral part of the social macrocosm. They have to play their part in accelerating the process of socio-economic development. To achieve this, they have to shed their exclusiveness and work for the upliftment of the society at large, transcending the regional, social and religious barriers.

7. The Teacher

In spite of the newly emerging methods of curriculum transaction, the teacher remains the pivot of the educational system. There is need for giving him the rightful place in the educational system as also in the social hierarchy. For this, it would be necessary to adopt measures for a continuous upgradation of his scholastic and professional competencies. His financial status also needs to be continuously upgraded.

8. Educational Finance

Educational development – quantitatively and qualitatively – needs adequate financial inputs. We have already brought out the inadequate, disparate nature of financial inputs.[2] We shall repeat that in case the country wants a good, relevant and productive system of education, it has to pay for it. There are no lesser options.

9. Cultural Rejuvenation

"There are four main cradles of civilisation from which elements of culture have spread to other parts of the world. These are, moving from east to west, China, the Indian sub-continent, the 'Fertile Crescent' and the Mediterranean. Of these areas, India deserves a larger share of credit than is usually given because in a minimal assessment, this has deeply affected the religious life of most of Asia and has provided very important elements in the culture of the whole of South-East Asia, as well as extending her influence, directly and indirectly to other parts of the World".[3]

The glorious Indian cultural heritage, described above in so glowing terms, has thrown up serious challenge, particularly to the educational system, which needs to be attuned to the sustenance and regeneration of the Indian culture. This has to be achieved regardless of religious, social and economic barriers that are prone to divide the Indian society.

As in the colonial era, the post-independence India has also produced a large number of luminaries, intellectuals, academics, thinkers and administrators, who have contributed substantially, among others, to educational policy formulation, programming and implementation of the schemes of educational developments as also teaching. They include stalwarts like Sri Aurobindo, M.K. Gandhi, Sarvpalli Radhakrishnan, Zakir Husain, Nobel Laureates C.V. Raman, Amritya Sen, D.S. Kothari, V. K. R.V. Rao and other intellectual giants. We have, however, hesitated to highlight their individual contribution to the cause of education. We are aware that most of them were, in some way or the other, associated with the academic programmes including policy formulation and educational transaction. We have, therefore, worked out the profile of an ideal teacher, who would represent these path breakers in the field of education.

It may be recalled that since times immemorial, Indian teacher *(Guru)* has occupied a place of utmost honour and respect that would be the envy of the high and mighty of the land. The seekers of knowledge regardless of their station in life, would flock to the hallowed precincts of the abode of the Guru, to receive education and training of all kinds including the aesthetic and martial arts. In fact, the Guru was considered as a person, who would not only impart education of the worldly type but would also help the student to attain celestial heights in the realm of spirituality. Kabir, the Sufi saint, poet and thinker, (1440-1518) in his inimitable style said:

> *"Guru Govind dono khade, ka ke lagoon pai;*
> *Balihari us Guru ke jis Govind diyo milaye"*

In this couplet, Kabir has expressed his dilemma, when he found himself in the presence of both his Guru and God. The question that he asked himself was to whom he should pay his obeisance first – the Guru or God?

He resolved his mental conflict by touching the feet of the Guru first because, according to him, it was he who was instrumental in bringing him face to face with the Creator of the universe.

It is difficult to imagine that, in the present day educational system, the teacher would be able to reach the sublime heights that Kabir's preceptor did. It is, however, hoped that he would encourage the students to think for themselves, have the freedom to express themselves and as suggested by Sri Aurobindo, show the students how to perfect their knowledge that lies within them, through their own initiatives.

We **conclude** here the story of education in a country, which was, once upon a time, famous for its educational institutions, its depth of thought, its preceptors, thinkers, mathematicians, astronomers, linguists, law givers, men of letters and strategists of war and peace.

It was a country, which was much sought after by seekers of knowledge from countries as far as China, Vietnam, Malaysia, Indonesia, Afghanistan and Iran. It was a country, which spread its gospel of truth, honesty, purity of thought – *Satyam, Shivam, Sundram* - not through coercion but through discussion, dissemination and exchange of thought.

Unfortunately, the country went into deep slumber for a millennium, when it was enslaved by foreigners, who attempted to destroy its culture, its civilisation and traditions. Its famous educational institutions were razed to the ground; its libraries were burnt to ashes; its men of thought were killed in cold blood, its abundant natural resources were plundered and its population was reduced to abject poverty.

Fortunately, this ancient land has been able to shrug off its centuries old yoke of slavery, which had stifled its conscience; dwarfed its faculties of reasoning, logic and freedom to act on its own.

Will this brazenly devastated land regain its lost glory? Will it be again counted among the comity of nations? Will its preceptors, thinkers, scientists, mathematicians, astronomers and men of letters be again revered and respected?

These are questions, which are difficult to be answered. Much will depend upon how our educational and techno-economic social systems rise to meet the challenges thrown up by the present day world.

We earnestly hope that they will! We have abounding faith in the resilience of the people of this ancient land, who have withstood the brutal onslaughts of the foreign invaders for a very long time and preserved their civilisation, culture and traditions, while many other civilisations perished by the way side. Iqbal has immortalised the inviolability of Indian civilisation in the following stanzas (in Urdu):

> *"Kucch baat hai ke hasti mitati nahi hamari;*
> *Sadiyon raha hai dushman daur-e zamman humara"*
> *"Unaan O Misr O Roma Sab Mit Gaye Jahaan Se;*
> *Ab Tak Magar Hai Baaqi Naam-O-Nishaan Hamaara"* [4]

In English:

> "There is some reason that our existence has not been extinguished;
> (Although) For centuries, we have been victims of the ravages of time;
> Greece, Egypt and Rome (their civilisations) have been effaced from the surface of the earth,
> But we have been able to keep our civilisation intact and vibrant"

References

1. For details, see chapter 10 – Educational Development: Progress, Problems and Perspectives.
2. See Chapter 11: '*Financing of Indian Education*'.
3. Basham, A.L.; *A Cultural History of India*, 1975; Oxford University Press, p. 1.
4. Mohamad Iqbal in *Baanq-e-Dira.*

Bibliography

(A) Despatches/Reports, Letters Maintained at the National Archives of India

Public Letter from the Court of Directors to the Governor General in Council dated 2nd June 1814; Appendix to Report from Common's Select Committee, dated 16th August, 1832.

Despatches of 1854 to 1868 – A collection of Despatches from the Home Department on the subject of Education.

Indian Educational Policy, Resolution of the Govt. of India in the Home Department, No. 199-2011 dated 11th March, 1904.

Progress of Education in India; 1897-98 to 1901-02; 1904.

Home (Education Department); Proceedings 13,14, 27-28, 31-32, December, 1902.

India during the year 1901-02 and the nine preceding years; Government of India.

Notes serial Nos. 1-9 File No. 2-1/35 E

Proceeding No. 210-238 (B); EO 53, 1918.

Proceedings No. 22, (Deposit); Note in the Finance Department on the Expenditure on the Education Commissioner and the Curator of the Bureau of Education, No. 103-108; March, 1913.

(B) Books

Altbach: P. G. (ed) Private Prometheus; Private Higher Education in the 21st Century 2000, Centre for International Higher Education, Massachusetts, USA.

Asha Gupta, (ed.) Private Higher Education, 2008; Shipra Publications.

Azad J. L., Financing Higher Education in India, 1975, Sterling.

________ Government Support for Higher Education and Research; 1986. Concept.

________ Higher Education in India, 1988, Radiant.

________ Financing and Management of Higher Education in India: The Role of the Private Sector, 2008, Gyan Publishing House.

Basham; A. L.; A Cultural History of India; 1975, Oxford University Press.

Basu A. N., Education in Modern India. A brief Review, 1947, Calcutta.

Basu, Aparna; The Growth of Education and Political Developments in India, (1888-1921) 1974; OUP, Delhi.

Bharadwaja, Chiranjeevi, Light of Truth; An English Translation of Satyarth Prakash, 1975; Sarvedishak Pratinidhi Sabha.

Biswas et.al; Development of Education in India, 1986; Concept Publishing Company.

Charles Grant, Observations on the State of Society among the Asiatic Subjects of Great Britain with Respect of Morals and Means of Improving it; London, 1813.

Carnoy Martin; Globalisation and Educational Reforms; 1999, IIEP; Paris.

Chatterji, Reena, Impact of Raja Ram Mohan Roy on Education in India, 1983, S. Chand and Co., Delhi.

Ghosh, Suresh Chandra, History of Education in India (2007); Rawat Publications.

Girjan, Shiv, et.al; Pandit Madan Mohan Malaviya, 2004, Commonwealth Publications, Jaipur.

Howell Arthur; Education in British India Prior to 1854 and in 1870-71, Calcutta, Government Press, 1872.
J. A. Richey, H. Sharp : Selections from Educational Records; 1920-22.
Kaul J. N. (ed); Higher Education, Social Change and National Development, 1975; Indian Institute of Advanced Studies, Shimla.
Majumdar R.C.; The History and Culture of the Indian People, Vol. IX, 1985, Bharatiya Vidya Bhavan, Bombay.
Malhotra Rajiv, et.al.; Breaking India; 2011, Amaryllis, Bhopal.
Manoj Das; Sri Aurobindo on Education; 1999, NCERT, New Delhi.
Manson A. H.; The Process of Planning, A Study of India's Five Year Plans; 1950-64.
Mccully S. T.; English Education and Origins of Indian Nationalism; 1940, New York, Columbia University Press.
Middlehurst, Robin; University Challenges; 2001; Minerva, Netherlands.
Mukerji, S. N., Education in India; Today and Tomorrow, 1964, Baroda.
Mukhopadhyay, M. (ed) Education in India, Shipra; 2007.
Myrdal Gunnar; Asian Drama, 1969, Penguin Ltd.
Nand Kishore Singh; Mahatma Gandhi and Non-Cooperation Movement; 1922;
National Planning Committee; 1949; Vora and Co. Publishers, Bombay;
Nurullah S. and Naik J. P., A Student History of Education in India during the British Period (1800-1861) 1962, Macmillan.
Raghu Mara; Debating Gandhi, 2006; Oxfored University Press.
Sadler Michael, The Calcutta University Commission, 1917-19, Calcutta.
Salamatullah; Zakir Hussain on Education, NCERT, New Delhi.
Shahabuddin, Iraqi (ed) Sir Syed Ahmed Khan; Vision and Mission, 2008; A.M.U., Aligarh.
Sharma J. M.; Swami Dayanand – A Biography; 1998; UBS Publications, New Delhi.
Sharma S. R.; Life and Works of Swami Dayanand; 2004; Book Enclave, Jaipur.
Sharma, Ram Nath; History of Indian Education, 2006, Gurgaon.
Sheen Vincent; Mahatma Gandhi, 1968; Publications Division, New Delhi.
Tilak J.B.G. (ed); Financing Education in India; NIEPA, 2003.
________ Economics of Inequality in Education.
________ Education for Development in Asia.
Thomas F. W.; History and Prospects of British Education in India; 1891, London.
Trevelyan, George O, The Life and Letters of Lord Macaulay, 1876; OUP.
UNESCO, Learning the Treasures within; 1996.
________ Statistical Year Books for Various Years.
World Bank: Higher Education, The Lessons of Experience; 1994, Washington;

(C) Important Commissions Appointed by the Department/Ministry of Education/ HRD from time to time:

(i) Under Colonial Rule
1. Education Commission; 1882-83
2. Indian University Commission; 1902
3. Calcutta University Commission, 1917-19
4. The Indian Statutory Commission, 1929

(ii) Under the Government of independent India
1. University Education Commission, 1948-49
2. Secondary Education, Commission, 1952-53
3. Education Commission, 1964-66

(iii) Statistical Reports (for various years)
1. Progress Reports – Annual, Quinquennial, Decennial (The first Report from 1897-98 to 1901-02 (published in 1904);
2. Selected Educational Statistics, Ministry of Human Resource Development, Government of India. New Delhi.
3. Budgeted Expenditure on Education, Ministry of Human Resource Development, Government of India. New Delhi.

(D) Other Reports

Annual Reports of: the University Grants Commission, All India Council for Technical Education, National Council for Educational Research and Training; National University of Educational Planning and Administration.

Reports of the Specialised Committees appointed by the Ministry of Human Resource Development, AICTE, UGC and NCERT.

Planning Commission: Annual Plans; Five Year Plans; Mid-term Reviews; other Reports on Specific Issues.

Index

A

B

C

D

E

P

Q

R